Fundamentals of Lighting

Fundamentals of Lighting

Susan M. Winchip
Illinois State University

Fairchild Publications, Inc. • New York

Director of Sales and Acquisitions:	Dana Meltzer-Berkowitz
Executive Editor:	Olga T. Kontzias
Senior Development Editor:	Jennifer Crane
Production Manager:	Ginger Hillman
Senior Production Editor:	Elizabeth Marotta
Art Director:	Adam B. Bohannon
Cover Design:	Adam B. Bohannon
Cover Art:	CSA Mod Art/Veer

Developed and Produced by Focus Strategic Communications, Inc.

Project Managers:	Ron Edwards, Adrianna Edwards
Developmental Editor:	Ron Edwards
Copy Editor:	Debbie Sawczak
Proofreader:	Linda Szostak
Index:	Ron Edwards
Art Director:	Adrianna Edwards
Interior Design and Layout:	Lisa Platt
Photo Research and Permissions:	Matthew Dudley

Library of Congress Catalog Card Number: 2007925961

ISBN: 978-1-56367-528-7

GST R 133004424

Printed in Malaysia

CH07, TP04

Brief Contents

Extended Contents

Preface

Fundamentals of Lighting evolved as a response to the need to develop a textbook on quality lighting from a design perspective. Many books written from an engineering perspective contain a great deal of technical and quantitative detail, but without enough content about quality lighting and its application to an environment. There are likewise numerous examples of "coffee-table" books filled with beautiful photographs, but these books lack the technical details that a designer or architect needs to create a functional and aesthetically pleasing environment. These books also lack the comprehensive, integrative approach that helps students to understand lighting within the context of the design process.

In teaching a lighting course at the university level, I have used several books, references, and articles to cover the essential content adequately. Not only is this approach expensive for the students, but extracting information from a variety of sources also inhibits the continuity of concepts and the integration of subject matter that can be accomplished in one textbook.

Fundamentals of Lighting is written for college students who are studying lighting in their quest to become interior designers. The textbook is an approach to quality lighting with a primary focus on the design process. Specifically, the textbook uses an integrative approach to lighting that not only includes the basics of lighting systems, but also demonstrates how lighting is interrelated with the design process, human factors, sustainability, global issues, design fundamentals, regulations, and business practices.

Many of the topics and suggestions provided in the text reflect the results of research studies. The exercises and pedagogical suggestions in the accompanying Instructor's Guide are written to reinforce the content of the textbook and help to develop critical skills for a practicing professional, such as programming, schematic design, concept development, design development, drafting, sketching, and teamwork.

The text can be used in a variety of courses and formats. It can serve as the primary textbook in introductory lighting courses, or as a supplementary resource in other courses, such as commercial and residential studio courses. Students should be encouraged to keep their books after an initial lighting course, and then use the text as a reference when they are required to develop lighting plans in other courses and in their future professional practices. The interdisciplinary nature of the content makes the book an excellent choice for reinforcing concepts throughout the curriculum. For example, in non-lighting courses, this textbook could be used as a reference when discussing topics such as sustainable design, energy standards, codes, or the phases of the design process.

Organization of the Textbook

This textbook is organized sequentially to develop a fundamental understanding of how to design quality lighting environments. It is divided into two parts. Part I explores basic concepts and elements of a quality lighting environment, including components of lighting systems, daylight integration, color, and directional effects of illumination. This content serves as the foundation for exploring specific applications in Part II. These applications include energy considerations, sustainability, human factors, and residential and commercial interiors. The last two chapters serve as the culminating experience of the textbook by reviewing comprehensive programming, schematic design, design development, contract documents, and contract administration.

For more information, go to http://www.fairchildbooks.com and search on _fundamentals of lighting.

Pedagogical Features

Every chapter in the textbook has pedagogical features that are designed to assist teaching and enhance learning. To help explain concepts and techniques, every chapter has hand-drawn line illustrations and numerous full-color illustrations. In addition, each chapter begins with a list of objectives, which can be used as an assessment tool at the beginning and end of a lesson. The summary, list of key terms, and exercises in every chapter are designed to reinforce the content and develop important professional skills.

The appendices are very important to learning the content of the book and can be an excellent reference for practicing professionals. The charts in the appendices include shapes of lamps and beam spread tables. The appendices also include a substantial list of contact information for lighting manufacturers, distributors, suppliers, professional organizations, government agencies, and trade associations.

The Instructor's Guide that accompanies this text offers additional activities and assignments designed to enhance teaching and learning. It explains in full detail the pedagogical approach of the text and elaborates on the content embodied in *Fundamentals of Lighting*.

Acknowledgments

An author is only one individual in the process of publishing a textbook. I am very grateful to all the other individuals who dedicated their best work and time to this endeavor. My first note of appreciation is extended to Olga Kontzias, executive editor, and Joseph Miranda, acquisitions editor, at Fairchild Books. I am extremely grateful to Olga for assigning a fantastic staff to work with me throughout the publishing process.

Timothy Bayley's extraordinary hand-drawn line illustrations are not only important for a quality presentation, but their creativity, details, and eloquent style help to communicate the essence of the book. I am enormously grateful to my dear friend, Tim, for our years of friendship and his beautiful drawings.

I want to express my sincerest gratitude to my incredible husband, Galen, and my three children, Kristi, Kyle, and Amy. They have supported my work and have provided encouragement throughout my academic career.

PART I
Principles of Lighting

CHAPTER 1

Introduction to Quality Lighting

- Comprehend and assess the importance of quality lighting.
- Identify the key characteristics of light and some of the effects light has on the human response.
- Analyze the basic parts of the eye and the vision process.
- Describe general, task, accent, and decorative lighting techniques.
- Identify fixtures that are used for general, task, accent, and decorative lighting.
- Develop a fundamental understanding of the factors that affect quality in general, task, and accent lighting.

Light is one of the essential elements of life; without it we could not exist. Designers must consider both natural and electrical sources of light when they plan a quality lighting environment. To understand natural and electrical light, it is important to review historical developments of light sources and how civilizations invented technologies to produce light. Electric light, the form to which we are accustomed, has been in existence for approximately 100 years. This is an extremely short period of time compared to the thousands of years of civilization. Advancements in lighting will continue to transform our lives and society.

As a form of energy, light travels through space and affects every living organism. Light sources and the physiological process of vision affect what we see. Poor lighting has a negative effect on vision, our ability to perform tasks, and our psychological responses. Designing functional and aesthetic interiors requires a focus on planning principles that include the fundamentals of illumination, elements of lighting systems, and specific interior applications.

Lighting requirements in a space can be divided into three main categories: general, task, and accent. The first is **general lighting**, or **ambient lighting**, which provides overall illumination in a space, including lighting that allows people to navigate an area safely. The second is **task lighting**, which is the lighting specified for each task (such as reading, for example) that is performed in a space. The third is **accent lighting**, which is used to create interest and to highlight special features such as architectural details, artwork, plant foliage, or decorative accessories. **Decorative lighting** is ornamental and should not be included in the three categories; it includes light sources that provide illumination and are also artistic pieces themselves. For a well-planned lighting environment, it is critical to include daylight as well as electrical light, and to specify general, task, and accent lighting in every space in an interior. Using a variety of types of lighting allows the designer to create a lighting plan that is adapted to the purpose of the space and the needs of its users. Decorative lighting is an optional source that could be used as a focal point in select locations.

What Is Light?

Technically, **light** is a form of energy that is part of the electromagnetic spectrum visible to the human eye. The spectrum also includes cosmic rays, microwaves, gamma rays, radar, radio waves, ultraviolet, and X-rays. The human eye is able to see light in only a relatively small spectrum, from violet (about 400 nanometers) to red (about 750 nanometers) wavelengths. (A nanometer is extremely small, about one billionth of a meter.) Light travels at a speed of 186,000 miles per second (or about 300,000 kilometers per second), theoretically the fastest speed in the universe. **Natural light** includes direct light from the sun and the stars. **Indirect natural light** is the result of reflection from clouds, structures, and the landscape. The unit for measuring the quantity of light emitted by a light source is the **lumen (lm)**.

general lighting/ ambient lighting
Overall illumination in a space, including lighting that allows people to walk safely through a room and that sets the mood or character of the interior.

task lighting
Illumination that is specific to each task performed in a space.

accent lighting
Illumination designed to highlight an object or area in a space.

decorative lighting
Luminaires that provide illumination and are also artistic pieces.

light
A form of energy that is part of the electromagnetic spectrum.

natural light
Illumination from the sun and the stars.

indirect natural light
Illumination reflected from clouds, the moon, and stars.

lumen (lm)
A unit of measurement of the light output of a lamp.

Quality Lighting

Quality lighting is a relatively new concept. The discovery of electricity and the invention of the incandescent lightbulb in the 1800s prompted engineers to develop new and better lamps and lighting systems. Since then, the focus has been primarily on the quantity of light needed in a space. Because we can measure light, it is fairly easy to have an adequate amount of lighting in a space. Now that scientists and engineers have developed systems that produce a large quantity of light, it is necessary for designers to focus on the quality of lighting. There is a subjective aspect to quality lighting that extends beyond scientific measurement into psychology and mood, making it complicated and difficult to accomplish. The *IESNA Lighting Handbook*, 9th edition, focuses on the importance of quality lighting and the quantity of lighting.

What is quality lighting? **Quality lighting** allows users to function comfortably in an interior, feel safe in it, and appreciate its aesthetic components. Achieving a quality lighting environment requires complete control over the lighting system. Environments with quality lighting are specifically designed for particular uses in special locations. These environments reflect a skillful application of the principles of design by integrating and layering light into the entire composition. **Layered lighting** includes natural light and multiple electrical light sources. With the focus on quality, lighting is no longer an afterthought that is simply added on to a design plan. Quality lighting includes the art of balancing and integrating daylight and general, task, accent, and decorative lighting. Designing quality lighting environments also results in reduced energy costs and conservation of natural resources. Throughout this text, the principles of quality lighting are applied to the fundamentals of lighting, elements of lighting systems, case studies, and presentations of lighting solutions. The goal of every chapter is to build the knowledge and skills designers need to create quality lighting environments.

quality lighting
A layered illumination plan that reduces energy costs, conserves natural resources, and allows users of the space to function comfortably, feel safe, and appreciate the aesthetic components of the environment.

layered lighting
An illumination plan that includes natural light and multiple electrical light sources.

Vision and Lighting

The vision process starts when light enters the pupil, the aperture of the iris of the eye (Figure 1.1). The lens adjusts the perception of light for near and far vision, and the cornea focuses light on the retina of the eye by refraction. This function is known as **accommodation**. The retina is the inner, light-sensitive lining of the eye, and the fovea of the retina is where light is focused. Rods and cones are detector cells located at the back of the retina. Rods are activated primarily at lower illuminance levels and are important in night vision; cones are activated by bright light, color, and detail. The fovea does not contain any rods. The cones and rods convert light energy into nerve impulses, which are sent by the optic nerve from the retina to the brain for interpretation. Through this entire process, brightness and color are adjusted and images are compared to experiences in memory.

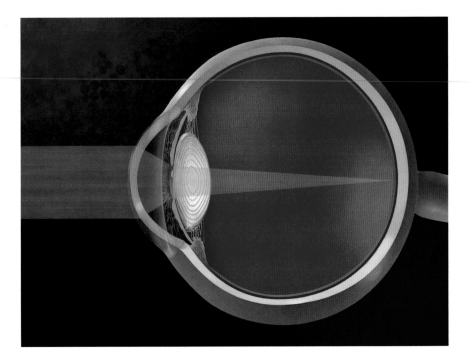

FIGURE 1.1
Cross section of the eye.

Adaptation is what happens when the eye adjusts itself to the amount of brightness entering the pupil. Similar to a camera lens, the pupil constricts in bright light and expands in the dark. The adaptation process can take some time. When you enter a dark movie theater on a bright sunny day, your eyes require more time to adjust from bright to dark than from dark to light. To assist the adaptation that occurs in the vision process, designers should consider a lighting system that provides a transition in light levels. For low-level illuminated interiors used during daylight times, a transitional system should begin with higher light levels as one enters the space, lowering gradually as one travels through the interior. If possible, the amount of time required for a person to reach the darkest space should be equal to the amount of time it takes for adaptation to occur in the vision process. Seating should be provided for those individuals, such as the elderly, who need more time for their eyes to adapt. During evening hours, to reduce the contrast in lighting from outdoors to indoors, the lighting levels should be decreased in the entry area and gradually reduced as one progresses through the interior.

The **eye's field of vision** is also an important consideration in designing quality lighting environments. It is most natural to see objects within a horizontal field. The field of vision includes a central and a peripheral area. The central field of vision for the eye is approximately 2 degrees above and 2 degrees below the direct line of sight (Figure 1.2). **Visual acuity**, the ability of the eye to see detail and color, is best in this small range. The peripheral area is the area to the sides of the central field of vision and above and below the central field of vision. Brightness and motion, such as flashing lights, are best seen in peripheral vision. Designers should consider the eye's field of vision when they plan the lighting for detailed visual tasks or when specifying bright or flashing lighting systems. For example, when planning the lighting for a work surface, a designer should position the light source to illuminate the work area in the central field of vision. Flashing emergency light fixtures are best located in areas within the peripheral field of vision. Since the location of the eye's field of vision changes when a person moves from a sitting to a standing position, a designer might have to specify several light sources to accommodate all the lighting needs.

eye's field of vision
The central and peripheral areas that are visible to the eye.

visual acuity
The ability of the eye to see details.

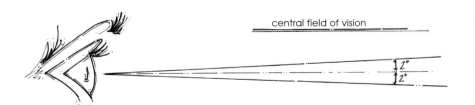

central field of vision

FIGURE 1.2
The central field of vision for the eye is approximately 2 degrees above and below the direct line of sight.

FIGURE 1.3
To honor the life
of President
John F. Kennedy, the
architect Philip
Johnson designed a
memorial with a ceno-
taph, an open tomb.

presbyopia
*A decrease in the
eye's ability to
change the shape
of the lens, affecting
an individual's ability
to focus on near or
distant objects.*

The aging process of the eye affects visual acuity, color identification, adaptation, peripheral vision, depth perception, and tolerance for glare. As one ages, the lens of the eye yellows and **presbyopia** occurs. That is the decline in the eye's ability to adjust the shape of the lens. As a result, when designing spaces for the elderly, designers must specify higher illumination levels, especially in areas where detailed tasks are performed and where there are potential hazards such as stairs.

Light and Emotive Responses

Light is a remarkable element that can be exciting, mysterious, magical, or terrifying. Paris, "the City of Light," evokes excitement. Fireworks, used in Chinese New Year's celebrations as early as the ninth century, are an excellent example of how lights can create a festive atmosphere. Lights are often used to inspire people during sorrowful times. To memorialize the victims of the 1995 Oklahoma City bombing, the Butler Design Partnership firm designed clear chairs, one for each of the 168 victims, which are illuminated during the evening. The life of President John F. Kennedy is honored in a memorial with a cenotaph, a monument, designed by the architect Philip Johnson. The words "John Fitzgerald Kennedy" are engraved in gold on black granite in the center of the sculpture (Figure 1.3). These are the only words on the sculpture and they are illuminated only by the reflections of the surrounding white walls. The words are dark during the evening hours, thus representing the loss of a leader. More recently, to honor the victims of the attack on the World Trade Center in New York City on September 11, 2001, the city had lighting designers project two vertical beams of light where the towers had stood (see Figure 1.4).

While these lighting examples demonstrate inspirational uses, light also can be very frightening, as with lightning or a severe fire. For example, lightning is often used in movies and on the stage to create a fearful setting. A raging fire can create panic in people and animals. Flashing red lights on fire trucks or ambulances cause apprehensive feelings of being in a crisis or a life-threatening situation.

FIGURE 1.4
To honor victims of the World Trade Center attack in New York City on September 11, 2001, two vertical beams of light were projected from the location of the structures.

Layered Lighting

The integration and control of daylight can be applied to each category of lighting, including general, task, and accent. This requires layered lighting utilizing multiple light sources, each with its own purpose. This gives the users of the space the flexibility of selecting and adjusting the lighting for each specific activity. An important element in achieving a flexible light plan is to have multiple switching and dimming controls. The overall theme of an interior should be reflected in the selection of the light fixtures and the illumination levels for each of the three categories of lighting—general, task, and accent.

General Lighting

As we saw earlier in this chapter, general lighting is sometimes referred to as ambient lighting, and is designed to provide uniform lighting to a space. Often, light fixtures for general lighting are designed for indirect illumination and are hidden from view. General lighting allows people to walk safely through a space by reducing sharp contrasts between light sources. This enables people to perceive the overall shape and size of a space. General lighting also establishes the mood or character of an interior.

The design of a general lighting plan should be based upon the purpose of the space and the needs of its users. General lighting is the source that establishes the overall impression of a space and is determined by the light level, light source, and fixtures. For example, the general lighting in a high-end restaurant or retail store will usually be dimmer than in a fast-food restaurant or discount store. High-end spaces usually have a flexible lighting system including electrical fixtures that promote a certain mood and image. Designers of low-end or discount settings plan systems that are functional but economize on electrical usage, maintenance, and fixtures.

Daylight can be the source of general lighting on sunny days in spaces with many windows or skylights. But those spaces should be designed to provide general lighting from electrical sources during the evenings or on dark, cloudy days. A variety of light fixtures and structural lighting systems are available to provide the lighting required for general illumination. (Lighting systems and styles of fixtures are discussed in Chapter 5.) To have an adequate level of illumination, the space must have several indirect fixtures in various locations. Any light fixture that provides indirect light could be used for general lighting, or it may be supplemented with light that is integrated into walls, ceilings, or furniture.

Task Lighting

Task lighting is another category of lighting that is used in both commercial and residential environments to provide quality lighting for specific activities and tasks. Task lighting is a direct form of lighting that enables users to see the critical details of an activity. A quality lighting environment includes the appropriate balance of general lighting and task lighting. The illumination level of task lighting should be approximately three times the level of general lighting. This ratio ensures a level of lighting that allows the eye to shift from the task to the surrounding area and vice versa with a minimum amount of adjustment in the eye's lens.

Some task lighting requires special consideration. For example, it is critical that lighting be excellent for activities that require precision, such as surgery. The more time is spent engaged in an activity, the more important it is to specify appropriate task lighting. Any quality task lighting design must take into account individuals with less than perfect eyesight, such as the elderly.

In planning a task lighting system, it is important to build in flexibility and control for the users of the space. For example, adjustable luminaires and dimmers can customize the lighting for the specific needs of a user at a particular time and save energy by localizing the high-illumination levels where they are required. Lighting plans that specify an illumination level for an entire area regardless of the specific needs of the users result in a waste of electricity because some individuals do not need a high level of illumination or are not always present in the space. Customized task lighting in a large, open, office space allows individual users to have flexibility and control, providing the appropriate illumination level at the brightness required for the duration of an activity.

Potential problems should be considered in planning quality task lighting. Task lighting can become a problem because the illumination levels needed for many activities can be very high, which can lead to difficulty for the eye in adapting to the varying light levels and contrasts. The light source may create glare, **veiling reflections**, or shadows. Glare and veiling reflections occur when the light source is reflected on the work space. For example, computer monitors can reflect fixtures mounted on a ceiling, or light can cause glare on shiny surfaces such as glossy magazines.

veiling reflection
Reduction in light contrast on a task as a result of a reflected image on a surface.

The eye can have problems adjusting between light and dark areas because of severe contrast in illumination levels between the task and its surrounding area. It is especially difficult to ensure the proper lighting levels for tasks that require high levels of illumination, such as sewing black fabric with black thread or reading very small type. Close work fatigues the eye by creating strain. Generally, the more light on the task, the less strain there will be on the eye.

To reduce strain on eyes, a designer can do other things besides increasing the brightness of the lighting. One possibility would be to increase the contrast or size of the objects used in a task. For example, most books are printed with black type on white paper because the extreme contrast between black and white results in the greatest amount of visibility. To improve visibility, a designer might also change the color of a work surface or the position of a piece of furniture. Designers can use computerized analytical tools to predict visibility patterns and illumination levels in an environment.

In planning task lighting, a designer must first identify the activities that occur in a space and then determine which characteristics of those tasks need to receive special lighting treatment. National codes and standards have been established for task illumination levels for commercial and residential spaces. Excellent sources for this information include the *National Handbook of the Illuminating Engineering Society of North America (IESNA)* and the *Chartered Institute of Building Services Engineers (CIBSE) Code for Lighting* in the United Kingdom. The recommended illumination levels are averages, not minimum requirements, which is why it is important to avoid overlighting an area while providing adequate illumination for special needs groups, such as seniors with aging eyes. For example, higher illumination levels should be specified for long-term care facilities for the elderly.

In addition to illumination levels for a task, a designer must consider the design and placement of each **luminaire**. Luminaires for task lighting include portable fixtures, pendants, and recessed, track, and structural lighting. Some office furniture has task lighting built into it. This lighting includes sources for both task lighting and ambient lighting, whereby direct light is positioned for tasks and indirect light for the general or ambient light surrounding the workstation. Task-ambient furniture systems can be an effective way to illuminate a large, open office space that accommodates users with a variety of needs.

Daylight can also be a part of task lighting. Daylight is excellent for helping people to discern critical details, for example, in reading and writing, and to make color distinctions. That is why daylight can be very effective in interiors such as schools, offices, and libraries. Supplemental electrical sources have to be planned, however, to meet the needs of the users on dark days and in the evenings.

luminaire
An element of a lighting system that includes a light source, housing elements, ballasts, transformers, controls, a mounting mechanism, and a connection to electrical power.

Accent and Decorative Lighting

Accent lighting is another layer of illumination in a quality lighting environment. It can be as simple as a single spotlight trained on a piece of art on a wall. Some of the illumination from accent lighting can also contribute to the interior's general lighting, but the purpose of accent or highlight lighting is to bring attention to an object or element in a space. Accent lighting creates drama, variety, interest, and excitement in an interior. The form and style of accent lighting should be designed to contribute to the room's atmosphere and theme.

In planning accent lighting, it is important for the designer to identify the things needing to be highlighted and the characteristics of the surrounding areas. Designers use accent lighting to emphasize artwork, sculptures, water, fabrics, architectural details, textures, forms, and plants. The location and aiming angle must be chosen so as to avoid direct glare to the eyes of users. To avoid problems with viewing, the preferred angle to a wall is 30 degrees (see Figure 1.5). Exterior views, especially in the evening, can also be excellent focal points of an interior.

Creating contrast and determining the best angle at which to position a light are key to successful accent lighting. To attract the eye to an object or area requires contrast, so the characteristics of the surrounding area of the accented object are important. A white object will blend into white walls around it, while a dark object will stand out by contrast

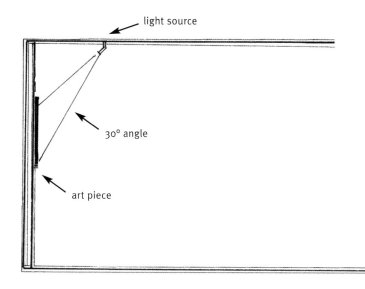

light source

30° angle

art piece

FIGURE 1.5
To accent artwork on a wall, the preferred angle to the wall is 30°.

(see Figure 1.6a). An illumination level that is the same for both the accented item and the surrounding area will not emphasize the item effectively (see Figure 1.6b). Contrasts in illumination levels enhance the accent item and distinguish it from the surrounding area (see Figure 1.6c).

FIGURE 1.6a
Creating contrast between the characteristics of the surrounding area and the accented object is important. The white walls surrounding the white object on the pedestal affect the visibility of the sculpture.

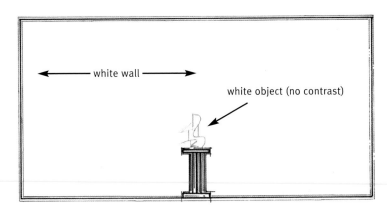

FIGURE 1.6b
An illumination level that is the same for both the accent item and the surrounding area will not effectively emphasize the object. A lack of contrast in illumination levels also reduces an emphasis on the details of the object.

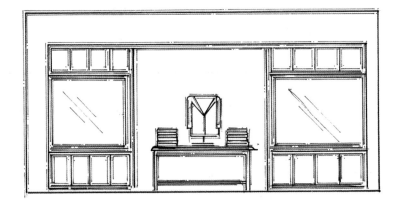

FIGURE 1.6c
Contrasts in illumination levels enhance the merchandise.

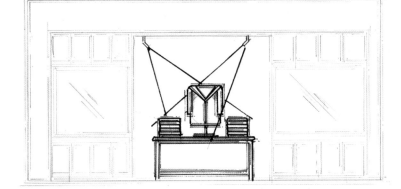

The drama and emphasis of extreme light and shadow is often illustrated in the *chiaroscuro* technique in paintings. This technique emphasizes patterns of light, shade, and shadows. One approach to achieving contrast is to illuminate the object to be accented with a greater amount of light than its surrounding area. Since the eye is attracted to light, the users of the space will focus their attention on the areas of the room with the highest illumination levels. Generally, to create enough contrast to accent an object requires a minimum ratio of 5 to 1 between the accent and general lighting. Ratios lower than this will generally not provide enough contrast to be considered accent lighting. Extreme drama can be accomplished with a 10 to 1 ratio, but the ratio should not exceed 20 to 1. Differentials higher than this create a setting that does not allow the eye to adjust to the contrasts between light and dark. Specifying effective contrast ratios is difficult in spaces that have many accented areas or objects. For example, a retailer might want to emphasize several displays that are close to one another in the store. But this may result in the objects blending together, eliminating the contrast required to bring attention to the individual items (Figure 1.7). In addition to varying the illumination levels, a designer might have to contrast other elements in the space by employing complementary colors and varying textures, forms, shapes, and lines. Motion is also an excellent technique for attracting the eye, especially peripheral vision.

Direction and angle of a source are also key considerations in accent lighting. The perceived shapes of three-dimensional objects can be affected if the direction and angle of light are not well planned (see Figure 1.8). Plant foliage can provide interesting patterns and shadows on walls and ceilings if a light source is placed close to a plant. In fact, revealing the textures and form of an object often requires that the light source be close to the object (see Figure 1.9). This technique is referred to as **grazing**. In contrast, **backlighting** will create a silhouette of an object (see Figure 1.10). A specific direction and angle of light can also create dramatic shadows that the designer wants to emphasize.

FIGURE 1.7
Several highlighted displays located next to each other can result in a lack of emphasis.

grazing
A lighting technique that places the light source close to a surface or object to highlight interesting textures and produce dramatic shadows.

backlighting
Illumination that is directly behind an object. Also referred to as silhouetting.

Accent lighting is especially effective in modeling, which enhances the shape and form of three-dimensional objects.

Accent lighting allows a designer to be very creative in highlighting areas or objects. It can often be more interesting and effective if the

FIGURE 1.8
The direction and angle of illumination can affect the perceived shapes of three-dimensional objects.

FIGURE 1.9
By positioning the light source close to an object, this example of the grazing technique reveals textures and form.

designer selects a specific point of emphasis on an accent piece. For example, instead of providing a uniform distribution of light to a painting or architectural detail, it might be far more dramatic to illuminate only portions of a painting or only one interesting detail of a column on a fireplace. Highlighting flower petals that have fallen from a bouquet sitting on a table, rather than the entire arrangement, is another creative example of accent lighting. Spotlighting the specific element and having the appropriate contrast in illumination levels can focus the emphasis on the focal point. The best approach to accenting a sculpture or objet d'art is to have two light sources aimed at the piece from two different angles.

FIGURE 1.10
Backlighting is used to create silhouettes of the objects on the top shelf.

Shadows play an important role in accent lighting. A strong spotlight can create some undesirable shadows on a surface. For example, the frame of a painting could create a shadow from the spotlight on the artwork. It is therefore critical to position the spotlight at the proper mounting location and aiming angle. Of course, shadows can be planned as unique focal points of an area or object, such as shadows of foliage on a ceiling and on walls (see Figure 1.11). The shadow of a unique form, such as an abstract sculpture, could also be the accented element. Shadows of architectural details of an interior enhance the sculptural elements and the three-dimensional aspect of a façade; the location and aiming angle are critical to ensure that a façade is viewed as having three dimensions rather than two. Depending on the intensity of a light source, its distance

FIGURE 1.11
The proper location of a luminaire can create interesting shadows on walls and ceilings.

from the object, and the aiming angle, shadow lines can be hard or soft. From a design perspective a hard shadow line will project an image that is dramatic and harsh. A soft shadow line does not attract the eye easily and promotes a subdued theme.

Light fixtures used for accent lighting include **uplights**, **recessed spots**, **spotlight projectors** with optical control, and wall brackets. Depending on their location in a space, luminaires for accent lighting can form a decorative element of an interior or they can be hidden from view. Some furniture is designed with accent lighting hidden from direct view. Curio cabinets, breakfronts, and other cabinets often have accent lighting to enhance crystal, china, and objets d'art. As with general lighting, it is often intriguing to hide the light source when specifying accent lighting. Viewing an object or area enhanced by illumination without seeing the source of the light adds mystery and drama to a setting (see Figure 1.12).

Since accent lighting is often a small, bright light source, unexpected glare can create a safety concern. Daylight could be a bright source that accents an object or area in a space through narrow slits or small openings. The variability of daylight, depending on the weather, the time of day, and so on, will affect the quality of the accent.

uplight
Luminaire that directs the light up; generally a portable luminaire.

recessed spot
Luminaire mounted in a ceiling or furniture piece, with a lamp that distributes the light in a concentrated area.

spotlight projector
Device that allows designers to select a very precise area to be illuminated.

FIGURE 1.12
Viewing only the effects of light can add mystery and excitement to a room.

Decorative lighting is designed to be a focal point in a space. It can be a fixture that is designed to be an ornamental element of the interior, or it can be a specialty architectural lighting solution. Chandeliers, Tiffany glass shades, neon tubes, lasers, holograms, holiday lights, wall sconces, and some fiber optics are examples of decorative lighting. Daylight can be a source of decorative lighting when it illuminates a stained glass window. To appreciate the stained glass window in the evening, exterior lighting should be included in the lighting plan. Decorative lighting can also be an art form. Candles and flames in a fireplace are decorative sources that add warmth and enhance the appearance of people and objects in an environment. Whenever possible, candles should be considered an important element of the layered lighting in a space.

The purpose of a decorative fixture should remain ornamental. For example, while most chandeliers are designed to be only decorative, quite frequently a chandelier in a dining room is used as the source for general, task, and decorative lighting. As a result, the high illumination level required to meet all three needs could discourage people from viewing the chandelier, negating the purpose of having it as a decorative fixture. This is especially problematic if the chandelier has exposed **flame-shaped lamps**, which are quite common. Decorative lighting serves an important role in reinforcing the theme and style of the space. These sources should supplement the lighting specified for general, task, and accent purposes.

flame-shaped lamp
Small, decorative lamp in the shape of a flame. The bulb is clear or frosted glass.

To design quality lighting environments, an interior designer must understand the power and effect of light on people within the context of the setting. This requires an understanding of the purpose of the space and characteristics of the users. For example, low levels of illumination are appropriate for a romantic restaurant, but they would be very wrong for a workplace. Flashing lights can promote excitement in a nightclub, but they would be very annoying in a museum. An important element in addressing the needs of the users of the space focuses on the variability of the vision process. Quality lighting must support the basic functions of vision. This requires an understanding of what happens when light enters the eye and the conditions that alter the vision process.

SUMMARY

- Light is a form of energy that is part of the electromagnetic spectrum visible to the human eye. Light has the ability to elicit significant emotional responses from people.

- Quality lighting environments allow users to function in a space, feel safe in it, and appreciate its aesthetic components. These environments reflect a skillful application of the principles of design by integrating and layering lighting into the entire composition.

- The vision process starts when light enters the pupil. The lens adjusts the light for near and far vision, and the cornea focuses light on the retina by refraction. Rods and cones are detector cells located at the back of the retina. Rods are activated primarily in lower illumination levels, and cones are activated by bright light, color, and detail. The optic nerve sends impulses from the retina to the brain for interpretation.

- Because light/dark adaptation occurs in the vision process, designers should consider a lighting system that provides a transition in light levels.

- The eye's field of vision includes a central and peripheral area.

- The aging of the eye affects visual acuity, color identification, the adaptation process, peripheral vision, depth perception, and tolerance for glare.

- General or ambient lighting is a category of lighting designed to provide uniform lighting to a space.

- Task lighting is a direct form of lighting that enables users to see the critical details of an activity.

- The purpose of accent or highlight lighting is to bring attention to an object or element in a space. Creating contrast and determining the direction and angle of a source are key considerations in accent lighting.

- Decorative lighting is designed to be an ornamental element of an interior.

accent lighting

accommodation

adaptation

backlighting

decorative lighting

eye's field of vision

flame-shaped lamp

general lighting/ambient
   lighting

grazing

indirect natural light

layered lighting

light

lumen (lm)

luminaire

natural light

presbyopia

quality lighting

recessed spot

spotlight projector

task lighting

uplight

veiling reflection

visual acuity

Exercises

1. Identify several experiences you have had with changes in lighting, such as entering a movie theater on a bright, sunny day. Describe what occurs in the vision process as you experience these changes.

2. Developing observational and problem-solving skills is critical to success as a designer. Identify five public spaces you can observe during various times of the day and on different days of the week. Write a report that could include sketches and photographs responding to the items listed below:

    a. Determine whether the space meets all the criteria for a quality lighting environment.

    b. Given the users and elements of the space, identify special needs for vision.

    c. Determine the human response elicited from the space and identify the lighting techniques that contribute to the response.

    d. Compare and contrast how the space would work with non-electrical light fixtures.

3. Select photographs of five residential interiors and five nonresidential interiors. Identify the electrical fixtures in the space and determine the category (general, task, accent) of each fixture. If a fixture does not exist for a category of lighting, suggest an effective fixture. The identification and analysis should be submitted in written form. Photographs must be included.

4. The purpose of this project is to develop an understanding of how to integrate daylight with general, task, and accent lighting. As a designer you have been commissioned to create layered lighting plans for an elementary school in a warm climate and for a discount retail store in a cold climate. You are to submit to each client a written document, optionally accompanied by sketches and photographs, that includes the following information:

   a. Critical spaces for integrating daylight.

   b. For each space in the interior, an identification of the needs for general, task, and accent lighting.

CHAPTER 2

Natural and Artificial Light Sources

OBJECTIVES

- Identify the advantages and disadvantages of using daylight as a lighting source.
- Describe the factors and conditions that affect the quantity and quality of daylight in an interior.
- Identify the primary functional components of incandescent-filament, halogen, fluorescent, and high-intensity discharge lamps.
- Compare and contrast the advantages and disadvantages of incandescent-filament, halogen, fluorescent, and high-intensity discharge lamps.
- Identify the primary functional components and operating principles of fiber optics and light-emitting diodes (LEDs).
- Determine applications for fiber optics and light-emitting diodes (LEDs).

Creating a quality lighting environment requires a comprehensive plan based on both natural and artificial light. Integrating and controlling daylight involves an understanding of solar geometry, the distribution of daylight into spaces, glazing technologies, and energy considerations. **Solar geometry** is the movement of the earth around the sun.

This chapter covers characteristics of electrical sources that are utilized in interiors, including incandescent-filament, halogen (tungsten-halogen), fluorescent, high-intensity discharge (HID), fiber optics, and LEDs. Electrical sources are used to complement daylight and to provide general, task, accent, and decorative lighting in an environment.

solar geometry
The movement of the earth around the sun.

An electrical lighting system is composed of the electrical power, light source, luminaire, controls, maintenance, and service. All these elements affect the quantity and quality of illumination in an interior. In reviewing electrical sources, it is critical to study all the elements of quality lighting systems.

Daylight Integration and Control of Sunlight

Daylight is not only essential to life but critical to the psychological and biological well-being of people. From an architectural perspective, daylight enters an interior through **apertures** that include windows and skylights. Everyone appreciates windows in most interior spaces. Offices that have windows, especially on more than one side, are usually associated with status. Daylight is generally perceived as constant and is considered the standard for determining "true" colors. To determine an object's color accurately, people will often take the item outdoors or examine it near a window. Restaurants with a beautiful view of a city skyline, water, or golf course have prime seating close to these windows. Unfortunately, with the invention of electrical light sources and air conditioning, many contemporary buildings do not effectively integrate daylight into spaces. Many buildings have spaces with no windows or skylights. The integration of daylight into interiors is vital to creating quality environments. This practice includes **harvesting daylight**, that is, capturing daylight for the purpose of illuminating interiors.

The key to a quality lighting environment is distinguishing between sunlight and daylight. **Sunlight** is considered light that enters a space directly from the sun. This type of light is generally not good lighting for an interior. Direct sunlight can produce glare and excessive heat, and it can cause materials to fade. **Daylight**, or skylight, is the term that describes the desirable natural light in a space. Daylight results in a perceived even distribution of light that avoids the glare and ill effects of direct sunlight. A designer should always focus on ways to integrate daylight into an interior while avoiding the glare of sunlight.

aperture
An opening in a wall or ceiling, such as a window or skylight.

harvesting daylight
Capturing daylight for the purpose of illuminating an interior.

sunlight
Light from the sun that enters a space directly.

daylight (skylight)
Desirable natural light in a space.

Advantages and Disadvantages of Daylight

There are advantages and disadvantages to using daylight as part of a quality lighting plan. Advantages of integrating daylight into interiors include energy savings resulting from a reduction in electrical lights and from passive solar energy penetration in the winter. Another advantage to daylight is the even distribution of light that appears to reveal the "true" colors of objects and surfaces. Daylight also enhances visual acuity by providing better light for reading and writing. Advantages of integrating daylight into interiors also include benefits associated with windows, such as providing a view and ventilation.

In addition, daylight has positive psychological and physiological effects on people: it reduces stress, satisfies circadian rhythms, and encourages positive attitudes. A **circadian rhythm** is the biological function that coordinates sleeping and waking times through hormones and metabolic processes. Research done in hospitals, schools, and retail stores indicates that daylight has positive effects on human performance (Heschong, 1997; Heschong, 1999; Littlefair, 1996). Littlefair reported on the positive effects of using light shelves to maximize daylight in the patient rooms of hospitals. The Heschong Group (1999) found that students in classrooms with significant daylight had 7 to 18 percent higher scores than students working in classrooms with little or no daylight. It also found that retail stores with skylights reported 40 percent higher sales. (Human factors related to lighting are examined in detail in Chapter 8.)

Disadvantages of natural light are often a result of direct sunlight penetrating a space. The ultraviolet rays of the sun can fade fabrics and artwork. The fabric's fiber and weave determine how easily the material will be damaged. Natural fibers such as silk, cotton, or linen are more susceptible to damage than acrylics or polyesters, and tight weaves, shiny fabrics, and thick fibers are more resistant to damage from the sun. If direct sunlight cannot be avoided, a designer can specify a fabric that deteriorates less readily than others. Infrared rays of the sun also cause some woods to crack and peel. Disadvantages associated with windows include glare, noise penetration, the problem of cleaning and maintenance, lack of privacy, and heat gain in the summer. In addition, the beautiful views enjoyed during the day can become "black holes" at

circadian rhythm
A biological function that coordinates sleeping and waking times through hormones and metabolic processes.

night. Windows at night resemble mirrors by reflecting distracting images into the room. This problem can be resolved with appropriate window treatments and measures to reduce contrast, for example, by adding exterior lighting to the landscaping. The key to resolving problems associated with sunlight is first an awareness that these negative consequences exist, and then planning solutions that address the concerns. Many solutions include installing appropriate devices that help to control sunlight and layering light so that daylight penetration is integrated with electrical systems.

Solar Geometry and the Variability of Sunlight

Designing buildings that maximize penetration of daylight requires a great deal of analysis and planning, beginning with an understanding of solar geometry and the variability of sunlight. Solar geometry examines the movement of the earth around the sun. Sunlight changes daily, hourly, by the season, with the weather, and with geographical location. Colors, shadows, forms, and shapes vary during the day according to the sun's position. The oblique shafts of light produced by midmorning and late afternoon sun create long and soft shadows. The harsh shadows produced by sunlight at noon, on the other hand, emphasize the three dimensions of objects; this **modeling** is best achieved with side lighting rather than lighting from a ceiling (see Figure 2.1).

modeling
Emphasizing the three dimensions of a piece or surface through light, shade, and shadows.

FIGURE 2.1
Colors, shadows, forms, and shapes vary during the day according to the sun's position. Harsh shadows produced by sunlight at noon emphasize the shape of an object.

As illustrated in Figure 2.2, the path of the sun is dramatically different in summer and winter. In the northern hemisphere during the summer, the sun rises in the northeast and sets in the northwest. In contrast, the path of the winter sun is lower; it rises in the southeast and sets in the southwest. On October 21 and March 21, the sun's path is identical. The directional qualities of the sun are determined by the earth's latitude; a more northerly sunrise and sunset will occur in higher latitudes. To determine the sun's path in a specific location, one can contact the American Society of Heating, Refrigerating, and Air-Conditioning Engineers (ASHRAE).

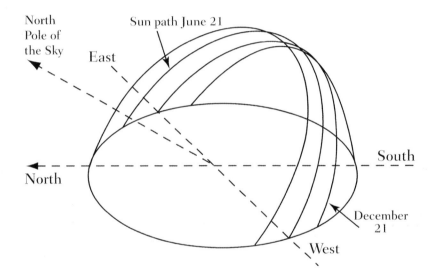

FIGURE 2.2
The path of the sun is different in the summer and winter.

To maximize quality daylight, a designer utilizes this solar geometry to specify the size, shape, and location of windows. Ideally, window and shielding units should be positioned to allow the maximum amount of sunlight into a space during the winter and the minimum amount during the hot summer. Shielding devices can include roof overhangs, louvers, and deciduous trees. A very sophisticated shielding device was designed for the Arab World Institute in Paris. The south side of the building is a glass wall (Figure 2.3) covered with photo-electrical control units. The metallic structure of the control units is aesthetically pleasing, and the photosensing mechanism allows the lenses to change according to the daylight levels. Functioning like a camera lens, on a cloudy day the aperture opens very wide to allow the maximum amount of daylight into the building. On a sunny day the lenses close to prevent a great deal of heat and sunlight penetration. This design helps to reduce energy costs, while the variability of daylight creates an ever-changing artistic composition on the south wall of the Institute.

FIGURE 2.3
The south side of the Arab World Institute in Paris is a glass wall covered with photo-electrical control units. The photosensing mechanism allows the lenses to change according to the daylight levels.

In addition to the geometry of the solar system, there are several other factors that influence the level and quality of daylight entering a space. These include clouds, weather, atmospheric pollution, orientation, landscaping, and surrounding structures. The amount and type of cloud affects the characteristics of daylight. Atmospheric pollution tends to create a hazy lighting condition, especially at sunset. Overcast days generally provide a uniform level of intensity that lacks the dynamic qualities of bright sunlight. Cloudy days reduce contrast and shadows. The U.S. Weather Bureau provides the number of overcast days per year by geographical location. A designer needs this information in planning the integration of daylight with electrical systems. For example, if a building is located in an area that experiences a high number of overcast days, it may be necessary to have extra large windows and an adequate number of electrical sources in order to have enough illumination.

Characteristics of Electrical Light Sources

An understanding of electrical light sources begins with an examination of the general characteristics of **lamps**. Lamps are commonly referred to as lightbulbs; they are the term for any source that produces optical radiation. Having a working knowledge of electrical light sources requires a review of a lamp's **light output**, efficacy, lamp life, color, maintenance factors, and cost.

The light level or **illuminance** that falls on a surface can be measured in **foot-candles** or **lux**. A foot-candle (fc) is a unit of illuminance equal to the amount of light that falls on a surface within a one-foot radius of the source (see Figure 2.4). It is appropriate for designers to review the guidelines established by the Illuminating Engineering Society of North America (IESNA) regarding the amount of light necessary to perform a specific task adequately. The **candlepower** of a light source, measured in **candelas (cd)**, is its intensity in a specific direction.

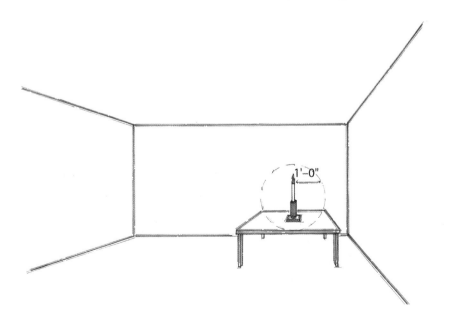

lamp
Commonly referred to as a lightbulb, a lamp is a source that produces optical radiation.

light output
The amount of illumination produced by a lamp, measured in lumens.

illuminance
The total amount of light on a surface; measured in lux (lx) or foot-candles (fc).

foot-candle (fc)
Unit measuring the amount of light that falls on a surface within a one-foot radius of the source.

lux (lx)
The International System of Units (SI) unit of illuminance.

candlepower
The intensity of a light source, measured in candelas.

candela (cd)
The SI unit of measurement of luminous intensity. One candela represents the luminous intensity from a source focused in a specific direction on a solid angle called the steradian.

FIGURE 2.4
A foot-candle is the amount of light that falls on a surface within a one-foot radius of the source.

The **watt (W)** is a unit measuring an electrical circuit's ability to do work, such as producing light and heat, in terms of the amount of electricity drawn. Therefore, a 20-watt lamp consumes 20 watts of electricity.

The **lumens per watt (lpW)** is a measure of the light output for each watt of electricity consumed and is used to determine energy efficiency. The resulting rating is known as the lamp's **efficacy**. The more lumens produced by a lamp per watt, the more efficient the lamp is and the more energy is saved. Typical lamp efficacies are provided in Table 2.1. **Lamp life** is a calculation derived from a record of how long it takes for approximately 50 percent of 100 lamps to burn out.

TABLE 2.1
Typical Lamp Efficacies

Lamps	Efficacies
Incandescent	10–40 lpW
Halogen incandescent	20–45 lpW
Fluorescent	35–105 lpW
Mercury	50–60 lpW
Metal halide	60–120 lpW
High-pressure sodium	60–140 lpW

Adapted from: GE Lighting Lamp Products Catalog, 2004.

Chromaticity and the color-rendering index are used to specify lamps and color. The **chromaticity** or the **color temperature** of a light source indicates the degree of red or blue in the light produced and is measured in kelvins (K). A lower number on the kelvin scale indicates warmer apparent color of a light source. For example, the warm color of light emitted from a candle is 2000K, and the color appearance of cool daylight is 5000K. A neutral color temperature is 3500K. Lamps of 3000K and 4100K provide a warm and cool appearance, respectively. The **color-rendering index (CRI)** measures how faithfully a light source reveals the colors of objects. The index range is from 0 to 100. The higher the CRI number, the better the color-rendering ability of the lamp.

Maintenance factors include replacement considerations based upon lamp life and reduced light output. Costs include the initial cost of the lamp, installation, energy requirements, and replacement considerations. The location of a lamp and the high cost of labor are factors to be considered when planning the replacement of lamps.

A lamp's size, wattage, shape, lpW, luminous intensity, life, color temperature, and CRI are provided in a lamp manufacturer's catalog. Figure 2.5 is a lamp manufacturer's chart for a halogen lamp. A designer should always refer to such charts when selecting and specifying lamps; the most current information will be found on the manufacturer's Web site. Figure 2.5 also explains how a designer uses the information in a specific application.

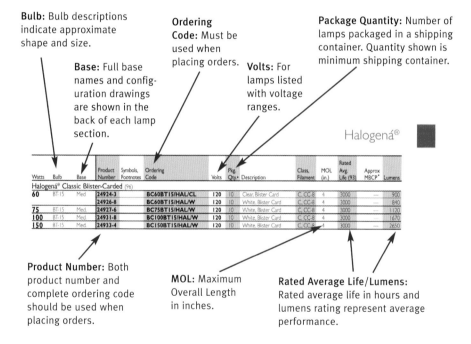

Bulb: Bulb descriptions indicate approximate shape and size.

Base: Full base names and configuration drawings are shown in the back of each lamp section.

Ordering Code: Must be used when placing orders.

Volts: For lamps listed with voltage ranges.

Package Quantity: Number of lamps packaged in a shipping container. Quantity shown is minimum shipping container.

Product Number: Both product number and complete ordering code should be used when placing orders.

MOL: Maximum Overall Length in inches.

Rated Average Life/Lumens: Rated average life in hours and lumens rating represent average performance.

FIGURE 2.5
A lamp manufacturer's chart for halogen lamps.

Incandescent and Halogen Lamps

The **incandescent carbon-filament lamp** is the oldest electrical light source and provides the greatest amount of flexibility for designers. Because of the simultaneous work conducted by Edison in the United States and Swan in England, 1879 is the year credited with the start of the lamp. Figure 2.6 illustrates a drawing of the basic components of an incandescent lamp. An electrical current heats the tungsten filament until incandescence is reached, at which point an incandescent lamp is said to be lit (Benya, Heschong, McGowan, Miller, and Rubinstein, 2001; Coaton and Marsden, 1997; IESNA, 2000). Tungsten is usually the conductive material used for this purpose because it has a high melting point and a low evaporation point.

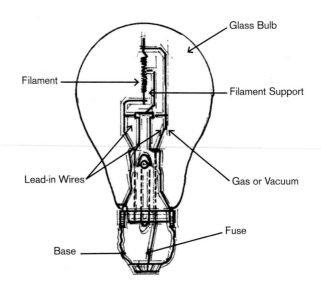

Glass Bulb

Filament

Filament Support

Lead-in Wires

Gas or Vacuum

Fuse

Base

FIGURE 2.6
The basic components of an incandescent lamp.

Heating the tungsten filament oxidizes it, causing fragments of tungsten to be deposited on the glass of the bulb. Eventually the tungsten accumulation will cause the bulb to burn out. Inert gases have been added to bulbs to reduce the oxidization of the tungsten filament. A standard incandescent lamp has argon with some nitrogen to prevent arcing. Adding krypton is expensive, but it increases the lumens per watt rating and extends the life of an incandescent lamp. Use of a halogen, either iodine or bromine gas, improves the performance of an incandescent lamp by redistributing the oxidizing tungsten on the filament rather than allowing it to accumulate on the glass (Benya, Heschong, McGowan, Miller, and Rubinstein, 2001; Coaton and Marsden, 1997; IESNA, 2000). These **tungsten-halogen lamps** are available in line (120 volts, typical household current) and low (generally 12 volts) voltage. Low-voltage lamps can produce more light output per watt.

tungsten-halogen lamp
Incandescent lamp that contains halogen.

The efficacy of the incandescent lamp is affected by the amount of heat produced by the lamp. Generally only 10 to 15 percent of the energy consumed to illuminate an incandescent lamp produces light, while 85 to 90 percent of the energy consumed produces heat. This can be observed by someone feeling the heat produced by an incandescent lamp after it has been on for a period of time. Heat generated by the lamp not only affects the lamp's life, but can damage artwork, fabrics, and other precious materials. In commercial environments the heat can seriously affect the load on air-conditioning systems. Dimming will reduce the amount of light and heat generated by the lamp.

Incandescent lamps are available in a variety of sizes, wattages, shapes, and colors. Sizes of incandescent lamps range from very small holiday lights to extremely large exterior search lamps. The variety in sizes corresponds to a wide range of wattages; a small night-light lamp can be just 4 watts, and large theater lamps can be as high as 10,000 watts. Incandescent lamps have been manufactured in a variety of shapes; however, there are standard shapes used throughout the industry (see Appendix). Codes developed by the American National Standards Institute (ANSI) include a letter that designates the shape of the lamp followed by a number that describes the diameter of the lamp in eighths of an inch. For example, in reviewing a lamp manufacturer's catalog, a designer will find an A19 listed in the incandescent lamp section. The A is the code for an "arbitrary" shape, and the lamp is $2\frac{3}{8}$ ($\frac{19}{8}$) inches wide at its widest point.

To improve the efficacy and directional qualities of the incandescent lamp, engineers developed the reflector (R) lamp. The R lamp replaced the standard incandescent lamp in tracks, recessed downlights, and accent luminaires. However, guidelines developed by the U.S. Energy Policy Act (EPAct) in 1992 imposed limitations on lamp energy consumption. To comply with the standards, some of the incandescent R and PAR (parabolic aluminized reflector) lamps are no longer manufactured. This includes the incandescent R30, R40, and PAR38 lamps. The PAR lamp has a heat-resistant glass that enables the lamp to be used outdoors.

Lamps with optical control systems are available in a variety of beam spreads ranging from **spot (SP)** to **flood (FL)**. Codes for descriptors of

spot (SP)
A narrow beam spread.

flood (FL)
A wide beam spread.

incandescent lamps are shown in Table 2.2. Lamps that are designed with a spot beam provide a very focused area of light. The size of the area illuminated is dependent upon the type of spot used. The traditional spot will illuminate a small area. An area will become more focused by

TABLE 2.2

Selected Codes for Descriptors of Lamps

Lamp Code	Description
A/*	Arbitrary
AR/	Aluminum Reflector
B/	Flame (smooth)
C/	Cone Shape
CA/	Candle
CMH/	Ceramic Metal Halide
ED/	Ellipsoidal Dimpled
F/	Flame (irregular)
**/FL	Flood
G/	Globe shape
GT/	Globe-Tubular
/H	Halogen
/HIR	Halogen Infrared Reflecting
/HO	High Output
MR/	Multifaceted Mirror Reflector
/MWFL	Medium Wide Flood
P/	Pear shape
PAR/	Parabolic Aluminized Reflector
PS/	Pear-Straight neck
R/	Reflector
/SP	Spot
S/	Straight side
T/	Tubular
TB/	Teflon Bulb
/VHO	Very High Output
/VWFL	Very Wide Flood
/WFL	Wide Flood

*Letters before / represent a lamp shape

**Letters after / represent a descriptor of a lamp

using a narrow spot (NSP) or a very narrow spot (VNSP). Flood lamps are designed to illuminate a large area. A traditional flood illuminates the smallest area. Wide flood (WFL), medium wide flood (MWFL), and very wide flood (VWFL) lamps illuminate larger areas. Figure 2.7 illustrates the candela distribution from a light source.

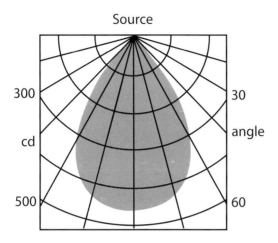

FIGURE 2.7
Candela distribution from a light source.

As a member of the incandescent family, the halogen lamp has the same positive qualities that other incandescent lamps have; however, the **halogen regenerative cycle** produces a much improved lamp in which the halogen gas and the compact size of the tube cause tungsten to be reapplied to the filament. This halogen regenerative cycle significantly reduces the amount of black sediment that accumulates on the inside of the glass. As a result, halogen lamps have a longer life than other incandescent lamps, and are 20 to 30 percent more efficient. The halogen lamp will emit more luminance using the same amount of electricity. Lumen maintenance is also improved because of the reduction or elimination of the bulb blackening.

halogen regenerative cycle *The operational process in which evaporated tungsten is redeposited on a halogen lamp's filament.*

To increase the efficacy of the halogen lamp, the halogen infrared reflecting (HIR) lamp was developed. With a coating on the glass, this lamp converts the infrared rays into visible light, resulting in an improved lpW rating. To improve the quality and quantity of light, General Electric recently announced a new halogen lamp that adds a silver coating to the IR film. Compared to the HIR PAR38, the additional silver coating on the

"Optimum" PAR38 results in a lamp that is more efficient and has a longer life. There is also a slight increase in energy savings.

An increase in the size of the filament of the incandescent lamp produced low-voltage lamps. Halogen and HIR lamps are available for line voltage and low-voltage systems. Line voltage in the United States is between 110 and 220 volts; a low-voltage application is between 6 and 75 volts. For a low-voltage application, a transformer is most often used to step down the electrical voltage. For luminaires with multiple fixtures, it is important not to exceed the maximum wattage permitted by a transformer; therefore, luminaires may require more than one transformer to accommodate high wattages. The low-voltage halogen lamp has excellent qualities including precise beam control, good resistance to vibration, high efficacy, high lumen output, and an extremely compact size.

Fluorescent Lamps

fluorescent lamp
An electric-discharge light source that generally uses electrodes, phosphors, low-pressure mercury, and other gases for illumination.

electric-discharge lamp
Electrical light source that produces illumination without filaments and operates on low or high pressure. An electric current passes through a vapor or gas.

ballast
A control device used with an electric-discharge lamp to start the lamp and control the electrical current during operation.

The **fluorescent lamp** is one of the discharge lamps. **Electric-discharge lamps** operate on low or high pressure and do not have the filaments that exist in incandescent lamps. Discharge lamps are made of glass, use mercury or sodium vapor, and require a **ballast** to start the lamp and control the electrical current. The majority of these lamps have electrodes and maintain a fairly consistent color. Fluorescent lamps are used extensively because they are energy-efficient, have a high lumen output, have a long life, radiate less heat than incandescent lamps, have a moderate initial cost and low operating cost, and have a variety of color options. Fluorescent lamps use up to 80 percent less energy and can last up to 18 times longer than incandescent lamps. Some fluorescent lamps are rated to last 40,000 hours.

As shown in Figure 2.8, the fluorescent lamp operates by having an electrical current pass through hot tungsten cathodes at either end of a long tubular shape (Benya, Heschong, McGowan, Miller, and Rubinstein, 2001; Coaton and Marsden, 1997; IESNA, 2000). The glass tube is filled with low-pressure mercury gas and other inert gases including argon, neon, and krypton. The cathodes emit electrons that excite the mercury gas, which produces radiant energy primarily in the form of invisible ultraviolet rays. The phosphorous coating on the inside of the glass tube reradiates the ultraviolet rays into the visible spectrum. As visible light is produced, the phosphor coating fluoresces. Since this glow occurs at a very low temperature, fluorescent lamps require very little electricity.

The phosphorous coating determines the color of the light produced. Initially, fluorescent lamps were manufactured with a chemical substance that limited the range of colors. The development of triphosphors made from rare-earth phosphors improved the color properties and efficacy ratings of fluorescent lamps.

Fluorescent lamps can operate only in a system that includes a ballast.

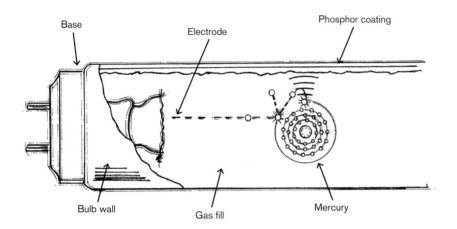

Base
Electrode
Phosphor coating

Bulb wall
Gas fill
Mercury

FIGURE 2.8
A fluorescent lamp operates by having an electrical current pass through hot tungsten cathodes at either end of a long, tubular shape.

The ballast starts the lamp and then regulates the flow of electrical current to it. The operating life of a ballast is approximately three times that of a fluorescent lamp. Ballasts are available in magnetic and electronic versions, the electronic ballast being generally preferred because it is more energy-efficient, is quieter, and weighs less than the magnetic ballast.

Fluorescent lamps are available in three lamp-ballast circuits, including preheat, instant start, and rapid start. The preheat system operates by heating the cathodes electrically at the start of the illumination and is used for lower-wattage lamps. To start the luminaire, the button must be held down for a short time. The instant-start lamp functions without a starter and has a high, open-circuit voltage that slightly reduces the life of the lamp. The rapid start operates by continuously heating the cathodes and is the most common system used today. It can illuminate lamps at high wattages and has a longer life than the other two lamp-ballast circuits. Dimming can be used only by a rapid-start system.

Fluorescent lamps are available in a variety of sizes, shapes, and wattages, but the most common are the straight tubes—T12, T8, and T5 (see Appendix). These designations are derived from the industry's nomenclature for fluorescent lamps. For example, an F40T8/835 is the nomenclature for a fluorescent (F) lamp of 40 watts (40), with a tubular shape (T) that is $\frac{8}{8}$" in diameter (8), a CRI rating in the 80s (8) and with a chromaticity of 3500K (35). Nomenclature can vary among lamp manufacturers, so a designer must refer to the manufacturer's key to ascertain the nomenclature for that company.

For many years, the T12 was the fluorescent lamp most frequently specified by designers and architects. For energy conservation purposes, the T12 should no longer be specified. The T8 has become the most successful because of its improved efficiency, enhanced color, and small one-inch diameter. The T8's lpW is approximately 25 percent better than the T12's. The smaller T5 lamp, on the other hand, is only slightly more efficient than the T8 and poses retrofit problems. The T5 lamp is available only in metric sizes and its mini-bipin bases can be installed only in luminaires that are specifically designed for it. The primary shapes of fluorescent lamps are the straight tube, U shape, and circle. Bending a straight tube makes the U shape and the circle. To comply with the 1992 U.S. Energy Policy Act (EPAct), standard 40-watt fluorescent lamps are no longer produced.

As an energy-efficient alternative to the incandescent lamp, the **compact fluorescent lamp (CFL)** or the energy-saving lightbulb has become a very popular choice. One or two of the linear fluorescent tubes is folded to create the CFL. Some of the CFLs have a screw base that replicates the base of an incandescent lamp. CFLs are available in twin, triple, and quadruple tubes. To maximize the light output while reducing the size of the lamp, manufacturers have developed the spiral-shaped CFL. The ballast for the lamp is either a separate control gear (see Figure 2.9a), or is built into the unit (see Figure 2.9b). These lamps produce a high lumen output and can yield energy savings of up to 75 percent compared to the incandescent lamp. Some CFLs are not designed to be dimmed and should not be used in a luminaire that has a dimming control.

compact fluorescent lamp (CFL)
A lamp made with one or more small, folded fluorescent tubes and equipped with a screw base. The ballast is a separate control gear or is built into the unit as an integral part of the system.

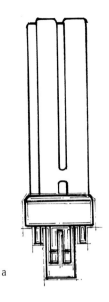
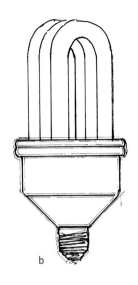

a b

High-intensity Discharge Lamps

Mercury, metal halide, and high-pressure sodium are **high-intensity discharge (HID) lamps** (see Figure 2.10). These are electric-discharge lamps with a light-producing arc that is stabilized by the temperature of the bulb (IESNA, 2000). A **mercury (MV) lamp** uses radiation from mercury vapor for illumination. A **metal halide (MH) lamp** utilizes chemical

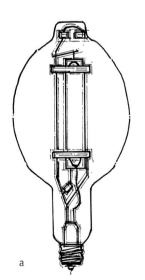
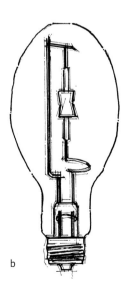
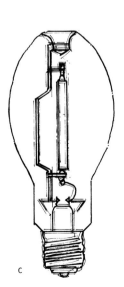

a b c

compounds of metal halides and possibly metallic vapors such as mercury. A **high-pressure sodium (HPS) lamp** uses sodium vapor for illumination.

HID lamps operate in a manner fairly similar to the fluorescent lamp. As with a fluorescent lamp, illumination from HID lamps begins with an arc between two electrodes, operates in a gas-filled cylindrical tube, requires ballasts, and uses radiant energy created by means of gases and metal vapors. Different lamps and wattages cannot be interchanged because HID ballasts are made for specific ones. Electronic ballasts are the best choice for HID lamps because they are more efficient than magnetic ballasts and can best control voltages.

HID lamps have been excellent choices for applications that require high efficacy, long life, high lpW performance, operation in a wide range of ambient temperatures, and positive long-term economics. Metal halide (MH) lamps have high efficacy, good color rendition, long life, good lumen maintenance, and a wide spectrum of colors and wattages. They are available in the shape of the arbitrary incandescent lamp and have warm and cool color renditions. Because of its excellent optical control and ability to be operated in a variety of temperatures, the MH lamp has many indoor and outdoor applications. The high-pressure sodium (HPS) lamp has an extremely high lpW rating, exceptionally long service, and excellent long-term economics. HPS lamps can last 40,000 hours, but over-wattage can shorten the life of the lamps. Lamp life ratings are based upon ten hours per start.

Disadvantages of HID lamps include the required start-up time, color shifts during the life of the lamp, variations in color between lamps of the same type, strict ballast requirements, and the fact that they are not easily dimmable. Start-up times for some HID lamps are between two and ten minutes. The **restrike** time can be several minutes because the lamp must cool down before starting again. This is especially problematic in applications where safety and security are critical issues. Good restrike time is necessary when there is a power interruption or reduction in voltage in the system. Some instant-restrike HID lamps are available, but only at high wattages, and they must be used with special luminaires and ballasts. In applications that require illumination at all times, a designer should specify an additional luminaire that would illuminate the space during the restrike time, or specify an HID lamp with a built-in auxiliary unit that lights up when the lamp shuts down. Because of the warm-up and restrike characteristics of HID lamps, it is not advisable to use these lamps on units that have motion detectors.

The technology of MH and HPS lamps is continually improving. The compact MH lamp is available in lower wattages, making it an ideal solution for display and track systems. The Pulse Start and the Ceramic MH lamps (CMH) are improvements on the standard MH lamp. The CMH lamp has the best performance characteristics, including better color consistency over the life of the lamp. The newest CMH lamps have improved efficacy, lumen maintenance, color rendition, and lamp life.

Remote Source Illumination Systems: Fiber Optic Lighting

Fiber optic lighting is one of the newest forms of electrical light and can be used for general, task, accent, and decorative applications. Fiber optics utilizes a remote source for illumination, from which light is transmitted through a bundle of optical fibers. Fiber optic lighting is used in a variety of applications, including architectural, custom, landscape, and signage.

The light source used for fiber optics is housed in a box called the **illuminator**, and the directional lamp is usually metal halide or tungsten-halogen (see Figure 2.11). Metal halide lamps are used for

fiber optic lighting
An electrical light source that utilizes a remote source for illumination. Light is transmitted from the source through a bundle of optical fibers.

illuminator
The box that contains the light source for a fiber optic lighting system. The fiber optics originate from the illuminator.

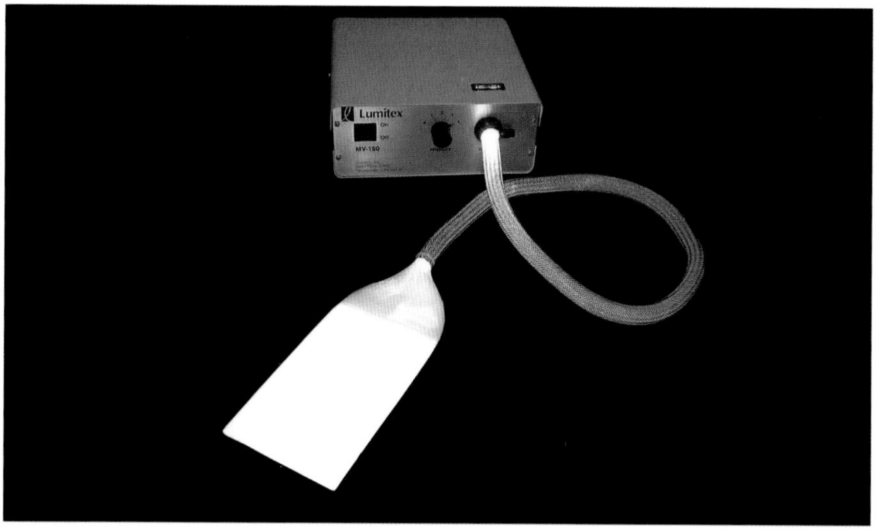

FIGURE 2.11
The light source for a fiber optic system is housed in the illuminator.
The directional lamp, located in the illuminator, is usually metal halide or tungsten-halogen.

applications that require long lamp life, though some systems are starting to use LEDs as the light source. The optical fibers are bundled together at the "port" or opening in the side of the illuminator. They are made from glass or plastic, and hundreds of optical fibers can be used in the system. Glass is the preferred material because it transmits excellent color, transmits light well, lasts long, requires minimum maintenance, and bends easily. Light produced from fiber optics is a result of internal reflection; in an **end-emitting** system, light is visible at the end of the fibers (see Figure 2.12a), while in a **side-emitting** system, light is visible along the sides of the entire length of the fibers (see Figure 2.12b).

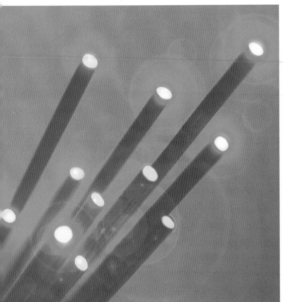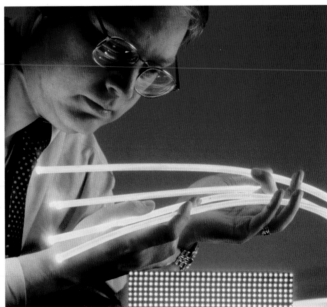

a

b

FIGURE 2.12
In fiber optic systems, light is visible by (a) end-emitting or (b) side-emitting fibers.

End-emitting fiber optic systems produce directional illumination and are made from glass. End fittings are available in a variety of finishes and styles. The most common interior end fittings are fixed or adjustable downlights (see Figures 2.13a and 2.13b). The fittings are small, approximately two inches in diameter; crystal end fittings produce sparkle and are only one inch in diameter. Side-emitting systems are made from glass or plastic and produce an even distribution of illumination over the length of the fibers. The longest optical fibers are made from plastic and can be 100 feet long. A variety of special effects are available that are housed in the illuminator. Wheels can be installed to provide color changes or twinkling. The twinkling wheel provides a touch of animation to the light. Fiber optic systems can also be dimmed.

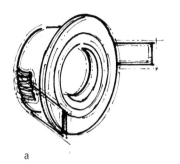
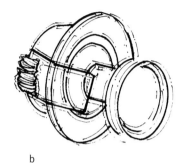

a   b

FIGURE 2.13
The most common interior end fittings for fiber optic systems are (a) fixed or (b) adjustable downlights.

There are many advantages to using fiber optic lighting, including safety, ease of maintenance, low transmission of heat to objects being illuminated, and very small amounts of the infrared (IR) and ultraviolet (UV) wavelengths. Since the light source in fiber optic systems is located in the illuminator, the fibers only transmit light and do not carry an electrical current. This makes it possible for a designer to place the fibers in wet spaces such as swimming pools, ponds, saunas, spas, steam rooms, and showers, while the illuminator is installed at a remote dry location.

Fiber optic lighting is easy to maintain because there are few lamps to replace and the illuminator can be mounted in a location that is easily accessible. Fewer lamps also result in energy savings. Because of the intense heat produced by some lamps, fans should be installed in the illuminator. Installing the lamp at a remote site eliminates the detrimental effects of heat and IR and UV rays on objects being illuminated. Thus, fiber optic lighting is an excellent choice for heat-sensitive products, artwork and other decorative objects, and fragile museum artifacts.

There are many design options with fiber optic lighting. The tiny point of light emitted by fiber optics can be quite decorative, presents a high-tech look, and attracts attention without glare (see Figure 2.14). Designers use end-emitting systems in display cases to highlight jewelry

and crystal. Cabinetmakers install fiber optic lighting in a variety of furniture pieces including curio cabinets, breakfronts, bookcases, and entertainment units. Fiber optic lighting is also very effective for illuminating steps and pavers.

Electroluminescent Lamps

**electroluminescent
lamp**
*Electrical light source
that operates
through an
interaction between
an electrical field
and a phosphor.*

**light-emitting diode
(LED)**
*Semiconductor
device consisting of
a chemical chip
embedded in a
plastic capsule. The
light is focused or
scattered by lenses
or diffusers.*

In 1907 Henry Joseph Round discovered the phenomenon of electroluminescence. **Electroluminescent lamps** operate through an interaction between an electrical field and a phosphor (Benya, Heschong, McGowan, Miller, and Rubinstein, 2001; Coaton and Marsden, 1997; IESNA, 2000). Electroluminescent lamps include **light-emitting diodes (LEDs)** and lamps used for instrument panels and liquid crystal displays. These lamps are lightweight, have long life, require high-voltage drivers, and use very little electricity. Some lamps have operated for over 10 years.

LED is the first solid-state electronic light source for lighting, and the technology has improved dramatically since the mid-1990s. Currently, a tremendous amount of research is being conducted to create LED light that is viable for interior lighting. This light is expected to be available by 2010. An LED is a semiconductor in the form of a chemical chip embedded in a plastic capsule (see Figure 2.15). A volt from a direct current energizes the chip, making visible light. A transformer is needed to operate the lamps with a direct current. The light is focused by lenses or scattered by **diffusers**. The lamp life of LEDs is calculated as the mean time between failures (MTBF).

The chemicals contained in the chip determine the color of the light. The first colors were red, green, and amber; the development of blue in the 1990s enabled lamp manufacturers to produce white, significantly improving the application of LEDs for general illumination. One method used to produce the color white is through color mixing by combining red, green, and blue LEDs in one unit. This approach is not very successful because the white produced is altered as the individual LEDs deteriorate. The preferred way to create a white light is to use an LED with phosphors that absorb blue and hence produce a white color. However, the white produced is a "cool" white that is generally undesirable for interior applications. Scientists and engineers are working to develop phosphors that will produce a warmer white LED light with a high level of illumination.

diffuser
Cover on a luminaire that scatters light in many directions, made from white plastic or etched glass.

FIGURE 2.15
An LED consists of a chemical chip embedded in a plastic capsule.

LEDs are available in stand-alone or networked applications. Solar LEDs are also available. Many stand-alone applications are similar in shape and configuration to incandescent, halogen, fluorescent, and neon lamps. For example, LEDs have been installed in a unit that allows a drop-in replacement for a halogen flood or accent light. A tube

LED system that resembles the tube systems in neon lamps provides colored illumination throughout the element.

Networked arrangements include several luminaires and one controller. Digitally controlled LEDs provide flexibility in colors, brightness, and special effects such as twinkling or synchronization with music. These systems are especially effective for specialty architectural lighting and in retail stores, restaurants, and nightclubs. Software and hardware LED systems allow a user to manage, design, and control large-scale installations. For example, LED systems are available that use a series of tiles, or panels, to create scenes. Each tile is edged with red, blue, and green LEDs, allowing the user to create every possible color. Computer graphics programs can be used to create images from the tiles; a programmable controller creates synchronous color that changes the LED light in each tile. This same technology is also available for tube lighting systems.

As an illumination source in its infancy stage, LEDs have advantages and significant disadvantages. LED lamps are durable and small, have a long life, use minimal electrical power, have a directional source, and do not emit UV or IR radiation. Their efficacy is better than that of incandescent lamps. In addition, LEDs do not have glass or filaments that can break.

FIGURE 2.16
Interior applications using LEDs focus on settings that require decorative lighting in various colors.

As a new illumination technology, LEDs have not been used in many interior applications. LEDs are primarily used for signage, display backlights, automobiles, and pedestrian signals. Interior applications have focused on settings that need decorative lighting in various colors, such as bars, restaurants, or retail stores (see Figure 2.16). As LEDs improve, especially in color rendition properties and levels of illumination, designers will be able to use them for a variety of general, task, and accent applications. The LED light is a significant emerging technology, and designers should be alert to new developments.

SUMMARY

- It is essential to distinguish between sunlight and daylight. Direct sunlight can produce glare, excessive heat, and fading of materials. Daylight is the term that describes the desirable natural light in a space.

- Advantages to integrating daylight into interiors include energy savings resulting from a reduction in electrical lights and from passive solar energy penetration in the winter. Another advantage of daylight is the even distribution of light that appears to reveal the true colors of objects and surfaces. Daylight enhances visual acuity by providing better light for reading and writing.

- Designing buildings that maximize penetration of daylight begins with an understanding of solar geometry and the variability of sunlight.

- Factors that influence the level and quality of daylight entering a space include clouds, weather, atmospheric pollution, orientation, landscaping, and surrounding structures.

- An understanding of electrical light sources and their advantages and disadvantages requires a review of a lamp's light output, efficacy, lamp life, color, maintenance factors, and cost.

- An incandescent lamp operates by having an electrical current heat the tungsten filament until incandescence is reached. A standard incandescent lamp uses argon with some nitrogen to prevent arcing.

- Use of a halogen, either iodine or bromine gas, improves the performance of an incandescent lamp by redistributing the oxidizing tungsten on the filament rather than allowing it to accumulate on the glass. These lamps are halogen and are available in line and low voltage.

- The fluorescent lamp is a discharge lamp. Discharge lamps are made from glass, use mercury or sodium, and require a ballast to start the lamp and control the electrical current.

- Fluorescent lamps are available in three lamp-ballast circuits including preheat, instant start, and rapid start. Fluorescent lamps are available in a variety of sizes, shapes, and wattages, but the most common are the straight tubes of the T12, T8, and T5.

- Compact fluorescent lamps (CFL) produce a high lumen output and can achieve up to 75 percent energy savings compared to the incandescent lamp.
- The three basic types of high-intensity discharge (HID) lamps are mercury vapor (MV), metal halide (MH), and high-pressure sodium (HPS).
- HID lamps have been excellent choices for applications that require high efficacy, long life, high lpW performance, operation in a wide range of ambient temperatures, and positive long-term economics.
- Fiber optic lighting utilizes a remote source for illumination. The light source is housed in a box called the illuminator, and the directional lamp is usually metal halide or tungsten-halogen. The fibers are made from glass or plastic, and hundreds of optical fibers can be used in the system.
- There are many advantages to using fiber optic lighting, including safety, ease of maintenance, low transmission of heat to objects being illuminated, and very small amounts of the infrared (IR) and ultraviolet (UV) wavelengths.
- An LED is a semiconductor consisting of a chemical chip embedded in a plastic capsule. A volt from a direct current energizes the chip, making visible light. A transformer is needed to operate the lamps with a direct current. The light is focused or scattered by using lenses or diffusers.

Key Terms

aperture	compact fluorescent lamp (CFL)
ballast	daylight (skylight)
candela (cd)	diffuser
candlepower	efficacy
chromaticity	electric-discharge lamp
circadian rhythm	electroluminescent lamp
color temperature	end-emitting fiber optic
color-rendering index (CRI)	lighting system

fiber optic lighting	light-emitting diode (LED)
flood (FL)	light output
foot-candle (fc)	lumens per watt (lpW)
fluorescent lamp	lux (lx)
halogen regenerative cycle	mercury (MV) lamp
harvesting daylight	metal halide (MH) lamp
high-intensity discharge (HID)	modeling
lamp	restrike
high-pressure sodium (HPS)	side-emitting fiber optic
lamp	lighting system
illuminance	solar geometry
illuminator	spot (SP)
incandescent carbon-filament	sunlight
lamp	tungsten-halogen lamp
lamp	watt (W)
lamp life	

Exercises

1. Select two types of lamps from the following categories: incandescent, fluorescent, and HID. Locate the lamps in the catalogs of three different lamp manufacturers. In a summary essay, compare and contrast the performance of the lamps.

2. Identify several commercial and residential applications for end-emitting and side-emitting fiber optic systems. Write an essay that identifies the applications and discusses the advantages and disadvantages of using the two major types of fiber optic lighting.

3. In an essay, provide examples of how fiber optics and LEDs could be used for general, task, accent, and decorative lighting.

4. In an essay, provide examples of how incandescent, fluorescent, metal halide, and high-pressure sodium lamps could be used for general, task, and accent lighting. This discussion should also include how daylight can be successfully integrated with these electrical light sources.

5. Developing observation and problem-solving skills is critical to the success of a designer. Find installations of incandescent, fluorescent, and HID lamps in residential or commercial interiors. For each installation, respond to the items listed below.

   a. Identify the purpose of the space.

   b. Identify the purpose of the lighting, including an identification of general, task, and accent lighting.

   c. Evaluate the appropriateness of the illumination level.

   d. Based upon the definition of quality lighting environments described in Chapter 1, evaluate the overall quality of lighting in each space.

   e. Based upon your observations and reflections, provide recommendations for improving the lighting environment.

CHAPTER 3

Color and Directional Effects of Lighting

OBJECTIVES

- Summarize the basic concepts associated with color and lamps.
- Explain how chromaticity and the color rendering index can be used to specify lamps and color.
- Identify the elements of an environment that contribute to brightness and glare.
- Provide design solutions that maximize the positive attributes of brightness and control glare.
- Describe the reflectance properties of colors and materials.
- Apply the principles of reflectance and optical control to an environment

In Chapter 2 we saw that color was an important element in integrating and controlling daylight and electrical lights. Generally, people perceive daylight to reveal an object's "true" color. However, weather conditions, reflections, and the time of day can affect perceived color. The type of light source will affect perceived color, which influences the work of an interior designer. This is especially challenging with electrical light sources. Chapter 2 introduced chromaticity and the color rendering index (CRI) to assist designers in selecting electrical light sources that enhance colors.

Designing a quality lighting environment requires an understanding of the impact of the intensity and direction of a light source on an object's appearance, the effect of architectural features, the ability to perform a task, and the quantity of illumination. In layered lighting plans, an interior designer must coordinate the intensity and directional effects from all the light sources. A lighting plan must be developed that is in harmony with the physical attributes of furniture, objects, walls, floors, window treatments, and interior architecture. Colors, textures, shapes, forms, and size are affected by the intensity and directional qualities of light sources. Concurrently, the elements of design can affect the quantity and direction of light.

Lamps and Color

The eye can detect over five million colors. The perception of all these colors is affected by numerous factors, but most importantly by the source of light. For example, the wavelengths of daylight vary according to the time of day, sky conditions, time of year, and geographic location. Daylight at sunset appears to be redder than it does at noon, because the light will have more red and yellow wavelengths than blue or green ones. Northern daylight has more blue and green wavelengths than does southern daylight, resulting in a cooler appearance. Impressionist artists studied extensively how the appearance of colors and objects changed with the conditions of light and atmosphere. For example, Claude Monet painted the western façade of Rouen Cathedral at many different times of the day and under a variety of weather conditions (Figures 3.1a and 3.1b). From 1892 to 1894, he created 20 paintings of Rouen Cathedral.

Color cannot be seen without light. To prove this to yourself, walk through a room at dusk and attempt to identify and distinguish colors. You will notice that you can see objects but that it is nearly impossible to discern the colors of these objects and surfaces. Once the lights are turned on, the colors become visible. These facts are important when a lighting designer selects a light source. If a light source does not have a balanced spectrum of colors, the color of the object being illuminated will be altered. In specifying a quality lighting system, a designer selects lamps that will enhance the colors in the environment. To assist designers with the lamp selection process, lamp manufacturers provide data about lamp color specifications, such as chromaticity ratings and the color-rendering index (CRI).

a   b

Chromaticity

The chromaticity, or color temperature, of a light source helps to create the atmosphere of a space and often reflects the quality of the interior. The color temperature indicates the degree of red or blue in the light supplied by a light source. It is measured in kelvins (K) and is part of the information provided by lamp manufacturers about their lamps. On a kelvin scale, the warmer the apparent color of a light source, the lower the number of kelvins will be. A higher number on the scale represents a cooler or bluer color. For example, the warm color of light emitted from a candle is approximately 2000K, while the color of cool daylight is 5000K. A neutral color falls at about 3500K. Lamps that provide a warm and cool appearance have chromaticity ratings of 3000K and 4100K respectively.

FIGURE 3.1a
Effect of noon sunlight on the façade of Rouen Cathedral as painted by Claude Monet.

FIGURE 3.1b
Effect of a cloudy day on the façade of Rouen Cathedral as painted by Claude Monet.

One way to understand the scale is to imagine the heating of a hard material such as steel. As the steel is heated, it will first turn red, followed by yellow, then white, and finally blue-white, so that the temperature of the steel is reflected in the relative coolness of its color. Similarly, an interior that has a warm glow will have a relatively low chromaticity rating (3000K). In contrast, an interior that appears to be cool and bright will have a relatively high chromaticity rating (4100K). To comply with state energy codes, the most common chromaticity ratings for fluorescent sources are 3000K, 3500K, and 4100K. These lamps are available with CRIs in the 70s and 80s; some manufacturers produce lamps with CRIs in the 90s.

In an attempt to measure color, an international organization for color, the International Commission on Illumination or Commission Internationale de l'Eclairage (CIE), developed a diagram consisting of a graph on which colors ranging from red to violet are plotted on *x* and *y* axes (Figure 3.2). The diagram represents **correlated color temperature (CCT)**. The mathematics of the colors form the triangular-shaped diagram: the wavelengths of the colors, in nanometers, are identified around the perimeter of the color triangle, and all colors in the spectrum blend in the center to become white.

The *x* and *y* coordinates on the diagram help designers locate a color. In the center of the triangle is the "black body locus." This black curved line demonstrates the progression in color temperature in kelvins (K). As illustrated in Figure 3.2, one of the circles on the black body locus represents sunlight at noon, with a color temperature of 4870K. The light from a lamp with warm color appearance is shown to have a color temperature of 3000K. In practice, designers can use the CIE chromaticity diagram to determine quickly how a specific lamp compares to sunlight or the cool northwest sky.

correlated color temperature (CCT)
A color temperature in kelvins determined by the x and y coordinates on a color diagram (developed by the International Commission on Illumination).

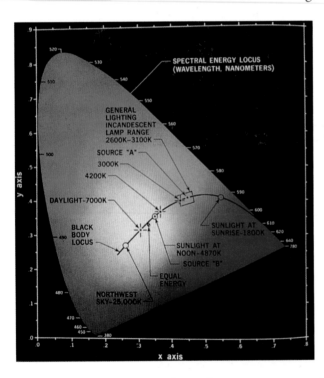

FIGURE 3.2
CIE chromaticity diagram for natural and artificial light sources.

For example, 3000K lamps are located on the black curved line midway between sunlight at sunrise and sunlight at noon, indicating that these lamps tend to enhance warm colors. Another lamp is located in the blue-green colored area, indicating that it tends to enhance cool colors. The diagram also makes it easy for a designer to compare the chromaticity ratings of various lamps.

Color Rendering Index

A designer must know the color temperature and rendering ratings of lamps in order to specify those that are appropriate. The color rendering index (CRI) measures how faithfully a light source reveals the true colors of objects, and is another piece of information provided by manufacturers of lamps. The index ranges from 0 to 100. The higher the CRI number, the better the color rendering ability of a lamp. The number is based upon an average of how eight colors appear in the light of different lamps in comparison to a standard test lamp. Thus, a source may be very good on most of the hues but not as good on others. Incandescent lamps have a CRI of 95 to 100 because they produce nearly perfect renditions of colors.

When color is important, select a lamp with a CRI in the 80s or higher. A CRI in the 90s should be specified in settings where color appearance is very important. Compared to lamps with a CRI in the 70s, the cost of lamps with a CRI in the 80s or higher is greater because of additional rare earth phosphors used and a slightly lower efficacy rating. To determine the colors of objects and surfaces, an interior designer should always examine samples under the lamps and/or any daylight in the space.

To integrate a lamp's color temperature and rendering ability, General Electric developed a chart that demonstrates the relationship between chromaticity in kelvins and the CRI (Figure 3.3). As shown in Figure 3.3, a warm (3000K) fluorescent lamp has approximately the same chromaticity as a different fluorescent lamp. However, the color rendering ability of the two lamps is approximately 80 and 50, respectively. Thus, because their chromaticity is similar, both lamps will appear to be a cool light source, but color rendering will be better with the lamp having a CRI of 80. A designer selecting lamps for a high-end retail store could first select lamps with a low chromaticity rating, and then select from within this grouping the lamp with the highest CRI.

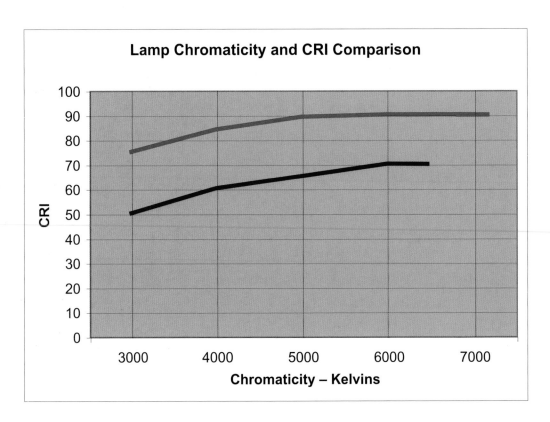

Lamp Chromaticity and CRI Comparison

FIGURE 3.3
The CRI and chromaticity of artificial light sources.

Table 3.1 summarizes color properties of common lamps produced by three major manufacturers. (It also indicates initial and mean lumens; according to the chart, a 4100K fluorescent lamp with a CRI in the 80s has initial and mean lumens of 2860 and 2710, respectively. Initial lumens is the light output when the luminaire is first installed, and mean lumens is the average light output over the life of the lamp.) It should be noted that for each of the major CCT ratings (3000K, 3500K, 4100K), fluorescent lamps are available in two CRI ratings (70s and 80s). Table 3.1 also provides some lamp suggestions for specific applications. For example, according to the chart, a 5000K fluorescent lamp is excellent for checking the color of textiles during the printing process and other situations where the quality of color is evaluated.

TABLE 3.1
Lamp Color Specifications and Suggested Applications

Lamps			CRI (approx.)	CCT (K) (approx.)	Suggested Applications
Incandescent			97–100	2500–2800K	Residential, special applications, such as niches, historic fixtures, sconces, night-lights, pendants
Halogen			97–100	2800–3000K	Residential, hospitality, gallery, retail (high-end)
Fluorescent F32T8's					
General Electric Initial/Mean Lumen	Osram Sylvania	Phillips			
SPX50/ECO 2715/2580	850/ECO	TL850/ALTO	5000K	80s	Color-critical areas in galleries, printing, jewelry displays, medical examinations
SP50/ECO 2665/2530	750/ECO	TL750/ALTO	5000K	70s	Galleries, printing, jewelry displays, medical examinations
SPX41/ECO 2860/2710	841/ECO	TL841/ALTO	4100K	80s	Color-critical areas in offices, retail (discount), and hospitality, florists, classrooms, conference rooms
SP41/ECO 2715/2580	741/ECO	TL741/ALTO	4100K	70s	Offices, retail (discount), and hospitality, florists, classrooms, conference rooms
SPX35/ECO 2860/2710	835/ECO	TL835/ALTO	3500K	80s	Color-critical areas in offices, reception areas, retail, hospitality, hospital, residential
SP35/ECO 2715/2580	735/ECO	TL735/ALTO	3500K	70s	Offices, reception areas, retail, hospitality, hospital
SPX30/ECO 2860/2710	830/ECO	TL830/ALTO	3000K	80s	Color-critical areas in offices, retail (high-end); and hospitality, libraries, hospital, residential
SP30/ECO 2715/2580	730/ECO	TL730/ALTO	3000K	70s	Offices, retail (high-end), and hospitality, Libraries, hospital, residential
Ceramic Metal Halide Initial/Mean Lumen					
General Electric Initial/Lumen	Osram Sylvania	Phillips	3000K–4200K	80–93	
CMH70/PAR38 4800/NA	MCP70PAR18	CDM70/PAR38	3000K	80s	Offices, retail, hospitality, hospital
CMH150/T6 13000/11000	MC150T6	CDM150/T6	4000K–4200K	90s	Offices, retail, hospitality, hospital
High Pressure Sodium Initial/Mean Lumen					
LU250/D 28000/27000	LU250/D	C250S50/D	2100K	22	Efficiency critical: industrial, outdoors
LU250/DX 22500/20700	N/A	C250S50/C	2200K	65	Industrial, outdoors

Directional Effects of Lighting

Brightness and Glare

brightness
An effect from a light source at a high illuminance level that can be perceived as either positive or distracting.

To have a quality lighting environment, an interior designer must develop a plan that maximizes the positive attributes of **brightness** and that controls glare. Brightness is a subjective concept that has positive and negative connotations. The bright lights we see during the Christmas holidays are exciting and contribute to the gaiety of festivities. In contrast, the bright lights of an automobile's high beams directed toward a driver on a dark highway are distracting and dangerous. Ideally, an interior designer plans an environment that results in only positive reactions to brightness.

Technically, brightness is the result of the interaction between an illumination level and the amount of light reflected off various surfaces, known as reflectance. An interior designer can measure the quantity of light in a space that results from the reflectance of objects and surfaces. (Measuring illumination is reviewed in Chapter 4.) However, illuminance and reflectance are only two factors that affect brightness. Illumination levels can be significantly increased without appearing to be brighter. For example, even though foot-candle levels are very high on a cloudy day, people perceive the day as gloomy. Furthermore, an increase in illumination levels does not necessarily improve the quality of lighting; sometimes, changing the direction of a light source, rather than increasing the quantity of lighting, is the best way to improve a dark work area. To deal with brightness successfully, an interior designer must consider all the factors involved, including subjective responses, the context of the situation, the vision attributes of the individuals using the space, light sources, directional qualities, and characteristics of elements of the design.

Brightness is generally a subjective reaction to an environment and is dependent upon individuals' expectations and comparative contexts as well as the physical condition of their eyes. In analyzing the perceived brightness of an environment, an interior designer must anticipate expectations of a setting within the variability of different times of the day and year. Through their accumulated experiences, people develop expectations for illumination levels and perceived brightness. For example, people generally expect light levels to be lower in the evening than during the day, and higher during the summer months than in the winter. Expectations of brightness are also related to the specific activity to be undertaken in a space. For example, a lighting plan for an office may not appear to be too bright, whereas the same illumination level in a romantic restaurant would most likely be perceived as too bright.

Perceived brightness is also affected by the physical condition of the eyes. Elderly people might not consider a light source bright because age affects their vision. A younger individual, on the other hand, might perceive the same environment as very bright. The eye has the ability to adjust to an enormous range of illumination levels; however, this adaptation affects perceived brightness. For example, if an individual moves from a very dark space to a lighter area, the lighter area may appear very bright until the eye adjusts to the higher illumination level.

The perceived brightness of an environment is also affected by light sources and their directional qualities. The design of a luminaire and the type of lamp used affect the perceived brightness of electrical sources. A luminaire that provides direct illumination can be perceived as bright, while the light from indirect light sources generally appears softer (Figures 3.4a and 3.4b). Exposed lamps, especially those with clear glass, can appear to be bright. The perceived brightness of a light source also depends upon the location of the luminaire in relation to users: if a luminaire appears to be bright only when one looks directly at the exposed lamps, the perceived brightness can be altered by moving the location of the task or changing the direction of the light source.

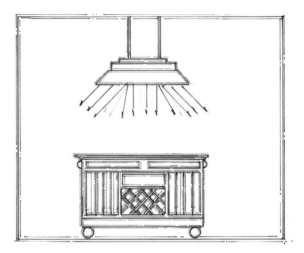

FIGURE 3.4a
Light dispersion of a direct luminaire.

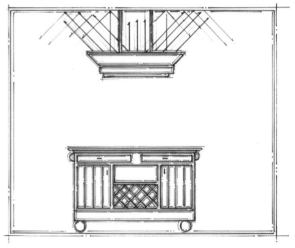

FIGURE 3.4b
Light dispersion of an indirect luminaire.

The perceived brightness of a setting is affected by its surroundings: an object will appear to be brighter when the area surrounding the light source is dark, and dimmer when the surrounding area is lighter. For example, high-beam headlights on an automobile appear to be bright at night, but not during the day.

The color, texture, and finish of objects also affect the perceived brightness of an interior. White and light colors will appear to be brighter than black and dark colors. Smooth and shiny textures will be perceived as brighter than rough and matte finishes. For example, a room painted white in a high-gloss finish will appear to be brighter than a room paneled in a dark, rough wood.

Excessive brightness is known as **glare**. As with perceived brightness, there are a variety of factors that affect glare. Glare can easily occur in illumination settings that require contrast for effective visibility and attention. For example, retail displays designed to attract attention to a product will often have a higher illumination level on the product than on the surrounding area. If the contrast between the two areas is too great, glare can occur. When the eye has to adjust to contrasting light levels, there is a loss in visual acuity and a potential for eye fatigue and strain, resulting in a negative subjective reaction. Glare due to contrast and high illumination levels can also occur with activities that require task lighting, for example, if concentrated light is shed on a task while the rest of the room is in darkness, or when bright, concentrated light sources are located above and in front of where the task is performed (Figure 3.5).

glare
A distracting high-illuminance level that can cause discomfort or be disabling.

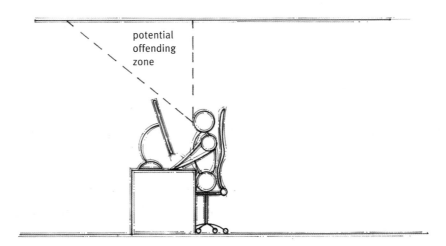

FIGURE 3.5
Luminaire locations that can cause glare to the user of the desk.

Direct or indirect glare occurs as a result of the intensity and direction of a light source. **Direct glare** occurs when a light source is at a high-illumination level and is usually not covered or shielded. It also often occurs on a bright sunny day if there is no window treatment. Any lamp that is exposed and illuminated at a high level can cause direct glare. Generally, any unshielded lamp greater than 25 watts can cause glare. A flame-shaped lamp in a chandelier can cause glare at a high-illumination level, but the same lamp appears to glitter or sparkle at lower light levels. (For more information regarding types of luminaires, refer to Chapter 5.) Direct glare can also be the result of extreme contrast in illumination levels between rooms. This can occur in a residential interior, for example, when the living room and dining room are located next to each other, and one of these rooms is in darkness while the other is highly illuminated. To help reduce glare, all spaces adjoining a room should have some illumination.

Indirect glare occurs from light that is reflected from surfaces or objects. It is important to examine how an individual can be affected by the reflections from indirect light sources. For example, on a sunny day, one can experience indirect glare from the sunlight reflected off light-colored surfaces or materials such as snow, concrete, or sand. Indoors, indirect glare can be the result of reflection of a light source from a light-colored or shiny surface. Glass, mirrors, and high-gloss surfaces, such as highly polished wood or the ink on a printed page, can cause indirect glare when the light source is directed toward these specular materials. Often an indirect light source can cause glare on visual display terminal (VDT) screens. As discussed in Chapter 1, indirect light that is reflected from a surface in a task area is termed *veiling reflections*.

Discomfort glare and disability glare are terms that describe the degree of disturbance caused by a bright light source. **Discomfort glare** occurs when a natural or electrical light source causes glare that is uncomfortable, but still allows an individual to see objects and perform tasks. Discomfort glare can be especially annoying when an individual is exposed to the glare for a long time. **Disability glare** arises when the glare from a light source is so severe that the individual is unable to see. This can happen, for example, when an individual is unable to see objects on a windowsill on a sunny day, or has difficulty seeing the faces

direct glare
A distracting high-illuminance level, frequently caused by viewing a bare light source or by extreme contrast in illumination levels.

indirect glare
A distracting high-illuminance level caused by reflection of a light source off a surface or object.

discomfort glare
A distracting high-illuminance level that is uncomfortable but still allows one to see.

disability glare
A distracting high-illuminance level that makes it impossible or difficult to see.

FIGURE 3.6
Disability glare in this hallway is the result of a bright light source.

of people approaching in a dark hallway with windows behind them (Figure 3.6). Disability glare can also occur when an individual is unable to read text on a glossy magazine page because of the reflection of the light on the surface. The high gloss of oil paints can cause disability glare on artwork. Some interior designers rely upon disability glare to discourage users from looking at undesirable elements in an interior, such as mechanical systems in an exposed ceiling.

Glare must be controlled in a quality lighting environment, and there are many approaches for an interior designer to consider depending upon the specific elements of an interior and the users of the space. Glare is easier to control when using more luminaires with lower wattages compared to fewer high-wattage luminaires. Locating luminaires out of the field of vision can also control glare. This requires an examination of the direction of a light source and all locations where people are sitting, standing, or walking. Unshielded downlights can be problematic because they are permanent installations and because of the direct angle of the beam of light. For example, a restaurant lighting plan that utilizes downlights above the tables can result in glare. The original lighting plan might have the downlights located directly in the center of the tables, avoiding glare for the patrons; however, tables in restaurants are frequently moved to accommodate various groups of people, to clean the floor, or through carelessness. When the tables are moved, the downlights are no longer centered and might cause glare by being positioned directly over the faces of people. The glare is disturbing, and the mottling effect on faces can be very unflattering. Shielding lamps with a material, such as a **shade**, **baffle**, **louver**, or lens, can reduce glare.

shade
A device, either opaque or translucent, that shields a bare lamp from view.

baffle
A linear or round unit in a luminaire designed to shield light from view.

louver
A grid-shaped unit of a luminaire designed to shield light from view.

Reducing brightness ratios is a means of controlling glare and is achieved by examining a variety of factors in the environment, including the illumination levels between areas in a space and the size of the opening in the luminaire. Generally, smaller luminaire openings have a greater potential for glare than larger apertures. Therefore, a luminaire that disperses light from a large area can help to reduce glare. An interior designer must also reduce brightness ratios from daylight by specifying window treatments that either prevent direct sunlight from entering the room or soften the light penetration. Exterior devices, such as awnings or roof overhangs, can also be used to reduce glare from sunlight.

reflectance
The ratio of incident light to the light reflected from a surface or material.

angle of incidence
The angle at which rays of light emitted from a light source strike an object or surface before reflection.

Reflectance, Optical Control, and Transmission

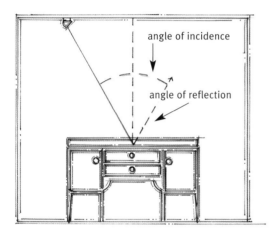

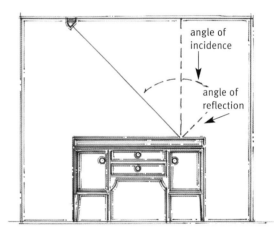

An object's appearance, the architectural features of an interior, the quantity of illumination, and the ability to perform a task are all affected by reflectance, optical control, and transmission. **Reflectance** is another factor that is affected by the direction of a light source and demonstrates the interaction between lighting and surface qualities of objects and materials. Determining the reflectance of a surface or object involves examining the **angles of incidence** and reflection (Figure 3.7). Changing the angle of the light source affects the angle of reflection (Figure 3.8). The type of lamp and shielding device on a luminaire also affects the angle of incidence. For example, a lamp with a clear glass covering allows light to travel in a straight direction. Frosted or milky materials alter the

FIGURE 3.7
Angle of incidence of light coming from a light source, striking a surface, and reflecting to the interior.

FIGURE 3.8
Changing the direction of the light source alters the angle of reflection.

angle of direction; light emitted from a frosted incandescent lamp will be diffused. Luminaires may be designed with shielding devices that direct incident light in one or multiple directions. Some luminaires, such as a pendant globe with a white painted finish, will emit a multi-directional angle of incidence. **Interreflection** occurs when light is contained within a structure and is continuously reflected from its surfaces. As discussed in Chapter 2, this occurs in fiber-optic lamps that are encased in a black tube (Figure 3.9).

Reflectance is affected by the color and texture of an object or surface. Depending upon the characteristics of a material, when light strikes a surface, it is reflected or absorbed. A specular object is one that reflects light. **Specular reflectance** results when all the falling light is reflected (Figure 3.10a). This occurs when light strikes a glossy surface. When most of the light is reflected, **semi-specular reflectance** occurs (Figure 3.10b). This can occur when light strikes a surface that has some specular or reflecting qualities but is irregular, such as etched glass or a hammered finish. **Diffused reflectance** (Figure 3.10c) arises when the light is scattered at a variety of angles, such as when light strikes a matte finish. Reflection from a shiny material or bright color can cause discomfort or disability glare.

Materials can also be rated according to their reflecting ability. Smooth and shiny materials will reflect more light than rough and heavily textured materials. Reflectance values of various materials are provided in Table 3.2. To compensate for luminous reflectance values in an interior with light colors and smooth surfaces, the illumination level may need to be reduced. In contrast, in an environment that has dark colors and rough materials, the illumination level might have to be increased. However, before increasing or decreasing the illumination level, an interior designer must examine other environmental factors that affect reflectance values in a space, including the size of the room, the location of a surface, and light sources.

interreflection
Result of light bouncing back and forth within an enclosed space or structure.

FIGURE 3.9
Interreflection is occurring as light reflects back and forth within an enclosed area.

specular reflectance
The phenomenon that occurs when a shiny material causes light to be reflected in one direction.

semi-specular reflectance
The phenomenon that occurs when a partially shiny material causes light to be reflected primarily in one direction.

diffused reflectance
The phenomenon that occurs when a material with a matte finish causes light to scatter in a variety of directions.

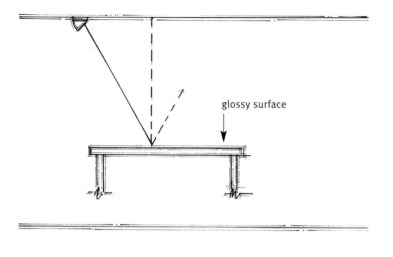

FIGURE 3.10a
Light coming from
a light source, striking
a glossy surface,
and reflecting to
the interior.

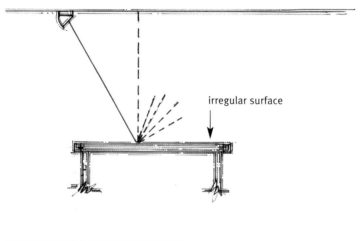

FIGURE 3.10b
Light coming from
a light source, striking
an irregular surface,
and reflecting to
the interior.

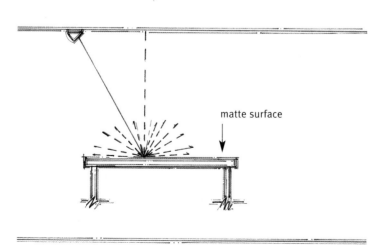

FIGURE 3.10c
Light coming from
a light source, striking
a matte surface,
and reflecting to
the interior.

TABLE 3.2
Reflecting Materials

Material	Reflectance [a,b] (percent)	Characteristics
Specular		
Mirrored and optical coated glass	80–99	Provide directional control of light and
Metallized and optical coated plastic	75–97	brightness at specific viewing angles.
Processed anodized and optical coated aluminum	75–95	Effective as efficient reflectors and for
Polished aluminum	60–70	special decorative lighting effects.
Chromium	60–65	
Stainless steel	55–65	
Black structural glass	5	
Spread		
Processed aluminum (diffuse)	70–80	General diffuse reflection with a high
Etched aluminum	70–85	specular surface reflection of from
Satin chromium	50–55	5 to10 percent of light.
Brushed aluminum	55–58	
Aluminum paint	60–70	
Diffuse		
White plaster	90–92	Diffuse reflection results in uniform
White paint b	75–90	surface brightness at all viewing
Porcelain enamel b	65–90	angles. Materials of this type are good
White terra cotta b	65–80	reflecting backgrounds for coves and
White structural glass	75–80	luminous forms.
Limestone	35–65	

[a] Inasmuch as the amount of light transmitted depends upon the thickness of the material and the angle of incidence of light, the figures given are based on thickness generally used in lighting applications and on near-normal angles of incidence.

[b] These provide compound diffuse-specular reflection unless matte finished.

Source: Reprinted from the IESNA Lighting Handbook (9th ed.), pp. 1–22, with permission from the Illuminating Engineering Society of North America.

Because light reflects off surfaces and between surfaces—known as interreflection—reflectance levels are affected by the size of a room. In a small room the walls are close together, so the light reflected from the walls strikes other walls and increases the reflectance level of the color. In a large room with high ceilings, the surfaces may be too far apart to cause interreflection, thus resulting in a lower reflectance level. Remember, even light-colored walls absorb some light. The location of a surface also affects reflectance levels. For instance, ceilings and walls cause interreflection because of their location, while floors reflect less light. Light sources that are close to a light-colored surface and have a high-illumination level will elicit the greatest amount of reflection. Recommended reflectance levels for surfaces are summarized in Table 3.3. This is a guideline and can be important when energy conservation is a design criterion.

TABLE 3.3
Recommended Reflectance for Interior Surfaces of Residences

Surface	Reflectance (percent)	Approximate Munsell Value
Ceiling	60–99	8 and above
Curtain and drapery treatment on large wall areas	35–60	6.5–8
Walls	35–60*	6.5–8
Floors	15–35*	4.0–6.5

* In areas where lighting for specific visual tasks takes precedence over lighting for the environment, the minimum reflectance should be 40 percent for walls, 25 percent for floors.

Source: Reprinted from the IESNA Lighting Handbook (9th ed.), pp. 18–22, with permission from the Illuminating Engineering Society of North America.

Some lamps and luminaires are designed to control illumination. Reflector lamps, such as R, PAR, and MR lamps, have an optical system designed within the lamp to control light. As described in Chapter 5, shielding devices, reflection, refraction, and diffusion are all elements of luminaires that are designed to control illumination. Shielding devices for luminaires include baffles, louvers, and fascias. Since light cannot penetrate the shielding units within the luminaire, additional illumination is produced by reflection. Luminaires designed to control light through reflection have materials such as shiny aluminum on the inside surfaces. These materials are known as specular because they reflect light. Light is emitted from the lamp and is reflected off the material to a surface or object (Figure 3.11). A luminaire with an interior surface made from a specular material can reflect a high percentage of the lamp's illumination. However, these luminaires can also cause glare. Luminaires made from a specular material but having a brushed or etched finish, on the other hand, will diffuse some of the incident light rays, while matte finishes and dark colors will diffuse more. Some luminaires are designed with **reflector contours** to maximize the amount of illumination emitted from a lamp by increasing reflection into a space. Common shapes for these luminaires include ellipses, parabolas, and circles.

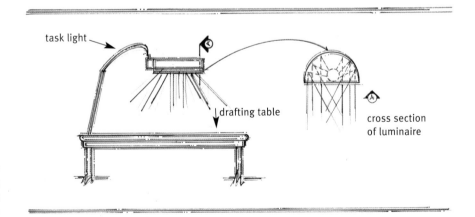

task light
drafting table
cross section
of luminaire

reflector contour
A design feature of a luminaire serving to help maximize the reflection of light into a space.

FIGURE 3.11
Light strikes the interior of a luminaire and then reflects into an interior space.

Some luminaires are made of materials designed to let light through rather than control it. **Transmission** is the term used to describe the passage of light through a material. The three types of transmission are direct, diffused, and mixed (Figures 3.12 a–c). Direct transmission

transmission
The passage of light through a material.

occurs when the majority of the light passes through the material (Figure 3.12a). Clear glass is an example of a material that allows direct transmission. Material that creates diffused transmission, such as plastic, causes the light to be scattered in many directions (Figure 3.12b). Mixed transmission occurs with materials that allow most of the light to pass through in a semi-scattered manner (Figure 3.12c). Etched and sandblasted glass are examples of such materials. Keep in mind that white plastics can be a source of glare. (For more information on the design of luminaires, see Chapter 5.)

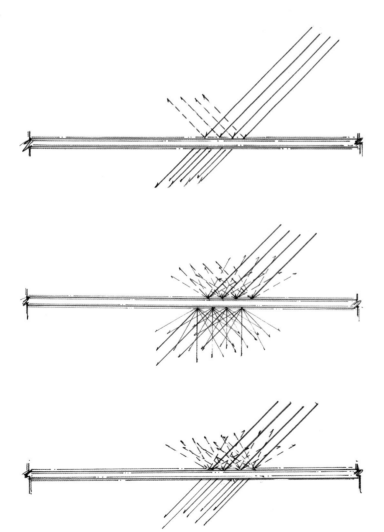

FIGURE 3.12a
Direct transmission occurs when most of the light passes through clear glass in a straight direction.

FIGURE 3.12b
Diffused transmission occurs when some of the light passes through a plastic material in a scattered direction.

FIGURE 3.12c
Mixed transmission occurs when most of the light passes through an etched glass in a semi-scattered direction.

Color and the directional effects of lighting explored in this chapter are important elements in a lighting system. In specifying a lighting plan, an interior designer must consider how color and the intensity and direction of a light source affect an object's appearance, the architectural features of a space, the ability of people in the space to perform a task, and quantity of illumination. The next chapter covers how to determine the quantity of illumination required in a quality lighting environment.

SUMMARY

- The wavelengths of daylight vary according to the time of day, sky conditions, time of year, and geographic location.
- Chromaticity ratings and the color rendering index are two types of data about lamp color.
- Chromaticity, or the color temperature of a light source, helps to create the atmosphere of a space and often reflects the quality of the interior. The color temperature indicates the degree of red or blue in the light emitted by a light source. Chromaticity of a light source is measured in kelvins (K) and is part of the information provided by lamp manufacturers.
- The warmer the apparent color of a light source, the lower the number on the kelvin scale. For example, the warm color of light emitted from a candle is 2000K, while the color appearance of cool daylight is 5000K.
- The color rendering index (CRI) measures how faithfully a light source reveals the color of objects. The index ranges from 0 to 100. The higher the CRI number, the better the color rendering ability of the lamp.
- The ability to perform a task or view an object is affected by a variety of factors, including glare, contrast, colors, illumination levels, and the physical condition of the eyes.
- The direction of a light source can affect the quantity of light required in a space.
- To ensure a quality lighting environment, an interior designer must develop a plan that maximizes the positive attributes of brightness and controls glare.
- Brightness is generally a subjective reaction to an environment and is

dependent upon individuals' expectations, their comparative contexts, and the physical condition of their eyes.

- A variety of factors affect glare, including individual perceptions, condition of the eyes, and extreme contrast in illumination levels.
- Reflectance is an example of the interaction between lighting and the surface qualities of objects and materials.
- Controlling the directional qualities of light sources is a key element in creating the desired atmosphere in an environment and in ensuring effective accent lighting.

Key Terms

angle of incidence

baffle

brightness

correlated color temperature
  (CCT)

diffused reflectance

direct glare

disability glare

discomfort glare

glare

indirect glare

interreflection

louver

reflectance

reflector contour

semi-specular reflectance

shade

specular reflectance

transmission

Exercises

1. In groups of three to four individuals, select four fabrics with warm and cool colors in a variety of textures, and four wall coverings with warm and cool colors. Take the material samples to a variety of commercial settings, including a grocery store, retail stores, a residence, and a library. Examine the fabrics and wall coverings under the various light sources. For each of the settings, record the type of light source and each group member's subjective reactions to the appearance of the colors.

2. Draw a CRI and chromaticity graph similar to General Electric's chart illustrated in Figure 3.3. Using the data in Table 3.1, identify and locate on the graph three lamps, each with chromaticity ratings in the ranges of 3000K, 4000K, and 5000K.

3. Identify five different commercial spaces and ask at least ten people in each space whether they perceive any of the light sources as bright. Be sure to ask people of various ages. Record their responses, the type of luminaire, lamp, illumination level (high, medium, low), and the location of the light sources. Analyze the data and write a report that summarizes the results and provides recommendations for future illumination applications.

4. Select eight different materials having a variety of textures. Utilizing a clamp light, direct the light source at each material and record the resultant reflection properties. Position the light source at a variety of angles and distances from the material. Record all results and write a report that provides a summary and recommendations for future practice.

5. Using the World Wide Web, locate luminaires that are designed with each of the following control devices: (a) reflection, (b) diffusion, and (c) shielding unit. Print the pictures of the luminaires and mount them in a notebook. Identify the advantages and disadvantages of each.

CHAPTER 4

Quantity of Light

- Describe the basic units of measurement used in lighting, including luminous intensity, luminous flux, illuminance, luminance, and luminance exitance, and comprehend the relationships among them.
- Understand candlepower distribution curves and how to apply the data they provide.
- Identify key factors to consider when specifying illumination levels for a quality lighting environment.
- Determine the average illuminance for an interior using the lumen method.
- Determine illuminance levels for a point in a space.

A quality lighting environment must have a plan for flexible illumination levels that reflects changes at different times of the day, a variety of activities, and the users of the space. Too often, designers forget that the quantity of illumination is only one consideration in a lighting system. Unfortunately, many environments are planned with only one lighting level.

Reducing the quantity of lighting and creating flexible illumination levels is essential to sustainable interior environments. Managing the quantity of lighting used reduces the consumption of energy and natural resources, and decreases the amount of waste that is deposited in landfills. Interior designers must understand the factors that affect the quantities of illumination in a space and develop strategies for the management of lighting systems.

Units of Measurement

International System of Units

Measuring the quantity of lighting in an environment is based upon the principles of radiometry and photometry. **Radiometry** is a scientific discipline dealing with the measurement of radiant energy in the form of electromagnetic waves. Radiant energy is heat energy transferred through space. **Photometry** is a science derived from radiometry that includes the human response to a source of illumination. The world-wide standard for the units of measurement is the International System of Units (SI). The properties measured include luminous intensity, luminous flux, illuminance, luminance, and luminous exitance.

In photometry, **luminous intensity** (abbreviated as I) is the intensity of a light source, measured in candelas (cd). One candela represents the luminous intensity from a source pointing in a specific direction on a solid angle called the **steradian** (Figure 4.1). Originally, a candle was used to measure luminous intensity, but it was impossible to arrive at a standard with so many types of candles; hence the international use of the candela, from which other units of measurement are derived. Candlepower and candela are considered interchangeable terms.

radiometry
A scientific discipline dealing with the measurement of radiant energy in the form of electromagnetic waves.

photometry
A scientific discipline dealing with the measurement of light, including the effects of vision.

luminous intensity
The intensity of light from a source pointing in a specific direction on a solid angle called the steradian.

steradian
A solid angle used to measure luminous intensity from a source in a specific direction.

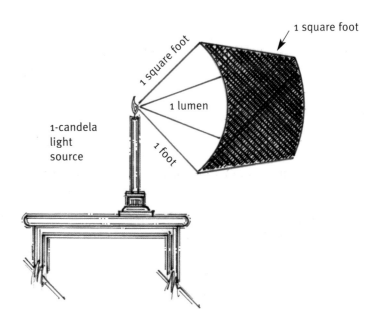

1 square foot

1 square foot

1 lumen

1-candela light source

1 foot

FIGURE 4.1
One candela from a source pointing in a specific direction on a solid angle, the steradian.

Luminous flux is the total amount of illumination emitted by a light source, measured in lumens (lm). The SI symbol or abbreviation is F. Lamp manufacturers provide this information about their products. As discussed in Chapter 2, the number of lumens produced by a lamp per watt of electricity consumed determines the lamp's efficacy. The **luminaire efficacy ratio (LER)** is a ratio of the lumens per watts consumed for the entire luminaire system, which includes the total lamp lumens, ballast factor, and photometric efficiency.

The unit of measurement used to determine the total amount of light falling on a surface is illuminance. The abbreviation for illuminance is E, and it is measured in lux (lx) or foot-candles (fc) in the metric and customary systems, respectively. An illumination of 1 lux is produced by 1 lumen of light shining on an area of one square meter. Ten lux equals approximately one foot-candle. Thus, a recommendation for 400 lux of illumination on a work surface would be equivalent to 40 foot-candles. By way of context for these measurements, the foot-candle levels for a full moon and for sunlight at noon are .01 fc and 10,000 fc respectively. Many work areas in homes, offices, and conference rooms utilize 30 to 50 fc (300 to 500 lx). As discussed in previous chapters, there are many factors to consider in determining illumination levels, including the lamp, design of the luminaire, maintenance procedures, reflectance values, and distance and angle from the light source to the task.

Luminance is a measure of the objective brightness of a light source. It indicates the amount of light in the eyes of users of the space after reflection or transmission from a surface. Thus, illuminance and reflectance affect luminance. The unit of measurement is candela per square meter (cd/m^2), and L is the abbreviation for the term. Brightness is the term used to refer to an individual's perception of the light in a space and, being somewhat subjective, is not a measurable property. Luminance affects the apparent brightness of a surface or material and is dependent upon the location of the user as well as colors, textures, and interior architecture. **Luminous exitance** is another term associated with luminance. This is a measure of the total quantity of light reflected and emitted in all directions from a surface or material. Luminous exitance is measured in lumens per square foot (lm/ft^2).

luminous flux
The total amount of illumination emitted by a light source; measured in lumens (lm).

luminaire efficacy ratio (LER)
A ratio expressing the lumens per watts consumed for the entire luminaire system.

luminous exitance
The total quantity of light reflected and emitted in all directions from a surface or material.

Photometric Data

To determine the direction, pattern, and intensity of light from reflector lamps and luminaires, interior designers refer to **candlepower distribution curves**, as provided by lamp and luminaire manufacturers (see Figure 4.2). Interior designers often use the term "bat-wing graphs" to refer to specific curves that resemble the shape of a bat's wings. These curves result from a bat-wing lens. On a polar candlepower distribution curve, zero, or the **nadir** (straight down), is the location of a light source. The concentric circles on the graph indicate the intensity expressed in candelas and the radiating lines are the angles of distribution.

Figure 4.2 illustrates a photometric data chart of a direct fluorescent (2-T8s) luminaire manufactured by Prudential Lighting. Directly above the candlepower distribution graph are summary data related to the luminaire. D = 100% and I = 0%, indicating that the luminaire is a direct fixture (100% direct light) and does not give any indirect (0 percent) light. The lamp lumens are 2950 with input watts of 59.

The chart also provides spacing criteria data. The spacing criterion (SC) is a metric measurement that indicates luminaire locations for spaces requiring consistent illumination levels. The height of direct luminaires is measured from the bottom of the fixture to a work surface that is 2' 6" above the floor (Figure 4.3). The measurement for indirect luminaires is from the ceiling to the work surface. Luminaire manufacturers provide SC ratio recommendations with other photometric data (see Figure 4.2). The SC for the length of the luminaire is referred to as the "parallel" or "along," and the short side of the luminaire is the "perpendicular" or "across." For the luminaire depicted in Figure 4.2, the SC along is 1.1, and the SC across is 1.3. Deviations from the recommended SC locations may result in illumination levels that are too high in some areas or too low in others.

Reflected light can be put to use. To maximize the amount of illumination derived from reflectance, luminaires should be installed close to walls, but not so close that they cause excessive brightness on the walls. Generally, the ideal distance from a wall to a fixture is half the center-to-center distance between fixtures. The formula for calculating the center-to-center distance between fixtures is: Spacing Intervals (SI) = SC ratio x Mounting Height (MH), where the mounting height is the

photometric data

OLYP-2T8-04-SPL-TMW-D1

Report # LSI15526   D=100% I=0.0%
Spacing Criteria: Along 1.1; Across 1.3
Lamp Lumens: 2950   Input Watts: 59

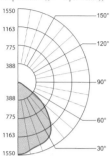

Candlepower Summary

Vertical Angle	Horizontal Angle 0	22.5	45	67.5	90	Output Lumens
0	1526	1526	1526	1526	1526	
5	1519	1513	1511	1508	1511	145
10	1480	1474	1466	1459	1458	
15	1419	1406	1400	1414	1417	397
20	1347	1329	1341	1376	1396	
25	1262	1245	1287	1347	1379	598
30	1160	1158	1233	1299	1334	
35	1045	1062	1156	1206	1241	708
40	913	956	1045	1057	1077	
45	771	830	885	866	884	651
50	605	668	678	656	684	
55	414	482	462	427	411	394
60	215	253	261	198	157	
65	103	106	106	103	105	117
70	53	49	46	70	75	
75	26	23	19	39	48	33
80	11	11	9	14	21	
85	3	3	3	5	6	5
90	0	0	0	0	0	

Zonal Lumen Summary

Zone	% Lamp	% Luminaire
0-90	51.66	100.00
90-180	0.00	0.00

Efficiency = 51.7%

Luminance Summary (cd/m ^{2})

Angle	0	45	90
45	3612	4162	4156
55	2388	2678	2380
65	804	835	829
75	338	244	616
85	120	121	228

Coefficients of Utilization (%)

Floor	effective floor cavity reflectance = .20											
Ceiling	80				70				50			
Wall	70	50	30	10	70	50	30	10	50	30	10	
RCR 0	62	62	62	62	60	60	60	60	57	57	57	
1	58	56	54	53	57	55	53	52	53	52	51	
2	54	51	48	46	53	50	48	46	48	46	45	
3	50	46	43	40	49	45	42	40	44	42	39	
4	47	42	38	36	46	41	38	35	40	37	35	
5	43	38	34	31	42	37	34	31	36	33	31	
6	40	34	30	28	39	34	30	27	33	30	27	
7	37	31	27	25	37	31	27	24	30	27	24	
8	34	28	24	21	34	28	24	21	27	24	21	
9	32	25	21	19	31	25	21	19	24	21	19	
10	29	23	19	17	29	23	19	17	22	19	16	

installation

Adjoining Detail

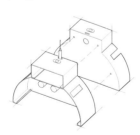

Mounting Locations

Cable mount   x = 1 1/2"
Cable/cord mount   x = 1 1/2"
Stem mount   x = 1 1/2"
Surface mount   y = 5"
(Finish plates not shown)

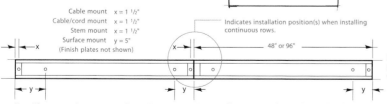

Indicates installation position(s) when installing continuous rows.

48" or 96"

Note: When connecting two or more fixtures in a row, mounting assemblies are required on both ends of the first fixture, with only one mounting assembly required on each additional fixture.

Suspension (x1)

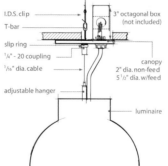

I.D.S. clip
T-bar
slip ring
1/4" - 20 coupling
1/16" dia. cable
adjustable hanger
3" octagonal box (not included)
canopy
2" dia. non-feed
5 1/2" dia. w/feed
luminaire

Suspension (x3)

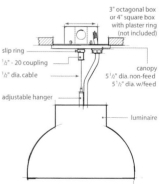

slip ring
1/2" - 20 coupling
1/2" dia. cable
adjustable hanger
3" octagonal box or 4" square box with plaster ring (not included)
canopy
5 1/2" dia. non-feed
5 1/2" dia. w/feed
luminaire

In an effort to continually provide the highest quality products, Prudential reserves the right to change design specifications and/or materials, without notice.

distance from the bottom of the luminaire to the work surface. The spacing intervals for a luminaire that is 7' 6" from a work surface and an SC of along 1.1 and across 1.3 are 8' and 10' on center along the length and along the short side of the fixture, respectively. This is determined by the SI = SC x MH equation as follows:

$$SI = 1.1 \times 7.5 = 8.25$$
or 8 feet on center along the length of the fixture
$$SI = 1.3 \times 7.5 = 9.75$$
or 10 feet on center along the short side of the fixture

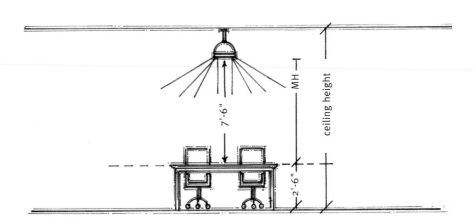

FIGURE 4.3
In calculating lighting quantities, the height measurement for direct luminaires is determined from the bottom of the fixture to a work surface that is 2'-6" from the floor (Mounting Height = MH).

To read the candlepower distribution graph, identify a specific angle of view, and then read the associated candelas. For example, for the direct linear luminaire, illustrated in Figure 4.2, the emitted candelas at a vertical angle of 30° are approximately 1160. This number is also available in the candlepower summary table. To locate the candelas at a vertical angle of 30° in the candlepower summary, refer to the vertical angle column. Find 30° and look to the right to locate the horizontal angle column for 0°. Moving to the right in the same row will provide the emitted candelas at horizontal angles of 22.5°, 45°, 67.5°, and 90°. For example, at a vertical angle of 30°, the emitted candelas at the 45° horizontal angle are 1233. The last column in the candlepower summary chart indicates the output in lumens at various vertical angles. For example, at a vertical angle of 25°, the output in lumens is 598.

The zonal lumens summary table provides a quick overview of lumens in two zones. Since the luminaire has a direct distribution of light, all the light is emitted in the zone between 0° and 90°, that is, in the downward zone. The zonal lumens table also indicates the efficiency of the luminaire and lamp combination, which is 51.7%. In addition, the cutsheet provides luminance summary (cd/m^2) data. For this luminaire, the luminance levels are higher at the lower vertical angles. For example, at a vertical angle of 45°, the luminance is 3612, while at 75°, it is 338. The table containing coefficients of utilization (percentage) data is explained later in this chapter.

As illustrated in Figure 4.2, luminaires and reflector lamps with a symmetrical distribution are often illustrated on only one side of the graph, since each half will be identical. It is important to note that indirect/direct luminaires have a candlepower distribution curve above and below nadir. If the luminaire distributes a high level of illumination toward the ceiling, to avoid annoying brightness or glare, it might be necessary to locate the fixture at a considerable distance from the ceiling. Luminaires that emit light from the top and sides of the fixture will have candlepower distribution graphs for vertical and horizontal light angles.

Calculations

Calculations for determining illuminance can be done by hand or by using a lighting software package. This section reviews both methods. To ensure a quality lighting environment, it is critical to recognize that the illuminance level identified through the calculations is only one of the variables to be considered in arriving at the final specifications. All the criteria discussed throughout this textbook, and the uniqueness of a site and its users, must be synthesized for the final lighting plan.

Lumen Method

The lumen method described in this section is an abbreviated method used to determine the average illuminance on horizontal surfaces in a room. These data can be useful in the initial stages of the lighting design process.

room-cavity ratio (RCR)
A formula designed to take into account the proportions of a space and the potential distance from the luminaires to a work surface.

coefficient of utilization (CU)
The ratio of initial lamp lumens to the lumens on a work surface.

light loss factor (LLF)
The amount of illuminance lost because of the type of lamp, ambient temperature of the space, time, input voltage, ballast, lamp position, interior conditions, or burnouts.

lamp lumen depreciation (LLD)
A measure of the loss of lumens resulting from the design of a lamp.

luminaire dirt depreciation (LDD)
A measure of the loss of light that results from dirt and dust accumulation.

To determine more accurate illuminance calculations, refer to IESNA (2000) or advanced lighting software programs. IESNA annually publishes a review of current lighting software in *Lighting Design and Application*.

To perform illuminance calculations, several elements must be identified, including the proportions of a room, luminaire, lamps, location of work surface, distance between the work surface and the luminaires, and reflectance values of ceilings, walls, and floors. In addition, the calculations require the **room-cavity ratios (RCR), coefficient of utilization (CU)** for luminaires, **light loss factor (LLF), lamp lumen depreciation (LLD),** and **luminaire dirt depreciation (LDD)**.

The RCR is a formula designed to take into account the proportions of a space and the potential distance from the luminaires to the work surface. In the formula, H is the height of the ceiling from the work surface; L is the length of the room; and W is the width of the room.

$$RCR = \frac{5(H)\ (L + W)}{L \times W}$$

The room-cavity ratio (RCR) is used to determine the coefficient of utilization (CU) (see Figure 4.2). The CU depends on the space to be illuminated and the design of the luminaire. The CU indicates the ratio of initial lamp lumens to the lumens on a work surface for a particular luminaire, lamp, location of the task plane, and space. CU percentages are available from luminaire manufacturers (see Figure 4.2). The CU table in Figure 4.2 is based upon a floor cavity reflectance of .20. Ceiling reflectance percentages are 80, 70, and 50. Wall reflectance percentages are provided for 70, 50, 30, and 10.

LLF indicates the illuminance that is lost as a result of the type of lamp, the temperature of the space, time, input voltage, ballast, lamp position, interior conditions, and burnouts. There can be a 25 percent loss of lumens because of dirt, dust, and lamp depreciation. IESNA (2000) has identified recoverable and nonrecoverable LLFs. The recoverable LLFs include room surface dirt depreciation, lamp lumen depreciation, lamp burnouts factor, and luminaire dirt depreciation. Nonrecoverable factors include ambient temperature, input voltage, ballast factor, and luminaire surface depreciation.

TABLE 4.1
Lamp Lumen Depreciation (LLD) Factors for Selected Lamps

Lamps	Typical LLD Factors
Incandescent	.85
Halogen	.92
Fluorescent	
T8/730	.90
T8/830	.93
Compact fluorescent	.85
Metal halide	.73
Ceramic metal halide	.89
High-pressure sodium	.80

For an abbreviated method of determining the average illuminance on horizontal surfaces in a room, LLF can be calculated by multiplying LLD x LDD. LLD is a metric measurement of the loss of lumens due to the design of a lamp. Table 4.1 provides a list of LLD for selected lamps. LDD accounts for the loss of light caused by dirt and dust accumulation. Important considerations for LDD are the design of the luminaire, the atmosphere of the space, and how often the lamps are cleaned. Table 4.2 and Figure 4.4 produced by IESNA (2000) illustrate maintenance categories for various luminaires, atmosphere considerations, and dirt conditions. This information serves as a reference for determining LDD. As defined by IESNA (2000), the categories include "very clean" (VC), "clean" (C), "medium" (M), "dirty" (D), and "very dirty" (VD). Lamps mounted in an exposed luminaire, in an environment that has a great deal of dust, such as a woodworking studio, would have to be cleaned very frequently to reduce significant light loss.

A simple method for determining average illuminance is the lumen method, also referred to as the zonal cavity calculation. This method provides only the average illuminance in a space and does not factor in variation in light levels. The basic formula for determining the average maintained illuminance on a work surface is:

$$\text{Maintained fc} = \frac{\text{Number of lamps x Initial lamp lumens x LLF x CU}}{\text{Area}}$$

TABLE 4.2
Procedure for Determining Luminaire Maintenance Categories

Maintenance Category	Top Enclosure	Bottom Enclosure
I.	1. None	1. None
II.	1. None 2. Transparent with 15 percent or more uplight through apertures 3. Translucent with 15 percent or more uplight through apertures 4. Opaque with 15 percent or more uplight through apertures	1. None 2. Louvers or baffles
III.	1. Transparent with less than 15 percent upward light through apertures 2. Translucent with less than 15 percent upward light through apertures 3. Opaque with less than 15 percent uplight through apertures	1. None 2. Louvers or baffles
IV.	1. Transparent unapertured 2. Translucent unapertured 3. Opaque unapertured	1. None 2. Louvers
V.	1. Transparent unapertured 2. Translucent unapertured 3. Opaque unapertured	1. Transparent unapertured 2. Translucent unapertured
VI.	1. None 2. Transparent unapertured 3. Translucent unapertured 4. Opaque unapertured	1. Transparent unapertured 2. Translucent unapertured 3. Opaque unapertured

Source: Reprinted from the IESNA Lighting Handbook (9th ed.), pp. 9–20, with permission from the Illuminating Engineering Society of North America.

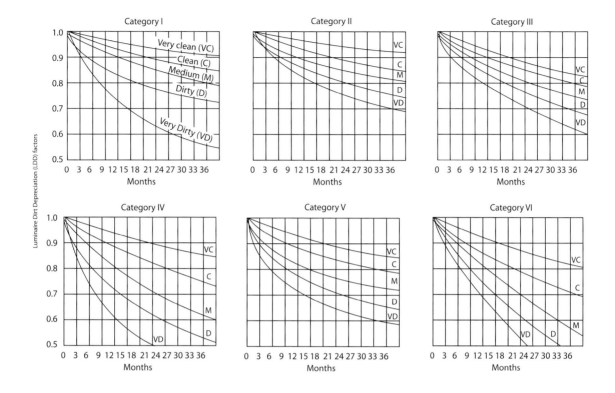

For example, let us consider a classroom with the following factors:
- a space 30' x 30' with a 10' ceiling and a task plane 2' 6" (AFF)
- clean space
- lamp cleaning twice a year
- 12 surface-mount luminaires with two F32T8 lamps in each luminaire
- 80 percent ceiling reflectance, 50 percent wall reflectance, and 20 percent floor reflectance

The average maintained illuminance on a work surface in this space is 30 fc. This is determined by performing the six steps listed below:

1. Determine the total number of lamps by multiplying the number of lamps per luminaire (2) x the number of luminaires (12). Use the SC to determine an approximate number of luminaires. For this example, the total number of lamps is 24.

FIGURE 4.4
Luminaire Dirt Depreciation (LDD) factors for six luminaire categories (I through VI) and for five degrees of dirtiness.

2. Refer to the lamp manufacturer's catalog to determine the initial lamp lumens. For this example, the approximate initial lumens for an F32T8 lamp is 2800.
3. Calculate the LLF by first identifying the LLD (see Table 4.1). In this example, the LLD for an F32T8 lamp is .93.
4. The information found in Table 4.2 and Figure 4.4 identifies the LDD. For this example, in Table 4.2, the two-lamp parabolic louver, surface-mount luminaire is found in the maintenance category III. In Figure 4.4, for a clean room in which lamps are cleaned every six months, the LDD is approximately .92. By multiplying the LLD x the LDD, the LLF is .85 (.93 x .92 = .85).
5. The CU is determined by first calculating the RCR. For this example:

$$RCR = \frac{5(7.5)\ (30 + 30)}{30\ x\ 30} = 2.5 \text{ or } 3$$

Given an RCR of 3 and a space with 80 percent ceiling reflectance (*pcc*), 50 percent wall reflectance (*pw*), and 20 percent floor reflectance (Figure 4.2 assumes a 20 percent floor reflectance), the CU is approximately .46 for the luminaire in Figure 4.2.

6. To determine the average maintained illuminance on the work surface, the values determined in steps 1 to 5 are then inserted into the formula:

$$fc = \frac{24 \text{ lamps x 2800 Initial lamp lumens}\ x\ .85\ x\ .46}{30\ x\ 30\ Area} = 29.2 \text{ or } 30$$

Note that when the LLF and the CU are factored in, illuminance levels are decreased. This reflects characteristics of luminaires, interior architecture, and environmental factors in the space. Without these two considerations, the illumination level would be approximately 75 fc at the initial installation, and would not take into account what could occur in the space throughout the life of the installation. This notation helps to illustrate why it is important to consider all the systemic factors that affect illuminance.

Point-by-Point Method

The basic point-by-point method determines the fc level for a focal point, or the amount of light needed to keep a plant alive. This method uses the inverse square law and cosine law, also referred to as Lambert's Law. The inverse square law is utilized only for point sources. The inverse square law formula is $E = I/d^2$, where E represents illumination (fc), I is the luminous intensity (cd) of the source, and d is the distance from the light source to the work surface. Luminous intensity is determined by examining a lamp's candlepower distribution chart, available from the lamp manufacturer (see Figure 4.5). The inverse square law is based on the principle that the illumination level on a surface decreases the farther the surface is from the light source. According to the formula, the factor by which the illumination on a surface is decreased is equal to the square of its distance from the source. For example, the illuminance on a surface 2' away from its source is one-fourth as much as the illumination 1' from the light source (Figure 4.6).

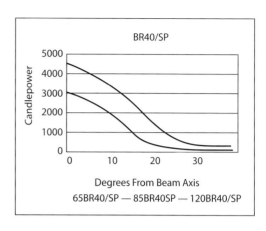

FIGURE 4.5
A candlepower distribution chart of a reflector BR40/SP.

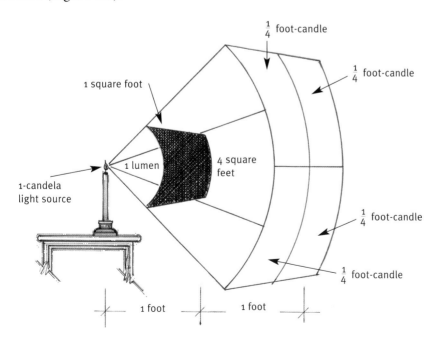

FIGURE 4.6
A demonstration of the inverse square law, whereby the level of illumination on a surface decreases the farther a surface is from the light source.

The inverse square law formula can be utilized for determining the illuminance on a point from a light source that is located directly above the surface (Figure 4.7). For example, for an 85 W reflector BR40 spot lamp located directly above a surface 7' 6" from the lamp, the approximate fc level would be 53. This is determined by the $E = I/d^2$ equation as follows:

$$E = 3000/7.5^2 = 53.3 \text{ or } 53 \text{ fc}$$

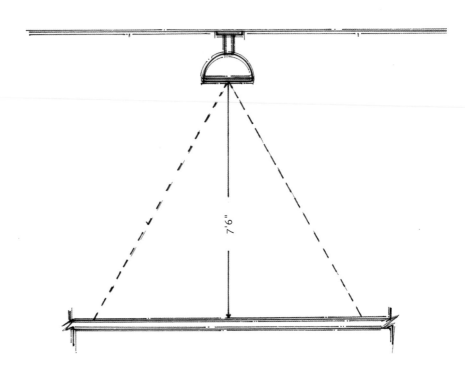

FIGURE 4.7
A light source located
directly above
a surface.

The formula for the cosine law is $E = I/d^2 \; 3 \cos\theta$, where θ (theta) is the angle between a ray from the luminaire falling on a point and a line perpendicular to the plane upon which that point is located. The cosine law indicates that the illuminance on a surface will vary according to the cosine of the angle of incidence. Cosine and sine are used for horizontal and vertical surfaces, respectively; the corresponding formula for determining the illuminance on a vertical surface is: $E = I/d^2 \; 3 \sin\theta$. Table 4.3 contains trigonometric functions that provide the cosine and sine for several angles.

Determining the illuminance for specific locations can be very complex because of the variety of areas within a space and the interdependence of the factors that affect lighting. For this reason, interior designers and engineers will generally use lighting software to perform the calculations. To facilitate a conceptual understanding of the process and the factors that are important to consider when determining illuminance for specific points, two representative examples follow.

The cosine law can be used to determine the illuminance on a horizontal surface when the luminaire, or the point to be lighted, is at an angle (Figure 4.8a). For example, for an 85 W reflector BR40 spot lamp located at an angle of 30° above a horizontal surface 7' 6" from the lamp, the illumination level would be approximately 3 fc. This is determined by the $E = I/d^2$ 3 $\cos\theta$ equation as follows:

$$E = 200 / 7.5^2 \text{ x } .866 = 3.08 \text{ or 3 fc}$$

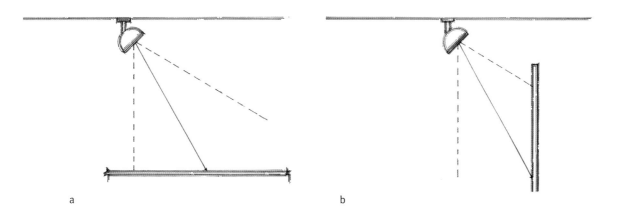

a   b

For an 85 W reflector BR40 spot lamp aimed at an angle of 30° at a vertical surface 7' 6" from the lamp, the illumination level would be approximately 2 fc (Figure 4.8b). This is determined by the $E = I/d^2$ 3 $\sin\theta$ equation as follows:

$$E = 200 / 7.5^2 \text{ x } .500 = 1.77 \text{ or 2 fc}$$

Interior designers conduct calculations for new construction as well as for the remodeling of existing spaces. Both applications utilize the

FIGURE 4.8a
A light source that is located at an angle to a horizontal surface.

FIGURE 4.8b
A light source located at an angle to a vertical surface.

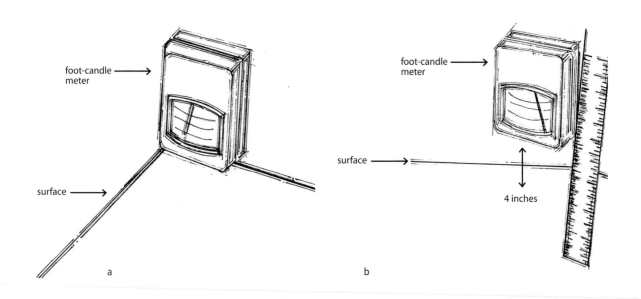

foot-candle meter

surface

a

foot-candle meter

surface

4 inches

b

FIGURE 4.9a
In the field, an interior designer can determine illumination levels by using a foot-candle meter.

FIGURE 4.9b
An interior designer can determine the reflectance of a surface by placing a foot-candle meter approximately 4″ away from the surface to record the fc level.

calculation methods discussed in this section. For existing spaces, an interior designer will frequently want to obtain current fc levels by taking illuminance measurements in the field using a foot-candle meter (Figure 4.9a). This instrument indicates the fc levels for any area within the space, as well as the reflectance values of surfaces. To determine a foot-candle level at a given location, an interior designer places the foot-candle meter in the specified location and reads the result. Usually, an interior designer will want the fc levels for both general and task lighting within a room. To obtain the general illuminance, an interior designer will establish a grid, take readings at each cross-section of the grid, and then average the results. Foot-candle readings for task lighting can be obtained by placing the foot-candle meter on each work surface. To determine an approximation of the reflectance of a surface, an interior designer will place the foot-candle meter approximately 4″ from the surface and record the fc level (Figure 4.9b).

Lighting software packages are available for basic and advanced illuminance calculations using daylight and electrical light sources. Basic programs, including AutoCAD extensions, will predict the brightness of surfaces and patterns of light distribution on vertical and horizontal surfaces. Advanced programs are able to calculate illuminance in rooms with unique shapes, including sloped ceilings (Figure 4.10).

FIGURE 4.10
Advanced lighting
programs can calcu-
late illuminance in
rooms with unique
shapes. This
shower/bathing room
is located in
Bali, Indonesia.

This chapter explores what is involved in determining the quantity of illumination in an interior. Many factors relating to the environment and the users of the space are covered, within the context of recommendations provided by IESNA and other international organizations. Quantity of lighting is only one of the factors that must be considered in designing a quality lighting environment.

SUMMARY

- Measuring the quantity of lighting in an environment is based on the principles of radiometry and photometry. Radiometry is a science that focuses on measuring radiant energy. Photometry is a science derived from radiometry that includes the human response to the source of illumination.

- The basic categories for measuring lighting include luminous intensity, luminous flux, illuminance, luminance, and luminance exitance.
- To determine the direction, pattern, and intensity of light from reflector lamps and luminaires, interior designers refer to photometric data reports, such as those provided by lamp and luminaire manufacturers.
- A simple method for determining average illuminance is the lumen method, also referred to as the zonal cavity calculation. This method provides only the average illuminance in a space and does not consider variance in light levels. The basic formula for determining the average maintained illuminance on a work surface is:

$$\text{Maintained fc} = \frac{\text{Number of lamps x Initial lamp lumens x LLF x CU}}{\text{Area}}$$

- The basic point-by-point method determines the fc level for a focal point, or the amount of light needed to keep a plant alive. Determining the illuminance for specific locations can be very complex because of the variety of areas within a space and the interdependence of the factors that affect lighting.
- Interior designers conduct calculations for new construction as well as for the remodeling of existing spaces. Both applications utilize the calculation methods illustrated in this chapter. For existing spaces, an interior designer will frequently take illuminance measurements in the field by using a foot-candle meter.

Key Terms

candlepower distribution curve

coefficient of utilization (CU)

illuminance

lamp lumen depreciation (LLD)

light loss factor (LLF)

luminaire dirt depreciation (LDD)

luminaire efficacy ratio (LER)	photometry
luminous exitance	radiometry
luminous flux	room-cavity ratio (RCR)
luminous intensity	steradian
nadir	

Exercises

1. Search the World Wide Web for three luminaire manufacturers. For each manufacturer, locate the photometric reports for three different luminaires. In a written report, provide the following information: (a) a summary of the photometric data for each luminaire; (b) comparison of photometric information of each manufacturer; and (c) an analysis of how an interior designer would utilize the photometric data in designing a quality lighting environment.

2. Visit three different spaces and record the following information about each space: (a) size of the room; (b) size and location of windows; (c) the type of luminaires and lamps and their location; and (d) the colors and textures of the ceiling, floor, and walls. Use a foot-candle meter to record the fc level for general and task illuminance. Also record the fc levels for each wall. In a written report, summarize the data collected and analyze the adequacy of illumination. Provide suggestions for improving the space, including the quality of layered lighting.

3. Search the World Wide Web for three luminaires for which data related to spacing criterion (SC) are provided. In a written report, summarize the SC for each luminaire and provide a rationale for differences between SC recommendations. Include how an interior designer would utilize the SC data for specifying luminaires.

4. Search the World Wide Web for three different lighting software packages. Write a report providing the following information for each program: (a) name of the program; (b) manufacturer; (c) computer power; (d) description of the program; (e) application

suggestions; (f) price; and (g) advantages and disadvantages of the program.

5. Identify a commercial and a residential space. Applying the lumen method, calculate a recommended illuminance level for each space. Also identify the recommended illuminance level for a task surface in each space by using the basic point-by-point method. In a written report, include the following items:

    a. floor plan of the spaces

    b. elevations of walls with windows

    c. summary of materials and colors in the spaces

    d. calculations resulting from the lumen method and the point-by-point method

    e. recommendations for luminaires and lamps

Lighting Systems: Luminaires

- Identify primary ways to distribute light: (1) direct, (2) indirect, (3) semi-direct, (4) semi-indirect, and (5) diffused.
- Understand how luminaires are designed to distribute light.
- Understand the advantages and disadvantages of the major categories of luminaires, including recessed, surface-mounted, suspended, track, structural, and furniture-integrated units.
- Apply an understanding of luminaires to the specification and placement of fixtures in an environment.
- Identify and apply selection criteria to the specification and placement of luminaires in an interior.

Earlier in this book, we saw how lamps and electricity are important as elements of a lighting system. In this chapter, we review another major component of the system, luminaires. In addition to exploring the role of luminaires in an interdependent system, this chapter demonstrates how the selection and the placement of luminaires affect the quality of lighting, quantity of illumination, and the directional effects of lighting. An interior designer must understand all the interdependent elements of the lighting system and have a working knowledge of the products available to successfully plan a quality lighting environment. This chapter focuses on luminaires for installation in ceilings, walls, floors, architectural elements, or cabinetry.

The design of luminaires blends science with art to resolve many of the contrasting characteristics of illumination, such as directing light up or down, flooding a space with light, or spotlighting a small art piece on a table. Many industrial designers, architects, and interior designers have been challenged to design a luminaire that successfully addresses these issues. Two interior elements that often define a designer are luminaires and chairs. Charles Rennie Mackintosh is an excellent example of a designer who is well known for the design of his chairs and luminaires (Figure 5.1).

The primary factors affecting the distribution of illumination are the shape of the luminaire, its materials and finishes, the location and size of the aperture, and the mounting position. Chapter 3 provides examples of how the shape, materials, and finish affect the directional effects of lighting. The location of the aperture, materials, and mounting position determine the primary ways in which light is distributed: (a) direct, (b) indirect, (c) semi-direct, (d) semi-indirect, and (e) diffused (Figure 5.2). **Direct** distribution occurs when at least 90 percent of the illumination is

direct light
Distribution of light when at least 90 percent of the illumination is downward.

downward. **Indirect** luminaires distribute at least 90 percent of the light toward the ceiling. **Semi-direct** luminaires distribute most of the illumination downward, and some of the light upward. **Semi-indirect** fixtures distribute most of the illumination upward, and some of the light downward. **Diffused** luminaires distribute illumination in all directions.

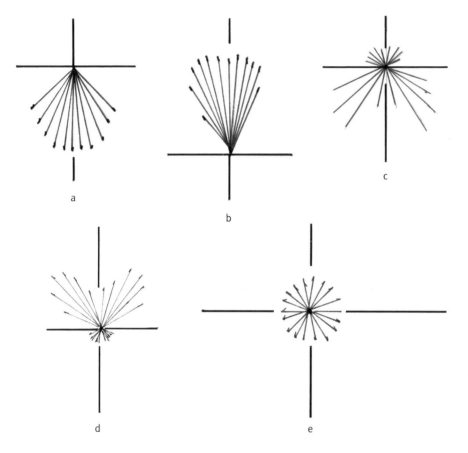

a

b

c

d

e

indirect light
Distribution of light when at least 90 percent of the illumination is directed toward the ceiling.

semi-direct lighting
Distribution of light when most of the illumination is directed downward and some is directed upward.

semi-indirect lighting
Distribution of light when most of the illumination is directed upward and some is directed downward.

diffused light
Distribution of light in all directions.

FIGURE 5.2
Photometric drawings of the five primary ways to distribute light: (a) direct, (b) indirect, (c) semi-direct, (d) semi-indirect, and (e) diffused.

Luminaire Types

Major categories of luminaires include recessed, surface-mounted, suspended, track, structural, and furniture-integrated units. These luminaires are designed primarily for incandescent, fluorescent, and HID lamps, and they are available in a variety of sizes, shapes, and materials. Most of these luminaires can be used for general, task, accent, or decorative lighting. Some manufacturers design a luminaire for multiple applications, such as a pendant, ceiling mount, and sconce. Such luminaires make it possible to employ various lighting techniques while maintaining unity of design.

There are large manufacturers who mass-produce luminaires, but there are also numerous small companies that produce luminaires, some by hand. Italian designers have a reputation for creating some of the most creative and classical pieces. The quality of construction and materials varies among manufacturers and product lines. To ensure a quality lighting environment, interior designers must be aware of the characteristics of the product they are specifying. This knowledge can be acquired by visiting manufacturer showrooms, discussing product attributes with manufacturer representatives, attending educational seminars, and reading current articles in trade journals.

Recessed Luminaires

recessed luminaire
Fixture installed above a Sheetrock or suspended-grid ceiling.

semi-recessed luminaire
Fixture whose housing is partly above and partly below the ceiling.

luminous ceiling
Ceiling whose lighting consists of rows of lamps behind diffused lenses.

Recessed downlight luminaires are fixtures that are installed above a Sheetrock or suspended-grid ceiling. New developments in the design of **recessed luminaires** allow a flangeless installation, so that the ceiling surface is flush with the aperture of the recessed fixture. The installation has a clean appearance and helps to conceal the fixture. Recessed luminaires whose housing is partly above and partly below the ceiling are called **semi-recessed luminaires**. A recessed luminaire generally creates direct lighting in a space. The most common recessed luminaires are troffers, downlights, wall wash, and accent. Common sizes for recessed troffers are 6" to 8" x 4' (15 to 20 cm x 122 cm), 1' x 4' (31 cm x 122 cm), 2' x 2' (61 cm x 61 cm), and 2' x 4' (61 cm x 122 cm) (Figure 5.3). These sizes accommodate the various lengths of fluorescent lamps. The interior of a troffer is generally painted white or has a specular metal reflector, while the most common devices at the aperture are acrylic prismatic lenses and parabolic louvers. As demonstrated in Figure 4.2, the photometric distribution for a fluorescent fixture with silver parabolic louvers is direct. Parabolic louvers with large cell depths (1.5" to 4" or 4 cm to 10 cm) have higher luminaire efficiency than smaller cells because the large cells have more surfaces with high reflectance. **Luminous ceilings** utilize rows of lamps behind diffused lenses.

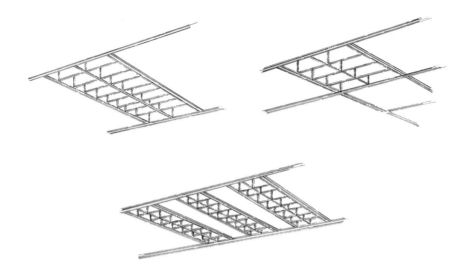

FIGURE 5.3
Examples of recessed
troffer luminaires.

Recessed downlights are also referred to as **high hats** or cans. The most common shapes for recessed downlights are round and square. The size of a downlight aperture can be as small as 2". The finish applied to the rim affects the efficiency of the luminaire, with white and aluminum finishes providing the highest luminaire efficiency. Dark-colored and black rims have lower luminaire efficiency ratings, but the reflectance values help to reduce glare. The efficiency of a downlight is also affected by the existence of a reflector in the luminaire. To maximize the lumens emitted from downlights without reflectors, reflector lamps should be specified.

The type of device used at the aperture affects the photometric distribution from downlights. In general, light emitted from a downlight with a bare opening will be dependent upon the type of lamp. For example, a narrow halogen spot lamp mounted in a recessed downlight will emit a narrow beam of light. Recessed downlights with a bare opening can cause discomfort or disability glare because of the exposed lamp. There are many devices available for this purpose, including baffles, louvers, and specialized lenses. Special recessed luminaires are designed for floor installations. These recessed uplight luminaires include a floor-mount plate and are often used to enhance architectural details.

Recessed downlights may also be designed to direct light to a vertical surface. For grazing techniques, the distance from the downlight to the

recessed downlight
Recessed ceiling-mounted luminaire, also referred to as a high hat or high-hat luminaire.

high hat
Recessed ceiling-mounted luminaire, also referred to as a downlight.

FIGURE 5.4
Recessed linear
wall washer.

wall should be approximately 6" to 8" (15 cm to 20 cm). The distance between downlights depends upon whether a scalloped pattern on the wall is considered desirable; luminaires that are close together are less likely to create a scalloped pattern. Recessed linear or round wall washers distribute light over a large area on a wall (Figure 5.4). The typical photometric distribution for a recessed wall washer illustrates how light strikes a vertical surface (Figure 5.5); a reflector or an angled lens causes the light to strike the wall at a different angle. Wall washer luminaires should be located at least 30" (76 cm) from the wall to prevent hot spots. To avoid scalloped patterns on the wall, the distance from the luminaire to the wall and between luminaires should be approximately one-third the height of the ceiling.

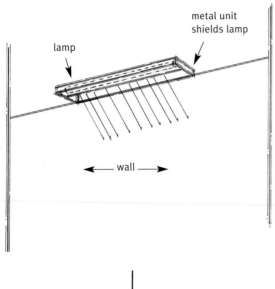

lamp

metal unit shields lamp

← wall →

Recessed accent or spot downlights emit a narrow beam of light. Recessed accent downlights have an aiming angle of 30° to 45° and can rotate at least 350° and are either fixed or adjustable. Common directional trims for recessed accent downlights include slotted, baffled, eyeball, and pinhole apertures (Figure 5.6 a–c). Multiple recessed luminaires have two to six spots in one rectangular opening (Figure 5.7), enabling them to spotlight three different points of emphasis with only one hole in the ceiling. For interiors with angled ceilings, recessed, sloped-ceiling luminaires can be used to dis-

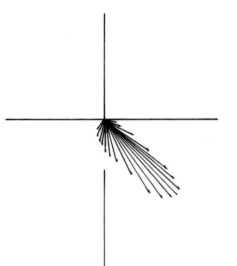

FIGURE 5.5
Photometric
distribution of
a recessed wall
washer, showing
how light strikes a
vertical surface.

tribute light downward, provide a wall-wash effect, or spotlight objects.

One advantage of recessed luminaires is that they can direct light to a variety of locations while maintaining the appearance of a clean ceiling line, often making a space appear larger. Recessed luminaires can provide task lighting for an area that has a decorative luminaire. Miniature

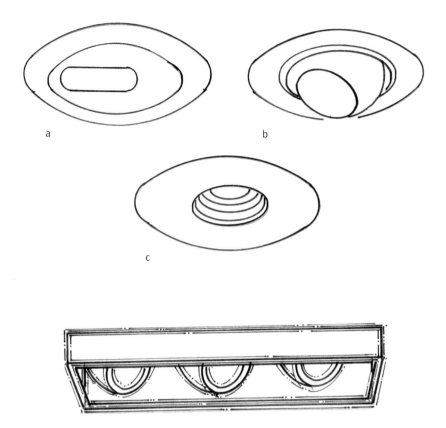

a

b

c

FIGURE 5.6
Directional trims for
recessed accent
downlights: (a) slotted,
(b) eyeball, and
(c) baffled pinhole.

FIGURE 5.7
Multiple recessed
downlights.

recessed luminaires can be hidden to promote an element of mystery. Some disadvantages of recessed lighting include the clearance space required for installation, the need for space allowances between insulation and the housing unit, and the need for ventilation to remove heat. Because of the mounting requirements, the need to accommodate a fire-rated ceiling, and the holes in the ceiling, recessed luminaires should always be planned early in construction. In addition to the structural mounting requirements, there are other challenges related to recessed luminaires. They must be placed in the proper location to avoid problems associated with direct lighting, including glare and unflattering shadows on people. The fixed distance from the ceiling to an object or surface makes it very important to select a luminaire and lamp that can perform to suit the parameters of the specific site. The removal of recessed luminaires can be costly and disrupts the surface adhere to the principles of design. For example, luminaires should reflect the theme of the design concept, the scale must be appropriate for the shape and size of the room, and the placement of fixtures should be balanced on the ceiling. Some surface-mount luminaires cast a light and shadow pattern on a wall or ceiling, which could negatively distort the appearance of a patterned or textured surface.

Suspended Luminaires

suspended luminaire
Fixture installed on a ceiling and extending into the room by a cord, chain, pole, or wire.

Suspended luminaires are fixtures that are installed on a ceiling and extend into the room by cords, chains, poles, or wires. Some luminaires have a mechanism that allows for easy cord length adjustments. Suspended luminaires can emit direct, indirect, semi-direct, and diffused lighting. The most common suspended luminaires include pendants, chandeliers, ceiling fans, linear fluorescent fixtures (indirect and bidirectional), and luminaires forming an element of a track system. Many of these are for decorative purposes only.

Linear fluorescent luminaires are frequently designed for task lighting. Bidirectional (direct–indirect) luminaires for general or task lighting should have materials, reflectors, baffles, or louvers with reflectance values greater than 90 percent. To avoid hot spots, or glare, suspended luminaires giving indirect light should be mounted at least 18" (46 cm) from the ceiling; those in a circulation area should be at least 80" (203 cm) from the floor. The distance from a dining table to the bottom of the luminaire should be 30" (76 cm) or more. An appropriate distance is determined by the height of the ceiling and the scale of the room and the luminaire.

The primary advantage of using a suspended luminaire is decorative. Therefore, the design of the luminaire must reflect the design concept of the interior and adhere to the principles of design. Because suspended luminaires are generally focal points in an interior and can visually divide the space, they can make an interior appear smaller depending upon the location, size, and material of the luminaire. Suspended luminaires can also be difficult to maintain because of their location and the high accumulation of dirt and dust. Two important considerations for mounting suspended luminaires are avoidance of glare and prevention of collision with people moving through the space. To specify an

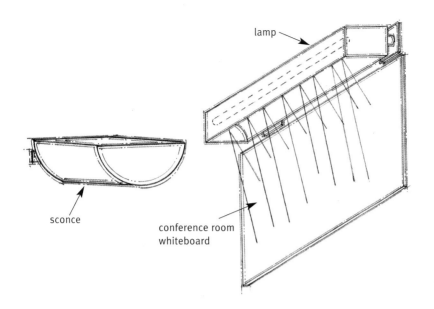

lamp

sconce

conference room
whiteboard

FIGURE 5.9
Surface-mount
luminaires.

Whiteboard lighting is mounted on a wall and provides direct light on a whiteboard or chalkboard. Generally, fluorescent lamps are used for whiteboard lighting. The internal reflector emits a soft light on the vertical surface without shadows or glare.

Surface-mount luminaires also include fixtures that are installed under a shelf or cabinet. The most common shapes are linear, round, and square. Generally, the linear luminaires have fluorescent lamps, and the round and square shapes use incandescent lamps. The punch of light emitted from miniature, surface-mount luminaires is an excellent way to highlight objects on a shelf.

Surface-mount luminaires have the advantage of simultaneously being decorative and providing illumination. The potential to direct and diffuse light provides flexibility in addressing the multiple lighting requirements in an environment. Compared to recessed luminaires, surface-mount fixtures are easier to install. In specifying the location of a surface-mount luminaire, an interior designer does not have to consider clearances for insulation or mechanical and plumbing restrictions. Some of the disadvantages of surface-mount luminaires have to do with the location of the fixtures. Relamping at the ceiling level can be difficult, and removing the luminaire can result in severe damage to finishes and materials. Since a surface-mount luminaire can become a focal point in a room, selection and location of the fixtures must adhere to the principles of design. For example, luminaires should reflect the theme of the design concept, the scale must be appropriate for the shape and size of the room, and the placement of fixtures should be balanced on the ceiling. Some surface-mount luminaires cast a light and shadow pattern on a wall or ceiling, which could negatively distort the appearance of a patterned or textured surface.

Suspended Luminaires

Suspended luminaires are fixtures that are installed on a ceiling and extend into the room by cords, chains, poles, or wires. Some luminaires have a mechanism that allows for easy cord length adjustments. Suspended luminaires can emit direct, indirect, semi-direct, and diffused lighting. The most common suspended luminaires include pendants, chandeliers, ceiling fans, linear fluorescent fixtures (indirect and bidirectional), and luminaires forming an element of a track system. Many of these are for decorative purposes only.

Linear fluorescent luminaires are frequently designed for task lighting. Bidirectional (direct–indirect) luminaires for general or task lighting should have materials, reflectors, baffles, or louvers with reflectance values greater than 90 percent. To avoid hot spots, or glare, suspended luminaires giving indirect light should be mounted at least 18" (46 cm) from the ceiling; those in a circulation area should be at least 80" (203 cm) from the floor. The distance from a dining table to the bottom of the luminaire should be 30" (76 cm) or more. An appropriate distance is determined by the height of the ceiling and the scale of the room and the luminaire.

The primary advantage of using a suspended luminaire is decorative. Therefore, the design of the luminaire must reflect the design concept of the interior and adhere to the principles of design. Because suspended luminaires are generally focal points in an interior and can visually divide the space, they can make an interior appear smaller depending upon the location, size, and material of the luminaire. Suspended luminaires can also be difficult to maintain because of their location and the high accumulation of dirt and dust. Two important considerations for mounting suspended luminaires are avoidance of glare and prevention of collision with people moving through the space. To specify an appropriate location, an interior designer should consider how the location affects people standing and sitting. Whenever possible, the location of the luminaire should not interfere with decorative focal points in an environment, such as artwork on a wall or a beautiful view from a window. When using multiple, suspended luminaires in rows, take care to ensure that the fixtures are hung in a perfectly straight line.

Track Luminaires

Track luminaires are fixtures that have multiple heads and are mounted on an electrical raceway (Figure 5.10). Tracks are available in a variety of lengths, and connectors are used to create shapes such as L, T, or X. Generally, one end of the track connects to the main circuit wiring while the other end is dead. Multitracks are available for separate switching arrangements, as are low-voltage track systems with remote transformers. Track systems can be suspended from a ceiling by cables, recessed into the ceiling plane, or surface-mounted on a ceiling or wall. Track-mounted luminaires, known as track heads, are available in a variety of styles, colors, sizes, lamp types, and materials; they also come with built-in transformers. Some track heads are connected to the end of a long, flexible cable that can be shaped to aim light in numerous directions. A monopoint luminaire is used for installations that require only one track head. Track luminaires have evolved to designs that include low-voltage cable and rail systems (Figure 5.10). The heads on these systems are attached to

track luminaire
Fixture that has multiple heads mounted on an electrical raceway.

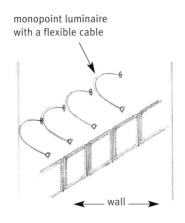

monopoint luminaire
with a flexible cable

wall

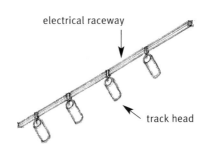

electrical raceway

track head

FIGURE 5.10
Examples of track luminaires.

a cable or rail, which can be adjusted and shaped at the site of installation. The flexibility of the system allows for designs in curves and soft angles.

Light distribution from the heads of a track system is direct, indirect, direct–indirect, or diffused. The most common applications for track systems are accent, wall wash, and downlight. Many heads are designed merely to hold the lamp and do not allow any adjustment or control; for these heads, it is critical to select the lamp that will have the desired beam spread and intensity. To control glare, heads are available with louvers, lenses, and solid or mesh shielding devices. Suspension kits for track systems, and extensions for each track head, are available for use on high ceilings.

The primary advantage of a track system is flexibility, in that it is relatively simple to re-aim and reposition the heads. This is why they are frequently used to highlight items on display in retail stores. Tracks also provide the flexibility of having different types of illumination from one fixture. Disadvantages of a track system include difficulty in reaching the heads, a strong potential for glare, and a high accumulation of dirt and dust. When it is difficult to reach the track heads, they are seldom re-aimed or repositioned, negating the most important advantage of a track system and increasing the potential for glare. To reduce the potential for glare, avoid track locations where users can see the lamps, or add a shielding device to the heads.

In specifying a track system, it is important to be aware of the quality of the product. Some tracks are made of flimsy aluminum and are not suitable for applications that require frequent re-aiming and repositioning. There are also some safety concerns associated with track systems. Generally, components are not interchangeable from one manufacturer to another, especially for track systems that are rated specifically for one manufacturer and one product line. In addition, the ease of adding heads to a track increases the likelihood of exceeding the maximum wattage for the system.

Structural and Furniture-Integrated Luminaires

structural luminaire
Illumination technique that is an element of the architectural interior.

Structural luminaires are those that form an element of the architectural interior. The major types of structural luminaires are cove, valance, cornice, soffit, and wall brackets (Figure 5.11 a–e). **Cove lighting** is mounted on a wall, with the light directed up toward the ceiling. Cove lighting is especially effective in rooms with high ceilings, and can be integrated with crown molding. **Valance lighting** is mounted above a window, with the light directed up and down. **Cornice lighting** can be mounted on a wall or above a window, with the light directed down. **Soffit lighting** is a built-in wall element close or next to the ceiling and extends 12" to 18" (31 cm to 46 cm) from the wall, generally directing the light down onto a task although some units can include indirect lighting. Soffit lighting is frequently used over work areas, such as kitchen counters, desks, and bathroom sinks. **Wall bracket lighting** is mounted on a wall, with the light directed up and down. A **wallslot** is integrated in the ceiling system and distributes light down on vertical surfaces. They are sometimes used around the perimeter of a room. New developments in seamless fluorescent systems eliminate dark zones in continuous rows. This results in a continuous band of illumination on walls and ceilings.

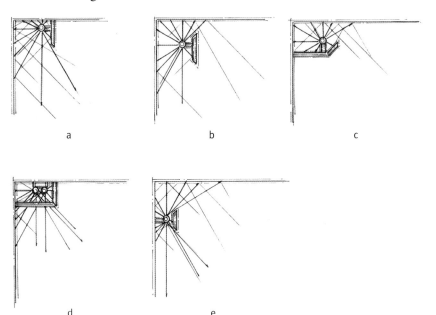

a   b   c

d   e

The most common materials used for structural luminaires are wood, metal, and gypsum board. The board shielding the light source is called a fascia. To achieve the maximum amount of light from structural

---

cove lighting
Illumination technique mounted on a wall or ceiling, directing the light up toward the ceiling.

valance lighting
Illumination technique mounted above a window, directing the light up and down.

cornice lighting
Illumination technique mounted on a wall or above a window, directing the light down.

soffit lighting
Illumination technique that is a built-in wall element close or next to the ceiling; directs the light down onto a task.

wall bracket lighting
Illumination technique mounted on a wall and directing the light up and down.

wallslot
A structural lighting system integrated in the ceiling and distributing light down onto vertical surfaces.

FIGURE 5.11
Examples of structural luminaires: (a) cove (b) valance, (c), cornice, (d) soffit, and (e) wall bracket.

luminaires, the interior surfaces should be painted white and the fascia should have an angled cutoff. Generally, linear fluorescent lamps are used in these units. To ensure consistency in color and intensity level, all lamps installed in a unit should be from the same manufacturer. To reduce glare, some structural luminaires include a device that shields the light source, such as a baffle, lens, or louver.

The size of the unit and its location on a wall are also important to the success of structural luminaires. The unit must have the proper dimensions so as to maximize reflectance and adequately shield the lamps from multiple angles of view. The location on the wall affects reflectance, illumination levels, and the potential for glare. The dimensions that follow are applicable for cove, valance, cornice, and wall bracket lighting. Structural luminaires should be mounted at least 18" (46 cm) from a ceiling. The distance from the wall should be 6" to 12" (15 cm to 31 cm). Lamps should be mounted at least 4" (10 cm) from the wall and 2" (5 cm) from the fascia. The height of the fascia should be 8" to 12" (20 cm to 31 cm). Soffit luminaires should be 6" to 12" (15 cm to 31 cm) high and mounted 12" to 18" (31 cm to 46 cm) from the wall. Modifications to recommended dimensions may be necessary for rooms with high ceilings or for very large or small rooms. For example, in a large room, the dimensions of cove lighting may need to be modified in order to avoid dark areas in the center of the room. Some luminaires distribute light more evenly and avoid hot spots from the lamps. The integration of built-in reflectors assists in distributing the light along a surface.

Structural luminaires have the advantage of enhancing the interior by being well integrated with the interior architecture. Outlining the shape and size of an interior can make a space appear larger and can serve as a means of following the rhythm of the structure. Another advantage of this type of lighting is that the even distribution imitates one of the positive qualities of daylight, making it excellent for general lighting purposes. Structural luminaires can also add an element of mystery to an environment, because the light sources are hidden from view and the light appears to be floating. Disadvantages of structural luminaires are the potential for glare, damage to ceiling and walls when removing the elements, and difficulties associated with cleaning the lamps and relamping. In the case of large rooms, structural applications may leave the center of the room in darkness. In addition, any cracks or imperfections in walls or ceilings can become very noticeable when the light grazes the surfaces, though this effect can be minimized by use of a matte finish paint.

Furniture-integrated luminaires are mounted in a cabinet and generally hidden from view. The most common furniture pieces that have integrated lighting are office systems, curio cabinets, breakfronts, and bookcases (Figure 5.12). Office-system integrated furniture has lamps for ambient and task lighting, while furniture designed for the purpose of highlighting objects generally has downlights or spots. Furniture-integrated luminaires can provide excellent light for their intended purpose. Concerns related to these luminaires focus on the amount of heat that can collect in the cabinets and the difficulties associated with relamping.

Luminaires

FIGURE 5.12
Furniture-integrated luminaires.

furniture-integrated luminaire
Fixture mounted in a cabinet and generally hidden from view. The most common furniture pieces with integrated lighting are office systems, curio cabinets, breakfronts, and bookcases.

Specifying Luminaires

To specify luminaires, an interior designer must be knowledgeable about the products offered by various manufacturers of luminaires, lamps, and devices used to control fixtures.

Manufacturers' Specifications

The specification process begins with researching current products. The Internet is an excellent resource for identifying and comparing products, as Web sites are being developed that have specification-driven product categories. For example, a Web site lists several product categories, such as type of fixture, lamp, and applications (Figure 5.13). A user selects the desired categories, and the Web site locates the products that fit the specifications.

In reviewing various products, it is critical to locate specification data supplied by the manufacturer. These data include installation instructions, application guides, specification sheets, photometric information, and costs. The photometric data include spacing criterion (SC), coefficient of utilization (CU), and luminaire distribution curves and tables. An interior designer needs this information in order to select and specify luminaires and lamps. Data are also used to perform calculations and provide maintenance recommendations to a client.

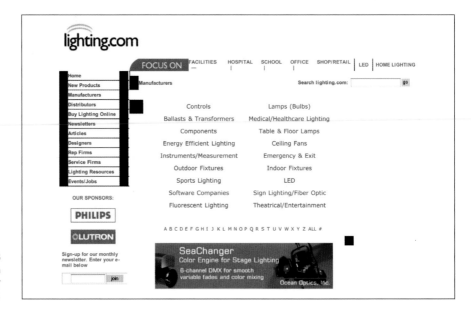

FIGURE 5.13
A specification-driven product category Web site.

Selection Considerations

Selecting luminaires for a quality lighting environment begins with an analysis of the site and the users of the space. (Information about the lighting design process is provided in Chapters 11 and 12.) Ideally, lighting is considered at the beginning stages of a project. A major factor that can affect the lighting plan is whether the project is new construction or work being done on an existing structure. Both situations can present unique challenges that an interior designer must resolve before specifying the luminaires.

In reviewing the specifics of the project, it is important for the designer to prioritize criteria associated with luminaires. For example, when an existing building has significant structural limitations, the first priority would be to ensure that the luminaires specified can in fact be installed in the rooms. Economic considerations could be a major priority for a client who has a building in a community with high electrical costs. A priority for an expensive jewelry store is to enhance the sparkle of jewels. Prioritized criteria are very helpful when specifying categories of luminaires.

Within the context of these priorities, the purpose of the luminaire must be identified. How will the luminaire be integrated with the layered lighting plan? Will the luminaire provide general, task, accent, or decorative lighting? An interior designer must also determine whether the luminaire should be the focal point of the space, blend into the interior, or be completely hidden. Once these decisions have been made, the next step in selecting luminaires involves evaluating specific characteristics of lighting systems, including quality of product, photometric data, lamp characteristics, economics, installation methods, operational considerations, maintenance, and design considerations.

The desired quality of the luminaire is often dependent upon the priorities of the client. However, in order to make informed decisions, it is the responsibility of the interior designer to know the quality differences between products. Well-constructed luminaires made from quality materials are always a good investment. Quality luminaires are especially important for long-term installations and when durability is critical. High-end interiors should also have quality luminaires.

Photometric data should be reviewed to determine the light distribution of the luminaire; the designer should perform the calculations necessary to make this determination. Specification data will also indicate the suggested lamps for the luminaire. Characteristics of the suggested lamps should be reviewed to determine whether they meet the objectives of the lighting plan. Some of the considerations are efficacy ratings, color characteristics, life of the lamp, aiming qualities, operating position, wattages, heat accumulation, optical control properties, control features, and availability of lamps. When searching internationally for luminaires, it is critical to know the plug and outlet compatibilities and the rating because different countries have different electrical systems and requirements. The economics associated with luminaires include the costs of the fixture, lamps, ballasts, controls, electricity, installation, and maintenance. (See Chapter 7 for more information about energy efficiency and luminaires.)

In selecting luminaires, there are many installation factors to consider. To determine the feasibility of installing a luminaire, the electrical, mechanical, plumbing, and structural components of the building must be surveyed. This process includes reviewing local building and electrical codes. Historical buildings have strict renovation codes and regulations that must be followed throughout a project. The interior must be surveyed to determine access for installation and maintenance. Space requirements may include ballasts, transformers, output boxes, and climate control. There must be adequate support in ceilings and walls for mounting luminaires. Materials such as Sheetrock, plaster, wood, and acoustical tile are the most common surfaces for mounting luminaires. Masonry walls and irregular surfaces can pose installation difficulties. In addition, unusual surface configurations may require a luminaire that can be modified or adjusted at the field site. The horizontal and vertical impact on the space must also be considered when installing a luminaire, as well as any effect on the placement of art on the wall. A review of installation considerations should also take into account the directional effects of lighting on the space and users.

Operational considerations are another aspect of specifying luminaires. Factors to examine include use of controls, adjustability, future requirements, ergonomics, environmental factors, and safety. An interior might require special controls, such as dimmers, occupancy detectors, and daylight photosensor systems. For a successful operation, a luminaire must be selected that is compatible with the specific requirements of the controls. (Controls for luminaires are covered in Chapter 6.)

Adjustability of a luminaire could be critical for lighting that is used by a variety of users and for a variety of tasks. It may be necessary to move luminaires to different locations or to completely remove the lighting system at a later date. For these situations, luminaires should be selected that allow for easy relocation and removal. Ergonomic and environmental factors should always be considered when specifying luminaires and lamps. (For more information about these topics, see Chapter 8.) In addition, there are safety concerns: a luminaire with an exposed lamp poses the danger of someone being burned or a flammable material igniting on contact. Inadequate light to perform tasks may result in injury or damage due to an inability to see work materials properly. The stability of the luminaire should also be examined, especially when children, elderly people, and pets are users of the space.

Maintenance is another important consideration for specifying a luminaire. A luminaire that cannot be easily cleaned or relamped reflects badly on the reputation of an interior designer. The cost of labor is a critical expense related to maintenance. Luminaires mounted in a location that is easily accessed generally do not pose maintenance problems; for locations that are difficult to reach, such as 20' ceilings, the luminaire should relamp from the front and be equipped with a shield to reduce the accumulation of dirt or dust. Lamps that have long life should also be considered. A product that requires special tools can hamper luminaire maintenance. The material of the luminaire could also pose maintenance problems. For example, shiny aluminum scratches easily and shows fingerprints.

The luminaire must reflect the theme of the interior and reinforce the principles of design. Interior designers should approach the selection of a luminaire with the same aesthetic criteria they would use for other elements in the space. To select a luminaire of a specific period often requires historical research. To be in concert with the theme of an interior, some interior designers have luminaires custom-made. This is frequently done for hotels and restaurants. The principles of design should also be applied to locating luminaires in a space. Ceiling-mounted luminaires should be balanced with other elements on the ceiling, including diffusers, returns, smoke alarms, and emergency lights. Symmetrical or asymmetrical balance can be used depending upon the type of fixture and the purpose of the lighting. Luminaires should be selected that reinforce the rhythm, emphasis, unity, proportion, and scale of a space and its furnishings. When high ceilings are emphasized in a room, luminaires should be selected that provide a vertical focus. Low-level lighting should be used in a space that is intended to be intimate. The size of the luminaire should be proportionate to the size of the room and the installation area. In addition, for nonresidential projects, the number of different types of lamps should be limited so as to avoid confusion when maintenance people must relamp the fixtures. When there are many different types of lamps, it is very likely that the correct lamp will not be placed in the proper luminaire during relamping.

The proper selection and placement of luminaires is essential to a quality lighting environment. To conserve energy, designers should choose luminaires that emit as many lumens as possible. The key to success is having a thorough knowledge of the products, understanding the interdependence of the elements in a lighting system, and considering how luminaires affect the overall design of an interior. Controls are another important element of the system. A discussion of controls, and how they affect the performance of luminaires, is covered in the next chapter.

SUMMARY

- Primary ways to distribute light are: (a) direct, (b) indirect, (c) semi-direct, (d) semi-indirect, and (e) diffused.
- Major categories of luminaires include recessed, surface-mounted, suspended, track, structural, and furniture-integrated units. These luminaires are designed primarily for incandescent, fluorescent, and HID lamps, and they are available in a variety of sizes, shapes, and materials. Most of these luminaires can be used for general, task, accent, or decorative lighting.
- The major types of structural luminaires are cove, valance, cornice, soffit, wall bracket, and wallslot.
- To specify luminaires, an interior designer must be knowledgeable about the products offered by various manufacturers of luminaires, lamps, and controls. It is critical to locate specification data supplied by the manufacturer.
- Selecting luminaires for a quality lighting environment begins with an analysis of the site and the users of the space. Within the context of established priorities, the purpose of the luminaire must be identified.
- To determine the feasibility of installing a luminaire, the electrical, mechanical, plumbing, and structural components of the building must be surveyed.

- Operational considerations include use of controls, adjustability, future requirements, ergonomics, environmental factors, and safety. Maintenance is another important matter when specifying a luminaire.
- A luminaire must reflect the theme of the interior and reinforce the principles of design.

Key Terms

cornice lighting	semi-direct lighting
cove lighting	semi-indirect lighting
diffused light	semi-recessed luminaire
direct light	soffit lighting
furniture-integrated luminaire	structural luminaire
HID high-bay	surface-mount luminaire
high hat	suspended luminaire
indirect light	track luminaire
luminous ceiling	valance lighting
recessed downlight	wall bracket lighting
recessed luminaire	wallslot

Exercises

1. For each major luminaire type (recessed, surface-mount, suspended, track, and structural), identify effective applications for general, task, and accent lighting. Summarize your suggestions in a written report; you may include illustrations and sketches.
2. Locate five different commercial or residential interiors. For each interior, respond to the following items: (a) identify the overall design theme of the space; (b) identify the luminaires; (c) evaluate the luminaires according to the principles of design, including balance, rhythm, emphasis, proportion, scale, variety, and unity. In a written report, summarize each interior and include illustrations.

3. Create a product resource file. Search the World Wide Web for 20 luminaire and 5 lamp manufacturers. The products should include all the types of luminaires. Locate all specification data for each product. Compile the resources in a file that is organized by types of luminaires and lamps. For each manufacturer, locate the photometric reports for three different luminaires.

4. Interior designers must write specifications for lighting plans. Identify two interiors and write the lighting plan specifications for the luminaires and lamps. Specifications should include all the information needed to order the luminaires and lamps. Refer to manufacturers' product data for the specification details. Specifications may be presented in a table.

Lighting Systems: Controls

- Describe the role of transformers and ballasts in a lighting system.
- Differentiate between magnetic and electronic versions of transformers and ballasts.
- Describe how lighting controls can conserve energy and enhance an environment.
- Identify the primary ways in which controls can conserve energy, including scheduling, daylight integration, monitoring lamp maintenance, and load shedding.
- Describe the basic equipment for lighting controls, including switches, dimmers, timers, occupancy sensors, photosensors, and central units.
- Understand how to specify auxiliary and lighting controls for a quality lighting environment.

Controls are mechanisms designed to regulate a lighting system, and are an important component. In the past, controls were not a major consideration, but advancements in digital technologies have increased the performance and options available to an interior designer. As controls become even more sophisticated, interior designers will have many ways to improve the efficiency of lighting systems and provide flexibility for users. Constant improvements in the technology of controls require that interior designers routinely read product literature and articles in professional journals.

This chapter explores auxiliary and lighting controls and how they affect a quality lighting environment. Auxiliary controls include transformers and ballasts. Lighting controls include a broad category of techniques and equipment that are designed to enhance an environment and conserve energy. Lighting controls operate either manually or automatically and include switches, dimmers, timers, occupancy sensors, photosensors, and central controls.

Auxiliary Controls

Transformers and ballasts are devices that are essential in the operation of some lighting systems. These controls must be compatible with a lighting system and they consume a small amount of electricity.

Transformers

transformer
An electrical device that increases or decreases voltages in a system.

A **transformer** is an electrical device that raises and lowers voltage in a system. Step-up transformers raise the quantity of voltage and step-down transformers lower the voltage for specific commercial and residential applications. For lighting purposes, a transformer is either integral to the design of the luminaire, or it is a separate unit concealed under a ceiling or behind a wall (Figure 6.1). The vast majority of line-voltage lighting applications operate at 120 V. Low-voltage lighting applications usually operate at 12 V. Thus, for low-voltage lighting, a transformer is needed to step-down the line voltage to 12 V. Another type of transformer converts alternating current to direct current for devices such as LEDs.

Transformers are available in magnetic and electronic versions. Magnetic transformers have a steel core, are encased in copper wire, and

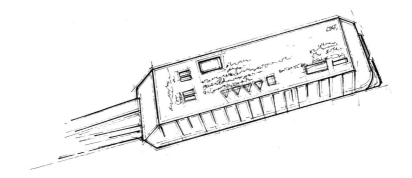

FIGURE 6.1
A 60 W transformer utilized in lighting systems.

are inexpensive and very reliable. They are also heavier, larger and noisier than electronic transformers. Electronic transformers are composed of an electrical circuit and generally do not last as long as a magnetic unit. The advantages of electronic transformers include smaller size, less weight, and quieter operation. Since electricity is required to operate transformers, the energy consumed by the device must be included in determining the watts-per-square-foot calculations in a space.

Each transformer is rated with a maximum wattage; this information is provided by manufacturers. For safety purposes and proper operation of the luminaire, it is critical to match lamps and the transformers to be used with them so that neither exceeds the maximum wattage. Also, the transformer should be installed as close as possible to the luminaire, as there can be a noticeable voltage drop and reduced light output when the distance between the transformer and luminaire is too great. The maximum distance from a luminaire to a transformer is dependent upon the wattage and the wire gauge. For example, a single-fixture luminaire with a 16-gauge wire at 12 V can accommodate 150 W when the transformer is 50' (15 m) from the luminaire. A single-fixture luminaire with a 12-gauge wire at 12 V can accommodate 250 W when the transformer is 50' (15 m) from the luminaire. A 24 V system is available to help alleviate problems associated with distances between the transformer and luminaires. All these data are available from luminaire manufacturers.

Most transformers work with standard incandescent dimmers. There are some options available for transformers, including automatic reset, soft starting, resettable circuit breakers, thermal protection, and short-circuit protection. There are also special devices designed for unique installation requirements, such as expandable hanger bars that provide support for suspended fixtures. Very small transformers with dimmers can be used in cabinets or display shelves. Plug-in transformers are available for 12 V fixtures.

Ballasts

A ballast is a control device used with an electric-discharge lamp to start the lamp; it also controls the electrical current during operation (Figure 6.2). Fluorescent and HID discharge lamps require ballasts to operate. The ballast for a lamp is either a separate control gear or an integral system and generally lasts longer than the discharge lamp itself. Ballasts are available in magnetic and electronic versions. Magnetic ballasts are made with a steel core wrapped with copper or aluminum wire. They may produce a humming sound that can be a problem. Based on the level of sound in decibels, ballasts have been rated on a scale from A, the quietest (20 to 24 dB), to F, the loudest (greater than 49 dB). Electronic ballasts are produced with solid-state circuitry, and some are designed to operate on high-frequency power to improve the efficiency of lamp/ballast systems. Electronic ballasts can accommodate only rapid- and instant-start fluorescent lamps. Multiple-lamp ballasts are available to accommodate several lamps.

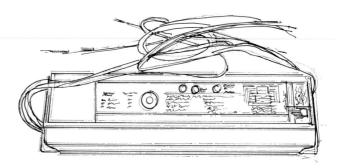

FIGURE 6.2
An electronic ballast for a fluorescent lamp.

As with transformers, the electronic version is generally preferred over the magnetic because the unit is more energy-efficient, quieter, and weighs less. Also, electronic ballasts use less electricity for the light output and operate at cooler temperatures, thereby saving energy. The cooler operating temperature improves lamp life and helps to reduce the energy required for air-conditioning. (For more information about energy and the environment, refer to Chapter 7.) Electronic ballasts eliminate flicker and can accommodate multiple-lamp operations. However, the initial cost of electronic ballasts is slightly more than that of magnetic ballasts.

Ballasts are designed to operate in a parallel or series circuit. In a series circuit, lamps operate together as one system. If one lamp burns out, the remaining lamps do not work. Lamps operating with a parallel ballast circuit function independently and continue to operate when one of the lamps burns out.

Ballasts must always be considered as forming a system together with specific lamps. Generally, ballasts are designed to work with the specific characteristics of lamps, such as type of source, wattage, and controls. For example, there are ballasts made specifically for metal halide lamps operating at a designated wattage. Fluorescent lamp/ballast circuits are uniquely designed for preheat, rapid-start, and instant-start systems. Moreover, variations among lamp manufacturers result in lamps and ballasts that may not be interchangeable.

Lamps and ballasts operate as an interdependent unit, and should be selected to maximize the performance of the system. For example, high-frequency electronic ballasts were developed to accommodate the efficacious T-8 fluorescent lamp. The union of a T-8 lamp and high-frequency electronic ballast results in low energy consumption, long lamp life, and improved maintenance. HID lamps, on the other hand, are no more efficient operating at high frequencies than at low ones. Thus, to maximize the operating potential of a lamp/ballast system, all characteristics must be reviewed, including how the individual units affect one another. Ballast characteristics and operating factors are used in determining light loss factors (LLF) and the watts-per-square-foot calculations for an interior.

The technology of ballasts is constantly improving in areas such as system efficacy, control abilities, and daylight integration. The goals are to provide greater flexibility, enhance control, improve light output, and conserve energy and natural resources. Energy-saving ballast/lamp systems, such as a 32 W T-8 lamp, reduce the consumption of watts. Circuits are being improved by allowing control of several lamp wattages on one circuit and reading input voltages and lamp types. These enhancements reduce the number of ballasts needed for an interior, facilitating specification and maintenance requirements. Improvements in controls include devices, such as smart circuitry, that regulate starts and restarts. Circuits can also monitor the end-of-life of a lamp, dimming, and photocells. To protect the environment, materials used to fabricate ballasts have also been improved. Some ballasts produced prior to 1978 contained the toxic substance **polychlorinated biphenyls (PCBs)**. Ballasts without PCBs are labeled "No PCBs."

polychlorinated biphenyls (PCBs)
A toxic substance used in ballasts produced prior to 1978.

Lighting Controls

Lighting controls are available in manual, automated, or a combination of both. The newest integrated control systems allow access to interiors from anywhere. Lighting control systems can be monitored, programmed, and managed using building networks or Ethernet/Internet. System software features allow a user to customize a graphic depicting the lighting system on floor plans, elevations, or any other illustration that helps to visualize illumination throughout a space and building. For example, via Ethernet/Internet, people sitting in their office can view a floor plan of their home and learn which lights are on or off. They can also review the status of any system integrated with the centralized control unit, such as security and fire alarms, and can control elements of any of these systems from the office.

Criteria for Specifying Controls

There are many criteria an interior designer should consider when specifying lighting controls, including energy considerations, economics, and aesthetics. Controls can be used to conserve energy by turning lights off when they are not needed, integrating daylight, monitoring lamp maintenance, and load shedding. Conserving energy requires examining the activity patterns of the users of the space. Based upon an analysis of how people function in a space, controls can be programmed for various types of schedules. Predictable scheduling is used to control the lights in a space when there is a set routine. For example, many offices have a fixed schedule for people arriving at work, taking lunch breaks, and leaving at the end of the day. A control system can be designed to turn lights on and off automatically according to the designated time and day of the week. Unpredictable scheduling is designed to accommodate unusual activities in a space. For example, a local control could be installed in a private office to turn the lights off when a person is out sick or away on vacation. Unpredictable scheduling could also be used in spaces such as retail dressing rooms, washrooms, or stacks in a library. IES (2000) estimates that predictable and unpredictable scheduling can reduce energy by up to 40 percent and 60 percent respectively.

Controls can also conserve energy by orchestrating daylight and electrical light sources. Dimming and switching plans can be programmed to complement daylight by maintaining an appropriate illumination level regardless of the weather conditions and time of year. Controls can also be adjusted to ensure that areas located far from windows have adequate illumination for required tasks. Multiple switching plans, dimmers, and photoelectric control units are excellent techniques for conserving energy by integrating daylight.

New technology has allowed very sophisticated system integration. For example, a centralized lighting control system in an office can connect electrical sources and shade control. Automated window shades are installed in front of windows, and a small photocell is suspended close to the window to monitor the level of daylight illumination. As the level of daylight increases, the translucent shades automatically come down and the light from electrical luminaires is reduced. Throughout the day and evening, the lighting control system is constantly balancing the amount of light and glare in a room using window shades and electrical sources. This results in a consistent foot-candle level in the space and conserves energy by eliminating or reducing electrical sources when daylight is sufficient. In addition, to customize lighting requirements for users, the system will allow individuals to control the light level in their space.

Energy can also be conserved by programming controls to monitor lamp maintenance. For example, controls can notify users when lamps are operating at an unacceptable lumen output level. Lamps operating at less than optimum levels require more energy to function. The low lumen output could be the result of the lamp's end-of-life, or the accumulation of dirt and dust. Upon notice of lamp lumen depreciation, relamping procedures could be activated automatically.

Reducing the electrical needs of a space is known as load shedding. A load represents all the lights on one switch. New, centralized lighting control systems will produce power consumption reports for every fixture in a building and indicate the foot-candle level for any surface or area in a space. This information can be used to carry out load shedding.

One form of load shedding is to reduce illumination during peak times. For example, because of high air-conditioning requirements, summer is a peak electrical demand period. Thus, during the summer, one way to minimize electrical consumption could be to dim or turn lights off on sunny days. Another peak electrical period is during normal working hours. Any load shedding that can be done during the week on a regular basis will conserve energy and natural resources. Task tuning is another method of conserving energy in work areas. This is accomplished by having lighting systems that individualize luminaires for each person in the space.

Generally, using controls to conserve energy will result in economic savings; of course, the cost of controls must be considered when calculating the cost of a lighting system. Control costs include the control unit itself, installation, electricity, and maintenance. Generally, these expenses can be offset by proper specification, installation, and use of controls. To conserve energy and reduce costs for existing lighting systems, there are retrofit control kits.

Controls are often specified for aesthetic purposes. General, task, accent, and decorative light sources should all have controls that will enhance the purpose of the light source. Controls can be adjusted to create the mood and atmosphere required by the environment and the activity taking place at a given time. They can also be used to create the perfect balance for accenting a piece of artwork, or they can establish the ideal levels between illumination zones in a space. Controls also enhance an interior by balancing natural and electrical light sources. For example, when illumination levels in an existing lighting plan are not balanced, controls can be added to lower or increase light levels for specific luminaires.

Controls provide the flexibility to accommodate a variety of activities in the same space. A lighting system with properly designed controls can transform a working conference room into an evening dining area. Controls also enable individuals to take notes while watching a presentation on a screen or monitor (Figure 6.3), and can improve visibility and reduce eyestrain by providing gradual adjustments in light levels. The proper placement of controls can assist individuals with visual impairments or challenging visual tasks. In addition, programming

lights either to fade off or to delay switching off can help provide an element of safety to a space.

Planning for controls requires a thorough analysis of the current and future needs of the space in terms of users and their activities. Key to successful planning is providing a system that allows for flexibility and individual control. Unfortunately, sometimes an expensive, well-planned control system is turned off, or is not used to the greatest advantage because individuals do not know how to do so. To inform people of the proper operation and maintenance of controls, written documentation and training sessions are very helpful.

Equipment

The basic equipment for lighting controls includes switches, dimmers, timers, occupancy sensors, photosensors, and central controls. In specifying equipment, designers must ensure that the controls are compatible with the entire lighting system, including the specific light source. Lighting controls operate manually, automatically, or by a combination of the two. The needs of the environment and users of the space should determine the type of control specified. (Chapters 11 and 12 discuss the process of designing a quality lighting environment.) The greatest flexibility for users is provided by automatic controls having a manual-off override. Designers should also consider how easy it is for individuals with disabilities to use the equipment. It is important to keep in mind that, because of the ever-changing technological advancements, the industry related to lighting controls is expanding. To optimize a lighting plan, an interior designer must keep current in the field and be knowledgeable regarding the interface between controls and other elements of a lighting system.

A **switch** is the easiest and oldest means of controlling lights. The function of an electrical switch is to stop the flow of electricity. A circuit is closed when a light is on and is open when the light is off. Relays, solenoids, or contactors are used for remote-control switching and for switching large lighting loads. The most common switch is a single pole that is operated manually. Switches are available in toggles, rockers, push buttons, rotary, or touch-plate mechanisms (Figure 6.4). Generally, they are mounted on a wall 48" (122 cm) above the floor, next to the opening side of a door. Systems with more than one switch are known as multigang configurations. Multilevel or bilevel switching provides the flexibility of obtaining different levels of illumination from the same luminaires.

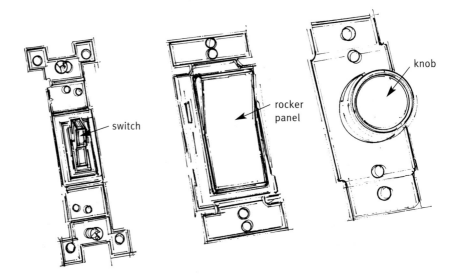

knob

switch

rocker panel

FIGURE 6.4
Different types
of switches

Switches can be localized or mounted in a central switching system. A double pole with a single throw operates two different electrical devices at the same time. A three-way switch operates a circuit from two different locations. A four-way switch will turn a light on or off from three different locations. When dimming a three-way switch, the dimming function will operate on only one of the switches. (For information on how to draw switching arrangements on electrical plans, see Chapter 12.)

Dimmers are used to conserve energy and enhance the aesthetics of an environment. Generally, reducing the power in a lamp conserves energy, affects color, and can extend the life of some lamps. Architectural dimming is the term describing a system that can be reduced to a light output of one percent to 2 percent. Dimmers have maximum wattages, indicated by manufacturers as part of their product information, that must be adhered to for proper performance and safe operation. Low-voltage lamps require a transformer designed for dimming. Generally, a rotary unit, toggle, linear slide, or touch plate operates dimmers. Plugs and adapters are available for dimming portable luminaires.

dimmer
Electrical device designed to decrease light output by reducing power to a lamp.

Dimming affects each light source in different ways. For incandescent and tungsten-halogen lamps, dimming results in energy savings, longer lamp life, and a warmer color. To accommodate the halogen regenerative cycle, manufacturers may suggest that tungsten-halogen lamps be operated at full power periodically. Fluorescent and HID lamps are difficult to dim. Dimming these lamps requires special ballasts and reduces lamp life. Also, some dimmers cause fluorescent lamps to flicker at low light levels. HID lamps do not perform well with dimmers because of the required warm-up and restrike times. Moreover, the color changes resulting from dimming HID lamps are undesirable.

There is a range of dimming equipment. Multilevel ballasts for discharge lamps can be used to create a smooth transition between light levels. Sophisticated dimmers will adjust the speed of raising or lowering light levels to accommodate the adaptive function of the eyes. For example, the eye takes longer to adjust from bright to dim than from dim to bright light levels. Thus, dimmers can be programmed to take a longer period of time to change the light level from bright to dark.

This can be very useful in a conference room when lights need to be dimmed for events such as viewing audiovisual presentations.

Timers control lighting systems by turning lights on and off at designated times. A timer can be a very simple device that a homeowner sets manually and plugs into a wall socket, or it can be a component in a very sophisticated computer program. Some of the computer programs include astronomical data that automatically adjusts the timer function according to the amount of daylight at a particular time of year in a specific geographical location. Many timers have backup systems for power outages. While they are most useful for predictable schedules in areas of high use, or for HID lamps that should not be switched frequently, timers can also be used in spaces that are not often occupied, such as restrooms or storage facilities. Unless there is supplementary lighting, they should not be used in areas where there is concern for safety or security.

Occupancy sensors are designed to turn lights on or off based upon whether there are people in a room. Research indicates significant energy savings from the use of occupancy sensors (Jennings, Rubenstein, and DiBartolomeo, 2000; Maniccia, Von Neida, and Tweed, 2000). Generally, occupancy sensors are practical in spaces that are used sporadically or unpredictably. They are also useful for security purposes. Sensors detect the presence of people in a space by discerning sounds, movements, or body heat. Ultrasonic sensors detect movement by analyzing changes in wave patterns, and are therefore not recommended for interiors with a high degree of air movement, which may interfere with their operation. Passive infrared (PIR) sensors detect body heat and require an unobstructed view of all areas of a room in order to function properly. Generally, ultrasonic sensors are more successful than PIR units. There are also dual-technology sensors that combine the functions of ultrasonic and PIR. Occupancy sensors can be used with switches, dimmers, timers, photosensors, and central controls, providing maximum flexibility in designing a system for a variety of spaces and users.

The success of occupancy sensors is dependent upon a thorough analysis of the interior and how people function in the space. Physical characteristics of the space and the users will determine the appropriate

timer
Device designed to control lighting systems by turning lights on and off at designated times.

occupancy sensor
Device designed to turn lights on or off depending on whether people are present in a room.

sensor and the ideal mounting location. Generally, PIR sensors are effective in open spaces that are free of obstructions, rooms with ceilings higher than 14' (427 cm), and remote areas. Ultrasonic or dual-technology sensors should be used in rooms with ceilings lower than 14' (427 cm), partitions, or large furniture.

Occupancy sensors can be mounted in a variety of ways—on the ceiling, on walls, or in the corners of a room. There are units available for wall switches and for plugging into electrical outlets, as well as portable units that can be located next to an individual. Each type of sensor has a designated angle of coverage and an effective range; manufacturers' literature provides these performance characteristics. In determining the location of the sensor, the most important consideration is to maintain an unobstructed view. The wrong type of sensor or an inappropriate location will cause lights to turn on or off at the wrong time. For example, when a PIR sensor is unable to detect a person working behind a high partition, the lights will automatically turn off. If this continues to happen, users of the space become frustrated and may eventually deactivate the system. To help avoid false readings, installations should include commissioning adjustments. This involves testing and adjusting the occupancy sensor to accommodate any nuances present in an interior.

Photosensors are devices that detect the amount of illumination in a space, and then send signals that control electrical light sources by switching lights on and off or by adjusting illumination levels to reach the optimum point. Photosensors adjust electrical light sources to accommodate fluctuations in the quality and quantity of daylight in a space or on a task, and research indicates the result is a savings in energy (Jennings, Rubenstein, and DiBartolomeo, 2000; Pacific Gas & Electric Company, 1999; Rundquist, McDougall, and Benya, 1996). Photosensors are available as separate units or may be integrated in a luminaire.

As with occupancy sensors, photosensors must be properly mounted. Photosensors can be mounted on a ceiling close to a task, directly on a work surface, or next to a window or skylight. Locating a photosensor close to exterior openings can be done with an indoor or outdoor mount. For the most accurate readings, a photosensor should not be

photosensor
Device that detects the amount of illumination in a space, and then sends signals to control electrical light sources.

mounted in direct view of electrical sources or sunlight. In addition, each photosensor should be connected to luminaires sharing one set of lighting requirements. For example, in a large classroom, the general perimeter lighting has a lower illumination level than the task lighting located above the desks. Therefore, different individual photosensors should be connected to the general and task luminaires respectively.

A **central control system** uses a microprocessor to monitor, adjust, and regulate lighting in many areas or zones within a building. Some units are designed to integrate lighting with other electrical units, including mechanical, energy, and security systems. Electrical units can include motorized window treatments, whirlpool jets, ceiling fans, kitchen appliances, sprinkler systems, garage door openers, security systems, skylights, sound systems, and audiovisual equipment. Mechanical systems can include heating, ventilation, air-conditioning, and plumbing. Central control systems can be connected to switches, dimmers, timers, occupancy sensors, and photosensors. For flexibility and safety purposes, central control systems should always have manual options for operating the luminaires.

> **central control system**
> An electronic system that uses a microprocessor to monitor, adjust, and regulate lighting in many areas or zones within a building, often in integration with other systems.

Central control systems can be programmed for preset "scenes." Each scene is designed for a specific space or activity and its illumination requirements, for example, security, entertainment, exterior lights, relaxation, or work. For example, if the button labeled "work" is pressed in a conference room, the central control system will adjust the luminaires to the programmed illumination levels for that activity in that space. Striking the "video" button will automatically adjust the luminaires for the task of viewing a video. Central control systems have become very sophisticated in residential buildings. Someone driving home from work can telephone the system and direct it to start running the bath water to a specific level and temperature, warm the towel bars, heat the tile floor, close the blinds, play music, and dim the lights. Central controls are activated by keypads, touch screens, computers, telephones, and handheld infrared remotes. Keypad buttons and faceplates are available in a variety of finishes and can be custom engraved for labeling purposes (Figure 6.5). High-humidity and waterproof versions of control units can be specified to resist the effects of mild moisture and water.

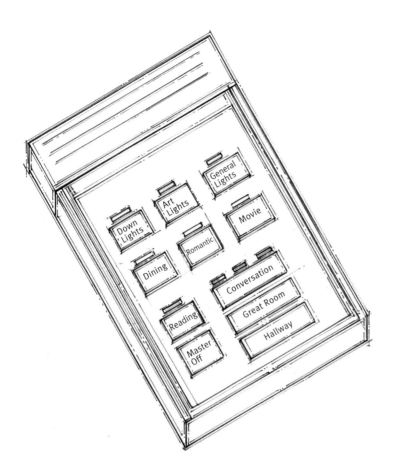

FIGURE 6.5
Control keypad
with custom
engraved labels.

Computer network control systems for lighting will continue to improve in the future. For digital lighting control, the developmental focus is on the digital addressable lighting interface (DALI). DALI is a means of communicating through low-voltage wires, allowing information to be distributed to the lighting system and allowing the luminaires to report back. DALI controls individual luminaires, groups of fixtures, occupancy sensors, dimmers, photosensors, timers, scenes, transition fades, and other networked systems. Luminaires communicate with DALI when a lamp is close to burning out, has low lumen output, or has ballast irregularities.

Controls play a very important role in a quality lighting environment by fine-tuning the system. Effective use of lighting controls can conserve energy and natural resources, provide users with flexibility, vary illumination using the same fixtures, and create an atmosphere conducive to the purpose of a space. Controls can also help to support safety and security systems. The progressive nature of the technology associated with controls requires that interior designers stay abreast of developments in the field.

SUMMARY

- Magnetic and electronic transformers convert voltages in a system. For lighting purposes, a transformer is either integral to the design of the luminaire or is a separate unit concealed above a ceiling or behind a wall.
- Magnetic and electronic ballasts are control devices used with electric discharge lamps; they start lamps and control the electrical current during operation.
- Generally, electronic transformers and ballasts are preferable to magnetic units because they are more energy-efficient, make less noise, and weigh less.
- Lighting controls operate either manually or automatically, and include switches, dimmers, timers, occupancy sensors, photosensors, and central controls.
- Controls can be used to conserve energy by turning lights off when they are not needed, integrating daylight, monitoring lamp maintenance, and load shedding.
- Generally, using controls to conserve energy will result in economic savings. The cost of controls includes the unit itself, installation, electricity, and maintenance.
- Controls can be adjusted to create the mood and atmosphere required for an activity or space.
- The function of an electrical switch is to stop the flow of electricity. A circuit is closed when a light is on and open when the light is off.
- Dimmers can conserve energy and enhance the aesthetics of an environment. Reducing the power to a lamp conserves energy, affects color, and can extend the life of some lamps.
- Timers control lighting systems by turning lights on and off at designated times.

- Occupancy sensors are designed to turn lights on or off based on whether there are people in a room.
- Photosensors are devices that detect the amount of illumination in a space, and then send signals to control electrical light sources. Photosensors are often used for daylight integration applications.
- Research indicates that the use of occupancy sensors and photosensors saves energy.
- Proper mounting location is key to the success of occupancy sensors and photosensors.
- A central control system uses a microprocessor to monitor, adjust, and regulate lighting in many areas or zones within a building. Some units are designed to integrate lighting with other electrical systems, including mechanical, energy, and security systems.

Key Terms

central control system

dimmer

occupancy sensor

photosensor

polychlorinated biphenyls
  (PCBs)

switch

timer

transformer

Exercises

1. Review the literature for the past two years to identify the newest developments in transformers and ballasts. In a written report, summarize the results and identify how to apply the findings to lighting systems.
2. Identify effective methods for applying controls to general, task, accent, and decorative lighting, and provide the suggestions in a written report. The report may include illustrations and drawings.

3. Review current literature regarding lighting controls. For each major type of lighting control, including switches, dimmers, timers, occupancy sensors, and photosensors, provide recommendations for effective interior applications. Write a report that includes your research and effective applications.

4. Identify three commercial and two residential spaces that will use central controls. For each space, develop preset scenes that integrate lighting with other systems. In a written report, describe the preset scenes and indicate how the programming will enhance the quality of the lighting environment.

PART II
Lighting Design Applications and the Design Process

CHAPTER 7

Energy, the Environment, and Sustainable Development/Design

OBJECTIVES

- Describe international energy requirements through 2020.
- Analyze the energy required for lighting, including consumption by type of building and practices described by producers, conveyors, and consumers.
- As prescribed by energy codes and standards, understand minimum requirements for energy-efficient design of new and existing buildings.
- Determine the factors that should be considered in an economic analysis.
- Define sustainable design and apply an understanding of it to lighting systems.
- Identify the factors that should be considered when specifying a sustainable lighting system.

Interior designers have an ethical responsibility to safeguard the health, safety, and welfare of the occupants of the interiors they specify. As our planet experiences growth in population and the depletion of natural resources, protecting the environment has become increasingly essential for the health and welfare of future generations. As global citizens, interior designers can play an active role in educating consumers and making a conscious effort to specify products and materials that minimize the impact on the environment.

During the past several years, the field of interior design has become more focused on the environment than it had been previously. This is made evident by the emergence of sustainable design. **Sustainable design** is design focusing on products and processes that protect the environment while conserving energy for future generations. Whenever possible, lighting specifications should reflect the principles embodied in sustainable design, including energy conservation and compliance with standards, codes, and regulations. Such design will involve incorporation of the information reviewed in previous chapters of this textbook, the most germane topics being daylight integration, characteristics of lamps, directional effects of lighting, design of luminaires, electricity, and controls. These areas and the principles of sustainable design are also to be considered in a lighting system's energy and maintenance management plan.

Energy

A quality lighting environment requires luminaire systems that protect the environment and conserve energy.

Global Energy Consumption

The Energy Information Administration (EIA) is an independent statistical and analytical agency that issues the annual *International Energy Outlook* (*IEO*) publication. In projecting international energy consumption, the EIA indicates "world energy consumption is projected to increase by 71 percent from 2003 to 2030" (IEO, 2006, 1). The EIA further examines world energy consumption specifically for the purpose of generating electricity, and projects increases in consumption of all primary energy sources, including coal and natural gas. Increases in the consumption of fossil fuels deplete nonrenewable resources, while the associated combustion process increases world carbon dioxide emissions. Specifying energy-efficient lighting systems can assist in reducing future international energy consumption and subsequent emissions.

The EIA divided the world into the following Organization for Economic Cooperation and Development (OECD) groupings: (1) North America, (2) OECD Europe, and (3) OECD Asia (Japan, South Korea,

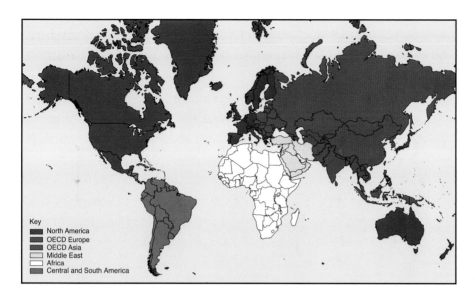

FIGURE 7.1
Map of OECD and
non-OECD members.

and Australia/New Zealand). The non-OECD regional subgroups are: (1) non-OECD Europe and Eurasia (including Russia), (2) non-OECD Asia (including China and India), (3) Africa, (4) the Middle East, and (5) Central and South America (Figure 7.1).

According to the EIA (2006), by the year 2030 world energy consumption will be 722 quadrillion British thermal units (Btu). The developing countries, primarily those in non-OECD Asia and Central and South America, will experience the greatest demand for energy. In reviewing energy consumption by type of fuel, the EIA reports that the greatest increase in demand is for natural gas (Figure 7.2). Most of the increase in the consumption of natural gas is attributed to the use of gas turbine power plants for the generation of electricity. This technology is appealing to producers and consumers because natural gas has many environmental and economic benefits. Natural gas burns more cleanly than other fossil fuels, thus reducing the ill effects derived from gas emissions.

World Delivered Energy Consumption by End-Use Sector, 2003–2030

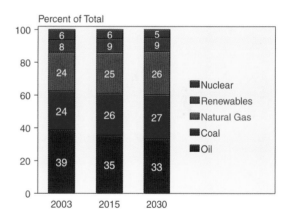

Note: Fuel shares may not add to 100 percent due to independent rounding.

Sources: 2006: Energy Information Administration (EIA), International Energy Annual 2006 (May–July 2005), Web site www.eia.doe.gov/iea/. 2015 and 2030: EIA, System for the Analysis of Global Energy Markets (2006).

FIGURE 7.2
World energy consumption by fuel type for 2003, 2015, and 2030.

World Electricity Generating Capacity by Fuel Type, 2003–2030

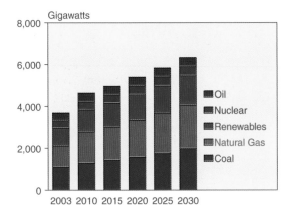

Gigawatts

Oil
Nuclear
Renewables
Natural Gas
Coal

2003 2010 2015 2020 2025 2030

Sources: 2006: Derived from Energy Information Administration (EIA), International Energy Annual 2006 (May–July 2005), Web site www.eia.doe.gov/iea/. 2010–2030: EIA, System for the Analysis of Global Energy Markets (2006).

FIGURE 7.3
World Electricity
Generating Capacity
by Fuel Type,
2003–2030.

Table 7.1 illustrates the history and projections for electrical consumption by region. The EIA postulates that electrical consumption for developing Asia and Central and South America will increase by 4.5 percent and 3.9 percent, respectively, per year. Currently, some areas in developing countries do not have electricity. Thus, the EIA anticipates that the increase in electrical usage will be derived primarily from improvements in the standard of living in these countries. The EIA also estimates the demand for the types of fuel used to generate electricity (Figure 7.3). The report indicates that coal will continue to be in high demand through 2030, but the largest increase in demand will be for natural gas.

Energy Consumption for Lighting

The EIA report does not provide a historical profile or projection of electrical demand by specific use, such as lighting. However, some of this information is available from the U.S. Environmental Protection Agency (EPA) and the International Association of Energy-Efficient Lighting (IAEEL). The EPA has determined that lighting consumes approximately 23 percent of the electricity used in buildings. In addition, approximately 20 percent of the electricity used for air-conditioning is required as a result of the heat generated by lamps. Most of the need for lighting occurs during weekdays, which is the time of peak demand for electricity. The purpose of a building affects the percentage of the electricity it uses for lighting. For example, a large percentage of the electricity consumed by a retail store is dedicated to lighting. In contrast, the percentage of electricity used for lighting by a factory is very small, because the highest demands are for operating machinery. Approximately half the electricity used in commercial buildings, and about 10 percent of the electricity consumed in residences, is for lighting.

TABLE 7.1

World Net Electricity Consumption by Region, 1990–2020

(Billion Kilowatt hours)

Region	History		Projections				Average Percent Change 1999–2020
	1990	1999	2005	2010	2015	2020	
Industrialized Countries	6,385	7,517	8,620	9,446	10,281	11,151	1.9
United States	2,817	3,236	3,793	4,170	4,556	4,916	2.0
EE/FSU	1,906	1,452	1,651	1,807	2,006	2,173	1.9
Developing Countries	2,258	3,863	4,912	6,127	7,548	9,082	4.2
Developing Asia	1,259	2,319	3,090	3,900	4,819	5,858	4.5
China	551	1,084	1,523	2,031	2,631	3,349	5.5
India	257	424	537	649	784	923	3.8
South Korea	93	233	309	348	392	429	3.0
Other Developing Asia	357	578	724	872	1,012	1,157	3.4
Central and South America	449	684	788	988	1,249	1,517	3.9
Total World	10,549	12,833	15,182	17,380	19,835	22,407	2.7

Note: EE/FSU = Eastern Europe and the former Soviet Union.

Sources: History: Energy Information Administration (EIA), International Energy Annual 1999, DOE/EIA-0219(99) (Washington, DC, February 2001). Projections: EIA, World Energy Projection System (2002).

The design of a building also affects the percentage of electricity used for lighting. Generally, buildings whose interiors have relatively little exposure to daylight require more electricity for lighting. Effective daylight integration can conserve energy; the amount of illumination from a window approximately 3' x 5' is equivalent to 100 incandescent 60 W lamps. Software is available to generate a simulation of the electrical needs for lighting in proposed buildings.

Based on a study of 38 countries, the IAEEL reports that "globally, electric lighting accounts for more than 2000 TWh electricity and 2900 million metric tons of carbon dioxide emissions (CO_2) per year" (2000, p. 1). The IAEEL study reveals that global electrical lighting needs are the highest in the service and residential sectors, suggesting that we should focus on designing efficient lighting systems for these two sectors.

To analyze lighting practices and attitudes, the Smithsonian National Museum of American History is collecting a written history of responses from those who make, sell, and use lighting. Questions and responses are available on the museum's Web site (http://americanhistory.si.edu/). The questions focus primarily on issues related to energy conservation. For example, one of the questions addressed to producers is: "Has your involvement with energy-efficient lighting led you to consider energy issues when you think about other products? Can you give examples?" (2003, p. 6). One conveyor question is: "Efficient lighting is increasingly seen as a system involving many integrated components. From your experience, how has this affected adoption of the technology?" (2003, p. 4). Consumers are asked: "Have you replaced entire lighting fixtures in order to use more efficient bulbs? If not, would you consider doing so?" (2003, p. 3).

The Web site includes selected responses to the questions. Since this is an ongoing study, findings and conclusions are not yet available at the time of publication of this text; however, by reading the responses from producers, conveyors, and consumers, an interior designer can gain insight into problems associated with making and distributing efficient lighting systems. For example, in response to the conveyor question identified in the previous paragraph, one respondent who is a designer and specifier noted, "This is a great concept that has only begun to crawl. I am currently working on a very complex project where we [lighting, HVAC, security, and IT designers] have integrated wide and local control of all systems with cross-compatibility. The various industries involved have yet to recognize the complexity of cross-compatibility and many say they have gone there, but have [actually] only scratched the surface. Once the walls are broken down and the various disciplines truly work together in development, only then will we see some highly efficient and sophisticated technologies" (2003, pp. 6–7). An understanding of the issues can facilitate discussion with industry representatives and lead to the design and use of more energy-efficient lighting systems.

An understanding of the perspectives of consumers can be invaluable in developing strategies to convince people to purchase energy-efficient lighting systems. For example, in response to being asked about using energy-efficient lighting equipment, a consumer commented, "Unfortunately, as a consumer I have no economic incentive to purchase energy-efficient fixtures. The premium for these types of bulbs is usually such that it is very hard to rationalize [buying them] as you are in the aisle of your local hardware store or Wal-Mart" (2003, p. 1). A homeowner responded, "It's a good idea but how much of our energy budget is consumed by lighting?" (2003, p. 2).

Energy Standards and Codes

To promote energy efficiency and sustainable development, standards and codes have been established worldwide. Because standards and codes are continuously being updated, an interior designer must always refer to the most current versions. Standards delineate minimum energy efficiency for lighting equipment and limit power for special interior applications, while codes are the laws enacted to apply these standards; in the U.S., states and local communities must enact laws that comply with federal standards. Many communities simply adopt the federal standards as their codes with no modifications; however, some states, such as California, have codes that exceed federal standards. Interior designers must always refer to the state and local codes that regulate their clients' buildings. This is especially important when designers have a project located in a different state or country from their own. Most standards and codes prescribe requirements according to the type of structure and whether it is existing or a new construction.

Important energy standards and codes that affect lighting efficiency are ASHRAE/IESNA 90.1-2001 (American Society of Heating, Refrigerating, and Air-Conditioning Engineers/Illuminating Engineering Society of North America), MEC-95 (Model Energy Code), IECC-03 (International Energy Conservation Code), and NFPA (National Fire Protection Act) 5000. Energy standards for lighting started in 1974 with a publication titled *Energy Conservation Guidelines for Existing Office Buildings*, developed by the General

Service Administration and the Public Building Services (GSA/PBS). During this time period, the ASHRAE worked with the IESNA to write a chapter on lighting in its standards document, ASHRAE 90-75. The chapter focuses on lighting-power budget-determination procedures and energy standards for specific applications. This standard has had several revisions, the most current editions being ASHRAE/IESNA 90.1-2001 for commercial buildings except low-rise residential buildings, and ASHRAE/IESNA 90.2-2001 for low-rise residential buildings. The standard specifies minimum requirements for the energy-efficient design of new buildings, as well as for additions or alterations to existing buildings.

The Energy Conservation Standard for New Buildings Act of 1976 mandated lighting efficiency standards. As a result of this legislation and ASHRAE 90-75, the Model Code for Energy Conservation in New Building Construction (MCEC 77) was developed by several professional organizations; in 1983, the title was changed to Model Energy Code (MEC). The International Code Council is the organization responsible for the IECC, mentioned above. This code includes a lighting section derived from ASHRAE/IESNA 90.1. The National Fire Protection Association (NFPA) 5000 Building Code is NFPA's complete building code and includes ASHRAE/IESNA 90.1 and 90.2 as the standard for energy provisions.

Since most lighting codes and regulations are based upon ASHRAE/IESNA 90.1, an interior designer should know this document well. Section 9 of the document is dedicated to lighting. Section 9.1 reviews general lighting applications, while Section 9.2 encompasses mandatory provisions, including lighting controls, tandem wiring, exit signs, installed interior lighting power, and luminaire wattage. The prescriptive path for interior lighting power allowance (ILPA) is described in Section 9.3. The ILPA is calculated in two ways: the building area method and the space-by-space method. The former involves the entire building and is determined by multiplying the gross lighted area by allowances provided in the standard's table of lighting power density. These allowances are based on maximum watts per square foot for a given type of building. For example, the maximum watts per square foot for a retail store are higher than for an office. In the near future, most office buildings in the United States will be limited to 1.1 watts per square foot.

The space-by-space method is a more flexible and accurate means to calculate the ILPA, because each area of a building is identified. The ILPA is determined by adding up all the lighting power allowances room by room. For example, in a school building, the ILPA would include the lighting power for classrooms, hallways, offices, restrooms, cafeteria, and gymnasium.

Compared to previous versions of the standard, ASHRAE/IESNA 90.1-2001 has more stringent interior lighting power requirements and mandatory control requirements. Lighting power calculations for installed interior lighting systems include lamps, ballasts, and controls for all permanent and portable luminaires. Some of the lighting power exemptions include luminaires for safety, exit signs, theatrical lighting, educational demonstration systems, areas for the visually impaired, plant growth, museum exhibits, medical and dental procedures, retail display windows, and registered historic landmarks. Except for safety and security lighting, controls must be accessible and mounted in a location that can be seen by users. Control devices are restricted to an area of 2500 sq. ft. in spaces less than 10,000 sq. ft. In spaces greater than 10,000 sq. ft., control devices are limited to an area of 10,000 sq. ft. Automatic shutoff controls are required for spaces greater than 5000 sq. ft. To simplify energy code compliance, the Department of Energy (DOE) has free software designed to perform the necessary calculations. REScheck and COMcheck are the compliance tools for residential and commercial buildings respectively (http://www.energycodes.gov).

The U.S. Energy Policy Act of 1992 (EPAct-92) has significantly affected energy-efficient lighting. The EPAct focuses on standards for lighting, energy-efficiency rating systems for windows, and demand-side management (DSM) programs. (DSM programs focus on strategies to reduce the consumption of energy by the customers of utilities providers.) The EPAct mandates that all states must have codes meeting or exceeding the standards in ASHRAE/IESNA 90.1. The EPAct energy code also requires lamp manufacturers to stop producing many lamps that are not energy-efficient, including standard 40 W fluorescent lamps and some incandescent reflector and PAR lamps. Lamps for special applications, such as emergency, safety, and cold temperature service, are excluded from meeting efficiency standards. As a result of the EPAct, lamp manufacturers have developed many energy-efficient lamps, including the T-8 and T-5/HO (high output). Figure 7.4 illustrates efficacy ratings for selected lamps. The Federal Trade Commission (FTC) has developed a labeling program that must be used by all lamp manufacturers to indicate the energy efficiency of their products. The label includes energy ratings for lamps and the estimated operating costs per year.

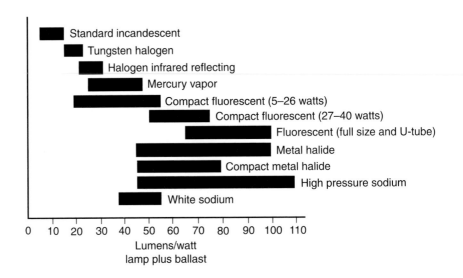

FIGURE 7.4
Efficacies for
selected lamps.

In addition to standards and codes, there are voluntary programs sponsored by the EPA and DOE that include recommendations for energy-efficient lighting practices. The EPA supports the Energy Star Buildings Program, and the DOE has established the Building America and Rebuild America programs. Energy Star is a program "helping businesses and individuals protect the environment through superior energy efficiency" (www.energystar.gov, p. 1). The program provides energy management strategies for businesses and recognizes buildings that perform efficiently. It also includes a residential voluntary labeling program to inform consumers of those products that meet strict energy-efficiency guidelines. The purpose of Building America is to provide energy solutions for production housing. The program is based on a systems engineering approach to create homes that consume less energy, improve builder productivity, and implement innovative technologies. Rebuild America encourages energy-efficiency improvements in existing commercial and high-rise residential buildings as well as in new education buildings.

Energy and Economics

An economic analysis of lighting should include all expenses associated with an installed system, including lamps, luminaires, ballasts, transformers, controls, electricity, maintenance, disposal, and labor. A lighting system accounts for approximately 5 percent of the total cost of a building. These capital costs are generally distributed over a ten-year period. Factors that affect the operation of a lighting system include the daylight factor, lamp life, and the efficiency of lamps and luminaires.

A lighting economic analysis can be conducted by examining simple payback or the life-cycle cost-benefit analysis (LCCBA). The LCCBA is complex and beyond the scope of this textbook. Chapter 25 in *IESNA Lighting Handbook*, 9th edition, provides a detailed illustration of how to conduct an LCCBA. Calculations include initial costs, annual power, maintenance costs, and the time value of money. IESNA recommends that LCCBA be used for large and complex projects. Many software tools are available to determine the costs and benefits of proposed energy conservation projects. The simple payback method is a quick estimate of the number of years required to pay back the money invested in a lighting system, and is convenient for comparing different lighting systems. For example, the payback period is five years for a lighting system that saves $3,000 in energy costs per year and costs $15,000 to purchase and operate.

$$\text{Payback} = \text{cost of system/savings per year}$$
$$5 \text{ years} = \$15,000/\$3000$$

Environment and Sustainable Design

Interior designers are in a unique position to encourage sustainable design because they specify millions of products and materials each year.

Sustainable Design

The U. S. Office of Technology Assessment (OTA) (1992) indicates that sustainable design consists of two major components: (1) waste prevention by reducing weight, toxicity, and energy use; and (2) better materials management by facilitating remanufacturing, recycling, composting, and energy recovery. The Environmental Protection Agency (EPA) (2001) has determined that the issues related to sustainable design include pollution prevention, multiple and systematic effects, an environmental life-cycle assessment (LCA), magnitude of impact (local and global), and specification of environmental attributes. The EIA study (2002) cited earlier in this chapter also examines world energy use and environmental issues. Figure 7.5 illustrates historical and projected world carbon dioxide emissions by region. The EIA reports that "the United States is currently the largest energy consumer in the industrialized world, accounting for the majority of its energy-related carbon dioxide emissions" (2002, p. 164).

All these areas are important when an interior designer specifies a lighting system. The manufacturing process, operations, and the disposal required for lighting systems consume resources, use energy, and cause pollution. In specifying lighting systems, the goals should be to: (1) reduce the use of nonrenewable resources, (2) control the use of renewable products, (3) minimize air, water, and soil pollution, (4) protect natural habitats, (5) eliminate toxic substances, and (6) reduce light pollution.

The many public and private energy and sustainable programs currently in

FIGURE 7.5 Historical and projected world carbon dioxide emissions by region, 1990–2020.

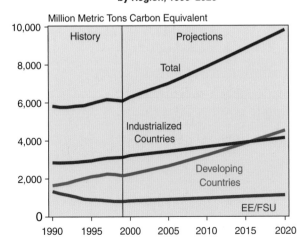

World Carbon Dioxide Emissions by Region, 1990–2020

TABLE 7.2

Energy and Sustainable Programs

Resources	Internet Address
Agencies	
U.S. Department of Energy	http://www.energy.gov
U.S. Environmental Protection Agency	http://www.epa.gov
Offices	
Office of Energy Efficiency and Renewable Energy	http://www.eere.energy.gov
National Fenestration Rating Council (NFRC)	http://www.nfrc.org
Programs and Research Laboratories	
Advanced Buildings	http://www.advancedbuilding.org
ASHRAE/IESNA 90.1-2001 (American Society of Heating, Refrigeration, and Air Conditioning Engineers/Illuminating Engineering Society of North America),	http://www.ashrae.org
Building America Program	http://www.eere.energy.gov/buildings/ building_america
Building Industry Research Alliance	http://www.bira.ws
Building Science Consortium	http://www.eere.energy.gov/buildings/ building_america/bsc.shtml
Consortium for Advanced Residential Buildings (CARB)	http://www.carb-swa.com
Dark Sky International	http://www.darksky.org
DesignLights Consortium	
Energy Star Program	http://www.energyace.com/ energy_star_program.htm
Environmental Energy Technologies Division (EETD)	http://www.lbl.gov
Energy Information Administration	
Industrialized Housing Partnership	
Integrated Building and Construction Solutions (IBA-COS)	http://www.ibacos-ba.com
International Association of Energy-Efficient Lighting (IAEEL)	http://www.iaeel.org
General Service Administration and the Public Building Services (GSA/PBS)	http://www.gsa.gov/Portal/home.jsp
IECC-03 (International Energy Conservation Code)	http://www.bocai.org/index.html
Lawrence Berkeley National Laboratory	http://www.lbl.gov
Leadership in Energy & Environmental Design	http://www.usgbc.org/LEED/LEED_main.asp
Lighting Systems Research Group	http://eetd.lbl.gov/btp/lsr
MEC-95 (Model Energy Code)	http://www.energycodes.gov
NFPA (National Fire Protection Act) 5000	http://www.nfpa.org/catalog/home/index.asp
National Renewable Energy Laboratory (NREL)	http://www.nrel.gov
National Science Foundation (NSF)	http://www.nsf.gov
National Wildlife Federation (NWF)	http://www.nwf.org
Oak Ridge National Laboratory (ORNL)	http://www.ornl.gov
Rebuild America	http://www.rebuild.org
U.S. Green Building Council	http://grove.ufl.edu/~usgbc

operation are valuable resources (Table 7.2). The EPA, DOE, National Wildlife Federation (NWF), and the National Science Foundation (NSF) all sponsor programs that encourage environmental conservation, minimization of waste, and maximization of energy. The former Green Lights Program has been subsumed by the Energy Star Buildings Program. The U.S. Green Building Council developed the Leadership in Energy and Environmental Design (LEED) system, which is quickly becoming the energy and environmental standard throughout the building industry. LEED is a voluntary national standard for developing high-performance, sustainable buildings. It was founded to "define 'green building' by establishing a common standard of measurement; promote integrated, whole-building design practices; recognize environmental leadership in the building industry; stimulate sustainable competition; raise consumer awareness of sustainable building benefits; and transform the building market" (www.usgbc.org/LEED, p. 1).

In addition to rating systems for buildings, voluntary labeling programs help to identify sustainable products. In the United States, the ecolabel and other labels developed by businesses and government-sponsored programs designate such products (Figure 7.6). Many countries throughout the world have created similar labels, which are used on lamps, materials, equipment, appliances, and floor coverings.

Successful sustainable practice requires teamwork in developing systems and procedures that maximize the overall efficiency and effectiveness of an entire building's system. For existing buildings, an assessment of the lighting system should be conducted, including an inventory of lamps, ballasts, luminaires, portable fixtures, controls, and daylight integration. A record should be made of the number of hours during which elements are turned on as well as the specific times of the day and week when this is the case. Effective sustainable practice recognizes the interdependency of lighting and all the other elements of the interior and the architecture. Thus, the assessment should include

FIGURE 7.6
The ecolabel used in the United States to recognize a green product.

the purpose of luminaires, room finishes, colors, materials, architectural features, electrical usage, air-conditioning loads, maintenance, and disposal policies.

Sustainable design includes proper placement of luminaires, as well as the use of colors and materials that maximize the reflectance of illumination. Luminaires should be located so as to provide effective lighting for specific tasks; layouts characterized by a uniform "blanket" distribution of light often waste energy. Specifying too many luminaires causes unnecessary consumption of natural resources involved in manufacturing and delivery. The lighting layout must be appropriate for the purpose of the luminaires and must control glare. The coefficient of utilization (CU) is an important calculation in determining how room proportions and the reflectances of walls, ceiling, and floors affect the quantity of lumens on a task. Colors of ceilings and walls should be light in value and should have a reflectance of at least 90 percent and 70 percent, respectively. Textures should be carefully chosen to avoid glare while enhancing reflectance.

Sustainable design requires the use of lamps that conserve energy and have a high efficacy rating, excellent light output, long life, high lumen maintenance, high color rendering, color stability, low mercury levels, and flexible disposal options. They should also be TCLP-compliant (TCLP = Toxicity Characteristic Leaching Procedure) and contain no additives. Lamps with high efficacy are often advertised as "energy-saving," "ultimate performance," or "long life." Discharge lamps, including fluorescent, metal halide, and high-pressure sodium are the most efficient white light sources, while incandescent lamps have low efficacy and should be used only for special applications. Compact fluorescent lamps (CFLs) are a good substitute for incandescent lamps because they consume approximately 70 percent less electricity and last six to ten times longer. They are available in several different shapes and in a variety of color temperatures; for warm light, specify a color temperature of 2700K to 3000K, and for cool light, 4500K to 6000K. To conserve energy and reduce maintenance costs, CFLs are beginning to be used in recessed downlights, wall sconces, and structural lighting. For applications that require excellent color rendition and precise optical control, such as accent lighting, halogen or halogen infrared (HIR) are good choices because they are more efficient than incandescent lamps.

Compared to incandescent lamps, fluorescent lamps produce the same light output while using one-third of the energy. Fluorescent lamps also last approximately 10 times longer than incandescent ones and utilize less hazardous materials. T8 and T5 fluorescent lamps are becoming very popular because they are energy-efficient, have improved color properties, and are small in size. The super-T8 is efficacious, and the T5/HO (high output) has a lumen level that equals that of some HID lamps. The F32T8 operated with an electronic ballast is a very popular retrofit system for the banned F40T12 with a magnetic ballast, as it reduces the number of ballasts and lamps required for an installation in addition to saving 8 W per lamp. Eliminating magnetic ballasts for electronic units will further reduce the watts required for operation.

HID lamps are efficacious sources, and generally produce more lumens per watt in higher wattages. HPS is the most efficacious, followed by metal halide, and then mercury vapor. High-pressure sodium or metal halide lamps should be substituted for mercury vapor lamps, and standard metal halide lamps should be replaced with energy-efficient ones. The pulse-start metal halide (PSMH) lamp is efficacious because it uses approximately 30 percent less wattage than a standard metal halide lamp. Metal halides are available in warm (3000K) and cool (4000K) colors, and the CRI ranges are 85 to 96.

LEDs are an excellent lighting source for exit signs, and fiber optics show promising development. The Lawrence Berkeley National Laboratory (LBNL) is developing a fiber optic illuminator that will absorb most of the light produced by the lamp and transport the lumens to the fiber optics. Once this is accomplished, fiber optics will be an energy-efficient light source.

The focus on sustainable design has encouraged some luminaire designers to create fixtures made from recycled products. This practice represents a major shift in thinking about the design process. Prior to sustainable design, a designer developed a concept for a luminaire based on using new materials, and then businesses identified products that could be made from recycled materials. Starting with recycled products allows new designs for luminaires that conserve resources. Interiors of luminaires should be semi-specular, low iridescent, or white.

In addition to environmentally friendly material composition, a sustainable fixture is designed for energy efficiency. This is accomplished primarily by maximizing the lumen output. The luminaire efficacy ratio (LER) can be used to compare the efficiency and effectiveness of different luminaires, with high LERs corresponding to high efficiency. To reduce the accumulation of dirt and dust on lamps, luminaires should also be sealed.

Luminaires in existing buildings should be evaluated to determine whether the fixtures should be replaced or retrofitted. The most common retrofit is the addition of a reflector to the interior of a luminaire, enhancing the lumen output by 20 to 30 percent. To improve optics, diffusers should be replaced with prismatic lenses made from either plastic or glass. "Egg crate" louvers should be replaced with parabolic louvers, because the contour parabolic shape maximizes lumen output and helps to control glare.

Energy consumed in a space is based upon wattage and duration. Controls are the element of a lighting system that can affect the length of time electricity is used, and should be installed with a thorough commissioning process, which ensures that a building system performs according to the specifications. Ideally, as controls are operating in a space, users should not notice changes in the illumination levels. Many studies have been conducted to examine practices relating to controls and to determine the energy savings obtained through their use. Pacific Gas and Electric Company (PG&E) (2000) conducted a study to examine the technology, current practice, and economics of lighting controls in relationship to Title 24, California's Energy Efficiency Standards for Nonresidential Buildings. The study reviewed occupancy sensors, automatic shut-off, and manual switches in single and bilevel dwellings and areas with daylight. As required by Title 24, most spaces must have "controls to reduce lighting." This generally involves bilevel controls and can be accomplished by a variety of methods, including "switching that turns off half the lights in a space; dimmers that reduce the entire space's light level by half; individual switches for two or more groups of luminaires in a space; or switching off the middle lamp of three-lamp luminaires" (PG&E, 2000, p. 1). There is little documentation to suggest the energy-effectiveness of Title 24. However, research studies provide support for saving energy by installing individual controls, and people seem to demonstrate more satisfaction with a lighting system that allows flexibility (Boyce, Eklund, and Simpson, 1999; Jennings, Rubenstein, DiBartolomeo, and Blanc, 2000; Rea, 1998).

Sustainable design emphasizes the importance of incorporating daylight in spaces. Daylight integration not only reduces energy consumption but helps to improve the overall health of the atmosphere in buildings. Energy savings are derived from switching patterns, window glazings, window treatments, and the addition of skylights, light pipes, and light shelves. Daylight switching plans include automatic switching and dimmers (Figure 7.7), which make it possible for lights next to windows to be turned off or dimmed while those further from windows are turned on. Heat gain or loss through windows can be controlled by installing windows with an efficient U-factor rating. The lower the U-value, the greater the resistance to heat transfer and the greater the insulation value. The National Fenestration Rating Council (NFRC) provides U-value ratings for windows.

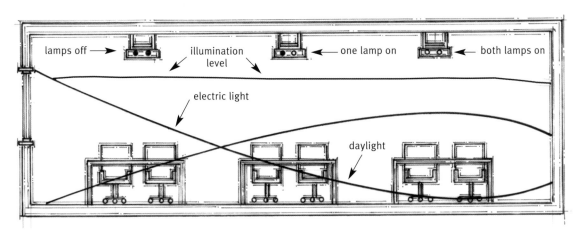

FIGURE 7.7
Daylight switching plan for lights that can be turned on or off depending on the amount of daylight entering a space.

A thorough maintenance plan that includes cleaning instructions, a relamping program, and disposal guidelines is another element of sustainable practice. Dirt, dust, and age affect lumen output. The IESNA reports, "the combined effect of equipment age and dirt depreciation can reduce illuminance by 25% to 50% depending on the application and equipment used" (2000, p. 28-1). Luminaires should be easily accessible to allow maintenance workers to clean and relamp fixtures.

Cleaning instructions should specify the proper detergent and the intervals at which luminaires, lamps, ceilings, walls, and windows should be cleaned. Abrasive detergents can scratch reflectors, causing a decrease in lumen output; manufacturers' product literature will indicate the proper cleaning detergent and method. Generally, the most energy-efficient time to relamp is when 70 percent of the lamp's rated life has elapsed, as lamps burning beyond this point generally consume a high amount of electricity for the lumen output. To save labor costs, group relamping should be specified.

Disposal Regulations

The primary goals of sustainable disposal practices are to decrease the amount of waste and reduce its environmental impact. To improve solid-waste disposal methods, the Solid Waste Disposal Act (SWDA) was enacted in 1965. In 1976, this act was amended to establish the Resource Conservation and Recovery Act (RCRA), whose objective was to: (1) protect human health and the environment; (2) reduce and/or eliminate the generation of hazardous wastes; and (3) conserve energy and natural resources (Department of Energy, 2003, p. 1). The RCRA regulates hazardous waste associated with mercury, lead, and sodium. Several agencies have responsibilities associated with the RCRA, including the EPA, whose guidelines and regulations significantly affect the field of lighting. The EPA regulates the "proper management of solid and hazardous wastes, oversees and approves the development of state waste management plans, and provides financial aid to agencies and firms performing research on solid waste" (Department of Energy, 2003, p. 1). The Toxic Substances Control Act (TSCA) and the Superfund Law (the Comprehensive Environmental Response, Compensation and Liability Act or CERCLA) regulate proper disposal of PCBs at the federal level.

To test the mercury content of lamps with a view to avoiding contamination of landfill sites, the EPA developed the **toxicity characteristic leaching procedure (TCLP)** in 1990. To pass the TCLP test, the range of mercury content in a lamp should be between 4 mg and 6 mg without additives. Some lamp manufacturers whose products have mercury levels exceeding the TCLP test include additives in the lamps in order to alter

toxicity characteristic leaching procedure (TCLP)
A procedure developed by the EPA to test the mercury content of lamps. To pass the TCLP test, the range of mercury content must be between 4 mg and 6 mg without additives.

their material composition in a manner that allows them to pass the test regardless. Local laws and regulations specify the maximum levels of mercury in lamps. Some states, such as California, have laws that mandate lower mercury levels than the TCLP. The Land Disposal Program Flexibility Act of 1996 is a law that addresses adjustments to land disposal restriction and water monitoring at solid-waste landfill units.

As a result of this legislation, there are many regulations that affect handling, removal, storage, transport, and disposal of lighting devices. Environmental regulations exist at the federal, regional, state, and local levels. The most current regulations should always be reviewed when lighting systems need to be removed, as a building owner can be held liable for failing to comply with environmental regulations. An interior designer should encourage a client to maintain records of lamps and ballasts operating in a building and keep track of subsequent disposal processes.

Primary concerns related to removing lighting systems are toxic leaks and lamp breakage. Once a lighting system has been determined to contain toxic materials, removal requires strict handling procedures, including the wearing of special protective clothing, gloves, and goggles. The equipment must be contained in special packaging, labeled as prescribed, and transported by means that will help ensure safe delivery with no breakage. Materials can be transported to recycling facilities, hazardous waste landfills, or incinerators. Each method of disposal presents various cost options, which should be included in the price of lighting systems. Contact the EPA to obtain information on the most current methods for hazardous waste disposal.

Many companies specialize in lamp and ballast disposal. The Appendix provides a list of firms associated with recycling and processing lamps and ballasts. In selecting a disposal company, research should be conducted to ensure that the company has updated permits, good standing with the EPA, proper training in hazardous waste handling, and adequate liability insurance. The EPA also publishes a list of companies associated with lighting waste disposal.

The environmental impact of the components of lighting systems includes the type of materials used for the products, the manufacturing process, delivery, use, and disposal practices. Information related to materials and delivery modes are available from manufacturers. Some manufacturers have made a conscious effort to create sustainable products and to be sustainable companies. Unfortunately, some manufacturers only appear to be sustainable; their claims prove to be superficial. Until formal standards have been developed that clearly define sustainable products and practices, interior designers must apply their own knowledge of sustainable design to information provided by manufacturers.

Ideally, materials used for the components of lighting systems should be derived from renewable resources, reused products, or recycled materials. In addition, the materials should have little or no toxic content. A primary area of concern is the use of mercury in fluorescent, HID, and neon lights. Currently, light for these lamps cannot be produced without mercury. Mercury is **PBT (persistent, bioaccumulative, toxic)**, meaning that it is poisonous, remains in water or land indefinitely, and accrues in the world's ecosystems. For example, when a fluorescent lamp is deposited in a landfill and breaks, mercury leaks into the ground. Water from rain can transport mercury to the air, lakes, and rivers. Once the mercury is in the water system, fish ingest the mercury, plant life is affected, and eventually people can develop high levels of mercury by eating fish. To reduce the environmental impact, lamps should be specified that have long life and low mercury content, both of which can be determined by consulting the information available from lamp manufacturers. Federal and state laws regulate the disposal of lamps containing mercury.

Another item of concern is the toxic substance polychlorinated biphenyls (PCBs). This chemical was used in ballasts before it was banned in 1978. Ballasts without PCBs are labeled "No PCBs." Federal and state laws also regulate the disposal of ballasts with PCBs. In addition to lamps, ballasts, and luminaires, other components of lighting systems should be examined with reference to the materials used to make them. These components include the housing unit, transformers, and controls. All products should be made from renewable resources, reused products, or recycled materials, and should not contain toxic substances.

In addition to the materials used for lighting systems, sustainable design takes into account the manufacturers' production processes and delivery of goods. A sustainable manufacturing company will promote energy efficiency and sustainable development by reducing electrical

PBT (persistent, bioaccumulative, toxic)
A classification indicating that a substance is toxic, remains in water or land indefinitely, and accrues in the world's ecosystems.

usage, using renewable resources, recycling, and preventing toxic waste. These practices should be evident throughout the life cycle of the manufacturing process, packaging, and delivery. Packaging should be made from recycled materials and on the smallest scale possible, minimizing the resources needed to create the packaging and the space required in delivery trucks. A sustainable focus on delivery is important because a lot of nonrenewable resources are used for transportation. A sustainable manufacturer will focus on minimizing the number of trucks needed to transport products and the distances each vehicle must travel.

SUMMARY

- According to the EIA (2002), by the year 2030, world energy consumption will be 722 quadrillion British thermal units (Btu).
- The EIA estimates that electrical consumption for developing Asia and Central and South America will increase by 4.5 percent and 3.9 percent, respectively, per year.
- The EPA has determined that lighting accounts for approximately 23 percent of the electricity used in buildings.
- Based on a study of 38 countries, the IAEEL reports that "Globally, electric lighting accounts for more than 2000 TWh electricity and 2900 million metric tons of carbon dioxide emissions (CO_2) per year."
- To promote energy efficiency and sustainable development, standards and codes have been established worldwide. An interior designer must always refer to the most current standards and codes because they are continuously updated.
- Important energy standards and codes that affect lighting efficiency are ASHRAE/IESNA 90.1-2001, MEC-95, and IECC-03.
- The U.S. Energy Policy Act of 1992 (EPAct-92) has significantly affected energy-efficient lighting. EPAct focuses on standards for lighting, energy-efficiency rating systems for windows, and demand-side management (DSM) programs.
- An economic analysis of lighting should include all expenses associated with an installed system, including lamps, luminaires, ballasts, transformers, controls, electricity, maintenance, disposal, and labor.

- An economic analysis of lighting can be conducted by examining the simple payback, or the life-cycle cost-benefit analysis (LCCBA). Many software tools are available to determine the costs and benefits of proposed energy conservation projects. The simple payback method is a quick estimate of the number of years required to pay back the money invested in a lighting system.
- The Environmental Protection Agency (EPA) has determined that the issues related to sustainable design include pollution prevention, multiple and systematic effects, an environmental life-cycle assessment (LCA), magnitude of impact (local and global), and specification of environmental attributes.
- In specifying lighting systems, the goals should be to: (1) reduce the use of nonrenewable resources; (2) control the use of renewable products; (3) minimize air, water, and soil pollution; (4) protect natural habitats; (5) eliminate toxic substances; and (6) reduce light pollution.
- The primary goals of sustainable disposal practices are to reduce the impact on the environment and decrease waste.
- Sustainable design requires the use of lamps that conserve energy and have high efficacy ratings, excellent light output, long life, high lumen maintenance, high color rendering, color stability, low mercury levels, and flexible disposal options. They should also be TCLP-compliant without additives.

Key Terms

PBT (persistent, bioaccumulative, toxic)

sustainable design

toxicity characteristic leaching procedure (TCLP)

Exercises

1. Locate the study of the written history of responses from lighting producers, conveyors, and consumers conducted by the Smithsonian

National Museum of American History. Analyze and summarize the results in a written report. Show how the results of the study can influence energy-efficient lighting practices in the future.

2. Research local state laws and regulations affecting sustainable design and energy-efficient lighting systems. In a written report, summarize the findings and discuss the implications for designing lighting systems.

3. Research international policies and regulations promoting sustainable lighting systems. In a written report, compare and contrast policies, and provide suggestions for improving the regulations in your hometown.

4. Visit an office and a department in a retail store. For each space, conduct an analysis of the lighting systems from the perspective of sustainability and energy conservation. Develop recommendations for improving the lighting systems, including retrofit applications. Summarize the results in a written report and include illustrations, photographs, or sketches.

5. Interview facility managers to determine sustainable and energy-conserving lighting practices. In a written report, summarize your findings and provide suggestions for improving energy efficiency and sustainability.

CHAPTER 8

Illumination and Human Health and Behavior

OBJECTIVES

- Describe the results of research that indicate both negative and positive effects of lighting on a person's health.
- Understand how light affects the body's circadian rhythm.
- Understand the behavioral and psychological effects of light on people.
- Apply the principles of universal design to a lighting environment.

Research indicates that lighting can affect the health, behavior, and psychological well-being of people. The fundamental basis for this research is the concept of the interaction between people and their environment. According to Wapner and Demick, the person-in-environment system assumes that the individual is "comprised of mutually defining physical/biological (e.g., health), psychological (e.g., self-esteem), and sociocultural (e.g., role as worker) aspects; and the environment is comprised of mutually defining aspects, including physical (natural and built), interpersonal (e.g., friend, spouse), and sociocultural (rules of home, community, and culture) aspects" (2002, p. 5). An awareness of the interaction between a person and the environment is key to understanding how illumination can affect people. In designing a lighting system, the interior designer must know the users of the space within the context of the specific environment.

A quality lighting environment is planned to optimize the person-in-environment system. Such planning involves knowledge of current research and a thorough assessment of the project. Early lighting research focused on visual aspects of illumination as it related to workplace performance and perceptions of the environment. Current research still explores behavioral and psychological effects of illumination, but the emerging topic is how lighting affects biological processes in people. An assessment of a project includes the purpose of the space and the characteristics of the users of the space. (Chapter 11 reviews the client and project assessment process.) Understanding the effects of illumination on people can assist an interior designer in fulfilling the purpose of the environment. By knowing the specific characteristics of people, through observation, the designer can specify lighting to accommodate special needs of individuals within the context of the environment.

The effect of illumination on people includes physiological and psychological factors. Physiological aspects are related to health, vision, and the needs of special populations. Illumination can affect the psychological well-being of people by altering behavior and eliciting subjective impressions of an environment. The lighting in the United States Holocaust Memorial Museum in Washington, D.C. was specifically planned to evoke simultaneous feelings of compassion, sadness, and outrage in the viewers. The permanent exhibit begins with two images that have an immediate impact on viewers (Figure 8.1). A large photograph of people who were killed is directly in front of visitors as they come off the elevator, while the words "THE HOLOCAUST," next to the photograph, bring an immediate connection to the tragedy. High-contrast lighting emphasizes the images and enhances the viewer's emotional response. The physiological and psychological effects of lighting on people should be applied to the design of the environment. Considerations should include the design of a layered lighting system, layout, physical attributes of the space, and ergonomic factors.

The effects of illumination on vision are discussed in previous chapters in this textbook and should serve as background to the information covered in this chapter. An overview of the vision process is presented in Chapter 1, while Chapter 3 reviews the subjective experience of brightness. Generally, the effects of illumination are dependent upon subjective responses, the context of the situation, personal vision attributes, type of light source, directional qualities of light, and characteristics of elements of the design.

Physiological Factors

The person-in-environment system examines the interaction between an individual's health and the natural and built environments. Daylight and electrical light are elements of the natural and built environments, respectively, that can affect health.

Lighting Effects on Health

Photobiology is the science that examines the interaction of light and living organisms (http://www.pol-us.net, 2003). Research indicates that lighting has negative and positive effects on a person's health. Some of the negative effects from bad lighting include eyestrain, headaches, dizziness, skin cancer, and premature aging of skin and eyes. Individuals with epilepsy may experience seizures when exposed

FIGURE 8.1
One of the first images seen in the permanent exhibition space of the United States Holocaust Memorial Museum in Washington, D.C. The high-contrast lighting emphasizes the images and enhances emotional responses from visitors to the museum.

photobiology
The science that examines the interaction of light and living organisms.

to flickering lights. Only a very small percentage of the population can detect flicker in a properly operating discharge lamp, but some groups have difficulties with such lamps. Kleeman (1981) found that fluorescent lighting affected hyperactive children by causing nutritional problems and a reduced attention span. Some diseases or medications can cause an individual to be more sensitive to high illumination levels. Current research is exploring the effects of lighting on the growth and development of infants (Giradin, 1992; Miller, White, R., Whitman, O'Callaghn, and Maxwell, 1995; Quinn, Shin, Maguire, and Stone, 1999; Phelps and Watts, 1997; Reynolds, Hardy, Kennedy, Spencer, van Heuven, and Fielder, 1998).

Photomedicine is the science dedicated to using light to improve human health. Some of the positive effects of light on people are derived from the body's production of Vitamin D, which aids in the absorption of calcium. This can help to prevent osteoporosis and rickets. Ultraviolet light is used to cure jaundice in infants. In addition, the medical profession is exploring light therapy as a means of curing certain forms of cancer, leukemia, and skin conditions. Light is also being used to regulate hormones, improve growth in children, and enhance the immune system. Research is examining the possibility that light can even affect biological functions through means other than just vision. A newly discovered photoreceptive mechanism in the eye could lead to a better understanding of the effects of illumination on biological and psychological functions.

Light therapy has been successful in helping to regulate the biological clock associated with the body's circadian rhythm (National Mental Health Association, 2003; Rea, 2002; Rea, Bullough, and Figueiro, 2002; Rea, Figueiro, and Bullough, 2002). The circadian rhythm coordinates bodily functions for waking and sleeping, and affects hormone levels and metabolic processes. High levels of illumination are required to initiate the circadian process, and lower light levels trigger the production of melatonin, a hormone required for sleeping. People who experience jet lag or work night shifts often have difficulty regulating their circadian rhythms. The role of light on disrupting or maintaining circadian rhythm was a major area of discussion at the 2002 LRO (Lighting Research Office) Symposium. Other topics included human cancer development, productivity, and jet lag (Figueiro and Stevens, 2002; Lockley, 2002; Stevens, 2002). For the most part, problems associated with regulating circadian rhythms did not exist prior to electrical lighting, because people functioned with the earth's natural clock of daylight and evening hours. Electrical lighting allows people to maintain high levels of illumination 24 hours a day, every day of the year. Most of the effects resulting from this are still unknown.

However, problems related to circadian rhythms are associated with **seasonal affective disorder (SAD)**, which is a condition associated with an individual's inadequate exposure to sunlight. Some of the effects of SAD are depression, weight gain, lack of concentration, and sleeplessness. Many people experience SAD during the winter months when the days are shortest. This is especially problematic for people living in the northern region of the northern hemisphere, because of the few hours of sunlight. Research indicates that females are more likely to experience SAD than males. People with SAD are encouraged to spend more time outdoors, preferably on sunny days, early in the day. Some physicians will prescribe light therapy to alleviate SAD. This treatment consists of exposure to high levels of illumination at the start of the day. Light therapy has also been helpful in regulating sleep patterns with dementia patients (Mishimia, Okawa, Hiskikawa, Hozumi, Hori, and Takashi, 1994; Satlin, Volicer, Ross, Herz, and Campbell, 1992). People who have a severe case of SAD need a professional diagnosis of the disease, since medication may be needed. SAD can be very serious, in extreme cases even resulting in suicide.

seasonal affective disorder (SAD)
A condition associated with an individual's inadequate exposure to sunlight.

Psychological Factors

Wapner and Demick (2002) indicate that the person-in-environment system includes the effect of the environment on the psychological well-being of individuals as well as its effect on interpersonal relations. Lighting research has focused on the role of illumination in these factors, including characteristics of natural and electrical light sources and their behavioral and psychological effects on people. For example, Veitch, Gifford, and Hine (1991) conducted a research study, "Demand

Characteristics and Full Spectrum Lighting Effects on Performance and Mood." Chapter 2 of this book discusses research studies that found positive effects of daylight on activities in hospitals, schools, and retail stores (Heschong, 1999; Heschong, 1997, Littlefair, 1996; Littlefair, 1991; Wu and Ng, 2003). In addition, Beauchemin and Hays (1996) found that individuals in psychiatric units who had rooms with natural daylight stayed approximately three days less than patients living with electrical light sources.

Researchers have been interested in understanding which characteristics of electrical light sources affect people. The topics investigated include specific lamps, color rendering index, color temperature, quantity and intensity of light, spectral composition, and distribution patterns. Some studies have explored lighting effects on certain groups, such as people with Alzheimer's disease, cancer, and AIDS, as well as infants and the elderly (Figueiro, Eggleston, and Rea, 2002; Graham and Michel, 2003; Miller, 2002; Noelle-Waggoner, 2002).

In examining the effects of lighting on behavior, research has focused on the performance of office workers, on cognitive processes, and on wayfinding. The types of psychological effect studied include attitude, stress, satisfaction, interpersonal communication, perception of space, motivation, control, and stimulation. The following two sections provide a summary of the effects of lighting on the behavior and psychology of people. For additional research studies, refer to the reference list at the end of the book.

Lighting Effects on Behavior

Some of the earliest lighting research investigated the effects of quantity of light on productivity in the workplace (Blackwell, 1946; Boynton and Boss, 1971; Boyce, 1973; Hughes and McNelis, 1978; Simonson and Brozek, 1948; Weston, 1962). At that time, electrical light sources were relatively new, and the lighting industry was trying to persuade employers to invest in lighting systems. The cost–benefit approach served as a rationale; research studies demonstrated that quality lighting improved worker productivity, and the increase in performance offset the cost of the lighting system.

Owing to the interdependence of the many factors that can affect performance, including noise, stress, ambient temperature, and daylight, current research regarding the effect of lighting on productivity is inconclusive. Some studies have demonstrated that improved performance may be the result of a higher level of satisfaction with working conditions, rather than a direct relationship between lighting and productivity (Boyce, Akashi, Hunter, and Bullough, 2003; Ducker, 1999; Isen, Daubman, and Nowicki, 1987). Research has indicated that control over one's environment, including lighting, is a significant factor in employee satisfaction (Boyce, Eklund, and Simpson, 2000; Hedge, Erickson, and Rubin, 1992; Sherrod and Cohen, 1979; Veitch and Newsham, 1998; Veitch and Newsham, 1999).

In an attempt to determine the direct effect of illumination on performance, research studies have examined specific characteristics of lighting systems, including fluorescent lamps, ballasts, and types of luminaire. Extensive research on the effect of full-spectrum fluorescent lamps generally indicates that there is no effect on performance or mood (Berry, 1983; Boray, Gifford, and Rosenblood, 1989; Food and Drug Administration, 1986; Veitch, 1997; Veitch and McColl, 1995; Veitch, Gifford, and Hine, 1991). However, some studies do suggest that fluorescent light flicker can increase headaches and stress (Veitch and McColl, 2001; Kuller and Laike, 1998; Wilkins, Nimmo-Smith, Slater, and Bedocs, 1989). Veitch and Newsham (1998) found that the performance of clerical workers was improved by using electronic, rather than magnetic, ballasts in the workplace. Moreover, the use of electronic ballasts reduced headaches (Wilkins, et al., 1989).

In addition to eliminating light flicker, electronic ballasts might be preferred because they operate more quietly than magnetic ones. Many studies have shown a significant relationship between noise and quality of worker performance (Banbury, Macken, Tremblay, and Jones, 2001; Evans and Cohen, 1987; Gawron, 1982; Hygge, 1991; Hygge and Knez, 2001; Nelson, Nilsson, and Johnson, 1984). Certain types of luminaire might also contribute to noise in an environment, as fixtures made from hard materials and having relatively large flat surfaces can reflect sound.

Generally, research indicates that worker performance is unaffected by type of luminaire and light distribution patterns (Eklund, Boyce, and Simpson, 2000; Veitch and Newsham, 1998). However, studies have demonstrated that proper lighting for a computer's visual display terminal (VDT) is required to enhance worker productivity (Clark, 2001; National Lighting Bureau, 1988). To reduce eyestrain and dry eyes, physicians recommend frequent eye movement. This can be accomplished by creating an interesting environment around the VDT screen and varying illumination levels.

Universal Design

Lighting systems should be planned to accommodate all people, whenever possible, without modifications. This can be accomplished by specifying a lighting plan that meets the physical and psychological needs of the users of the space.

Physical Environment

universal design
An approach to the physical environment that focuses on accommodating the needs of all people, whenever possible, without modifications.

A quality lighting environment reflects the principles of **universal design**. In order to be able to design environments that meet the needs and abilities of all people, an interior designer should review the current literature. Research studies are invaluable in providing guidance and recommendations for effective environments.

There are many aspects of lighting that should be considered when applying the principles of universal design, including visual acuity, manual dexterity, and the placement of luminaires, switches, and outlets. Visual acuity is affected by illumination level, type of lamp, distribution, color temperature, color rendering, ballast, and the ability to control lighting. The needs of individuals with visual impairments and diseases must be addressed in order to ensure visual acuity. Specifying value contrasts—such as white/black—for tasks can also enhance visual acuity.

The operation of wall switches and luminaires should be intuitive and easy for users. Generally, rocker or touch switches are the easiest; devices that have to be pinched or twisted should be avoided. Switches and dimmers should be accessible and simple to operate. Avoid portable luminaires with switching mechanisms on the cord. Luminaires that allow the user to change the direction of the light source should be weighted, and the shade should be designed to prevent burns from the heat from the lamp. The Research Group for Inclusive Environments (RGIE) (2002) conducted a study with elderly subjects to determine which portable luminaire was the most satisfactory for people with visual impairments in an office environment. The results indicated a preference for the Anglepoise luminaire with a 60 W tungsten pearl lamp, primarily because of ease of use (Figure 8.2). The model had a reach of 43" (1100 mm), and the shade used was 8" (200 mm) in diameter. According to RGIE, people reported that the Anglepoise luminaire was "easy to use, easy to get the light where it was wanted, quite flexible" (2003, p. 1).

Luminaires, switches, and outlets should be placed so as to be accessible to people with disabilities, including individuals in wheelchairs. Luminaires should always be positioned to avoid shadows on work surfaces. Portable luminaires designed to allow the user to adjust the direction or control the level of illumination should be located within

FIGURE 8.2
People with visual impairments in an office environment selected the Anglepoise tungsten luminaire as the preferred portable luminaire, primarily because of ease of use.

a convenient distance of the user; the average range of reach is 24" (610 mm). The American Disability Act (ADA) (2003) specifies that wall-mounted luminaires mounted between 27" and 80" (685 mm and 2030 mm) above a finished floor (AFF) should not extend more than 4" (100 mm) from the wall. Luminaires at or below 27" (685 mm) AFF may protrude any amount. The lowest element of a suspended luminaire should allow for 80" (2030 mm) of clear headroom. Freestanding luminaires mounted on posts may overhang 12" (305 mm) horizontally and 27" to 80" (685 mm to 2030 mm) AFF.

Wall switches and outlets should be mounted at a level accessible to people standing or sitting in a wheelchair. Universal access is 15" to 48" (380 mm to 1219 mm) AFF. ADA specifies that electrical receptacles on walls shall be mounted no less than 15" (380 mm) AFF. However, in following the principles of universal design, a convenient location for wall switches and outlets is 38" and 18" (965 and 457 mm) AFF, respectively. With respect to intensity of illumination, the ADA requirements for signage are in the range of 100 to 300 lux (10 fc to 30 fc), and a minimum of 50 lux (5 fc) for elevator thresholds.

The results of research should be applied to lighting planning. Lighting research is a relatively new field of study and is continuously improving and expanding. Thus, to specify a lighting environment that addresses the health, behavior, emotions, and perceptions of people, an interior designer should always refer to the most current research. In analyzing the research, it is critical to scrutinize the specifics of a study. Each study is conducted with specific subjects and parameters, and can be applied to practice only when the conditions of the research study are similar to those of the interior project on which a designer is working. The material discussed in this chapter and the preceding chapters in this textbook should be applied to the lighting design process covered in Chapters 11 and 12.

SUMMARY

- The person-in-environment system examines the interaction between an individual's health and the natural and built environments.

- Research indicates that lighting can have both negative and positive effects on a person's health. Some of the negative effects from lighting include eyestrain, headaches, dizziness, skin cancer, and aging of skin and eyes.
- Light therapy has been successful in helping to regulate the biological clock associated with the body's circadian rhythm.
- Lighting research has focused on the characteristics of natural and electrical light sources and their behavioral and psychological effects on people. Topics studied include specific types of lamp, CRI, color temperature, quantity and intensity of light, spectral composition, and distribution patterns.
- To determine the effect of illumination on performance, research studies have examined specific characteristics of elements of lighting systems, including fluorescent lamps, ballasts, and types of luminaire.
- A quality lighting environment reflects the principles of universal design. Lighting systems should be planned to accommodate all people, whenever possible, without modifications.

Key Terms

photobiology   universal design

seasonal affective disorder (SAD)

Exercises

1. Interview people in an office, restaurant, retail store, and health-care facility to determine their perceptions of the interior. Analyze the results and determine the positive and negative attributes of each space. Summarize the results in a written report and include illustrations, photographs, or sketches.
2. Select five photographs of the interiors of public places. For each space identify the purpose of the space, the most frequent users, and

the anticipated behavioral response to the lighting environment. Summarize your results in a written report and include photographs.

3. Research a disease that affects the psychological and physical needs of the individuals who have it. Write an essay that includes specific lighting requirements for individuals with the disease. Illustrations of luminaires should be included.

CHAPTER 9

Residential Applications

OBJECTIVES

- Apply an understanding of the content covered in previous chapters to the practice of designing lighting for residences.
- Identify and apply important criteria for illuminating transitional spaces.
- Identify and apply important criteria for illuminating activities that occur in multifunctional and dedicated spaces.

Residential design encompasses an enormous variety of structures throughout the world in cities, suburbs, small towns, and even on water. Residences have been constructed in every conceivable style, in an extremely broad range of sizes, and in an amazing array of configurations. The complexity increases when one factors in the diversity of furniture, floor coverings, wall coverings, colors, materials, equipment, and accessories, which are unique to every residence. This tremendous diversity creates an exciting challenge for interior designers, particularly for lighting systems tailored to each particular client and the characteristics of his or her residence.

Quality lighting requires an approach that integrates the users of a space with their activities and the specific elements of the environment, including orientation, colors, textures, materials, furniture, accessories, and the geometry of the space. Lighting must also be designed to accommodate the client's budget, preferred taste, and lifestyle, as well as the installation limitations of the residence.

Transitional Spaces

Quality residential lighting environments are complex to design, but their integration with other interior elements should appear seamless. The holistic approach involves content covered in the previous chapters, including daylight integration, layered lighting, illumination zones, color, directional effects of illumination, and lighting systems. Designers of residential lighting should also consider energy conservation, sustainable practice, safety, security, and human factors related to physiology and psychology.

Layered lighting is important for all rooms in a residence, including bathrooms. Residential rooms often have only one layer of lighting, such as a task light over a bathroom mirror. Layered lighting does not have to be expensive and can be accomplished with portable luminaires; the challenge is remembering to plan layered lighting in every room. In determining lighting techniques and the lighting system, all options should be considered for every room. It is frequently taken for granted that a certain type of luminaire is always appropriate for a specific room or task in a residence. For example, a popular approach for a kitchen is a surface-mounted fluorescent fixture in the center of the ceiling. An entryway will often have a glass and brass pendant suspended on a chain. Of course, there may be rooms where these luminaires would be perfect, but assuming that they are always appropriate in prescribed places is a mistake. A quality residential lighting environment is designed expressly for the unique needs of clients, their style of living, and all the elements of each room.

Entryways and Foyers

The transitional spaces in residences include entryways, foyers, hallways, and staircases. Often the terms entryway and foyer are used interchangeably. For the purposes of this section, *entryway* or *entry* is the term referring to the space located immediately outside the front entrance of a residence, and *foyer* is the interior area. Often, entry lighting includes one or two luminaires located next to the front door. This may be adequate for safety and security purposes; however, the lighting in this location should also set the tone for the overall design concept of the residence, as this is the first impression people have when approaching the residence. Some clients may want a very dignified, formal feeling for the entrance, and others may want a casual, informal atmosphere. Lighting can reinforce the desired impression by the design of the luminaires, illumination levels, and highlighted elements.

Luminaires for the entryway should reflect the architectural style of the home, and the size of the fixture should be on an appropriate scale for the size of the door and entryway as well as the home as a whole. A designer selecting exterior luminaires must analyze the entire elevation of the residence. Sometimes a luminaire next to a door is too small for the surrounding elements; one common practice is to use the same entry light on a residence regardless of whether the entrance has a single door or a set of double doors. To achieve good proportion, the residence with double doors needs larger entry luminaires.

The entry and foyer are major transition areas from the outside to the interior. As a result, the illumination level of the entry and foyer must accommodate daylight and evening light. To have a smooth adaptation transition during the day, the foyer should have natural light, supplemented by electrical lighting for cloudy days or if the windows are too small to provide adequate levels of daylight. For the evening hours, landscape lighting can help to ease the illumination level differences between the outdoors and the interior as people arriving move from a dark environment to a lighter one. In addition, appropriate levels should be planned for guests' departure from the residence, moving from a bright setting to a darker one. The eye takes longer to adapt when going from a bright to a dark setting. A transitional lighting plan should accommodate the variabilities of both situations.

Hallways and Staircases

Hallways and staircases are also transitional areas in a residence. Therefore, little time is typically spent analyzing elements in these areas, such as architectural details or artwork on the walls. Moreover, since people moving through a hallway or staircase are interested primarily in whatever room it is they are heading toward, their concentration is often diverted from the interior elements on the way. Most people are in a standing position as they walk through a hallway or progress up and down stairs. The combination of minimal time, movement, and a standing position creates unique lighting challenges that must be addressed in order to achieve a quality lighting environment.

Hallway challenges include layered lighting techniques, attracting attention to interesting elements that might exist on vertical planes, reducing the apparent length of long hallways, avoiding dark areas, creating safe passage during sleeping hours, and providing convenient switching arrangements. Layered lighting is often absent from hallways because people feel the only illumination necessary is task lighting. Illumination should be planned so that people can safely walk through hallways, but ambient and accent lighting are also important considerations. Variations in lighting, including accent lighting, can help to reduce the apparent length of a hallway and can help to avoid dark areas. For layered lighting, all vertical and horizontal planes should be considered, including structural luminaires in the ceiling, transoms above doors, and interior windows. Since hallways rarely have natural light, transoms and those openings known as interior windows on walls adjoining hallways can provide excellent illumination during the day.

A hallway that provides passage from bedrooms to bathrooms needs illumination that creates a safe environment during the sleeping hours. To assist the eye with adaptation, lighting during this time period should be low. The illumination level and location of the fixtures should be determined by the visual abilities of the users of the residence. Controls play an important role in safety and convenience. Switches for luminaires should be accessible at various locations in the hallway, including at the end of the space and next to bedroom and bathroom doors. To ensure adequate illumination at the appropriate locations, hallways can be equipped with occupancy sensors or photosensors.

The combination of movement and changes in elevation can pose safety issues for vertical circulation. Staircases should be illuminated in a manner that provides a clear distinction between the risers and treads. The projecting edges of the treads should be visible. This can be accomplished in a variety of ways, including locating luminaires at the top and bottom of staircases and lighting each step. Generally, lighting at the top of a staircase should be brighter than the luminaire located at the bottom. Recessed light sources along the wall or in the treads, low-voltage strip systems along the edges of the treads, or integrated light in the railing can illuminate each step. Accent lighting should highlight interesting elements, such as architectural moldings or artwork, on walls adjoining a staircase. Often, a staircase is a beautiful focal point in a residence, in which case accent lighting should highlight the most intriguing elements of the design. Silhouette lighting can be an effective technique for emphasizing an elegant staircase.

Task-Specific Illumination

Quality lighting environments enhance the way people live and work in their residences. This requires lighting that is client- and site-specific. A thorough assessment needs to be conducted to determine who performs which activities where in the residence. In determining lighting approaches, a distinction should be made between guests and people living in the residence. People who are not familiar with an interior, especially overnight guests, might require special lighting techniques.

Tasks Performed in Multiple Spaces

To design a task lighting plan that is client- and site-specific requires an assessment of all the variables associated with performing a particular task. This includes an analysis of the task, characteristics of the user(s), reflectance, illumination source, luminaire performance data, and dimensions of furniture. The needs of special populations must always be addressed as well.

Tasks that are visually demanding or require special accuracy require very precise illumination. Information must be collected regarding the visual abilities and anthropometric data of the users of the residence. Anthropometric data, or detailed measurements of the human body, are valuable for determining the proper location of luminaires, switches, and outlets; for example, the proper location for reading depends partly on the vertical distance from the seat to the eyes. Torso and head dimensions can be determined by measuring the user or referring to anthropometric charts. Sections that follow in this chapter identify criteria that are important for specific tasks, including appropriate dimensional factors. This information can be applied to the specific needs of users within the context of their environment.

People read in numerous locations in a residence; however, effective lighting should be planned for areas where frequent and prolonged reading occurs. Effective illumination for reading requires proper integration of the individual and the layers of lighting, the task light source, and the parameters of the furniture. The layers of lighting should have appropriately balanced illumination levels given the intensity of the light needed for reading. Since lighting for reading is typically at a high illumination level, appropriate levels for other lighting throughout the room will help to avoid extreme contrasts and the resulting eye fatigue.

The task light source should be directed at the reading material and should distribute the appropriate illumination level. The lamp should be concealed from the eyes of the reader. Luminaires with translucent shades in white or off-white can be effective because they provide direct and indirect illumination on the task. Opaque or dark-colored shades, on the other hand, restrict the quantity and distribution of illumination on a task.

Certain measurements are needed to provide effective light for reading with a portable luminaire on a table next to a chair. These include the vertical distance from the user's eye level to the floor, the size of the fixture, and the dimensions of the furniture (Figure 9.1). The ideal condition is for the bottom of the shade to be level with the reader's eyes. Thus, the total distance from the floor to the reader's eye level must equal the distance from the floor to the bottom of the shade. A change in any of the elements can affect the effectiveness of the lighting. For example, the situation shown in Figure 9.1 was created for a female adult with a seat-to-eye measurement of 32" (80 cm). If a child sits in the chair, the lighting is no longer effective because his or her eyes would be lower and therefore exposed to a bare lamp. An adult using a chair with a lower seat, or a higher table, would have the same result. Figures 9.2a and 9.2b provide additional examples of measurements needed for various approaches to task lighting for reading.

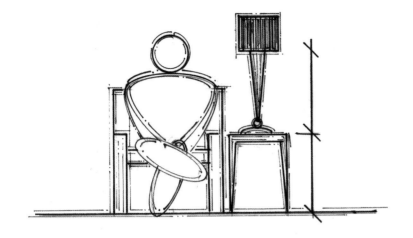

FIGURE 9.1
Determining the
appropriate location of
a luminaire for reading
requires multiple
measurements of
people, furniture, and
the fixture. Ideally,
for reading, the total
distance from the floor
to the reader's eye
level must equal the
distance from the
floor to the bottom
of the shade.

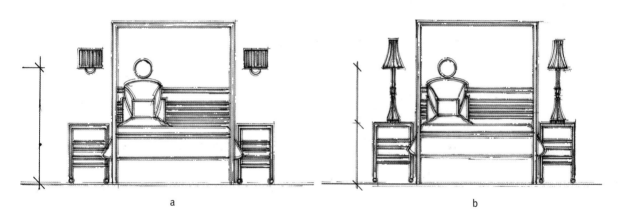

a   b

FIGURE 9.2
Various approaches to
task lighting for reading:
(a) a wall-mounted lumi-
naire next to the bed;
and (b) a portable lumi-
naire on a table next to
the bed. The placement
for (a) requires a
measurement of the eye
level of the user while
seated in bed. The
placement for
(b) requires measure-
ments of the height of
the fixture base to the
bottom of the shade,
the table height, and
the eye level of the user
while seated in bed.

Effective task lighting should also be planned for writing. People write in a variety of rooms in a residence, but most writing occurs on a horizontal surface. A luminaire mounted on the surface should be approximately 12" (30 cm) from the individual and 15" (38 cm) to the right or left of the paper (Figure 9.3). To avoid shadows on the task, the luminaire should be located to the left of a right-handed person and to the right of a left-handed person. The bottom of a shade should be level with the eyes of the writer. The other criteria described in the discussion related to reading can also be applied to the writing task.

Frequently, a surface used for writing is also used for operating a computer. Unfortunately, the two tasks have different illumination requirements because writing is performed on a horizontal surface

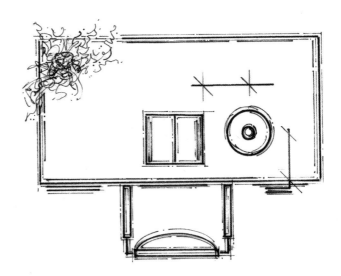

FIGURE 9.3
Plan view of the placement of a luminaire on a desk or table for the purpose of reading and writing. To avoid shadows on the task, the luminaire should be located to the left side of a right-handed person, and to the right side of a left-handed person. The bottom of a shade should be level with the eyes of the user.

while computer work is conducted on a vertical plane. The solution is to employ multiple luminaires, techniques, and controls. An effective method for illuminating a work surface with a computer is to locate diffused luminaires above the user, either in front of the individual or at the side (Figure 9.4).

People should not watch a television screen in the dark. A television screen can emit a high level of illumination, which contrasts significantly

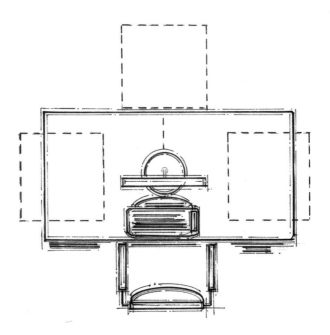

FIGURE 9.4
Plan view of the suggested placement of luminaires for working at a computer.

with dark surroundings. Illumination should exist in all areas of a room, including behind the television, next to the screen, and surrounding the viewer. As more residences are creating media rooms or home theaters, effective layered lighting techniques must be used to accommodate these unique illumination requirements.

Task lighting in residences must also be planned for hobbies or other activities perhaps related to an individual's profession. These tasks can include painting, sewing, playing the piano, playing cards or games, and other activities. Figure 9.5 provides an example of the measurements that are important to consider when designing illumination for a variety of tasks. For all of these activities, the lighting must be planned to avoid glare in the eyes of the users and prevent shadows of heads or hands from being cast on the tasks. The surrounding areas should always have lighting that creates smooth transitions between illumination levels.

Formal and informal conversation occurs throughout a residence; however, in rooms where conversations often occur, lighting should be designed to encourage and enhance the activity. Based on the lifestyle

FIGURE 9.5
Suggested placement of a luminaire for playing cards or games.

of the client, prime conversational areas could be the living room, kitchen, dining room, or bedrooms. Generally, lighting that is conducive to conversation is relaxing and enhances the facial features of people (Figure 9.6). This typically involves soft, indirect lighting at low to moderate illumination levels. Illumination on people can be reflected from surfaces, diffused through a soft fabric, or derived from a combination of the two. Avoid direct illumination that grazes the front of people's faces or is aimed at their eyes. Bright light sources behind people should also be avoided, because the silhouette effect can make it impossible for people to see the faces of those seated across from them.

FIGURE 9.6
Suggested placement of luminaires for a conversation area. To enhance facial features of people, the centers of the shades of luminaires should be approximately level with the faces of individuals. This placement requires the following measurements: (a) height of the fixture base to the center of the shade; (b) table height; (c) eye level of users; and (d) seat height.

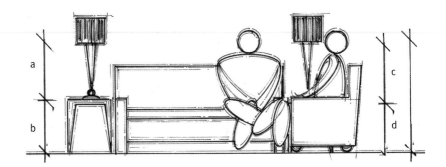

Tasks Performed in Dedicated Spaces

Food preparation and cleanup require special lighting considerations because of the danger of burns and cuts. Areas to consider include counters, ranges, and the sink. A variety of lighting techniques can be employed for the specific tasks done in kitchens. The horizontal nature of these tasks requires illumination from directly above the work area. Luminaires and their locations must be carefully planned to eliminate glare and shadows on tasks. Lamps should be selected with high CRI ratings so that the colors of food can be seen accurately. Layered lighting becomes very important in kitchens, because direct illumination of a fairly high intensity is needed for critical tasks, while ambient lighting helps to moderate the contrasts between brighter and darker areas. Accent lighting provides a work environment with visual interest, especially in a kitchen that is also used as a primary gathering place. Controls with a range of variability are useful for accommodating the multiple activities and tasks conducted in kitchens.

Illumination on counters, including islands, can be derived from luminaires mounted under wall cabinets or fixtures installed in soffits or the ceiling (Figure 9.7 a–c). Luminaires under wall cabinets can be located at the front or back edge of the cabinetry. Glare can pose a problem with this technique when the counter or backsplash has a shiny or glossy finish. Luminaires installed in soffits or the ceiling can be recessed or surface-mounted. The point of installation must be carefully planned to avoid casting an individual's shadow on the task and to allow adequate clearance space for cabinet doors.

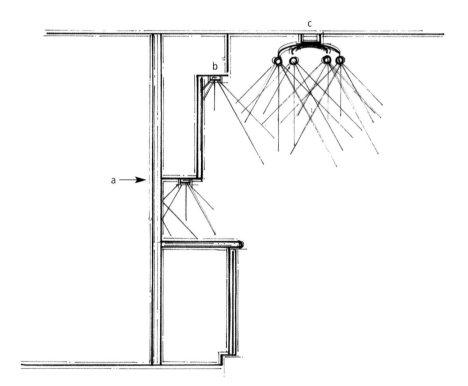

FIGURE 9.7
A side elevation showing suggested placements of luminaires for food preparation at counters: (a) luminaires mounted under wall cabinets; (b) fixtures installed in soffits; and (c) luminaires mounted on the ceiling.

Luminaires located above a cooktop or sink can be an effective method of illumination. As always, the light source should be positioned so as to eliminate glare and avoid having people work in their own shadow. Glare can be especially problematic for work conducted at the cooktop because frequently those surfaces are made up of highly reflective materials. Light directed from the right and left of the worker can help to eliminate shadows on a task (Figure 9.8). This **cross-lighting** technique can be effective because each light source serves as direct and fill lighting simultaneously. To facilitate cleaning associated with the grease from cooking, luminaires surrounding the cooktop should have sealed covers and surfaces that are easy to wash.

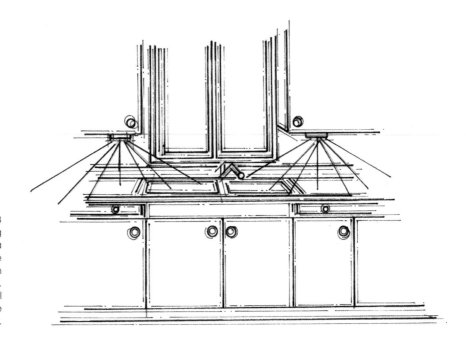

FIGURE 9.8
Cross-lighting technique used over a sink. Each light source can serve as both direct and fill lighting. Proper placement will help to eliminate shadows on the task.

There are many methods for illuminating kitchen cabinetry, and many techniques involve hiding sources within the structural elements of the cabinets. Whenever possible, the interior of cabinets in food-preparation areas should be illuminated; this is especially important for corner and base cabinets. The light source should be positioned to illuminate most of the items in the cabinet, including those in the back.

A variety of techniques and types of luminaires can be used to illuminate the eating area. Frequently, a pendant fixture is located over a table. While this can be an effective approach, other methods should always be considered. Furthermore, one fixture is never the answer for an entire room. In a dining room, luminaires should be expressly selected for the task of eating, but need not be located above the center of the table. For example, illuminating the four corners of a table can provide excellent task lighting and soft illumination on the faces of people seated at the table, especially if the table is relocated or expanded with table leaves (Figure 9.9).

luminaire

luminaire

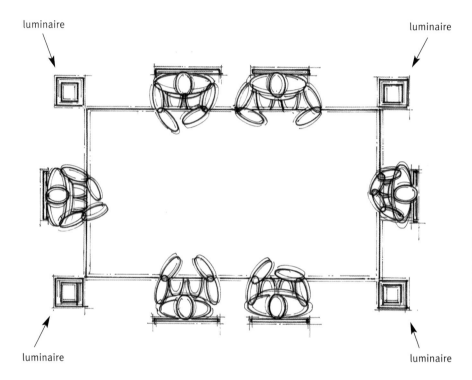

luminaire

luminaire

FIGURE 9.9
Plan view of a dining room with illumination close to the four corners of a table. This technique can provide excellent task lighting and soft illumination on the faces of people seated at the table.

The size and location of luminaires should be carefully planned in a dining room. In the case of a pendant fixture, the size must be appropriate for the dimensions of the table and room; frequently, a dining room fixture is too small or too large for the table and the size of the room. An appropriate size is determined by following the principles of the golden section. To avoid having people hit their head on a pendant fixture when they stand up, the luminaire should be approximately 6" (15 cm) from the edges of the table. A pendant should not interfere with artwork on a wall or a beautiful view from a window; for these situations, the space between a table and the ceiling should be unobstructed. This might be accomplished by using concealed light sources.

Rooms for sleeping and playing have some unique lighting considerations. The ages of the occupants are an important issue. Lighting and electrical outlets must be safe for children of all ages and the elderly. Cords on portable luminaires should not be accessible from any location in a room to avoid tripping, and also avoid luminaires that fall over easily. All outlets should be covered with protective seals. To promote eye development, young infants should have some level of illumination at all times of the day. The lighting in rooms for children should be planned to accommodate the changing activities that occur in the space as the children become older. Playing with blocks on the floor requires different illumination from studying at a desk or working at a computer. Whenever possible, projection of future lighting needs for children's spaces should occur during the construction phase of a project.

People of all ages need adequate illumination to move through rooms during the evening hours. Illumination that is kept on at a low level throughout the night or triggered by occupancy sensors or photosensors can provide sufficient evening illumination. People who share a room often awaken in the morning at different times. Separate lighting systems can provide illumination for the person who must get up, while maintaining a fairly dark environment for the person still sleeping.

Residences built during the past several years often have no lighting in closets. Illumination in closets is essential not only to enable people to see the items they are handling or retrieving but also to prevent accidents when belongings fall. The bare incandescent lamp, formerly a common approach for closets, should be avoided because the brightness can cause disability glare and the lamp poses a fire hazard. In a confined space, adequate clearance around a light source should always be provided. To illuminate items on shelves and hanging on rods, an effective approach is to locate a light source at a high position on the wall across from the objects (Figure 9.10). Low, supplementary lighting should be provided to illuminate objects on the closet floor.

Effective illumination is critical in grooming areas. Many accidents occur in bathrooms, so illumination should be designed to promote a safe environment. The combination of water and slick surfaces creates a treacherous situation requiring good illumination of all areas in a bathroom, including steps, bathtubs, showers, and any locations likely to

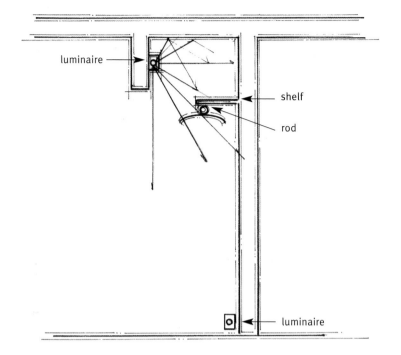

luminaire

shelf

rod

luminaire

FIGURE 9.10
A side illustration of a suggestion for providing illumination in a closet. Adequate clearance should be provided between the luminaire and objects in the closet, and the luminaire should have an element that covers the lamp.

have standing water. Illumination on handrails and grab bars can be very helpful. Luminaires in the shower must be rated for wet locations and should be positioned so as to minimize shadows and eliminate glare not only in the shower but throughout the bathroom. Glare should be determined based on both sitting and standing positions of residents.

Illumination for applying makeup and for shaving has special requirements. Some of the most important criteria include accurate color rendering properties, clarity in seeing details, and a uniform distribution of illumination. Lamps for facial grooming should have a CRI rating of 100. The desired color temperature of the lamp can vary with the ethnicity of the user; generally, Western and Eastern cultures prefer warm and cool light sources respectively. For accurate vision of facial details, illumination should be diffused and located next to the face, and all shadows on the face must be eliminated. The quality of illumination is affected by the interaction of lamp characteristics with the type of diffuser used on a luminaire. For example, an effective combination for facial grooming is an opal diffuser with fluorescent lamps. To determine the best lighting effect, various lamps and diffusers

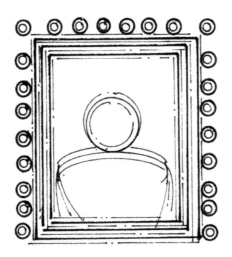

FIGURE 9.11
A suggested placement of luminaires for facial grooming: place illumination at the top and both sides of a mirror so as to surround the face of a person standing or seated in a chair. Lamps or the center of shades should be located at cheek level.

should be tested. Ideally, luminaires should surround a face on the top and sides (Figure 9.11), but at the very least they should be located next to both sides of the face. Lamps or the center of shades should be located at cheek level. A full-length mirror should have a fixture mounted above it.

Quality residential lighting should be unique to every combination of user, activity, and environment. Too often, prescribed lighting solutions have been applied to residences without regard for the specific characteristics of the situation. An interior designer should specify a lighting plan that incorporates relevant issues presented in previous chapters of this textbook within the context of the client's needs.

SUMMARY

- Layered lighting is important for all rooms in a residence, including bathrooms.
- Luminaires in an entryway should reflect the architectural style of the home, and the size of the fixture should be on an appropriate scale for the size of the door and entryway, as well as of the home as a whole.
- The entryway and foyer are major transition areas from the outside to the interior. As a result, the illumination level of the entry and foyer must accommodate daylight and evening hours.
- Hallway lighting considerations include layering, attracting attention to interesting elements on vertical planes, reducing the apparent length of long hallways, avoiding dark areas, creating safe passage during sleeping hours, and providing convenient switching arrangements.
- Staircases should be illuminated in a manner that allows clear distinction between risers and treads.

- Quality lighting environments enhance the way people live and work in their residences. This requires lighting that is client- and site-specific. A thorough analysis needs to be conducted to determine who performs which activities where in the residence.
- Anthropometric data, or detailed measurements of the human body, are valuable for determining the proper location of luminaires, switches, and outlets.
- Food preparation and cleanup require special lighting considerations because of the dangers of burns and cuts.
- Rooms for sleeping and playing represent some unique lighting considerations. The ages of the occupants are an important issue.
- Effective illumination is critical in grooming areas. In view of the high number of accidents that occur in bathrooms, illumination should be designed to help promote a safe environment.

Key Terms

cross-lighting

Exercises

1. Select photographs of entries, foyers, hallways, and staircases. Identify the electrical luminaires in the spaces and determine the lighting category (general, task, accent) of each. If a luminaire does not exist for a category of lighting, suggest one that would be effective. The identification and analysis should be submitted in written form. Photographs must be included.
2. Select photographs of areas for reading, conversation, writing, working at a computer, and watching television. Identify the lighting for the task involved and determine its effectiveness. Where necessary, provide suggestions to improve the effectiveness of the lighting for the specific activity. The identification and analysis

should be submitted in written form. Photographs must be included.

3. Select photographs of kitchens, dining rooms, bedrooms, and bathrooms. Identify the ambient, task, and accent lighting, and determine the effectiveness of illumination. Where necessary, provide suggestions to improve the effectiveness of the lighting for a specific purpose. The identification and analysis should be submitted in written form. Photographs must be included.

Commercial Applications

- Describe common lighting considerations in commercial facilities, including structural elements, needs of the end users, principles of universal design, and public areas.
- Identify and apply important lighting considerations in offices, educational facilities, and healthcare institutions.
- Identify and apply important lighting considerations in the hospitality industry and retail stores.

Important considerations in lighting residential interiors are discussed in Chapter 9. This chapter explores the most frequent commercial interiors that designers are commissioned to work on. Some of the most important issues affecting all commercial structures include designing for diverse populations, safety concerns, protecting the environment, and energy conservation. People with a wide range of abilities, communication skills, and perceptions work in or visit commercial buildings. Therefore, the principles of universal design are a critical component in designing a quality lighting environment for these spaces that is as safe as possible for all users. Also, because commercial interiors consume tremendous amounts of resources and electricity, energy codes are becoming more stringent every year. By implementing effective conservation practices, an interior designer can comply with the codes and help make a positive impact on our planet.

The principles of a quality lighting environment must be applied to all types of commercial structures and to every space within a building.

This chapter focuses on how lighting affects the end users in offices, schools, healthcare institutions, hospitality interiors, and retail establishments. Designing the lighting for commercial interiors requires a thorough understanding of the goals of the organization and the characteristics of the end users. The environment must be responsive to the needs of the client, the people who work in the building, and people who visit for a limited amount of time. Creating functional and aesthetic designs requires interaction with users of the environment and the application of observational skills. (Chapter 11 explores methodology in detail.) Designers must collaborate with multiple professionals engaged in the construction process, including architects, engineers, contractors, electricians, building inspectors, acoustical experts, and fire-prevention specialists.

Task-Oriented Commercial Interiors

The most common task-oriented commercial interiors are offices, educational facilities, and healthcare institutions. Designers need to plan, install, and evaluate lighting for commercial interiors within the parameters of the project, including the budget and schedule. This requires an extensive collaborative effort with the client, end users, and professionals who work on the project.

In designing lighting for a variety of users, it is critical to incorporate the principles of universal design. As discussed in Chapter 9, illumination must specifically address the needs of users, their activities, the site, interior architecture, furniture, equipment, and characteristics of the elements of the space. Even within the context of commercial spaces used for the same purpose, such as restaurants, every commercial building has unique requirements that must be addressed in the lighting.

Offices

Lighting for offices is affected by management philosophies and the technology that employees use. Management is always interested in operating a profitable business by producing quality work and retaining good employees. Throughout the history of office interiors, managers have attempted to identify the specific conditions that would ensure success and reflect the corporate culture. This includes the design of office space, furniture, equipment, and lighting.

Currently, a common management philosophy is to create an environment that is flexible to the changing needs of a business. This frequently involves downsizing, reducing excess, eliminating categories of workers, and instituting shared spaces. In addition, as a consequence of the 9/11 attack, many corporations are decentralizing their organizations. To reduce absenteeism and retain quality employees, management has focused on the personal needs of employees. For example, to create a homelike environment, "living rooms" in an office serve as locations for meetings or casual conversation. Many employees have flexible schedules, work in a variety of locations, and engage in telecommuting. These individuals often need hotels and work space when they come to the office. Customized lighting in these spaces helps to individualize an office that is shared by many people. Since collaboration remains important in the eyes of managers, the office needs space for interaction, such as touchdown areas. To encourage spontaneous collaborative activities, touchdown spaces are distributed throughout a building. To reduce travel expenses, many managers have elected to invest in video-conferencing facilities. All these changes in management philosophies require unique approaches to illuminating the office.

It is important to review how the technology that people use in an office helps to determine appropriate lighting environments. In the earliest offices, employees performed most of their work on the horizontal plane of a desk. The work involved writing, using a typewriter, and reading a variety of documents, including carbon copies. The lack of strong contrast and the importance of speed and accuracy prompted management to install lighting fixtures that emitted high quantities of illumination. In addition, to ensure bright illumination on a task, direct light sources were used without adequate shielding.

The next major development in office technology was the portable computer. Researchers are still developing the optimum lighting system that can provide effective illumination for people working at a computer and writing at a desk. Since manufacturers of computers are dramatically improving the surfaces of VDT screens, problems associated with glare and veiling reflections should eventually become obsolete.

The use of videoconferencing technology poses unique lighting challenges, as the interaction between the camera, transmission, and lighting are extremely complex. (The variables to consider when designing lighting for videoconferencing are discussed later in this chapter). The progression to wireless technology has enabled employees to work in various locations throughout a building. Designers will have to plan effective task lighting in a variety of locations in order to accommodate these new ways of working.

Critical to quality illumination in an office environment is the relationship between ergonomics and lighting. Tasks performed in an office can cause vision problems and repetitive stress injuries, such as carpal tunnel syndrome (CTS). Office workers report problems such as eyestrain, visual fatigue, and blurred vision. In addition, they indicate that problems associated with vision have indirectly caused other physical ailments, such as headaches. Musculoskeletal injuries can occur when people work in unnatural positions or engage in repetitive motions. For example, one cause of CTS is the repetitive wrist motion that occurs when people work at a keyboard for long periods of time.

Lighting has a role in helping to reduce vision problems and musculoskeletal injuries. Task lighting in offices should be designed to accommodate the specific needs of each end user. Even though employees might be engaged in the same tasks, each individual has different vision requirements. Therefore, an employee should be able to control the type of lighting he or she needs in order to perform tasks. This can be accomplished by specifying luminaires and controls that the end user is able to operate. **Localized lighting** techniques allow an employee to position light sources where they are needed and at the appropriate illumination level. Vision problems should decline when people can create the optimum lighting for their tasks and work environment.

Ineffective lighting can contribute to musculoskeletal injuries. For example, an end user may move to an unnatural or awkward position in order to avoid glare and veiling reflections, and develop back or neck problems as a result of working in such a position for a long period of time. To prevent CTS, individuals are encouraged to vary their working

localized lighting
A lighting technique that allows a user to position light sources where they are needed and at the appropriate illumination level.

positions. This might involve alternating between standing and sitting. For multiple positions to be successful, however, lighting must be designed to accommodate various locations. Localized lighting, controlled by the end user, can provide the flexibility required for changing lines of sight.

Allowing the end users to determine their lighting needs should also help resolve the problems associated with too much light in an office environment. Currently, many offices have excessively high illumination levels because of the historical belief that bright lights improve productivity and provide stimulation in the work environment. Effective lighting for computer tasks should take into account the light provided by luminous VDT screens, and ensure appropriate illumination levels between the screen, the immediate work area, and surrounding areas. Glare and veiling reflections can be avoided by eliminating a direct angle of light distribution from luminaires and windows.

Office environments have a variety of users, daylight conditions, configurations, furniture styles, and interior materials. Lighting should be customized to the unique requirements and needs of each client and should include layered lighting in every space. Many of the same tasks are performed in private offices and open-plan areas. For tasks performed in offices, lighting should be designed to eliminate glare on work surfaces, avoid severe contrasts in the distribution of lighting, illuminate vertical surfaces, diminish shadows, and provide effective localized lighting for end users. Open-plan offices can be complicated to illuminate because the potential for glare and veiling reflections is significant. To determine visual problems associated with multiple luminaires located throughout a large area, designers must analyze work areas for every station in the space.

Technology has significantly influenced the design of conference rooms. In addition to being the traditional place in which to hold meetings, conference rooms have become the location for viewing audiovisual presentations, working at computers, and conducting teleconferences. Lighting for such multifunctional spaces must accommodate the full range of activities, which occur at varying times of day, as well as the specific needs of each end user. Lighting for discussion purposes should be designed to enhance facial features, enable participants to view a whiteboard, and provide task lighting for note taking on paper or on a computer. When the purpose of the room changes to viewing an audiovisual presentation, perimeter lighting should be soft throughout the room and in the area surrounding a screen or television monitor. In addition, task lighting for taking notes should be available for every person in the room.

Educational Facilities

Lighting for educational facilities should be efficient and support philosophies of learning. Many research studies and reports have demonstrated the importance of daylight to learning (Benya, 2001; Duro-Test Lighting, 2003; Heschong, 1999; Lane, 1996; Plympton, Conway, and Epstein, 2000; Ravetto, 1994; Thayer, 1995). (See Figure 10.1.) As discussed in Chapter 2, daylight enhances visual acuity, which provides better light for reading and writing. Daylight also has positive psychological and physiological effects on people by reducing stress, satisfying circadian rhythms, and encouraging positive attitudes. The Heschong

FIGURE 10.1
Prior to the 1950s, large windows were specified in classrooms to provide daylight.

Group (1999) found that students in classrooms that had significant daylight had higher test scores than students working in classrooms with little or no daylight. The Alberta Department of Education in Canada and schools in Raleigh, North Carolina, reported health and educational benefits for children who were exposed to daylight. Research also found that absenteeism was lower in educational facilities illuminated by daylight.

A variety of activities occur in classrooms. Many educators believe that the best learning occurs when students are exposed to different approaches to teaching. These include lectures, discussion, deskwork, interactive media, or groupwork. Many classrooms are designed to accommodate a lecture format and collaborative small-group activities. Classroom activities can occur at desks, at tables, or on the floor. Technology has had a tremendous impact on education by presenting students with a variety of ways to learn. Educators can present information to students by means of computers, television monitors, screens, flipcharts, chalkboards, or whiteboards.

As demonstrated in research studies, daylight is important in the classroom. Every effort should be made to incorporate some daylight into every space, including corridors. For existing structures, this could include adding skylights, light wells, clerestories, roof monitors, light shelves, and tubular skylights. To accommodate times when a classroom needs to be dark, effective shading devices must be installed at every window in a room, including any glazing on partition walls. To supplement daylight, electrical lighting systems must be energy-efficient and easy to maintain, and must have a long life.

Pendant luminaires, whether direct or indirect, provide an excellent diffused quality of illumination. When properly spaced, they also ensure a uniform distribution pattern, which can help to eliminate dark areas in a classroom. Efficient ballasts should work in tandem with controls, such as daylight or motion sensors. Multilevel switching, with user override for automatic controls, can be coordinated to respond to daylight contours. The quantity of light in classrooms should follow the recommendations in the *IESNA Lighting Handbook*. The ninth edition recommends 40 fc to 50 fc (400 lux to 500 lux) in classrooms, and 20 fc to 40 fc (200 lux to 400 lux) for computer classrooms.

Layered lighting should be used throughout the school building. To conserve energy, it is preferable to limit accent lighting and specify energy-efficient lamps. When a lecture is occurring in a classroom, lighting should be directed on the speaker, task luminaires should be aimed at desks to enable students to write notes, and uniform, perimeter illumination should exist throughout the room. Perimeter lighting in a classroom is very important, because students must often read material that is on vertical surfaces, such as whiteboards, chalkboards, flipcharts, or bulletin boards. Specific lighting might have to be included to illuminate the walls surrounding windows, where teaching materials are frequently located. During the day, these vertical surfaces will be dark unless light is directed at the area (Figure 10.2).

FIGURE 10.2
Wall surfaces surrounding windows will be dark without the addition of artificial sources. Without balancing illumination, students could have difficulty seeing teaching materials in this area of a room.

Educators often combine lectures with audiovisual presentations. Many classrooms are not planned to accommodate the variable lighting needed to take notes in a dark environment. For these conditions, low levels of illumination should exist in the area around the speaker, on the surface used to hold the speaker's notes, at desks for note-taking, and at the perimeter of the room. Illumination that is close to a monitor or screen must be strategically planned to avoid washing out images. A dark setting can be problematic because of the bright and dark contrasts.

Computers are located in different settings throughout a school building. For example, some whole classrooms are dedicated to computer work. Many students use laptop computers in lecture halls while the teacher also uses a computer to access relevant materials and personal files. Every setting involving the use of computers must have lighting that supports the task. Illumination considerations for computers, discussed earlier in this chapter and textbook, apply to classrooms. Rooms should be glare-free and have a diffused, uniform distribution of illumination.

For situations in which students work in groups in a classroom, a different lighting effect should be planned. To encourage discussion and stimulate creative thinking, illumination for group discussions could be similar to the lighting conditions used for casual conversation in a living room. Changing the lighting environment is important in a classroom; the variance in illumination can be a psychological stimulus and can reinforce the transition to a different subject or activity. One of the reasons for having windows in the classroom is that the variability associated with climatic conditions and outdoor views stimulates the brain.

Healthcare Institutions

Healthcare institutions encompass a variety of facilities, such as hospitals, medical offices, clinics, and residential long-term care units. As with other commercial structures, the practices and policies of users affect lighting. Early healthcare facilities primarily focused on the needs of doctors rather than on patients and their families. Thus, rooms in medical buildings were designed primarily for medical purposes, and support facilities for family members did not exist. As the medical profession gained a better understanding of the importance of family and the environment for the recovery of patients, healthcare facilities improved the design of patient rooms and provided for the needs of family and friends. New facilities, such as birth rooms, hospice centers, healing gardens, and age-in-place residential units, focus on empowering patients. In addition to providing effective lighting for medical procedures, interiors

FIGURE 10.3
To assist people in moving through interiors, it is important to integrate lighting effectively with signage.

need lighting that improves the psychological well-being of patients and meets the needs of family members.

To assist people in locating rooms, especially in a crisis, it is desirable to design illumination that enhances wayfinding (Figure 10.3). Such lighting must be effectively integrated with signage. For safety, security, and aesthetic purposes, dark areas should not exist. Visitors often use reception areas and waiting rooms when they are waiting to hear about the results of surgery or a medical procedure; a serene lighting environment can help to reduce stress and anxiety associated with those situations. Lighting should also help to create some level of privacy for people who may have emotional responses to hearing results. Some ways of providing privacy include avoiding direct illumination on people's faces and using small pools of light to give the impression that a large room is divided into smaller, private areas.

Quality lighting is important in these settings because many of the tasks being performed demand accuracy. Appropriate lighting will eliminate glare and shadows while promoting a professional and positive impression. Daylight can also help significantly in creating a healthy and pleasing environment. Research indicates positive effects of daylight on patients in healthcare facilities. As noted in Chapter 2, Littlefair (1996) reported on the positive effects of reflected daylight in hospital rooms. The variability of daylight can serve as a stimulus for people who must stay in one location for a long period of time, and natural light can assist with the body's circadian rhythm. Coordinating the body's circadian rhythm is especially important for people who are disoriented after a long surgery or recovery period. Natural light can also be helpful in making skin tones more visible.

Electrical lighting in healthcare facilities must enable medical personnel to see accurately during tasks such as carrying out medical procedures, reading reports, recording health information, and performing tests. In addition, lighting should help to promote a healthy, professional, and clean impression of the facilities. Layered lighting should be included in most spaces, especially in public areas and patient rooms. Some medical procedures require specialist lighting fixtures. Specification of these fixtures must be done in consultation with medical personnel.

The most energy-efficient electrical sources should be specified for each task. Highly specialized lighting and illumination in critical areas might require less efficient lighting systems. However, most spaces in healthcare facilities should have efficient lighting systems because they require illumination 24 hours a day seven days a week. Ensuring illumination at the appropriate level requires strict enforcement of cleaning and maintenance guidelines for lighting systems. Medical personnel must be able to detect skin tones accurately and examine someone without shadows obstructing details. Lamps with CRI ratings of 100 should be used for spaces involving activities that require color rendition accuracy, such as examination rooms, recovery rooms, and laboratories.

Lighting must accommodate the needs of patients and medical personnel and must be flexible enough to accommodate a variety of positions and locations in a room. Controls should be accessible from different positions, including by someone lying or sitting up in bed or seated in a chair. Illumination must also be planned for tasks performed in a chair, for walking through the room, and for bathroom activities. The medical profession has become very specialized, and many different members of the medical staff work with patients in their room. For example, physical and occupational therapists often work with patients soon after surgery. Illumination must accommodate the tasks involved with their procedures and equipment.

Customer-Oriented Commercial Interiors

Interior designers are hired to design a variety of customer-oriented commercial interiors. The most common projects are hotels, restaurants, and retail spaces.

Hotels

The hotel industry is one of the largest retail businesses in the world. Hotels have a variety of amenities, prices, and room sizes, and they exist in a variety of locations, including on highways, in suburban and urban settings, and in resort areas. Hotels are operated as chains, franchises, or independents. Frequently, the design of chains and franchises is dictated by corporate standards. To reflect a sense of the community and reinforce a theme, some hotel designs are influenced by location. These variable traits of the hotel industry are important criteria for specifying a quality lighting environment.

People want a hotel to have a comfortable sleeping environment, clean bathrooms, and effective security. In order to exceed minimum expectations, many hotels are implementing a variety of personalized services that require special lighting. Guests must have a good night's sleep or they will not consider future visits. According to the National Sleep Foundation (NSF), sleep deprivation can have a negative effect on the physical and psychological health of people. The elderly, especially those with dementia, experience disruptions in their sleep. Sleep deprivation can become more pronounced when people travel because circadian rhythms are altered. Bright lights in guest rooms can disturb sleep and make it difficult for someone to adjust to a new time zone. Variable illumination levels and room-darkening window treatments in guest rooms can help to normalize biological clocks.

To create a calm and relaxing environment, some hotels are adding spas in guest rooms. These can include oversized bathtubs, multiple

pulsating showerheads, mood music, aromatherapy scents, and candles. Electrical lighting in guest bathrooms can contribute to the ambience by reinforcing the mood and enhancing the appearance of people (Figure 10.4). This requires a bathroom lighting system with the flexibility to have low levels of illumination for the bathing area and bright sources around mirrors for facial grooming.

In the commercial sector, lodging is the fourth most intensive consumer of energy in the United States. Bornholdt (2001) indicates that lighting can consume 40 percent of the property's overall electrical costs. To reduce energy consumption and conserve resources, lighting systems in hotels must be efficient and maintained on a regular basis. Daylight should supplement and replace electrical sources as often as possible. Among all the rooms in a hotel, guest rooms and meeting spaces consume the greatest amount of energy. Therefore, these spaces should have energy-efficient lighting systems and should be considered first in a retrofit operation.

Research on end-user practices and energy-consumption patterns has determined that lights remaining on in unoccupied spaces waste a great deal of energy in hotels. For example, at the Lawrence Berkeley National Laboratory, research focused on identifying which luminaires were used, how often, and the amount of time they were on in guest

FIGURE 10.4
A bathroom designed for a spa experience should have a lighting system with the flexibility to have low levels of illumination for the bathing area and bright sources around mirrors for facial grooming.

rooms and guest bathrooms. The findings indicate that luminaires are primarily used in the morning from six to ten o'clock, and after five o'clock in the evening. Bathroom fixtures and table luminaires in the guest room were on the most, an average of eight and five hours, respectively. The study recommends that occupancy sensors be used in guest bathrooms to conserve energy. To avoid upsetting guests, occupancy sensors should be calibrated with long set times of approximately two hours. Hotel staff should be told to turn off lights in unoccupied guest rooms and bathrooms.

Controls can play an important role in conserving energy in hotels. In addition to installing occupancy sensors in guest bathrooms, it is advisable to equip stairways and corridors with motion detector controls or timers. Controls can be calibrated to change lighting automatically in areas whose activities and illumination needs fluctuate. For example, a reception desk is typically busy with people checking in and out during the early part of the day. During the rest of the day, the reception area does not need high quantities of illumination at every station. Corridors surrounding meeting rooms can also vary in usage patterns. Controls should reduce the level of illumination in corridors when meetings are in session, since the corridors are typically unoccupied at such times.

Most hotels have a theme or an image that is projected in the design of the facilities. Lighting can reinforce the theme in various ways. The most obvious method is to select luminaires that reflect the theme and are integrated with the environment. For example, many of the luminaires at Walt Disney World have been custom-designed to blend with the overall design theme (Figure 10.5). Illumination levels and special lighting effects should support the desired mood of the hotel at various times of the day while taking into account any specific design element that functions as an overall theme. For example, a hotel in the mountains might have rough textures as the dominating concept. For this situation, lighting techniques that specifically enhance rough textures should be selected. Fabulous views of a city skyline or a sunset over the ocean are often focal points of a hotel. To maximize guests' ability to see the views, sunlight must be shielded from end users, and, in the evening, light sources must be carefully planned to avoid reflections of fixtures on the glass.

LIGHTING DESIGN APPLICATIONS AND THE DESIGN PROCESS

FIGURE 10.5
An illustration of a
custom-designed
luminaire that
reinforces the
theme of a Walt
Disney World hotel.

Lighting at the entrance of a hotel should give guests an impression of safety and security. As people enter the hotel, lighting should immediately help with wayfinding. Many people are first-time users of the facilities, so lighting can help direct people to the reception desk, public areas, and guest rooms. Lighting for the reception desk area should provide excellent illumination for people reading hotel statements and signing bills. To meet the needs of the hotel staff and guests, task illumination must be well planned on both sides of the desk. People use the lobby area for a variety of activities, including reading maps and brochures with fine print, meeting people, and having conversations. Lighting in lobbies must be flexible enough to accommodate this range of activities, making the faces of people easy to see from a variety of angles, and providing task lighting to serve the needs of reading. To respond to diverse moods and activities, lighting in the lobby should create a different atmosphere during the day from that in evening hours.

A primary goal of hotel operators is to create a homelike environment in guest rooms. This includes providing lighting to accommodate the diverse tasks performed in various locations in guest rooms. Technology has enabled people to use guest rooms for a variety of purposes, including working at a computer, playing video games, and watching movies. A focus on work-related amenities has given rise to 24-hour business centers and executive technology suites and floors. Lighting for work-related activities in these spaces must be appropriate for laptops, reading, and meetings. Illumination should also provide the appropriate atmosphere for relaxation, including creative applications involving the interplay of light with water in bathrooms.

Large public areas in hotels are used for a variety of activities, including conferences, meetings, receptions, and weddings. These spaces are often designed so they can be arranged into various configurations with the use of soundproof partitions. Lighting must accommodate the various tasks, including working at computers, viewing audiovisual presentations, taking notes, delivering and listening to speeches, dining, dancing, and conversation. Every possible room configuration should have lighting that will accommodate the various activities. In addition, corridor areas surrounding meeting rooms are often used to conduct business. Therefore, to ensure illumination that meets the needs of work-related tasks, these areas should have luminaires that can be controlled by end users.

Restaurants

All restaurants share the common goal of earning profits through customer satisfaction. People who are happy with the quality of food, service, and ambience become repeat customers and can further increase profits by communicating the positive attributes of the business to friends and family members. Consistency is a valued commodity for a successful restaurant. Once this is attained, any changes to the restaurant, including the lighting, may be perceived as altering the quality of the food. Since lighting is often considered the most important element in the design of a restaurant, it is important to be sure that the lighting is ideal from the start.

The perfect lighting approach provides appropriate illumination for tasks and creates an atmosphere. Lighting plays an important role in attracting people to a restaurant and helping them to feel comfortable while dining. Lighting on the outside of the restaurant must highlight characteristics outside that would entice people to come in. Lighting can also help to inform the customer about the degree of formality and price range: generally, understated lighting techniques are used for more formal and expensive restaurants, while bright, theatrical lighting schemes often reflect a more casual and moderate price range. Lighting that helps to communicate proper dress expectations and prices is especially useful for potential customers who are unfamiliar with the restaurant.

Lighting in the reception area should be exceptional, because this is the first impression customers have of the interior of the restaurant. As a transitional area from the outside, the reception area should have appropriate illumination levels that assist with the adaptive function of the eyes. A positive reaction will encourage people to stay and may reduce anxieties associated with waiting for a table. Lighting should also help to create the desired emotional response to the thematic concept of the restaurant. A fine restaurant often has soft, warm illumination. Restaurants catering to people who are looking for an adventurous evening have lighting that is bright, colorful, and perhaps synchronized with music.

Lighting for walking through the restaurant should serve several purposes. For safety reasons, effective illumination must be provided in the pathway, especially transitional areas involving steps. However, lighting should not emphasize pathways. As people walk through the restaurant, illumination levels should change to emphasize the focal points in the space.

Lighting at the tables should include adequate illumination for people to read menus. This is especially important for the elderly, who are likely to have vision problems. Table lighting should also enhance the appearance of food and of the people seated at the table. It is critical that lighting render the colors of food accurately. Deviations from true colors may be interpreted as spoiled food.

To accommodate all the purposes of lighting in restaurants, various sources should be coordinated through the use of layered lighting techniques. Whenever possible, daylight is a wonderful source of illumination for restaurants serving breakfast, lunch, and brunch. Electrical sources should have a warm color temperature and, whenever possible, should be energy-efficient. To enhance the appearance of food and skin tones, incandescent lamps are frequently used in restaurant lighting systems. For some applications, CFLs would serve as an excellent energy-efficient alternative, and fluorescent lamps help to reduce the heat generated by incandescent lamps. To help servers do their jobs efficiently, illumination at service stations should provide adequate lighting on beverages, utensils, and dishes while not creating an annoying source of brightness to patrons in the dining room.

Retail Stores

The earliest retail stores were located at street level in residential buildings. Later designs included bazaars and arcades. These structures were dependent upon daylight for their operations. A decorative approach to integrating daylight was to install skylights covered with beautiful stained glass (Figure 10.6). As electricity and electrical sources advanced, many retailers opted for eliminating the penetration of daylight, preferring the ability to control the environment by manipulating electrical lights.

Lighting must reinforce the store's image. There is a wide spectrum of retail stores representing every price range and a variety of products and services. Generally, lighting for a discount retail store provides uniform, bright illumination from industrial luminaires. Higher-end stores have lower ambient light levels and spotlights that create the contrast required to highlight products. Each of these lighting techniques reflects an image and promotes a value statement.

FIGURE 10.6
An Art Nouveau style stained glass in a cupola of Au Printemps department store in Paris. Designed by Brière, the unit has over 3,000 individual pieces of glass.

LIGHTING DESIGN APPLICATIONS AND THE DESIGN PROCESS

Lighting for store windows depends on the layout of the area. Window displays are designed with and without backs; a window display environment with a back is more controlled, so lighting can be planned specifically for the merchandise within the confined space. This setting is ideal for using spotlights to direct eyes to a product. Window displays without backs can be confusing to viewers because merchandise and lighting in the background create a diversion. However, many retailers prefer a window display with an open back because it enables people to see a lot of merchandise while walking by the store. To emphasize products in window displays without backs, illumination contrasts between the various areas should be carefully monitored, and other methods of attraction may be considered, such as using colored lights in the window or lighting with movement.

Once a customer has entered a store, lighting has a significant role in the overall plan of the space, circulation, and visual merchandising. As always, lighting should accommodate people with visual disabilities and assist in other aspects of the principles of universal design. Layered lighting techniques must support the plan of the space and the objectives of merchandising. Frequently, lighting is used to designate various areas within a store. For example, in a department store, the cosmetics, shoe, and women's departments might have different levels of illumination and luminaires. Retailers often use different ceiling heights, surfaces, and colors to designate different areas or products.

Lighting can assist in wayfinding by illuminating the path to departments and merchandise. Frequently, light from ambient and accent sources can help to provide illumination for aisles. Illumination should assist customers in finding merchandise and contribute to their safety by highlighting changes in elevation, surface materials, and sharp corners of displays. Since customers walk through aisles from a variety of directions, lighting must be carefully analyzed from multiple points to ensure a glare-free setting. This includes monitoring reflections from shiny finishes on walls and floors. For example, a highly polished marble floor can cause annoying glare from ceiling fixtures.

In addition to illumination in aisles, perimeter lighting can help customers to understand the size and shape of the store and locate merchandise. Quick apprehension of the store's configuration encourages customers to explore the entire store. Perimeter lighting can easily be integrated into vertical planes and must effectively illuminate signage and products found in areas of the store that are farthest from the entrance. Since people are drawn to light, perimeter wall illumination also encourages customers to walk to all areas within a store, including those at the edges. Customers will avoid dark spaces, on the other hand, so it is important to analyze a store plan carefully to determine the location of these areas. In addition, for security purposes and to help curtail theft, the sales staff must be able to see all areas within a store.

Quality lighting is critical to visual merchandising. Effective lighting must start with the product and an understanding of how to illuminate the most appealing characteristics of the merchandise. In stores with a lot of products in various colors, textures, and sizes, this is a significant challenge. Lighting must put the focus on one product, or on one detail of a product, within a setting that has many items in close proximity. This requires an understanding of the characteristics of the product, since obviously products are made from a wide variety of materials and in different colors, textures, shapes, and sizes. A visualization prioritization scheme can also be very helpful. Another important consideration is the necessary flexibility to accommodate the variables and changes in

FIGURE 10.7
The tiered shelving unit enables light to strike merchandise on each shelf.

LIGHTING DESIGN APPLICATIONS AND THE DESIGN PROCESS

displays throughout the year. For example, a retailer may elect to highlight a specific area or characteristic of a product, such as the texture of a woolen sweater. Lighting flexibility can include a variety of factors, such as aiming angles, illumination intensities, color temperatures, and degree of focus. To enhance the appearance of products and provide excellent visibility for evaluating merchandise, light sources should be as close to the merchandise as possible. Spotlighting merchandise on tables or gondolas, for example, is easier to accomplish with tiered units that expose merchandise on every shelf (Figure 10.7).

Serious consideration should be given to the areas within a store that are typically point-of-purchase locations. Important areas are dressing rooms and the sales transaction counter. Frequently, illumination in dressing rooms is derived from industrial types of luminaires, with light sources that have low color rendering ratings. Instead, lighting in dressing rooms should enhance the appearance of the merchandise and the customers, because this is one of the most critical decision points for a consumer. Lighting should surround mirrors and provide excellent color rendition. Lighting should also be excellent at the point where people are purchasing merchandise, because customers can easily change their mind and not buy the product.

Quality lighting for retail stores must balance the goals of the retailer, energy codes, and environmental concerns. To enhance merchandising and increase sales, retailers frequently use high-energy-consuming lamps, such as incandescent and halogen lamps. However, to comply with energy codes and maximum watts-per-square-foot requirements, designers should consider energy-efficient lighting systems with the lowest life-cycle costs. The watts-per-square-foot maximums prescribed by energy codes are based upon the type of retail space. For example, mass merchandising buildings have more stringent requirements than boutiques. Daylight integration can help to satisfy energy code requirements.

Ensuring energy-efficient lighting systems for retail stores also requires care in selecting the appropriate luminaire and electrical source. For example, in a retail environment calling for multiple highlighted areas, low-voltage track systems are more energy-efficient than line-voltage tracks. Highlights should use narrow beam spots rather than flood lamps. Lamps in a retail environment should have long life, excellent color rendition, and high light output. Currently, halogen, fluorescent, and metal halide lamps are the most energy-efficient sources. Tremendous technological improvements in metal-halide lamps have precipitated great interest in using this source for multiple retail applications. Improvements in LEDs and fiber optics will provide more energy-efficient solutions in the future.

Color rendition will always be critical in retail stores. Ideal sources have CRI ratings of 100 and warm color temperatures between 3000K and 3200K. Returns frequently occur because customers are not happy with a color after they leave the store. Thus, lighting should render colors as faithfully as possible, and daylight is an excellent source for this.

As with all commercial environments, controls have a significant role in conserving energy and creating various settings for different moods. Retail stores should have automatic controls calibrated with the store's operating hours. For limited applications, occupancy sensors could be set to dim lights when departments are unoccupied and to increase illumination levels when someone enters a space. Generally, occupancy sensors are effective only in retail establishments with low traffic. Controls can be programmed for various scenes in different departments at various times of the day. This should include a special arrangement for evening maintenance. Efficient lamp maintenance is critical in a retail environment because products in the dark do not sell. Lamps should be quickly replaceable, accessible, and easy to change. Such lamps help the maintenance staff and sales associates who must often replace lamps during store hours. The number of different types of lamps should be kept to a minimum, because relamping can be very confusing when multiple sources are used in various locations in the store.

Creating a quality lighting environment for commercial structures is a complex process that cannot rely on one-size-fits-all prescriptive solutions. All clients should receive a lighting plan that is unique to the needs of their users, the interior elements of each space, and the site. Illumination must accommodate a variety of people performing numerous tasks in very diverse settings. In addition, interior designers must be cognizant of how world events can affect corporate and institutional philosophies, because these philosophies will in turn affect interiors and lighting. Continuous changes in technology also have a significant influence on lighting systems. Therefore, designers should constantly monitor improvements in the lighting field so as to be able to specify the most energy-efficient technologies. This is especially critical for commercial buildings because of the enormous consumption of electricity.

SUMMARY

- Lighting systems for commercial interiors should enhance visual comfort while accommodating functional and aesthetic requirements. A lighting plan should always aim for minimal impact on the local and global environment.
- Tasks performed in an office can cause problems with vision and musculoskeletal injuries, such as carpal tunnel syndrome (CTS). Poor task lighting can encourage users to assume positions that contribute to such problems.
- Lighting for educational facilities should be efficient and support philosophies of learning.
- Healthcare facilities include hospitals, medical offices, clinics, and residential long-term care units. In addition to providing effective lighting for medical procedures, interiors need lighting that improves the psychological well-being of patients and meets the needs of family members.
- In designing hotel lighting, it is important to understand the concerns of the hotel industry and the client's corporate philosophy. Hotels are part of the service industry; thus, customer satisfaction is the primary focus.
- Lighting plays an important role in attracting people to a restaurant and making them feel comfortable while dining. To accommodate all the purposes of lighting in restaurants, various sources should be coordinated in layered lighting techniques.
- Quality lighting is critical in retail stores and should be determined by the quality and type of merchandise. The goals of retailers are to project an image to consumers, attract customers to the store, focus attention on merchandise, reduce or eliminate returns, and create a memorable experience, all of which translates into future visits. Lighting has a major role in accomplishing these goals.

localized lighting

Exercises

1. Identify an office, a school classroom, and a public area in a health-care facility to observe during various times of the day and week. In a written report that may include sketches and photographs, address the items listed below:

   a. Determine whether the space meets all the criteria for a quality lighting environment. How can the lighting be improved?

   b. Given the users and elements of the space, identify special vision needs.

   c. Determine the human response elicited from the space and identify the lighting techniques that contribute to the response.

   d. Evaluate the energy efficiency of the lighting system, including daylight integration. How can the space be improved to conserve energy and natural resources?

2. Identify a restaurant, a retail store, and a public area in a hotel and observe them during various times of the day and week. In a written report that may include sketches and photographs, address the items listed below:

   a. Determine whether the space meets all the criteria for a quality lighting environment. How can the lighting be improved?

   b. Given the users and elements of the space, identify special vision needs.

   c. Determine the human response elicited from the space and identify the lighting techniques that contribute to the response.

   d. Evaluate the energy efficiency of the lighting system, including daylight integration. How can the space be improved to conserve energy and natural resources?

CHAPTER 11

Lighting Design Process:
Project Planning Through Design Development

- Identify the activities involved in the seven phases of the lighting design process.
- Identify the information that should be collected during the comprehensive programming phase and then be applied to developing the lighting criteria.
- Understand relevant lighting-related information that should be collected by interviewing, surveying, and observing end users of an interior.
- Understand how to analyze and synthesize the data collected in the comprehensive programming phase.
- Describe the brainstorming process, including sketching techniques that can assist with the conceptualization of the lighting design.
- Identify the purposes of the design development phase.
- Apply an understanding of the design development phase to a lighting project.
- Understand and describe the most salient factors in conducting oral presentations.

Basic concepts and elements of a quality lighting environment, including components of lighting systems, daylight integration, directional effects of illumination, energy considerations, environmental factors related to lighting, and human factors, are explored in previous chapters. This content serves as the foundation for exploring specific applications in residential and commercial interiors. Chapters 11 and 12 serve as the culminating experience of the textbook. The primary purpose of these chapters is to explain the lighting design process within the context of the content reviewed in Chapters 1 to 10. Lighting design is performed by architects, interior designers, and lighting designers. Frequently, a lighting designer develops the lighting design for an architect or interior designer.

This analysis of the lighting design process is broken down into two chapters. Chapter 11 covers details regarding the project planning process, as well as methods for conducting the comprehensive programming phase, schematic design, and design development. As the concluding chapter in the textbook, Chapter 12 deals with contractual documents, contract administration, and evaluation.

An important element in the success of the lighting design process is obtaining client approval at the conclusion of each phase and before proceeding to the next stage. This approval process is important to ensure that the client is in full agreement with the lighting design, costs, and schedule. If a lighting designer proceeds to the next phase before receiving client approval, valuable time and resources may be wasted. A client may be reluctant to pay for services without having approved them, and a lack of communication can seriously affect the working relationship. An unhappy client will not use the designer's services again and may make negative comments to potential clients. This is a serious problem because a great deal of business in the field of interior design is generated by repeat business and word-of-mouth.

Initial Phases

The lighting design process may be divided into the following seven phases: (1) project planning, (2) comprehensive programming, (3) schematic design, (4) design development, (5) contract documentation, (6) contract administration, and (7) evaluation (Figure 11.1). Client involvement is essential at every phase of the lighting design process to ensure satisfaction with and approval of the elements of the program, including illumination plans, schedules, and budget.

As a result of gathering data through programming, the criteria of the lighting project are used as the foundation for developing schematic

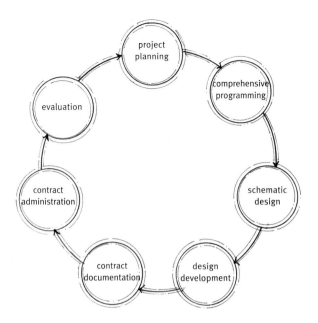

FIGURE 11.1
The lighting design process is divided into seven phases: (1) project planning, (2) comprehensive programming, (3) schematic design, (4) design development, (5) contract documentation, (6) contract administration, and (7) evaluation. As a cyclical process, the evaluation phase provides useful information to improve the lighting environment for the existing client and future projects.

designs. This is a conceptual phase in which many schematics of the lighting environment are explored with the client and the team of professionals involved in the project. Some of the schematic drawings used include bubble diagrams, lighting distribution diagrams, and task-lighting relationship sketches. A successful schematic design is then expounded and detailed in the design development phase. At this stage in the lighting design process, specific illumination methods, lighting systems, and layouts are presented to a client for discussion and evaluation. Upon approval by the client, registered professionals, such as architects and engineers, enter the contract documentation phase and begin developing working drawings, specifications, sections, cut sheets, and purchase orders. The contract administration phase is the implementation stage of the project.

The evaluation phase takes place after people are using the space or building. Often referred to as postoccupancy evaluation, this process is intended to determine user satisfaction with the lighting design. The data gathered during this phase should be used to improve any design problems. As illustrated by the directional arrows in Figure 11.1, information learned in the evaluation phase should also be used to benefit plans for future clients. A process focusing on continued improvement will result in the best possible quality lighting environments.

Project Planning

The primary purposes of planning are to develop a profile of the project and to determine the resources needed to achieve its objectives. A lighting designer may be hired by a variety of people associated with residential and commercial interiors, including the owner(s), an architect, an engineer, or a contractor.

To develop the best possible lighting plan, a lighting designer should be involved in the planning stage of the entire project. Within the context of the project's objectives and time line, determined in consultation with the client and other professionals, a lighting designer develops a plan for the lighting. Most lighting projects will have objectives related to users, tasks, interior elements, spatial geometry, technology, illumination methods, codes, time lines, budgets, and maintenance. Well-defined objectives outline the project and serve as the basis for the planning process.

The profile of the project, for planning purposes, should include a preliminary understanding of the needs of the owner, end users, and elements of the property. Understanding the scope of the work helps to determine the amount of time and resources needed to execute the project. This is critical information the lighting designer should acquire during the planning stages, because a client may have unreasonable expectations concerning the amount of time needed for construction, the feasibility of a design, or the cost of lighting systems.

For planning purposes, a lighting designer must know the location of the property and whether the project involves an existing building, new construction, or speculative construction. Developing a lighting design for an existing structure might involve minor adjustments to an installation, retrofitting, or a completely new lighting scheme for an interior project with extensive renovation. For new construction, the planning phase significantly affects the lighting plan. Ideally, the lighting plan should be developed in concert with the architectural concept. Planning at this stage gives the designer the opportunity to integrate daylight successfully and to create a design that enhances the appearance of the interior. The range of lighting possibilities diminishes as construction proceeds. Once walls, ceilings, and floors are finished, it can be difficult to integrate structural and portable luminaires, and they can be costly to install. Speculative construction projects require a lighting plan that appeals to a variety of people.

Early in the planning process, a lighting designer should visit the site with the client. A walk-through with the client provides an excellent opportunity for discussing existing lighting problems and constraints and the initial ideas. In consultation with the owner, it should be determined whether luminaires should be replaced, eliminated, left in the space, or retrofitted. Initial visits should also include the recording of significant architectural details, preliminary measurements of rooms, existing luminaires, and location of electrical outlets. The designer should take note of daylight integration as well as reflectance characteristics of interior surfaces, and should take photographs of the interior.

In consultation with the client, the team members should develop a comprehensive plan, which includes the list of activities, responsible individuals, time line, required resources, estimated costs, and billing dates. A project schedule includes the time line for activities, including important start and finish dates.

Programming

The programming phase includes interviews, observations, and an assessment of lighting systems and research initiatives. Preliminary information gleaned from the project planning phase provides the foundation for determining the type of data needed to design a quality lighting environment. It is during the comprehensive programming phase that data are collected about the end users, the physical characteristics of the space, and the applicable codes, ordinances, and regulations. Effective methods for obtaining information about end users and the interior include interviews, surveys, and field observation. In addition, a review of relevant literature and current research related to lighting should be conducted and documented. The results of such research can provide excellent insight and may be used to supplement project-specific data gathered in this phase. Interviews should be conducted with the client and, whenever possible, end users of the space, such as employees, customers, and perhaps visitors. The goal is to collect enough information to be able to make generalizations about the lighting environment.

Interviews and surveys provide good information regarding how the lighting design is perceived. However, it is difficult for people to describe in detail how they work or live in a space. Interviews and surveys cannot cover all the questions that might be relevant to understanding behavior in a space. That is where field observations come in. The use of multiple methodologies provides the greatest insight into human behavior and helps to validate results by checking data derived from one method against data from another. For example, in an interview a client might indicate that spotlights help to attract customers to a specific display. However, in observing customers in the store, it might be revealed that customers rarely look at the highlighted merchandise. Conflicting data need to be resolved through discussions with the client and perhaps further observation.

Effective interviews and surveys require research and preparation. Information learned from initial site visits and preliminary interviews with the client serve as the foundation for more specific questions. Questions can be written in a structured or semistructured format. A structured arrangement is a list of questions without flexibility for asking follow-up questions. A semistructured format includes a list of questions that enables the interviewer to ask additional questions for clarification purposes or to obtain more information.

Interview and survey questions should always include an assessment of the present situation and anticipated future needs. Table 11.1 provides examples of questions that might be asked in interviews or surveys of residential or commercial clients. Questions may be divided into the following: (1) characteristics of the end users, including physiological and psychological attributes, (2) activity assessment, (3) perceptions of lighting, and (4) anticipated future changes. The survey or interview questions should be modified to accommodate the unique needs and characteristics of each client. This is especially important when designing lighting for international clients, since different culture and life experiences can affect expectations and perceptions of a lighting environment. Therefore, understanding the end users' perceptions of lighting is important in planning an environment that will meet their needs.

TABLE 11.1

Name: **Age:**

Health Concerns (e.g., dementia, Alzheimer's disease, SAD, cognitive processing, hearing)

Visual Impairments	**Yes**	**No**
Cataracts	☐	☐
Glaucoma	☐	☐
Diabetic retinopathy	☐	☐
Difficulty seeing contrasts	☐	☐
Difficulty with visual acuity	☐	☐
Difficulty detecting motion	☐	☐
Difficulty with depth perception	☐	☐
Reduced field of vision	☐	☐
Color blindness	☐	☐
Problems with glare	☐	☐
Problems with flickering lights	☐	☐

Anthropometric Data (provide measurements in a range)

Distance from seat to eye level (inches or mm) ——————————————

Distance from floor to eye level (inches or mm) ——————————————

Reach distance (inches or mm)   ——————————————

Activity Assessment

Room	Location in Room	Activity	Special Lighting Needs	User(s)	Day(s) of Week	Time of day	Duration	Technology	Furniture	Luminaire(s)

TABLE 11.1 *(continued)*
Residential/Commercial Client Questionnaire

Perceptions of Lighting Assessment in Existing Spaces*

Client: Room: Lighting Method:

Perceptions of Lighting	Yes	No	Details
Appropriate level of illumination			
Appropriate mood and atmosphere for activities			
Appropriate amount of daylight			
Appropriate energy conservation			
Appropriate environmental conservation			
Appropriate accent lighting for artwork or a special collection			
Problems with distribution of light on a task			
Problems with glare			Time of day: Time of year:
Problems with shadows			Time of day: Time of year:
Problems with reflections on task surfaces			
Problems with flickering			
Problems with color accuracy			
Problems with the apparent color of a room			
Problems with seeing objects			
Problems with seeing people			
Problems with reaching controls			
Problems with manipulating controls			
Problems with heat from lamps			
Problems with electrical outlets			
Problems with the apparent size of the room			
Problems with safety			
Problems with security			
Additional comments			

* To be completed with the assistance of a lighting designer.

TABLE 11.1 *(continued)*
Residential/Commercial Client Questionnaire

Anticipated Future Changes

1. Changes in individuals living/working in the building:

2. Changes in number of rooms:

3. Changes in activities:

4. Anticipated renovation:

5. Furniture changes:

6. Changes in interior elements (floor coverings, wall coverings, ceilings, window treatments):

Understanding various perceptions of a lighting environment is important in commercial interiors as well as in residences. A demographic profile will help to identify characteristics of the end users. To determine perceptions of lighting, interview questions for commercial clients should be tailored to specific categories of end users. For example, in designing the lighting for a restaurant, different questions should be written for the owner(s), hostess, servers, maintenance crew, new customers, and returning patrons. Each group is engaged in different activities in the restaurant; hence, their satisfaction, expectations, and perceptions of the lighting environment may vary and should be taken into account in the new design. Table 11.2 provides examples of questions that may be used as a guide for developing a questionnaire for commercial interiors. The topics include business-related information, property data, end-user characteristics, activity assessment, and perceptions of lighting.

As noted earlier, interviews and surveys should elicit basic information about perceptions of the lighting environment. However, the ideal situation is to combine the results of surveys and interviews with field observations. Observing in a residence may be rather awkward and is therefore rare. In addition, observations in a residence are generally not all that informative because the frequent personal contact with

TABLE 11.2
Commercial Client Questionnaire

Project: Location:

Name: Role (owner, employee, customer):

Business-Related Data

Purpose of the business/organization:

Mission/goals/objectives of the business/organization:

Image of the business/organization:

Elements contributing to profits and ROI (return on investment):

Energy and environmental conservation policies and practices:

Current critical issues related to the industry:

Current societal events affecting the business/organization:

Anticipated changes in personnel:

Anticipated changes in activities:

Demographic profile of employees (sex, age, ethnic and cultural background):

Property Data

Geographic location:

Building owned or leased:

Anticipated changes in space needs:

Anticipated renovation:

Anticipated furniture changes:

Anticipated changes in interior elements (floor coverings, wall coverings, ceilings, window treatments):

residential clients allows a lighting designer to acquire the necessary information more naturally and easily. The arrangement of commercial interiors, on the other hand, often enables a lighting designer to conduct field observations of human behavior. Therefore, whenever possible, observations should be conducted in an interior that will be renovated. With new construction, sites similar to the proposed project should be observed. Research related to the project may be reviewed and integrated into plans.

The primary purpose of field observations is to watch how people behave in a specific lighting environment. Table 11.3 provides a guide that can be used for conducting field observations. As with all the guides included in this chapter, this document should be modified to address the specifics of the site, the lighting system, and the end users.

TABLE 11.3
Commercial Observations

Project: Location:
Observation Date: Observation Start Time: Observation Finish Time:

Describe people in the space (number of people, employee, customer, approximate ages, special needs):

Describe activities in the space:

Describe the role of lighting in conducting activities:

Describe unnatural movements that could be the result of poor lighting (e.g., shielding eyes, hesitations):

Describe any modifications or adjustments to the environment conducted by end users that could be the result of poor lighting:

Describe any problems associated with lighting and the principles of universal design:

Identify preferred area(s):

Identify any unoccupied area(s):

Observations should occur at different times of the day, on different days of the week, and perhaps during different seasons of the year. For example, observation of behavior in a retail store would reveal different activity on Monday mornings, Saturday afternoons, and during the Christmas season. To gain the most insight into the interaction between lighting and behavior, a site should be visited at the times that are most germane to the project. The frequency of visits depends on the consistency of results; a site should be observed enough times for the observer to be able to conclude that specific behavior is fairly constant. For example, in observing behavior in a restaurant, it might be noted that someone trips on a step located at the entrance. On subsequent visits, if many people trip on the step, then it would be recorded as a significant problem and might be addressed by adding illumination to the edge of the tread. However, if over the course of several visits only one person is observed to trip, and interviews with the employees reveal that they never noticed anyone having problems with the step, then perhaps additional illumination does not have to be installed at the entrance. By way of caution, note that a ramp must be provided to comply with the regulations found in the Americans with Disabilities Act (ADA) and International Building Code (IBC) regulations.

Programming involves an assessment of the lighting system and the physical attributes of an interior that might affect the quality of illumination. This involves visiting the site and creating an inventory of luminaires, lamps, controls, electrical outlets, daylight integration, architectural features, room configurations, furniture, colors, and material finishes. It is important to take photographs of the interior to assist with the schematic and design development phases of the lighting design process. In addition, sketches should be made of the floor plan, wall elevations, reflected ceiling plan, and perhaps light distribution patterns. Sketches should be drawn quickly; at this stage of the lighting design process, approximate dimensions are sufficient. For some projects, a floor plan and reflected ceiling plan might already exist. (Exact dimensions of interiors are recorded during the design development phase.)

As illustrated in Figure 11.2, each sketch of a room should include dimensions and the approximate location of interior elements such as luminaires, electrical outlets, controls, HVAC equipment, loudspeakers,

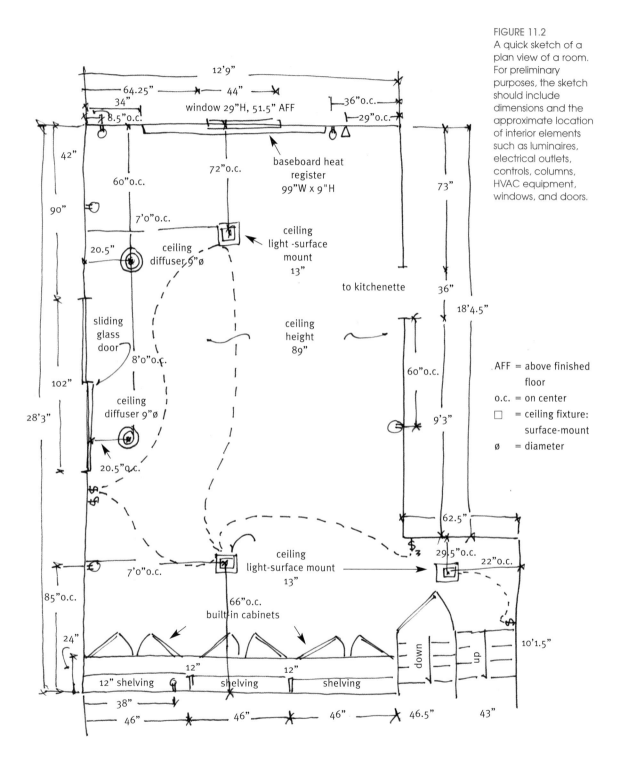

FIGURE 11.2
A quick sketch of a
plan view of a room.
For preliminary
purposes, the sketch
should include
dimensions and the
approximate location
of interior elements
such as luminaires,
electrical outlets,
controls, columns,
HVAC equipment,
windows, and doors.

12'9"

64.25" 44" 36"o.c.

34"

8.5"o.c. window 29"H, 51.5" AFF 29"o.c.

42"

60"o.c. 72"o.c. baseboard heat
register
99"W x 9"H

73"

90" 7'0"o.c. ceiling
light -surface
mount
13"

20.5" ceiling
diffuser 6"ø to kitchenette 36"

18'4.5"

sliding
glass
door ceiling
height
89"

8'0"o.c. 60"o.c.

102"

ceiling
diffuser 9"ø 9'3"

AFF = above finished
floor

28'3" o.c. = on center

□ = ceiling fixture:
surface-mount

ø = diameter

20.5"o.c.

62.5"

29.5"o.c. 22"o.c.

7'0"o.c. ceiling
light-surface mount
13"

85"o.c. 66"o.c.
built-in cabinets 10'1.5"

24" down up

12" 12"

12" shelving shelving shelving

38"

46" 46" 46" 46.5" 43"

sprinklers, smoke alarms, emergency fixtures, signage, windows, sky-lights, significant architectural details, structural members, cabinets, closets, and doors. For example, the floor plan in Figure 11.2 is the result of drawing a plan the approximate shape of the room. The overall room dimensions were recorded along with the approximate location of windows, electrical outlets, switching arrangements, wall-mounted luminaires, cabinets, and doors. Elevations should include the vertical dimensions of the location of windows, architectural elements, lumi-naires, switches, and electrical outlets (Figure 11.3). The reflected ceiling plan illustrates the location of columns, HVAC equipment, luminaires, ceiling tiles, and any other elements located on the ceiling (Figure 11.4).

The programming phase is an excellent time to research current local, state, and federal codes and regulations. Codes and regulations must also be identified for projects involving historic buildings. In addition, the designer should survey current literature to determine the most effective lighting systems and practices, and review current information regarding a specific setting, such as an educational facility.

FIGURE 11.3
A quick sketch of an elevation of a room. For preliminary purposes, the sketch should include vertical dimensions of the location of windows, architectural elements, luminaires, switches, and electrical outlets.

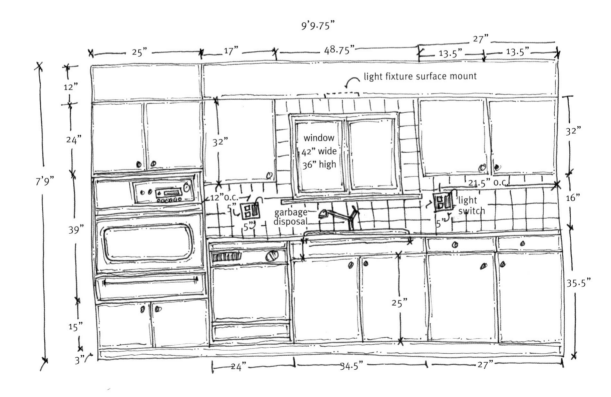

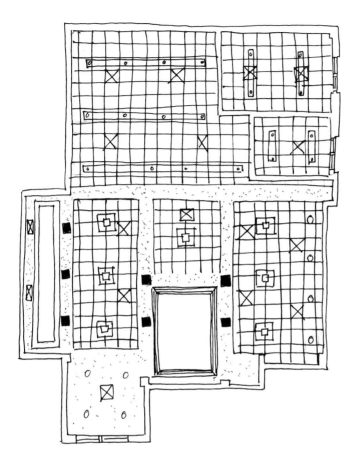

▣	= Pendant-mounted fixture
○	= Recessed fixture
⊠	= HVAC Ceiling Diffuser
■	= Column
⊡⋯⊡	= Pendant-mounted fixture

FIGURE 11.4
A quick sketch of a reflected ceiling plan of a room. For preliminary purposes, the sketch should include the location of columns, HVAC equipment, luminaires, ceiling tiles, and any other elements located on the ceiling.

To identify lighting products that use state-of-the-art technology, the designer should contact manufacturers' representatives and conduct a comprehensive review of product literature.

A thorough analysis of the data collected in the programming phase of the lighting design process provides the foundation for the project's lighting criteria. In general, lighting criteria should focus on the health, safety, and welfare of people and on protecting the environment. The needs and priorities of the client and end users and the characteristics of the environment determine specific lighting criteria. Considerations include accommodating the purpose of the space, lighting methods, structural constraints, budget, time line, and psychological and physiological factors. Lighting criteria should be developed in consultation with other team members working on the project.

Design Phases

Schematic Design

The schematic design phase consists of analyzing the results obtained during the comprehensive programming stage and then developing initial design concepts for the interior illumination. Data gathered in the programming phase include information about the client, end users, physical characteristics of the space, and applicable codes, ordinances, and regulations. For each category, a synopsis should be written that reflects information most germane to the project. The identification of salient facts requires a thorough analysis, synthesis, and evaluation of the data.

A summary of the data collected through interviews, surveys, and field observations may be produced by: (1) thorough analysis of the data by reading the content numerous times, (2) creating a detailed description of the results, (3) developing a prioritized list of lighting requirements, and (4) determining potential problems. The results of the analysis should be in written and sketch form. Responses from numerous interviews and surveys must be analyzed by identifying recurring themes or patterns. For example, in interviews of 50 people, only two might indicate the need for higher illumination in a corridor. This low response rate suggests that the existing illumination level might be appropriate and that perhaps the two people who mentioned the light in the corridor have different perceptions of brightness than most people do. Thus, new lighting for the corridor might not be included in the new lighting design. In contrast, if most of the people interviewed or surveyed identify a lighting problem in the corridor, then solutions should be developed.

The results of field observations should be a synthesis of all the visits. Multiple observations should be analyzed in the same way that responses from numerous interviews and surveys are analyzed, identifying only items that occur on a regular basis. The synopsis of people in the space should include a description of individuals, activities, unnatural movements, and modifications or adjustments to the environment that might be the result of poor lighting. A summary of how people are using the space should touch on the role of lighting in conducting activities, adherence to the principles of universal design, preferred areas, and unoccupied spaces. Many of the results related to specific locations within a building can be depicted in freehand sketches.

The various categories listed in the lighting assessment guide, including general lighting concerns, luminaires/lamps, lighting system controls, and safety/security/energy concerns, may all be summarized in written reports and sketches. These summaries are different from the results of an inventory of the lighting and interior. Inventory reports are an objective listing of the lighting elements. In contrast, the assessment process is a means of subjectively reviewing the lighting plan. Thus, the analysis focuses on problems, constraints, positive attributes, and perceptions of the lighting environment. The summary should include an analysis of the adequacy of power, complexities relating to access, and structural constraints. In addition to the written summaries, sketches can be developed using creative coding schemes that depict and reinforce the strengths and weaknesses of a lighting plan.

The results of the analysis serve as the basis for the conceptualization process of the schematic design phase. In this stage, a lighting designer and other professionals involved in the project engage in a comprehensive brainstorming process. There are a variety of brainstorming methods, and every team of professionals may have its own preferred method. Some of the most important factors in achieving effective results include allowing everyone to participate, expressing initial acceptance of all ideas, and exploring all possibilities to solve problems. In addition, the effectiveness of brainstorming depends on the articulation of a topical inquiry that is clearly understood by all members of the team. The topical inquiry is essentially the issue that will be explored during the brainstorming session. An example might be "What are the concerns involved in providing task lighting for the staff working on the third floor of the ABC building?" The inquiry needs to be concise and understood by the participants because brainstorming ideas that are irrelevant to a project can waste a great deal of time. This can be discouraging to people, and they might be reluctant to take part in future sessions.

Brainstorming sessions can be intensely creative. They should include written comments and sketches and explore all possible solutions for a lighting problem. For example, when exploring the options available for an existing lighting system, the team might consider whether the luminaires should be retrofitted, replaced, refurbished, renovated, rewired, or reconfigured. Options for improving lamps could include higher output, longer life, enhanced color, upgraded ballasts, relamping, or improved optics. Exploration of possible lighting methods might include recessed, surface-mounted, track systems, or pendants. Discussions should also focus on options that address the lighting criteria. For example, one of the lighting criteria for a project might stipulate a romantic mood for a restaurant during dinner hours. Brainstorming around this criterion could explore which lighting method, luminaire, lamp, and level of illumination would create a romantic feeling given the specific attributes of the restaurant's environment.

A variety of sketching techniques can be used in brainstorming sessions. During the sessions, it is common to review past drawings, so sketches should be saved, and a clean sheet should be used for each new concept under consideration. A preliminary drawing of a floor plan with furniture arrangements can serve as the basis for planning lighting. In brainstorming for lighting options, suggestions may arise related to improving the relationship among illumination, furniture arrangements, and architectural elements. By simultaneously considering all the elements that affect lighting, the team is likely to be able to produce a final plan for the interior that will result in a quality environment. One effective method for brainstorming lighting is to use tracing paper as an overlay for floor plans and elevations of the space. An overlay enables the team members to visualize the integration of lighting with the interior architecture, furniture, windows, doorways, and special features.

Sketches developed during brainstorming sessions should be compared to the schematics created during the analysis of the programming results. For example, Figure 11.5 demonstrates a sketch of a floor plan with a coding scheme that delineates safety, energy, glare, and shadow concerns. In this example, it would be essential to make sure that the conceptual schematics address items related to safety, energy, glare, and shadows. In addition, whenever possible, sketches should be created of anticipated changes concerning end users and the interior. A drawing of anticipated growth areas should be a separate overlay (Figure 11.6).

A series of overlays might be created to illustrate lighting changes with preset scene arrangements (Figure 11.7). Sketches of architectural details and schematics of custom-designed luminaires should also be developed during the conceptualization process (Figure 11.8).

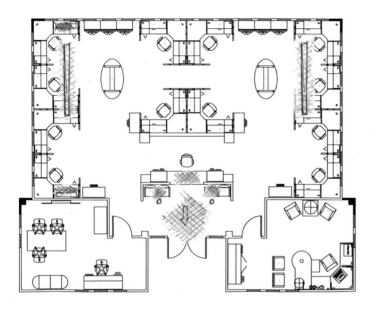

Legend
▤ = Energy
▧ = Shadow
▨ = Safety
▨ = Glare

FIGURE 11.5
An overlay sketch of a floor plan illustrating use of a coding scheme to indicate safety, energy, glare, and shadow concerns.

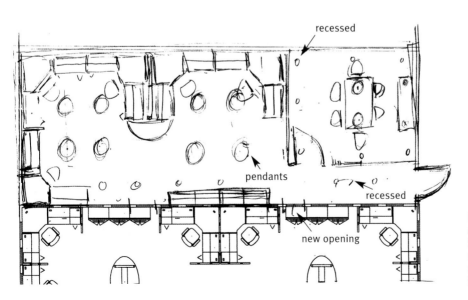

recessed

pendants

recessed

new opening

FIGURE 11.6
An overlay sketch of a floor plan illustrating anticipated growth areas and potential lighting needs.

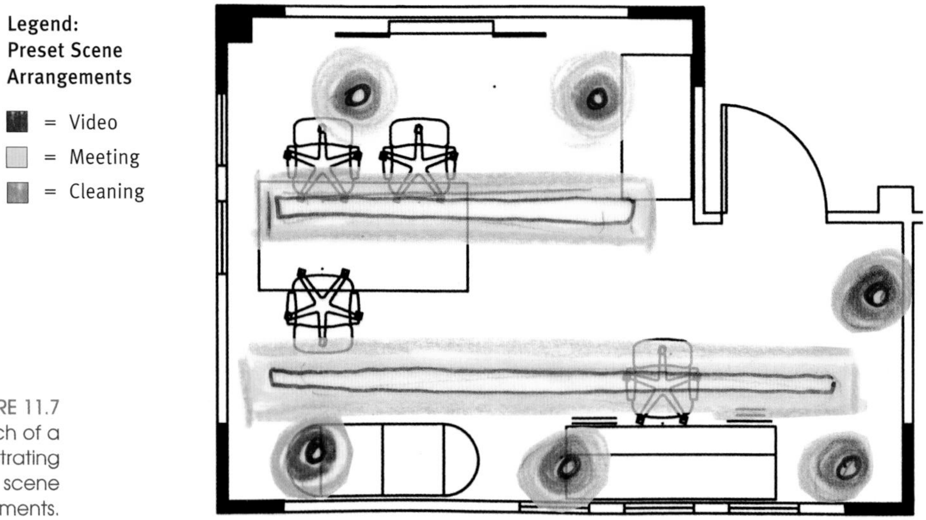

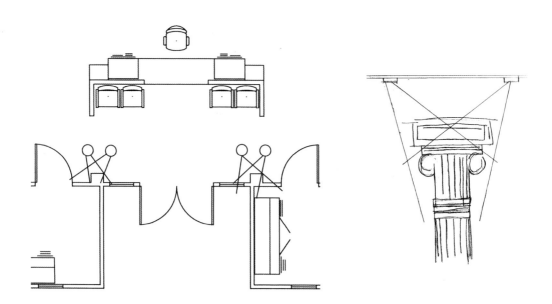

FIGURE 11.7
An overlay sketch of a
floor plan illustrating
preset lighting scene
arrangements.

FIGURE 11.8
A sketch of
architectural details
and illumination
patterns.

During the brainstorming sessions, the team must often identify several lighting plans. One good reason for developing multiple designs is to have alternatives to present to a client. The schematic design phase is the best time to make sure the client is pleased with the lighting design, because at this stage everything can easily be changed. Once a project proceeds beyond the schematic and design development phases, changes to the design can be expensive or even impossible. Alternatives presented to a client may take up a variety of themes, such as different lighting methods, styles of luminaires, price ranges, and approaches that require different time lines.

Design Development

The design development phase provides an opportunity to formulate the creative ideas. The purposes of the design development phase are to work through the details of the conceptual lighting design and produce presentation media and specifications for the client's approval. The design development phase begins after the client approves the concepts presented in the schematic design phase. The tasks involved in this phase are especially critical to the success of the project because the results are used to form the contractual agreements with the client, contractor, manufacturers, and suppliers. Therefore, it is important to think through and research all the details related to the lighting systems. In addition, a lighting designer should make sure that the client fully understands and approves the lighting design, the intended effect of the lighting on the environment, and appropriate operation and maintenance practices. Working through the details of the project requires a thorough examination of the lighting system in every room. The variables to consider include lamps, luminaires, controls, daylight integration, power sources, installation methods, and maintenance procedures. A comprehensive approach to gathering information from manufacturers, suppliers, and tradespeople involves obtaining exact costs of lighting systems, including materials and labor for fabricating structural units or custom-designed luminaires. The exact lamps required for the parameters of the selected lighting methods should be the first items specified, because the characteristics of the light source dictate the resulting lighting effects. For example, specific lamps must be selected to accommodate a project's lighting criterion that stipulates a particular beam spread or energy savings. Once the lamps are selected, luminaires and controls appropriate to these lamps can be researched and specified in turn.

Specifications and updates of the total project serve as the foundation for developing presentation media and requirements for the lighting

FIGURE 11.9
A virtual interior
developed by
the AGI32 lighting
software program.

design. The design team should determine the most appropriate presentation drawings and specifications. Common drawings include a floor plan with a lighting overlay, a reflected ceiling plan, elevations, lighting detail drawings, perspectives, and axonometric views. These drawings may be hard-line (drafted), freehand, or created using computer-aided design (CAD) or computer-aided design and drafting (CADD) technology. Lighting software programs can demonstrate virtual interiors and provide the flexibility to make quick changes to the lighting system or attributes of the interior (Figure 11.9). For example, the software allows a lighting designer to produce a virtual room of the project, with exact dimensions, architectural details, surface colors, textures, and a proposed lighting system. The software illustrates how the lighting system affects the interior within the parameters determined by the characteristics of the space. When presenting the virtual lighting design to the client, various solutions may be explored by immediately changing the type of lighting method, lamp, luminaire, point of installation, or characteristics of the interior. This tool is a tremendous help in enabling a client to visualize a lighting design. Furthermore, the ability to view multiple options in fairly quick succession assists a client in determining which design is most appropriate for the project.

Drawings must be consistent with details provided in specifications. For example, luminaires on a lighting plan must be the same dimensions as those described in the specifications. The quantity and type of luminaires must also be identical. Notes on a drawing can be helpful in explaining complex specification details of a lighting system. Working out the details of the specifications includes researching expertise that might be needed to help specify and install special lighting systems. Experts might not be available at the location of the project, making it costly to hire professionals from communities far from the site. This problem is common when specifying new technologies.

Presenting technical information to a client requires a format, such as a job or project notebook, that enables materials to be compiled in a professional manner. The job notebook may include a variety of documents, such as the concept statement, drawings, lighting specifications, manufacturers' cut sheets, sketches of custom-designed luminaires, samples of finishes, detailed budget estimates, revised consultation fees, bidding recommendations, maintenance guidelines, and projected time lines. It should be given to the client during the presentation.

Depending on the client's reactions, it may be necessary to make revisions to the lighting design. Once a client is in complete agreement with the lighting design, the contract documentation phase can begin. Upon approval by the client, a lighting designer develops recommendations for lighting specifications and submits the information to the registered professionals for review and final determination. Registered professionals, such as architects and engineers, begin the contract documentation phase by developing working drawings, specifications, sections, cut sheets, and purchase orders.

SUMMARY

- The lighting design process may be divided into the following seven phases: (1) project planning, (2) comprehensive programming,

(3) schematic design, (4) design development, (5) contract documentation, (6) contract administration, and (7) evaluation.

- The primary purposes of planning are to identify a profile of the project and to determine the resources required to achieve its objectives.
- In consultation with the client, the project's team members should develop a comprehensive plan that includes the list of activities, responsible individuals, time line, required resources, estimated costs, and billing dates.
- The comprehensive programming phase involves collecting data regarding the end users, physical characteristics of the space, and applicable codes, ordinances, and regulations.
- Effective methods for obtaining information about end users and the interior include interviews, surveys, and field observations.
- Interview and survey questions should always ask about the present situation as well as anticipated future needs.
- The primary purpose of field observations is to watch how people behave in a specific lighting environment.
- Comprehensive programming involves visiting the site and creating an inventory of luminaires, lamps, controls, electrical outlets, daylight integration, architectural features, room configurations, furniture, colors, and material finishes.
- Sketches should be developed of the floor plan, wall elevations, and reflected ceiling plan.
- The programming phase is an excellent time to research current local, state, and federal codes and regulations.
- Data collected in the programming phase of the lighting design process provide the foundation for the project's lighting criteria.
- The schematic design phase consists of analyzing the results obtained during the comprehensive programming stage and then developing initial design concepts for the interior illumination.
- A summary of the data collected through interviews, surveys, and field observations may be produced in the following ways: (1) thorough analysis of the data by reading the content numerous times, (2) creating a detailed description of the results, (3) developing a

prioritized list of lighting requirements, and (4) determining potential problems.

- The results of the analysis serve as the basis for the conceptualization process of the schematic design phase. In this stage, a lighting designer and other professionals involved in the project engage in a comprehensive brainstorming process.
- Brainstorming sessions should include written comments and sketches, and they should explore all possible options for a lighting solution.
- At the conclusion of the schematic design phase, materials presented to the client may include a concept statement, freehand sketches, photographs of luminaires, a list of lighting equipment, preliminary costs, and projected time lines.
- The purposes of the design development phase are to work through the details of the conceptual lighting design and produce presentation media and specifications for the client's approval.
- Presenting technical information to a client requires a format, such as a job or project notebook, that makes it possible for materials to be compiled in a professional manner.

Exercises

1. Identify three different public spaces. Use Table 11.3 as a model for creating an observation guide for each site. Visit each site as often as needed so that you will be able to present generalizations of how lighting affects behavior in the space. In a written report, include the following information: (a) a summary of the observations and the lighting system, (b) a summary of the strengths and weaknesses of the lighting in each space, (c) recommendations for improving the lighting environment, and (d) a list of questions that would be useful to ask the end users of the space.
2. Visit three buildings and conduct field observations. For each site, record how people are affected by the lighting design. Analyze and synthesize the observations. Make recommendations for improving

the space. Summarize your results in a written report and include illustrations, photographs, or sketches.

3. Select five photographs of public interiors. For each space, identify the purpose of the space and provide a description of the lighting systems. Identify the information that should be gathered for detailed analysis of the space. Summarize your results in a written report and include the photographs.

CHAPTER 12

Lighting Design Process:
Contract Documents Through Postoccupancy Evaluation

- Identify working drawings used to illustrate a lighting design.
- Describe details that should be included in lighting working drawings and specifications.
- Describe contracts that are frequently used for a lighting design.
- Identify the tasks associated with contract administration of a lighting project.
- Understand the purpose of the postoccupancy evaluation and how to apply the process to a lighting design.

The final phases of the lighting design process include the development of contract documents, contract administration, and evaluation. These phases are very exciting, because the project becomes a reality, but they can also be stressful. The lighting designer executes legally binding contracts with various businesses involved with the project, including the client, suppliers, contractors, and tradespeople. Changes to the original specifications can be costly and create delays, and a variety of problems and conflicts may occur during construction and installation. Since these stages do not involve creative processes, frequently a lighting designer is not as enthusiastic about fulfilling these responsibilities. Nevertheless, the final phases are absolutely critical to the success of a lighting design, and since these are the last experiences a client remembers, it is essential to conclude with a positive impression. Therefore, sufficient time must be allocated to developing accurate documents, consistent communication, careful supervision, and effective problem-solving.

In studying the content of this chapter, it is important to understand the material in terms of its generic application in the context of lighting. Specific architectural, engineering, and interior design firms develop a preferred format for drawings, specifications, and contracts. Standardized requirements are reviewed by an attorney and then serve as a template for developing contract documents. Moreover, each firm may have staff members who are responsible for developing particular documents, such as specifications or purchase orders. The information presented in this chapter is therefore intended to be a guide to the procedures and contractual requirements of engaging in the final phases of the lighting design process.

Contract Documents

Contractual documents include working drawings and written specifications. Working or construction drawings are a graphic representation of a lighting system and serve to supplement the specifications, which consist of a written description of the parameters of the lighting system. Together, working drawings and written specifications are the basis for ordering products, installing wiring, and determining the location of luminaires, outlets, and controls. In contrast to presentation illustrations, which are produced in the design development phase, working drawings represent a legal contract. Therefore, they must be accurately scaled, contain detailed illustrations, and demonstrate that the plans comply with local codes. Working drawings for a lighting design are developed in coordination with mechanical, plumbing, and structural systems. Laws mandate that registered professionals, such as architects and engineers, stamp working drawings and specifications to certify that they meet the necessary standards. Therefore, the drawings developed by a lighting designer must be submitted to registered professionals for review and further development. To ensure retention of the original intent of the lighting design, a lighting designer should ask to review the working drawings prior to their being submitted to the local building department, contract closures, financial institutions, or a bidding process.

Commonly used working drawings consist of a plan of the lighting, electrical, lighting/electrical, and reflected ceiling. Drawings may also include elevations, sections, and details. Lighting schedules and general notes located on drawing sheets provide additional information regarding the lighting system. The production format, including dimensions, should be coordinated with other professionals working on the project. Drawings may be printed on sheets or presented in a job notebook. Lighting plans generated by CAD software are typically developed in layers, enabling the designer to examine the relationships between lighting and other elements of a project. For example, a lighting plan can be viewed in conjunction with the HVAC system to make sure components do not overlap. An assessment of the electrical plan together with furniture arrangements can help to ensure access to power for portable luminaires. Any cross-referencing of details on working drawings must also form part of the written specifications.

Symbol legends located on working drawings are essential for describing the type of luminaires, wiring configurations, switching systems, and outlets included in the design. Symbols and abbreviations are used to communicate complex details. To promote standardization throughout the building industry, a task force of the American Institute of Architects (AIA) developed a set of universal symbols and abbreviations for architectural working drawings. Many of these symbols and conventions, such as door swings and mechanical systems, are also used on working drawings for a lighting design. In addition, there are specific symbols for electrical plans, including convenience outlets, switch outlets, auxiliary units, general outlets, and switching arrangements (Figure 12.1).

Complex structures require separate lighting and electrical plans. Drawings for residential and small commercial buildings, on the other hand, often have only one plan that illustrates both lighting and electrical requirements. As illustrated in Figure 12.2, a lighting plan includes the location of luminaires, switches, and control loops. The luminaire should be scaled and represent a close approximation to the shape of the fixture. Complicated drawings might not have enough

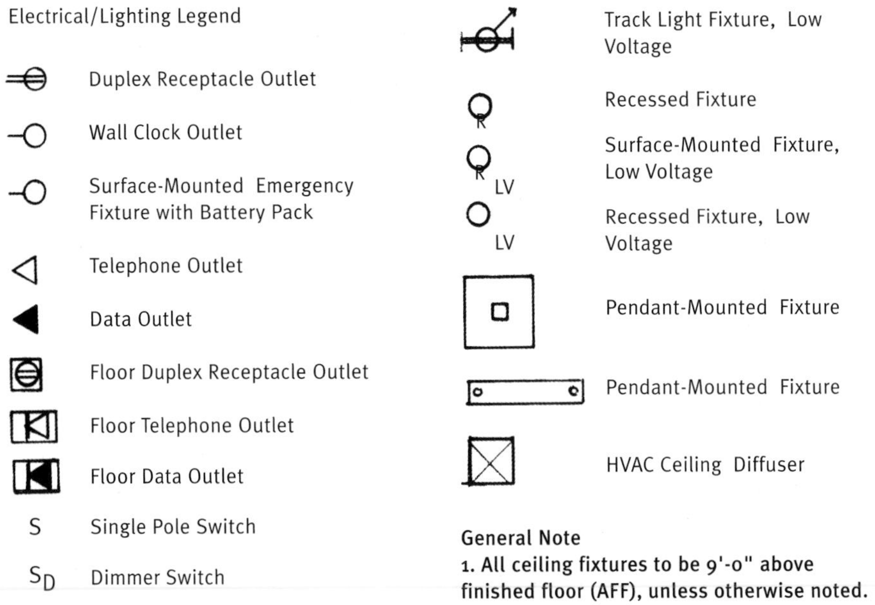

FIGURE 12.1
Symbols used in
electrical plans,
including symbols for
convenience outlets,
switch outlets, auxiliary
units, general outlets,
and switching
arrangements.

Electrical/Lighting Legend

⊖ Duplex Receptacle Outlet

◯ Wall Clock Outlet

◯ Surface-Mounted Emergency
Fixture with Battery Pack

◁ Telephone Outlet

◀ Data Outlet

⊖ Floor Duplex Receptacle Outlet

Ⓚ Floor Telephone Outlet

Ⓚ Floor Data Outlet

S Single Pole Switch

S$_D$ Dimmer Switch

Track Light Fixture, Low Voltage

Q$_R$ Recessed Fixture

Q$_R$ LV Surface-Mounted Fixture, Low Voltage

◯ LV Recessed Fixture, Low Voltage

▢ Pendant-Mounted Fixture

Pendant-Mounted Fixture

⊠ HVAC Ceiling Diffuser

General Note
1. All ceiling fixtures to be 9'-0" above finished floor (AFF), unless otherwise noted.

space to show scaled luminaires. In these situations, letters and subscripts may be used to identify specific luminaires, with either a circle or a hexagon surrounding the letters. The symbol and a brief description of the luminaire are then listed in the legends.

Dimension lines and notes may be used to identify the exact size and location of luminaires. Measurements are from the center (o.c.) of a luminaire to a fixed architectural element, such as the face of an exterior wall, window mullions, or the center of a partition. Spacing between multiple luminaires located in the same room is indicated by measurements from an architectural element to the center of each fixture. A plan may also include mounting heights of fixtures that are located on vertical planes or suspended from the ceiling. The mounting height of luminaires located on a vertical plane, such as a wall or column, is from AFF to the center of the fixture (o.c.). The distance for suspended fixtures is from AFF to the bottom of the luminaire.

Switching arrangements are illustrated by the applicable switch symbol and control loops. As demonstrated in Figure 12.2, control loops are drawn from the switch(es) to the luminaire that is controlled by the switch(es). Control loops on a lighting plan are curved, while straight lines are used to represent wiring runs on an electrical plan.

Whenever possible, furniture arrangements should be included in a lighting plan. Drawing techniques for this purpose include overlays, layers, or the simple addition of furniture to the plan. Combining the placement of furniture with the lighting plan can be very helpful in ensuring that the luminaire is accurately positioned for a specific task or that it fulfills the intended purpose. Specifying the exact location of a luminaire must take into consideration differences in furniture dimensions, the number of items in a room, and how a space is arranged. For example, to ensure that a chandelier will be centered over a dining table, it is best to position all the furniture on the plan and then determine the location of the luminaire. The dimensions and placement of furniture also affect the location of luminaires intended for unique purposes, such as highlighting artwork.

Electrical plans can be extremely complicated and technical. As with all working drawings, registered professionals must officially approve the documents. Generally, a lighting designer will be asked to describe only the lighting design, after which engineers determine power

Electrical/Lighting Legend

⊖	Duplex Receptacle Outlet
─○	Wall Clock Outlet
─○	Surface-Mounted Emergency Fixture with Battery Pack
◁	Telephone Outlet
◀	Data Outlet
⊖	Floor Duplex Receptacle Outlet
◰	Floor Telephone Outlet
◰	Floor Data Outlet
S	Single Pole Switch
S_D	Dimmer Switch
⚡	Track Light Fixture, Low Voltage
ℝ	Recessed Fixture
ℝ LV	Surface-Mounted Fixture, Low Voltage
○ LV	Recessed Fixture, Low Voltage
▫	Pendant-Mounted Fixture
▭	Pendant-Mounted Fixture
⊠	HVAC Ceiling Diffuser

General Note
1. All ceiling fixtures to be 9'-0" above finished floor (AFF), unless otherwise noted.

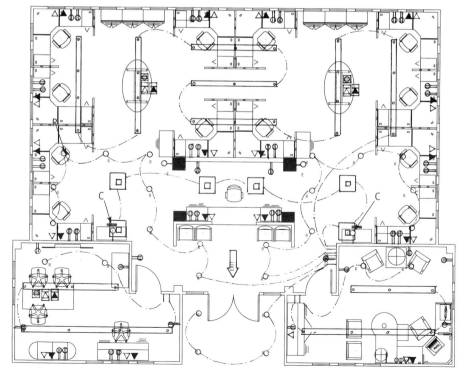

FIGURE 12.2
A lighting plan that indicates the location of luminaires, switches, control loops, dimension lines, and notes.

Duplex Receptacle Outlet

Wall Clock Outlet

Surface-Mounted Emergency Fixture with Battery Pack

Telephone Outlet

Data Outlet

Floor Duplex Receptacle Outlet

Floor Telephone Outlet

Floor Data Outlet

S — Single Pole Switch

S$_D$ — Dimmer Switch

Track Light Fixture, Low Voltage

® — Recessed Fixture

® LV — Surface-Mounted Fixture, Low Voltage

O LV — Recessed Fixture, Low Voltage

Pendant-Mounted Fixture

Pendant-Mounted Fixture

HVAC Ceiling Diffuser

General Note
1. All ceiling fixtures to be 9'-0" above finished floor (AFF), unless otherwise noted.

requirements. Detailed electrical plans illustrate the wiring runs from electrical panels to all equipment in a building, including lighting systems. Elements related to lighting systems in an electrical plan include luminaires, switches, outlets, junction boxes, and auxiliary units (Figure 12.3). As mentioned, small commercial buildings and residences often have a single plan (a lighting/electrical plan) that combines electrical and lighting specifications. Such a plan includes the location of luminaires, switches, outlets, auxiliary units, junction boxes, and control loops (Figure 12.4).

In addition to recommending lighting systems, a lighting designer should provide suggestions for the location of switches and outlets. The location of these elements can significantly affect how well people function in a space. As discussed in Chapter 8, switches and outlets should be located in a position that reflects the principles of universal design and coincides with how people function in a space. Switches should be located on the lock side of a door and at various other convenient locations within a room or space. Outlets should be convenient

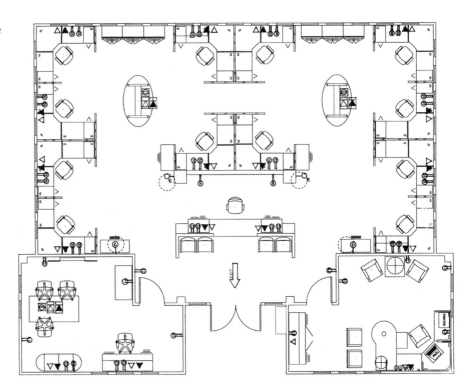

FIGURE 12.3
An electrical plan including outlets, junction boxes, auxiliary units, furniture, and telephone/data outlets.

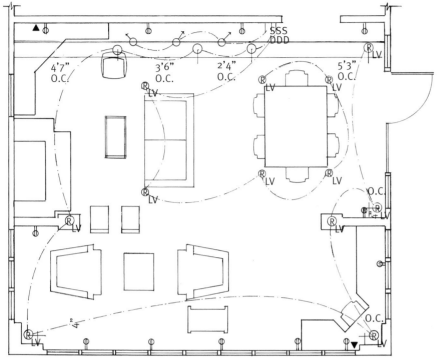

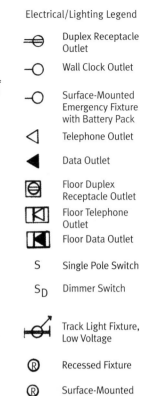

Electrical/Lighting Legend

⊕	Duplex Receptacle Outlet
⊖	Wall Clock Outlet
⊖	Surface-Mounted Emergency Fixture with Battery Pack
◁	Telephone Outlet
◀	Data Outlet
⊖	Floor Duplex Receptacle Outlet
⬚	Floor Telephone Outlet
⬚	Floor Data Outlet
S	Single Pole Switch
S$_D$	Dimmer Switch
⤢	Track Light Fixture, Low Voltage
ⓇR	Recessed Fixture
ⓇR LV	Surface-Mounted Fixture, Low Voltage
○ LV	Recessed Fixture, Low Voltage
□	Pendant-Mounted Fixture
▭	Pendant-Mounted Fixture
⊠	HVAC Ceiling Diffuser

to reach from a variety of positions. Since outlets are inexpensive to install during the construction phase, their number should be determined by power needs, not a standardized layout. Sufficient outlets should be installed to provide electricity to all portable luminaires without the need for extension cords, outlet adapters, or running the fixture's cord over a long distance.

The location of outlets should also be dependent upon the configuration of vertical planes and furniture arrangements. For example, the location of outlets should be coordinated with a fireplace, built-in cabinets, or artwork. Generally, outlets should not be centered on a wall, because electrical cords connected to the outlet may become a focal point. In addition, reaching an outlet can be very difficult when a large piece of furniture, such as a breakfront in a dining room, is placed in front of the outlet. The location of outlets should therefore take furniture arrangements into account. This can be especially challenging in rooms whose furniture is positioned away from the walls. A frequent solution to this problem is the use of floor outlets. On an electrical

FIGURE 12.4
A lighting/electrical plan indicating the location of luminaires, switches, outlets, control loops, and furniture.

plan, dimension lines extending from the outlet to fixed architectural elements indicate the location of floor outlets.

Since outlets and switches are elements of the interior, they should also harmonize with the style, colors, and furnishings of the environment. Specifications for switches and outlets should include recommendations for products that enhance the design concept.

A **reflected ceiling plan** is frequently included in working drawings. This plan is the image that one would see when looking in a mirror located on the floor; it illustrates the design of the ceiling, including the location of luminaires, architectural elements, and any HVAC equipment. A reflected ceiling plan is helpful for analyzing the functional and aesthetic components of the horizontal plane. Functionally, the plan is useful in determining whether the location of luminaires accommodates activities in the room and does not interfere with other structural elements on the ceiling plane. Aesthetically, the appearance of the ceiling affects the design of the interior space, especially in rooms with tall ceilings. In addition, a reflected ceiling plan helps the interior designer visualize how well the arrangement addresses the elements and principles of design.

A working drawing of a reflected ceiling plan includes the location of luminaires, switches, control loops, ceiling tiles, and any other element that intersects with the ceiling (Figure 12.5). These elements can include partitions, heating air ducts, diffusers, exposed beams, columns, speakers, skylights, cornices, coves, soffits, sprinkler heads, emergency lights, and signage. Ceiling materials and changes in ceiling heights should also be noted on the plan. Some plans include specific luminaire details such as lamp-aiming directions. The location of luminaires should be dimensioned following the same method used in a lighting plan. However, when a luminaire is located in the center of a ceiling tile, dimension lines do not have to be drawn. The arrangement of ceiling tiles should enhance the shape and size of the ceiling. When necessary, partial tiles are located along the perimeter of the room.

Elevation measurements provide a view of the arrangement of luminaires and other elements that can affect the visual composition of a wall, including furniture, objects, windows, or architectural features (Figure 12.6). Elevations are especially effective in demonstrating the location of wall-mounted luminaires, valances, coves, or soffits.

Working drawings of integrated lighting systems, such as bookcases, soffits, or kitchen cabinets, require detailed illustrations. Detailed working drawings must communicate precise information to a fabricator and an installer. As scaled drawings, details indicate the exact size and location of all elements contained in an integrated system, including lamps, lamp holders, ballasts, transformers, structural elements, return air slots, baffles, reflectors, glass, access grilles, cables, brackets, wiring, projectors, and mechanical support (Figure 12.7). Notes on detail drawings may include dimensions, material specifications, finishes, paint colors, and construction methods.

Supplementary to working drawings are written lighting specifications, which are important contract documents as well. Generally, information provided in specifications will override cross-referenced details illustrated in working drawings. Therefore, specifications must be accurate, comprehensive, and written in a clear and concise manner. Lighting specifications can be included in the furniture, furnishings,

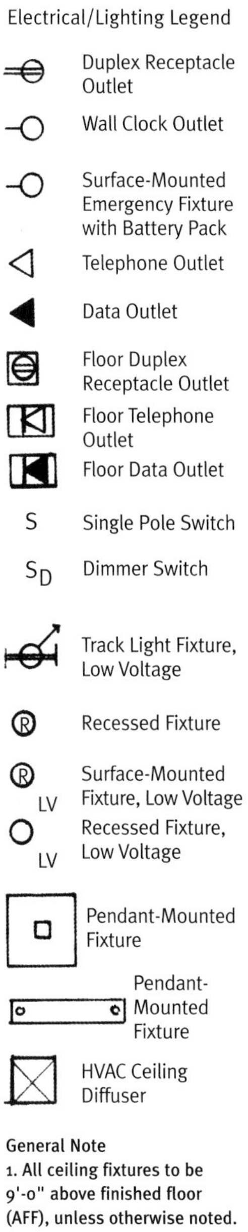

Electrical/Lighting Legend

⊖	Duplex Receptacle Outlet
⊸O	Wall Clock Outlet
⊸O	Surface-Mounted Emergency Fixture with Battery Pack
◁	Telephone Outlet
◀	Data Outlet
⊖	Floor Duplex Receptacle Outlet
◁	Floor Telephone Outlet
◀	Floor Data Outlet
S	Single Pole Switch
S_D	Dimmer Switch
⤙	Track Light Fixture, Low Voltage
Ⓡ	Recessed Fixture
Ⓡ LV	Surface-Mounted Fixture, Low Voltage
O LV	Recessed Fixture, Low Voltage
▢	Pendant-Mounted Fixture
▭	Pendant-Mounted Fixture
⊠	HVAC Ceiling Diffuser

General Note
1. All ceiling fixtures to be 9'-0" above finished floor (AFF), unless otherwise noted.

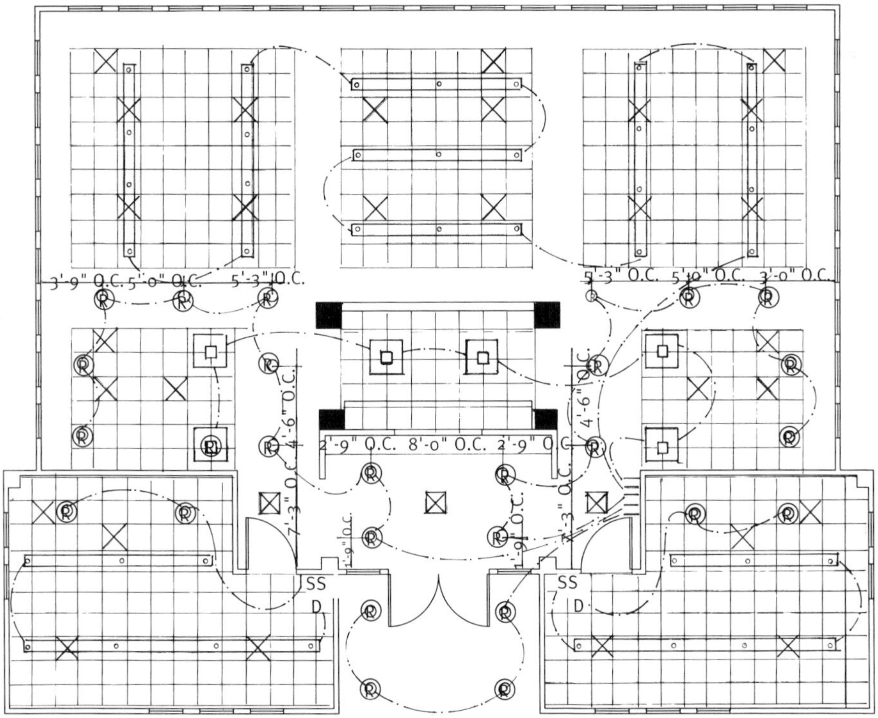

FIGURE 12.5
A reflected ceiling plan, including the location of luminaires, switches, control loops, ceiling tiles, and other elements intersecting with the ceiling.

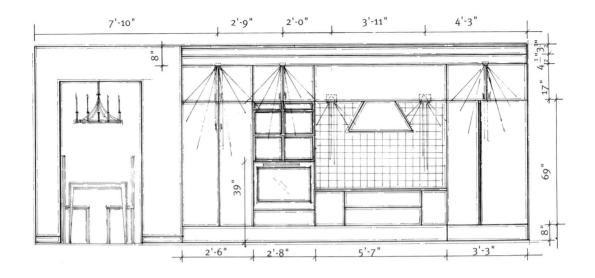

FIGURE 12.6
An elevation of a wall that indicates the arrangement of luminaires and other elements that can affect the visual composition of a wall.

and equipment (FF&E) document. To assist in the development of accurate specification of details, the International Association of Lighting Designers (IALD) published a manual entitled *Guidelines for Specification Integrity* (2002). Topics include: (1) building a foundation for specifying; (2) processes in the design; construction document, bidding, and construction phases; and (3) specification approaches and languages (IALD, 2002). These guidelines should serve as a resource in writing lighting specifications.

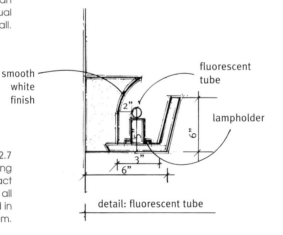

detail: fluorescent tube

FIGURE 12.7
A scaled detail drawing indicating the exact size and location of all elements contained in an integrated system.

Contract Administration

Contracts are used to initiate the construction phase of a project. A lighting designer prepares contracts with various individuals and businesses, including clients, manufacturers, suppliers, fabricators, vendors, independent contractors, and craftspeople. Contracts may be customized, or preprinted documents may be provided by various professional organizations. Any contract used by a lighting designer should be reviewed and approved by an attorney. A letter of agreement is frequently used as a contract between a lighting designer and another party when the designer is bidding on a project, requesting services, or purchasing products. Letters of agreement may also specify design fees, unit pricing, delivery charges, shipping instructions, time lines, and any other terms or applicable conditions.

A lighting designer may be involved in several activities associated with the construction phase, including reviewing documents, purchasing products, project management, monitoring costs, and site supervision. The construction phase is a critical stage of the lighting design process, because the work performed affects the quality and integrity of the design. Therefore, it is important for a lighting designer to be actively involved during this stage. The results of construction should reflect the design concept, working drawings, and specifications. Generally, monitoring a construction project requires a focus on service and management. Dedicating quality time to construction administration demonstrates to a client the designer's high level of professionalism and commitment. These positive impressions in turn foster loyalty on the part of clients.

Upon satisfactory completion of the lighting system, a lighting designer may assist with scheduling the move-in and on-site supervision. Being present during the move-in can be very valuable in making sure furniture, artwork, and other objects are positioned correctly for specific tasks or a desired lighting effect. Once move-in is complete, a variety of documents should be given to the client, including product warranties, operational recommendations, maintenance manuals, and recommendations for changes in the future. Operational recommendations should include any information relevant to using a lighting system, such as programming controls, adjusting luminaires to accommodate different users, maximum wattages, and instructions for aiming and focusing. The maintenance manual should include relamping recommendations, replacement instructions, and materials and methods for cleaning lenses, finishes, and lamps. Many of the instructions provided in the maintenance manual should be directly from manufacturers' product documentation. It is advisable to create a system for labeling the lamp(s) that correspond to specific fixtures so that the wrong lamp is not installed in a luminaire during relamping. Recommendations for future changes should include suggestions for modifying a lighting system to accommodate changes in tasks or in the interior environment, such as modifications to partitions, an increase in the number of employees, or changes in a display in a retail environment.

Postoccupancy Evaluation

The purposes of postoccupancy evaluation (POE) are to assess the effectiveness of the lighting design, make modifications whenever possible, and acquire information that may be used to improve future projects. Evaluations should be conducted at various intervals after move-in. A good approach is to visit the site within the first three months after move-in, then six months later, and then at least one year later. A follow-up after two years demonstrates a commitment to the integrity of the design and can lead to new work, because discussions will frequently revolve around the possibility of upgrades or new lighting systems. Visits after move-in are also a good opportunity to make sure new end users are acquainted with the proper operation of the lighting system and luminaires are accurately adjusted.

The primary focus of the evaluation should be to determine how well the lighting design achieves the goals of the project. A useful starting point is to re-examine data collected during the programming phase of the lighting design process. Questions used in surveys and interviews can serve as the foundation for determining the level of satisfaction with the lighting design. POE may consist of informal discussions with the client and end users, or it can be a formalized process involving considerable analysis of the data. Field observations may also be helpful in evaluating how well people interact with the lighting system. Many factors will determine the appropriate method, including the number of end users, the complexity of the project, and the uniqueness of the lighting design.

In determining the appropriate methodology, input should be derived from the client and other professionals involved with the project.

A client can provide valuable insight into what evaluation methods are appropriate for the end users and the working conditions of the environment. Where the lighting design is one component of an entire project, another professional, such as the architect or a contractor, could initiate POE. To determine the level of satisfaction with an entire project, a survey often uses general questions, such as "How satisfied are you with the quality of lighting?" A response to this question will provide information regarding the level of overall satisfaction, but it does not reveal which elements of the lighting design are the most satisfactory or whether there are any illumination problems. Whenever possible, items on a survey or an interview guide should be written in a manner that elicits specific information and details regarding various parts or aspects of the lighting design. The lighting design process is cyclical in the sense that the results obtained during the POE phase will inform subsequent projects. Combining this information with technological advances in lighting systems is invaluable to the success of designing a quality lighting environment in the future.

SUMMARY

- Working or construction drawings are a graphic representation of a lighting system. Together with written specifications, they are used to order products, install wiring, and determine the location of luminaires, outlets, and controls.
- Commonly used working drawings include a plan view of the lighting, electrical, lighting/electrical, and reflected ceiling. Drawings may also include elevations, sections, and details. Lighting schedules and general notes located on drawing sheets provide additional information regarding the lighting system.
- A lighting plan indicates the location of luminaires, switches, and control loops.
- A reflected ceiling plan includes the location of luminaires, architectural elements, and any HVAC equipment, seen as they would appear in a mirror on the floor.

- As a supplement to working drawings, lighting specifications are extremely important contract documents.
- Contracts are used to initiate the construction phase of a project. A lighting designer prepares contracts with various individuals and businesses, including clients, manufacturers, suppliers, fabricators, vendors, independent contractors, and craftspeople.
- Site supervision during construction and installations must be conducted in accordance with local laws and regulations.
- The purposes of a postoccupancy evaluation (POE) are to assess the effectiveness of the lighting design, to conduct modifications whenever possible, and to acquire information that can be used to improve future projects.

Key Term

reflected ceiling plan

Exercises

1. Review a set of working drawings and specifications prepared by an architectural firm. Analyze the lighting and electrical specifications. In a written report, address the following items: (a) a lighting inventory, (b) an electrical inventory, and (c) symbols and descriptions provided in the legends.
2. Identify a floor plan for a residential or commercial building. Develop a set of lighting working drawings for the structure, including a plan view of the lighting, electrical, and reflected ceiling. Follow IESNA (2000) guidelines for the lighting symbols.
3. Identify a commercial client and the end users of the space and develop a list of interview and survey questions for the purpose of conducting a POE. Questions should be specific to the end users of the space. In a written report, include the following information:

(a) a list of the questions, (b) an outline of the plan for interviewing and surveying the end users, (c) the rationale for different questions, (d) the rationale for who will be interviewed and surveyed, and (e) how the results will be used for future projects.

Glossary

A

accent lighting Illumination designed to highlight an object or area in a space.

accommodation A function of the eye that enables one to see objects at varying distances.

adaptation A function of the eye that adjusts to the amount of brightness entering the pupil.

angle of incidence The angle at which rays of light emitted from a light source strike an object or surface before reflection.

aperture An opening in a wall or ceiling, such as a window or skylight.

B

backlighting Illumination that is directly behind an object. Also referred to as silhouetting.

baffle A linear or round unit in a luminaire designed to shield light from view.

ballast A control device used with an electric-discharge lamp to start the lamp and control the electrical current during operation.

brightness An effect from a light source at a high illuminance level that can be perceived as either positive or distracting.

C

candela (cd) The SI unit of measurement of luminous intensity. One candela represents the luminous intensity from a source focused in a specific direction on a solid angle called the steradian.

candlepower The intensity of a light source, measured in candelas.

candlepower distribution curve A graph that illustrates the direction, pattern, and intensity of light emitted from a luminaire.

central control system An electronic system that uses a microprocessor to monitor, adjust, and regulate lighting in many areas or zones within a building, often in integration with other systems.

chromaticity The degree of warmness or coolness of a light source, measured in kelvins (K). Also referred to as color temperature.

circadian rhythm A biological function that coordinates sleeping and waking times through hormones and metabolic processes.

coefficient of utilization (CU) The ratio of initial lamp lumens to the lumens on a work surface.

color-rendering index (CRI) Measurement of how faithfully a light source reveals the colors of objects. The index range is from 0 to 100. The higher the CRI number, the better the color-rendering ability of the source.

color temperature The degree of warmness or coolness of a light source, measured in kelvins (K). Also referred to as chromaticity.

compact fluorescent lamp (CFL) A lamp made with one or more small, folded fluorescent tubes and equipped with a screw base. The ballast is a separate control gear or is built into the unit as an integral part of the system.

cornice lighting Illumination technique mounted on a wall or above a window, directing the light down.

correlated color temperature (CCT) A color temperature in kelvins determined by the x and y location on a color diagram (developed by the International Commission on Illumination).

cove lighting Illumination technique mounted on a wall or ceiling, directing the light up toward the ceiling.

cross-lighting Light directed from the right and left of a task or object.

D

daylight (skylight) Desirable natural light in a space.

decorative lighting Luminaires that provide illumination and are also artistic pieces.

diffused light Distribution of light in all directions.

diffused reflectance The phenomenon that occurs when a material with a matte finish causes light to scatter in a variety of directions.

diffuser Cover on a luminaire that scatters light in many directions, made from white plastic or etched glass.

dimmer Electrical device designed to decrease light output by reducing power to a lamp.

direct glare A distracting high-illuminance level, frequently caused by

viewing a bare light source or by extreme contrast in illumination levels.

direct light Distribution of light when at least 90 percent of the illumination is downward.

disability glare A distracting high-illuminance level that makes it impossible or difficult to see.

discomfort glare A distracting high-illuminance level that is uncomfortable but still allows one to see.

E

efficacy A rating based upon the lumens per watt consumed, reflecting the energy efficiency of a lamp.

electric-discharge lamp Electrical light source that produces illumination without filaments and operates on low or high pressure. An electric current passes through a vapor or gas.

electroluminescent lamp Electrical light source that operates through an interaction between an electrical field and a phosphor.

end-emitting fiber optic lighting system Light is visible at the end of the cylindrical optical fibers.

eye's field of vision The central and peripheral areas that are visible to the eye.

F

fiber optic lighting An electrical light source that utilizes a remote source for illumination. Light is transmitted from the source through a bundle of optical fibers.

flame-shaped lamp Small, decorative lamp in the shape of a flame. The bulb is clear or frosted glass.

flood (FL) A wide beam spread.

fluorescent lamp An electric-discharge

light source that generally uses electrodes, phosphors, low-pressure mercury, and other gases for illumination.

foot-candle Unit measuring the amount of light that falls on a surface within a one-foot radius of the source.

furniture-integrated luminaire Fixture mounted in a cabinet and generally hidden from view. The most common furniture pieces with integrated lighting are office systems, curio cabinets, breakfronts, and bookcases.

G

general lighting/ambient lighting Overall illumination in a space, including lighting that allows people to walk safely through a room and that sets the mood or character of the interior.

glare A distracting high-illuminance level that can cause discomfort or be disabling.

grazing A lighting technique that places the light source close to a surface or object to highlight interesting textures and produce dramatic shadows.

H

halogen regenerative cycle The operational process in which evaporated tungsten is redeposited on a halogen lamp's filament.

harvesting daylight Capturing daylight for the purpose of illuminating an interior.

HID high-bay Cone-shaped surface-mount fixture designed to accommodate the shape of HID light sources.

high hat Recessed ceiling-mounted luminaire, also referred to as a downlight.

high-intensity discharge (HID) lamp Electric-discharge lamp with a light-producing arc stabilized by bulb temperature, including mercury, metal halide, and high-pressure sodium.

high-pressure sodium (HPS) lamp A high-intensity discharge lamp that uses sodium vapor for illumination.

I

illuminance The total amount of light falling on a surface, measured in lux (lx) or foot-candle (fc).

illuminator The box that contains the light source for a fiber optic lighting system. The fiber optics originate from the illuminator.

incandescent carbon-filament lamp A light source that uses an electrical current to heat the conductive material until incandescence is produced.

indirect glare A distracting high-illuminance level caused by reflection of a light source off a surface or object.

indirect light Distribution of light when at least 90 percent of the illumination is directed toward the ceiling.

indirect natural light Illumination reflected from clouds, the moon, and stars.

interreflection Result of light bouncing back and forth within an enclosed space or structure.

L

lamp Commonly referred to as a light bulb, a lamp is a source that produces optical radiation.

lamp life The operational time of a lamp expressed in hours.

lamp lumen depreciation (LLD) A measure of the loss of lumens resulting from the design of a lamp.

layered lighting An illumination plan that includes natural light and multiple electrical light sources.

light A form of energy that is part of the electromagnetic spectrum.

light-emitting diode (LED) Semiconductor device consisting of a chemical chip embedded in a plastic capsule. The light is focused or scattered by lenses or diffusers.

light loss factor (LLF) The amount of illuminance lost because of the type of lamp, ambient temperature of the space, time, input voltage, ballast, lamp position, interior conditions, or burnouts.

light output The amount of illumination produced by a lamp, measured in lumens.

localized lighting A lighting technique that allows a user to position light sources where they are needed and at the appropriate illumination level.

louver A grid-shaped unit of a luminaire designed to shield light from view.

lumen (lm) A unit of measurement of the light output of a lamp.

lumens per watt (lpW) A rating that describes the amount of electricity consumed for a given amount of illumination.

luminaire An element of a lighting system that includes a light source, housing elements, ballasts, transformers, controls, a mounting mechanism, and a connection to electrical power.

luminaire dirt depreciation (LDD) A measure of the loss of light that results from dirt and dust accumulation.

luminaire efficacy ratio (LER) A ratio expressing the lumens per watts consumed for the entire luminaire system.

luminous ceiling Ceiling whose lighting consists of rows of lamps behind diffused lenses.

luminous exitance The total quantity of light reflected and emitted in all directions from a surface or material.

luminous flux The total amount of illumination emitted by a light source; measured in lumens (lm).

luminous intensity The intensity of light from a source pointing in a specific direction on a solid angle called the steradian.

lux (lx) The International System of Units (SI) unit of illuminance.

M

mercury lamp A high-intensity discharge lamp that uses radiation from mercury vapor for illumination.

metal halide (MH) lamp A high-intensity discharge lamp that utilizes chemical compounds of metal halides and possibly metallic vapors such as mercury.

modeling Emphasizing the three dimensions of a piece or surface through light, shade, and shadows.

N

nadir Zero on a polar candlepower distribution curve.

natural light Illumination from the sun and the stars.

O

occupancy sensor Device designed to turn lights on or off depending on whether people are present in a room.

P

PBT (persistent, bioaccumulative, toxic) A classification indicating that a substance is toxic, remains in water or land indefinitely, and accrues in the world's ecosystems.

photobiology The science that examines the interaction of light and living organisms.

photometry A scientific discipline dealing with the measurement of light, including the effects of vision.

photosensor Device that detects the amount of illumination in a space, and then sends signals to control electrical light sources.

polychlorinated biphenyls (PCBs) A toxic substance used in ballasts produced prior to 1978.

presbyopia A decrease in the eye's ability to change the shape of the lens, affecting an individual's ability to focus on near or distant objects.

Q

quality lighting A layered illumination plan that reduces energy costs, conserves natural resources, and allows users of the space to function comfortably, feel safe, and appreciate the aesthetic components of the environment.

R

radiometry A scientific discipline dealing with the measurement of radiant energy in the form of electromagnetic waves.

recessed downlight Recessed ceiling-mounted luminaire, also referred to as a high hat or high-hat luminaire.

recessed luminaire Fixture installed above a Sheetrock or suspended-grid ceiling.

recessed spot Luminaire mounted in a ceiling or furniture piece, with a lamp that distributes the light in a concentrated area.

reflectance The ratio of incident light to the light reflected from a surface or material.

reflected ceiling plan A contract working drawing that illustrates the design of the ceiling, including the location of luminaires, architectural elements, and any HVAC equipment, as it would appear if seen in a mirror located on the floor.

reflector contour A design feature of a luminaire serving to help maximize the reflection of light into a space.

restrike Result of a lamp having to start again because of a power interruption or reduction in voltage.

room-cavity ratio (RCR) A formula designed to take into account the proportions of a space and the potential distance from the luminaires to a work surface.

S

seasonal affective disorder (SAD) A condition associated with an individual's inadequate exposure to sunlight.

semi-direct lighting Distribution of light when most of the illumination is directed downward and some is directed upward.

semi-indirect lighting Distribution of light when most of the illumination is directed upward and some is directed downward.

semi-recessed luminaire Fixture whose housing is partly above and partly below the ceiling.

semi-specular reflectance The phenomenon that occurs when a partially shiny material causes light to be reflected primarily in one direction.

shade A device, either opaque or translucent, that shields a bare lamp from view.

side-emitting fiber optic lighting system Light is visible along the sides of the cylindrical optical fibers.

soffit lighting Illumination technique that is a built-in wall element close or next to the ceiling; directs the light down onto a task.

solar geometry The movement of the earth around the sun.

specular reflectance The phenomenon that occurs when a shiny material causes light to be reflected in one direction.

spot (SP) A narrow beam spread.

spotlight projector Device that allows designers to select a very precise area to be illuminated.

steradian A solid angle used to measure luminous intensity from a source in a specific direction.

structural luminaire Illumination technique that is an element of the architectural interior.

sunlight Light from the sun that enters a space directly.

surface-mount luminaire Fixture installed on a ceiling, wall, or floor, or under a shelf or cabinet.

suspended luminaire Fixture installed on a ceiling and extending into the room by a cord, chain, pole, or wire.

sustainable design Design focusing on products and processes that protect the environment and conserve energy for future generations.

switch A device that controls a luminaire by stopping and starting the flow of electricity. A circuit is closed when a light is on and is open when the light is off.

T

task lighting Illumination that is specific to each task performed in a space.

timer Device designed to control lighting systems by turning lights on and off at designated times.

toxicity characteristic leaching procedure (TCLP) A procedure developed by the EPA to test the mercury content of lamps. To pass the TCLP test, the range of mercury content must be between 4 mg and 6 mg without additives.

track luminaire Fixture that has multiple heads mounted on an electrical raceway.

transformer An electrical device that increases or decreases voltages in a system.

transmission The passage of light through a material.

tungsten-halogen lamp Incandescent lamp that contains halogen.

U

universal design An approach to the physical environment that focuses on accommodating the needs of all people, whenever possible, without modifications.

uplight Luminaire that directs the light up; generally a portable luminaire.

V

valance lighting Illumination technique mounted above a window, directing the light up and down.

veiling reflection Reduction in light contrast on a task as a result of a reflected image on a surface.

visual acuity The ability of the eye to see details.

W

wall bracket lighting Illumination technique mounted on a wall and directing the light up and down.

wallslot A structural lighting system integrated in the ceiling and distributing light down onto vertical surfaces.

watt (W) Unit measuring an electrical circuit's ability to do work, such as producing light and waste heat, in terms of the amount of electricity drawn.

Appendix A

Base Types and Bulb Shapes

INCANDESCENT LAMPS
Filament Designations, Base Types, Bulb Shapes

Filament Designations (Not Actual Sizes)

Filament designations consist of a letter or letters to indicate how the wire is coiled and an arbitrary number sometimes followed by a letter to indicate the arrangement of the filament on the supports. Prefix letters include C (coil) — wire is wound into a helical coil or it may be deeply fluted; CC (coiled coil) — wire is wound into a helical coil and this coiled wire again wound into a helical coil. Some of the more commonly used types of filament arrangements are illustrated.

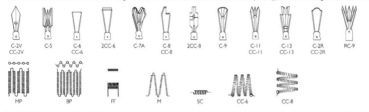

C-2V / CC-2V   C-5   C-6 / CC-6   2CC-6   C-7A   C-8 / CC-8   2CC-8   C-9   C-11 / CC-11   C-13 / CC-13   C-2R / CC-2R   RC-9

MP   BP   FF   M   SC   CC-6   CC-8

Base Shapes (Not Actual Sizes)

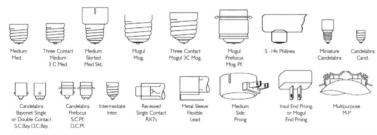

Medium Med.   Three Contact Medium 3 C Med.   Medium Skirted Med Skt.   Mogul Mog.   Three Contact Mogul 3C Mog.   Mogul Prefocus Mog. Pf.   S -14s Philinea   Miniature Candelabra   Candelabra Cand.

Candelabra Bayonet Single or Double Contact S.C.Bay. D.C.Bay.   Candelabra Prefocus S.C.Pf. D.C.Pf.   Intermediate Inter.   Recessed Single Contact RX7s   Metal Sleeve Flexible Lead   Medium Side Prong   Insul End Prong, or Mogul End Prong   Multipurpose M-P

Bulb Shapes (Not Actual Sizes)

The size and shape of a bulb is designated by a letter or letters followed by a number. The letter indicates the shape of the bulb while the number indicates the diameter of the bulb in eighths of an inch. For example, "T-10" indicates a tubular shaped bulb having a diameter of $\frac{10}{8}$ or $1\frac{1}{4}$ inches. The following illustrations show some of the more popular bulb shapes and sizes.

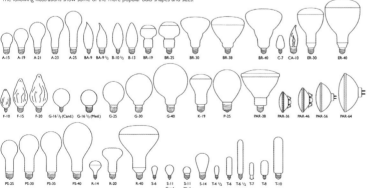

A-15   A-19   A-21   A-23   A-25   BA-9   BA-9½   B-10½   B-13   BR-19   BR-25   BR-30   BR-38   BR-40   C-7   CA-10   ER-30   ER-40

F-10   F-15   F-20   G-16½ (Cand.)   G-16½ (Med.)   G-25   G-30   G-40   K-19   P-25   PAR-38   PAR-36   PAR-46   PAR-56   PAR-64

PS-25   PS-30   PS-35   PS-40   R-14   R-20   R-40   S-6   S-11 Cand.   S-11 Med.   S-14   T-4½   T-6   T-6½   T-7   T-8   T-10

COMPACT FLUORESCENT LAMPS
Base Types and Bulb Shapes

Base Types (Not Actual Sizes)

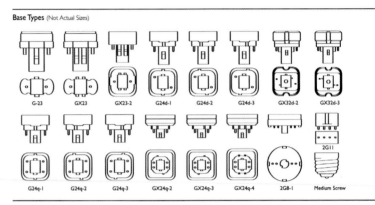

G-23 GX23 GX23-2 G24d-1 G24d-2 G24d-3 GX32d-2 GX32d-3

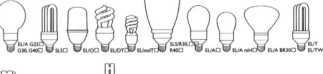

2G11

G24q-1 G24q-2 G24q-3 GX24q-2 GX24q-3 GX24q-4 2G8-1 Medium Screw

Bulb Shapes (Not Actual Sizes)

EL/A G25□ · G30, G40□ SLS□ EL/O□ EL/DT□ EL/mdT□ SLS/R30,□ · R40□ EL/A□ EL/A mH□ EL/A BR30□ EL/T · EL/TW

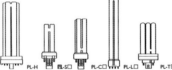

PL-H EL-S□ PL-C□ PL-L□ PL-T□

CFL

FLUORESCENT LAMPS
Fluorescent Base Types and Bulb Shapes

Base Types (Not Actual Sizes)

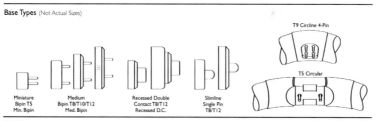

Miniature Bipin T5 Min. Bipin	Medium Bipin T8/T10/T12 Med. Bipin	Recessed Double Contact T8/T12 Recessed D.C.	Slimline Single Pin T8/T12	T9 Circline 4-Pin / T5 Circular

Bulb Shapes (Not Actual Sizes)

The size and shape of a bulb is designated by a letter or letters followed by a number. The letter indicates the shape of the bulb while the number indicates the diameter of the bulb in eighths of an inch. For example, "T12" indicates a tubular shaped bulb having a diameter of ¹²⁄₈ or 1½ inches. The following illustrations show some of the more popular bulb shapes and sizes.

T5 Miniature Bipin

T8 Medium Bipin

T10 Medium Bipin

T12 Medium Bipin

T8 Recessed Double Contact

T12 Recessed Double Contact

T12 Recessed Double Contact (Jacketed)

T8 Single Pin Slimline

T12 Single Pin Slimline

T12 Medium Bipin U-Bent Lamp (6")

T12 Medium Bipin U-Bent Lamp (3")

T8 Medium Bipin U-Bent Lamp

T5 Circular

T9 Circline 4-Pin

FLUORESCENT

HIGH INTENSITY DISCHARGE LAMPS
HID Bulb Shapes and Base Types; HID Warnings, Cautions and Operating Instructions

Base Types (Not Actual Sizes)

Medium☐ Admedium☐ | Mogul☐ | Extended Eyelet☐ | Position Oriented☐ | Medium Skirted☐ | Recessed☐ | Double Contact☐ | PG-12☐ | G-12☐ | G8.5☐ | PGJ5☐ | GX8.5☐
Med. E26☐ Admed.☐ | Mog. E39☐ | Mogul Base☐ | Mogul Base☐ | Med. Skt.☐ | Single Contact☐ | Bayonet, Med.☐
☐☐☐ | | EX39 Excl. Mog.☐ | POMB☐ | E26/50X39☐ | RX7s☐ | D.C. Bay

Bulb Shapes (Not Actual Sizes)

BD-17☐ | BT-37☐ | BT-56☐ | E-25☐ | ED-17☐ | ED-18☐ | ED-23½☐ | ED-28☐ | ED-37☐ | CDM-Tm☐ | T-4☐ | T-6☐ | TD-6☐ | TD-7☐ | T-10☐ | T-14 | T-17 | T-21☐ | TD☐ | Special

R111 | PAR-20☐ | PAR-30L☐ | PAR-38☐ | PAR-38☐ | R-40☐ | R-57☐ | R-60☐
☐☐ | | | WISO☐ | One Piece☐

WARNINGS, CAUTIONS AND OPERATING INSTRUCTIONS for MasterColor® Ceramic Metal Halide Lamps: Single Ended CDM-T G12, CDM-TC G8.5 and CDM-Tm PGJ5 (Universal); Double-Ended CDM-TD RX7 (Horizontal ± 45°, Enclosed Fixtures Only)

Warnings, Cautions and Operating Instructions

R **"WARNING:** These lamps can cause serious skin burn and eye inflammation from short wave ultraviolet radiation if outer envelope of the lamp is broken or punctured. Do not use where people will remain for more than a few minutes unless adequate shielding or other safety precautions are used. Certain lamps that will automatically extinguish when the outer envelope is broken or punctured are commercially available." This lamp complies with FDA radiation performance standard 21 CFR subchapter J. (USA:21CFR 1040.30 Canada:SOR/DORS/80-381)

If the outer bulb is broken or punctured, turn off at once and replace the lamp to avoid possible injury from hazardous short wave ultraviolet radiation. Do not scratch the outer bulb or subject it to pressure as this could cause the outer bulb to crack or shatter. A partial vacuum in the outer bulb may cause glass to fly if the envelope is struck.

WARNING: The arc-tube of metal halide lamps are designed to operate under high pressure and at temperatures up to 1000° C and can unexpectedly rupture due to internal or external factors such as a ballast failure or misapplication. If the arc-tube ruptures for any reason, the outer bulb may break and pieces of extremely hot glass might be discharged into the surrounding environment. If such a rupture were to happen, **THERE IS A RISK OF PERSONAL INJURY, PROPERTY DAMAGE, BURNS AND FIRE.**

Certain lamps that will retain all the glass particles should inner arc-tube rupture occur are commercially available from Philips Lighting Company.

RELAMP FIXTURES AT OR BEFORE THE END OF RATED LIFE. Allowing lamps to operate until they fail is not advised and may increase the possibility of inner arc tube rupture.

This lamp contains an arc tube with a filling gas containing Kr-85 and is distributed by Philips Lighting Company, a division of Philips Electronics North America Corporation, Somerset, New Jersey, 08875.

CAUTION: TO REDUCE THE RISK OF PERSONAL INJURY, PROPERTY DAMAGE, BURNS AND FIRE RESULTING FROM AN ARC-TUBE RUPTURE THE FOLLOWING <u>LAMP OPERATING INSTRUCTIONS</u> MUST BE FOLLOWED:

LAMP OPERATING INSTRUCTIONS:

1. RELAMP FIXTURES AT OR BEFORE THE END OF RATED LIFE. Allowing lamps to operate until they fail is not advised and may increase the possibility of inner arc tube rupture.

2. Use only in fully enclosed fixtures capable of withstanding particles of glass having temperatures up to 1000°C. Lens/diffuser material must be heat resistant. Consult fixture manufacturer regarding the suitability of the fixture for this lamp.

3. Do not operate a fixture with a missing or broken lens/diffuser. At high lighting levels or when illuminating light-sensitive materials the use of an extra UV filter is recommended.

4. Operate lamp only within specified limits of operating position.

5. Before lamp installation/replacement, shut power off and allow lamp and fixture to cool to avoid electrical shock

and potential burn hazards. When inserting a new CDM-Tm lamp, twist the lamp 45° clock-wise in the holder to ensure proper electrical and mechanical connection.

6. Use only auxiliary equipment meeting Philips and/or ANSI standards. Use within voltage limits recommended by ballast manufacturer.

   A. Operate lamp only within specified limits of operation.

   B. For total supply load refer to ballast manufacturers electrical data.

   C. Operate CDM-T (G12 base), CDM-TC (G8.5 base) and CDM-Tm (PGJ5 base) lamps only on thermally protected ballasts.

   D. Operate CDM-TC lamps (G8.5 base) and CDM-Tm (PGJ5 base) only on electronic ballasts.

7. Periodically inspect the outer envelope. Replace any lamps that show scratches, cracks or damage.

8. If a lamp bulb support is used, be sure to insulate the support electrically to avoid possible decomposition of the bulb glass.

9. Protect lamp base, socket and wiring against moisture, corrosive atmospheres and excessive heat.

10. Time should be allowed for lamps to stabilize in color when turned on for the first time. This may require several hours of operation, with more than one start. Lamp color is also subject to change under conditions of excess vibration or shock and color appearance may vary between individual lamps.

11. Lamps may require 4 to 8 minutes (10-15 minutes for CDM-Tm) to re-light if there is a power interruption.

12. Take care in handling and disposing of lamps. If an arc tube is broken, avoid skin contact with any of the contents or fragments.

HID

FEATURES

HOUSING

High quality metal housing.

Available in white (standard) or black finish. A variety of finishes also available.

Matte black baffle standard.

STEM

Extruded aluminum stem conceals fixture wiring and allows rotation up to 330°.

Pivot mechanism allows adjustment up to 90° from vertical.

ADAPTOR

Low-profile, injection-molded track mounting adaptor for easy attachment to Lithonia 1 or 2 circuit track. Snap lock secures adaptor to track.

ELECTRICAL SYSTEM

Medium-base porcelain socket.

LISTING

Fixtures are UL 1574 listed.

Listed and labeled to comply with Canadian Standards.

ACCESSORIES

Accepts a variety of lens, barn doors, filters and louvers. Shipped separately. See options and accessories tab for more information.

Catalog Number		
Notes		Type

Incandescent Line Voltage

LTC

Roundback

PAR16, 20, 30, 38 Lamps

Lamp Designation	Aperture (A)	Length (L)	Maximum Height (H)
PAR20/16	3-5/8 (9.2)	7 (17.8)	10-1/4 (26.0)
PAR30	5 (12.7)	8 (20.3)	11-3/4 (29.8)
PAR38	5-3/4 (14.6)	8-1/2 (21.6)	12-1/4 (31.1)

All dimensions are in inches (centimeters).

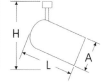

ORDERING INFORMATION

Example: **LTC RNDB PAR20 MB WH**

Choose the boldface catalog nomenclature that best suits your needs and write it on the appropriate line. Order accessories as separate catalog numbers (shipped separately).

LTC	RNDB			
Series	**Head Style**	**Lamp Designation[1]**	**Trim Type**	**Finish[3]**

Series	**Head Style**	**Lamp Designation**	**Trim Type**	**Finish**
LTC	RNDB Roundback cylinder	PAR20 PAR20 and PAR16 compatible (75W maximum)	MB Matte black baffle (standard)	**Architectural Colors** (powder finish)[4]
		PAR30 PAR30 long-neck compatible (75W maximum)[2]	WB White baffle	**Standard Colors**
				WH White (standard)
		PAR38 PAR38 compatible (Q250W maximum)		DBL Black
				DWHG Matte white, textured
				DBLB Matte black, textured
				Classic Colors
				DMB Medium bronze
				DNA Natural aluminum
				DSS Sandstone
				DGC Charcoal gray
				DTG Tennis green
				DBR Bright red
				DSB Steel blue
				Plated Finishes
				AB Antique brass
				PB Polished brass
				PCHR Polished chrome

Accessories

Order as separate catalog numbers.

LTFH500 Filter holder for PAR20 and PAR16. Specify white (WH) or black (DBL).

LTFH700 Filter holder for PAR30. Specify white (WH) or black (DBL).

LTFH800 Filter holder for PAR38. Specify white (WH) or black (DBL).

F500[5,6] Lens for use with 500 series filter holders and barn doors.

F700[5,6] Lens for use with 700 series filter holders and barn doors.

F800[5,6] Lens for use with 800 series filter holders and barn doors.

L500[6] Eggcrate louver for use with 500 series filter holders.

L700[6] Eggcrate louver for use with 700 series filter holders.

L800[6] Eggcrate louver for use with 800 series filter holders.

LTBD500 Barn door for PAR20 and PAR16. Specify white (WH) or black (DBL).

LTBD700 Barn door for PAR30. Specify white (WH) or black (DBL).

LTBD800 Barn door for PAR38. Specify white (WH) or black (DBL).

NOTES

1 For lamp ordering information, refer to options and accessories tab.

2 When utilizing short-neck lamps, socket extender is required. Order separately. TP30 SE.

3 White stem mounted fixtures have white stems and adaptors. All other stem-mounted fixtures have black stems and adaptors. For alternate stem/adaptor color add AWH (white) or ABL (black) after finish color. Example: DMB AWH

4 Additional architectural colors and custom color matches available; please see brochure 794.3.

5 For lens type (color selection information) refer to options and accessories tab.

6 A filter holder or barn door is required when ordering a louver or lens.

LTC Roundback

LAMP PERFORMANCE DATA

The lighting performance data charts shown provide lighting levels (footcandles), beam pattern (in feet), rated lamp life.

A Aiming angle	**FC** Footcandles, initial (centerbeam)	**W** Beam width (50% of CB candle power)
D Distance (feet)	**L** Beam length (50% of CB candle power)	**C** Distance to beam center (feet)

Lamp	Rated Life	Beam Spread	0° Aiming Angle					30° Aiming Angle					45° Aiming Angle					60° Aiming Angle				
			D	FC	W	L	C	D	FC	W	L	C	D	FC	W	L	C	D	FC	W	L	C
60PAR16/HAL/NSP	2000	10°	4	313	0.7	0.7	N/A	4	203	0.8	0.9	2.3	3	196	0.7	1.1	3.0	2	156	0.7	1.4	3.5
			6	139	1.1	1.1	N/A	6	90	1.2	1.4	3.5	4	110	1.0	1.4	4.0	3	69	1.1	2.2	5.2
			8	78	1.4	1.4	N/A	8	51	1.6	1.9	4.6	5	71	1.2	1.8	5.0	4	39	1.4	2.9	6.9
60PAR16/HAL/NFL	2000	30°	2	325	1.1	1.1	N/A	2	211	1.2	1.5	1.2	2	115	1.5	2.3	2.0	2	41	2.1	5.5	3.5
			4	81	2.1	2.1	N/A	3	94	1.9	2.2	1.7	3	51	2.3	3.5	3.0	3	18	3.2	8.2	5.2
			6	36	3.2	3.2	N/A	4	53	2.5	2.9	2.3	4	29	3.0	4.6	4.0	4	10	4.3	10.9	6.9
50PAR20/H/SP10	2500	10°	4	375	0.7	0.7	N/A	4	244	0.8	0.9	2.3	3	236	0.7	1.1	3.0	2	188	0.7	1.4	3.5
			6	167	1.1	1.1	N/A	5	156	1.0	1.2	2.9	4	133	1.0	1.4	4.0	3	83	1.1	2.2	5.2
			8	94	1.4	1.4	N/A	6	108	1.2	1.4	3.5	5	85	1.2	1.8	5.0	4	47	1.4	2.9	6.9
50PAR20/H/FL25	2500	25°	3	167	1.3	1.3	N/A	2	244	1.0	1.2	1.2	2	133	1.3	1.9	2.0	2	47	1.8	4.2	3.5
			4	94	1.8	1.8	N/A	3	108	1.5	1.8	1.7	3	59	1.9	2.8	3.0	3	21	2.7	6.2	5.2
			5	60	2.2	2.2	N/A	4	61	2.1	2.4	2.3	4	33	2.5	3.7	4.0	4	12	3.6	8.3	6.9
75PAR30/CAP/NSP	2500	9°	8	219	1.3	1.3	N/A	8	142	1.5	1.7	4.6	6	137	1.3	1.9	6.0	4	109	1.3	2.6	6.9
			10	140	1.6	1.6	N/A	10	91	1.8	2.1	5.8	8	77	1.8	2.5	8.0	6	49	1.9	3.9	10.4
			12	97	1.9	1.9	N/A	12	63	2.2	2.5	6.9	10	50	2.2	3.2	10.0	8	27	2.5	5.1	13.9
75PAR30/CAP/NFL	2500	30°	4	200	2.1	2.1	N/A	4	130	2.5	2.9	2.3	2	283	1.5	2.3	2.0	2	100	2.1	5.5	3.5
			6	89	3.2	3.2	N/A	6	58	3.7	4.4	3.5	4	71	3.0	4.6	4.0	3	44	3.2	8.2	5.2
			8	50	4.3	4.3	N/A	8	32	5.0	5.9	4.6	6	31	4.6	6.9	6.0	4	25	4.3	10.9	6.9
75PAR30/CAP/FL	2500	40°	4	125	2.9	2.9	N/A	3	144	2.5	3.1	1.7	3	79	3.1	5.0	3.0	2	63	2.9	9.7	3.5
			6	56	4.4	4.4	N/A	4	81	3.4	4.1	2.3	4	44	4.1	6.7	4.0	3	28	4.4	14.5	5.2
			8	31	5.8	5.8	N/A	5	52	4.2	5.1	2.9	5	28	5.2	8.4	5.0	4	16	5.8	19.3	6.9
120PAR/CAP/SPL/SP	3000	9°	10	250	1.6	1.6	N/A	10	162	1.8	2.1	5.8	6	246	1.3	1.9	6.0	4	195	1.3	2.66	6.9
			12	174	1.9	1.9	N/A	12	113	2.2	2.5	6.9	8	138	1.8	2.5	8.0	6	87	1.9	3.9	10.4
			14	128	2.2	2.2	N/A	14	83	2.5	2.9	8.1	10	88	2.2	3.2	10.0	8	49	2.5	5.1	13.9
120PAR/CAP/SPL/FL	3000	30°	4	313	2.1	2.1	N/A	4	203	2.5	2.9	2.3	4	110	3.0	4.6	4.0	2	156	2.1	5.5	3.5
			6	139	3.2	3.2	N/A	6	90	3.7	4.4	3.5	6	49	4.6	6.9	6.0	3	69	3.2	8.2	5.2
			8	78	4.3	4.3	N/A	8	51	5.0	5.9	4.6	8	28	6.1	9.2	8.0	4	39	4.3	10.9	6.9
120PAR/CAP/WFL	3000	50°	4	125	3.7	3.7	N/A	4	81	4.3	5.4	2.3	2	177	2.6	4.8	2.0	2	63	3.7	21.5	3.5
			6	56	5.6	5.6	N/A	6	36	6.5	8.0	3.5	4	44	5.3	9.5	4.0	3	28	5.6	32.2	5.2
			8	31	7.5	7.5	N/A	8	20	8.6	10.7	4.6	6	20	7.9	14.3	6.0	4	16	7.5	42.9	6.9
150PAR/SP	2000	12°	8	215	1.7	1.7	N/A	8	139	1.9	2.3	4.6	6	135	1.8	2.6	6.0	4	107	1.7	3.5	6.9
			12	95	2.5	2.5	N/A	12	62	2.9	3.4	6.9	8	76	2.4	3.4	8.0	6	48	2.5	5.2	10.4
			16	54	3.4	3.4	N/A	16	35	3.9	4.5	9.2	10	49	3.0	4.3	10.0	8	27	3.4	7.0	13.9
150PAR/FL	2000	30°	4	215	2.1	2.1	N/A	4	139	2.5	2.9	2.3	4	76	3.0	4.6	4.0	2	107	2.1	5.5	3.5
			8	54	4.3	4.3	N/A	6	62	3.7	4.4	3.5	6	34	4.6	6.9	6.0	4	27	4.3	10.9	6.9
			12	24	6.4	6.4	N/A	8	35	5.0	5.9	4.6	8	19	6.1	9.2	8.0	6	12	6.4	16.4	10.4
Q250PAR/SP10°	4200	10°	10	400	1.8	1.8	N/A	10	260	2.0	2.3	5.8	8	221	2.0	2.8	8.0	4	313	1.4	2.9	6.9
			15	178	2.6	2.6	N/A	14	133	2.8	3.3	8.1	10	141	2.5	3.5	10.0	6	139	2.1	4.3	10.4
			20	100	3.5	3.5	N/A	18	80	3.6	4.2	10.4	12	98	3.0	4.2	12.0	8	78	2.8	5.7	13.9
Q250PAR/FL30°	4200	30°	8	141	4.3	4.3	N/A	6	162	3.7	4.4	3.5	4	199	3.0	4.6	4.0	3	125	3.2	8.2	5.2
			12	63	6.4	6.4	N/A	8	91	5.0	5.9	4.6	6	88	4.6	6.9	6.0	4	70	4.3	10.9	6.9
			16	35	8.6	8.6	N/A	10	58	6.2	7.3	5.8	8	50	6.1	9.2	8.0	5	45	5.4	13.7	8.7

All data was calculated from each lamp manufacturer's published data and is subject to normal lamp variations. Maximum footcandle is usually at the aiming point, but not always on wider spread lamps. Lamp data supplied by manufacturers is approximate and individual lamp performance may vary.

LITHONIA LIGHTING

An *Acuity* Brands Company

Lithonia Lighting
Acuity Lighting Group, Inc.
Recessed Downlighting
One Lithonia Way, Conyers, GA 30012
Phone: 800-315-4935 Fax: 770-860-3106
In Canada: 1100 50th Ave., Lachine, Quebec H8T 2V3
www.lithonia.com

Sheet #: 105-LINE-RNDB   ©1999 Acuity Lighting Group, Inc. 10/99   105-LINE-RNDB.p65

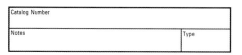

LITHONIA LIGHTING®

Catalog Number	
Notes	
	Type

Incandescent Low Voltage

LTC
Gimbal Ring
MR16, PAR36 Lamp

FEATURES

HOUSING
High quality metal lampholder ring.

Available in white (standard) or black finish. A variety of finishes also available.

YOKE
Heavy-gauge steel full-yoke for PAR36 fixtures and half-yoke for MR16 fixtures allows rotation up to 330°.

Pivot mechanism allows adjustment up to 90° from vertical.

ADAPTOR/ELECTRICAL SYSTEM
120V/12V solid-state, electronic transformer standard. Transformer is potted in low-profile, injection-molded adaptor housing which provides easy installation to Lithonia 1 or 2 circuit track. Snap lock secures adaptor to track.

Two-pin porcelain socket on MR16 fixtures. Spaded terminals on lamp leads on PAR36 unit with silicon terminal cover boot.

LISTING
Fixtures are UL 1574 listed.

Listed and labeled to comply with Canadian Standards.

ACCESSORIES
Accepts a variety of lens, barn doors, filters, and louvers. Shipped separately. See options and accessories tab for more information.

Lamp Designation	Aperture (A)	Length (L)	Maximum Height (H)
MR16	2-1/8 (5.4)	1-7/8 (4.7)	5-1/4 (13.3)
MR16 w/beam director	1-3/4 (4.4)	3-1/8 (7.8)	6 (15.2)
PAR36	5 (12.7)	2-3/8 (6.1)	7-5/8 (19.4)

All dimensions are in inches (centimeters).

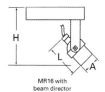

MR16   MR16 with beam director

ORDERING INFORMATION

Example: **LTC GMBR MR16 WH**

Choose the boldface catalog nomenclature that best suits your needs and write it on the appropriate line. Order accessories as separate catalog numbers (shipped separately).

LTC	GMBR			
Series	**Head Style**	**Lamp Designation**[1]	**Trim Type**	**Finish**[3]
LTC	**GMBR** Gimbal ring	**MR16** MR16 compatible, half-yoke mounted. 75W maximum.	**(blank)** Open (standard)	**Architectural Colors** (powder finish)[4]
		PAR36 PAR36 compatible, full-yoke mounted. 75W maximum.	**BMDR**[2] Beam director	**Standard Colors**
				WH White (standard)
				DBL Black
				DWHG Matte white, textured
				DBLB Matte black, textured
				Classic Colors

Accessories
Order as separate items

LTGCS Filter holder for PAR36.

F200 Lens for use with MR16 fixture only. Filter holder or barn door not required.[5]

F700 Lens for use with LTGCS clips or 700 series barn doors.[5,6]

L200 Honeycomb louver for use with MR16 fixture only. Filter holder or barn door not required.

L700 Eggcrate louver for use with LTGCS clips or 700 series barn doors.[6]

LTGBD200 Barn door for MR16. Specify white (WH) or black (DBL).

LTGBD700 Barn door for PAR36. Specify white (WH) or black (DBL).

Classic Colors
DMB Medium bronze
DNA Natural aluminum
DSS Sandstone
DGC Charcoal gray
DTG Tennis green
DBR Bright red
DSB Steel blue

NOTES

1 For lamp ordering information, refer to options and accessories tab.

2 MR16 fixtures only.

3 Yoke mounted fixtures have yokes that match fixtures. White adaptor utilized on white fixtures. black adaptors on all others. For alternate adaptor color add AWH (white) or ABL (black) after finish color. Example: DMB AWH

4 Additional architectural colors and custom color matches available; please see brochure 794.3.

5 For lens type (color selection information), refer to options and accessories tab.

6 A filter holder or barn door is required when ordering a louver or filter.

Downlighting and Track

Sheet #: 125-LOW-GMBR   LOW-150

LTC Gimbal Ring

LAMP PERFORMANCE DATA

The lighting performance data charts shown provide lighting levels (footcandles), beam pattern (in feet), rated lamp life.

  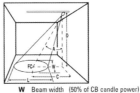

A Aiming angle   **FC** Footcandles, initial (centerbeam)   **W** Beam width (50% of CB candle power)
D Distance (feet)   **L** Beam length (50% of CB candle power)   **C** Distance to beam center (feet)

LAMP	RATED LIFE	BEAM SPREAD	0° AIMING ANGLE				30° AIMING ANGLE				45° AIMING ANGLE				60° AIMING ANGLE			
			D	FC	W	L	C	D	FC	W	L	C	D	FC	W	L	C
Q50MR16/C/FL40°-EXN	6000	40°	2	425	1.5	1.5	N/A	2	276	1.7	2.0	1.2	2	150	2.1	3.4	2.0	2	53	2.9	9.7	3.5
			4	106	2.9	2.9	N/A	4	69	3.4	4.1	2.3	3	67	3.1	5.0	3.0	3	24	4.4	14.5	5.2
			6	47	4.4	4.4	N/A	6	31	5.0	6.1	3.5	4	38	4.1	6.7	4.0	4	13	5.8	19.3	6.9
Q50MR16/C/WF55°-FNV	6000	55°	2	225	2.1	2.1	N/A	2	146	2.4	3.1	1.2	2	80	2.9	5.7	2.0	2	28	4.2	44.5	3.5
			4	56	4.2	4.2	N/A	4	37	4.8	6.1	2.3	3	35	4.4	8.6	3.0	3	13	6.3	66.8	5.2
			6	25	6.3	6.3	N/A	6	16	7.2	9.2	3.5	4	20	5.9	11.4	4.0	4	7	8.3	89.1	6.9
50MR16/T/NSP/10	4000	10°	6	319	1.1	1.1	N/A	6	207	1.2	1.4	3.5	4	254	1.0	1.4	4.0	3	160	1.1	2.2	5.2
			10	115	1.8	1.8	N/A	8	117	1.6	1.9	4.6	6	113	1.5	2.1	6.0	4	90	1.4	2.9	6.9
			14	59	2.5	2.5	N/A	10	75	2.0	2.3	5.8	8	64	2.0	2.8	8.0	5	58	1.8	3.6	8.7
50MR16/T/VWFL60	4000	60°	2	250	2.3	2.3	N/A	2	162	2.7	3.5	1.2	2	88	3.3	6.9	2.0	2	31	4.6	N/A	3.5
			4	63	4.6	4.6	N/A	3	72	4.0	5.2	1.7	3	39	4.9	10.4	3.0	3	14	6.9	N/A	5.2
			6	28	6.9	6.9	N/A	4	41	5.3	6.9	2.3	4	22	6.5	13.9	4.0	4	8	9.2	N/A	6.9
65MR16/T/NSP10	4000	10°	6	389	1.1	1.1	N/A	6	253	1.2	1.4	3.5	4	309	1.0	1.4	4.0	4	109	1.4	2.9	6.9
			10	140	1.8	1.8	N/A	10	91	2.0	2.3	5.8	8	77	2.0	2.8	8.0	6	49	2.1	4.3	10.4
			14	71	2.5	2.5	N/A	14	46	2.8	3.3	8.1	12	34	3.0	4.2	12.0	8	27	2.8	5.7	13.9
65MR16/T/VWFL60	4000	60°	2	263	2.3	2.3	N/A	2	171	2.7	3.5	1.2	2	93	3.3	6.9	2.0	2	33	4.6	N/A	3.5
			4	66	4.6	4.6	N/A	3	43	5.3	6.9	2.3	3	41	4.9	10.4	3.0	3	15	6.9	N/A	5.2
			6	29	6.9	6.9	N/A	6	19	8.0	10.4	3.5	4	23	6.5	13.9	4.0	4	8	9.2	N/A	6.9
Q71/MR16/C/NFL25°-EYJ	4000	25°	4	344	1.8	1.8	N/A	4	223	2.1	2.4	2.3	4	122	2.5	3.7	4.0	2	172	1.8	4.2	3.5
			8	86	3.6	3.6	N/A	8	56	4.1	4.8	4.6	6	54	3.8	5.6	6.0	3	76	2.7	6.2	5.2
			12	38	5.3	5.3	N/A	12	25	6.1	7.2	6.9	8	30	5.0	7.5	8.0	4	43	3.6	8.3	6.9
Q71/MR16/C/FL40°-EYC	4000	40°	4	138	2.9	2.9	N/A	4	89	3.4	4.1	2.3	2	194	2.1	3.4	2.0	2	69	2.9	9.7	3.5
			6	61	4.4	4.4	N/A	6	40	5.0	6.1	3.5	4	49	4.1	6.7	4.0	3	31	4.4	14.5	5.2
			8	34	5.8	5.8	N/A	8	22	6.7	8.1	4.6	6	22	6.2	10.1	6.0	4	17	5.8	19.3	6.9
50PAR36/CAP/NSP	4000	6°	12	174	1.3	1.3	N/A	8	254	1.0	1.1	4.6	6	246	0.9	1.3	6.0	4	195	0.8	1.7	6.9
			16	98	1.7	1.7	N/A	12	113	1.5	1.7	6.9	10	88	1.5	2.1	10.0	8	49	1.7	3.4	13.9
			20	63	2.1	2.1	N/A	16	63	1.9	2.2	9.2	14	45	2.1	2.9	14.0	12	22	2.5	5.1	20.8
50PAR36NSP	2000	10°	8	172	1.4	1.4	N/A	6	198	1.2	1.4	3.5	4	243	1.0	1.4	4.0	2	344	0.7	1.4	3.5
			12	76	2.1	2.1	N/A	10	71	2.0	2.3	5.8	8	61	2.0	2.8	8.0	4	86	1.4	2.9	6.9
			16	43	2.8	2.8	N/A	14	36	2.8	3.3	8.1	12	27	3.0	4.2	12.0	6	38	2.1	4.3	10.4
50PAR36WFL	2000	39°x27°	2	225	1.4	1.0	N/A	2	146	1.6	1.3	1.2	2	80	2.0	2.0	2.0	2	28	2.8	4.6	3.5
			4	56	2.8	1.9	N/A	4	37	3.3	2.6	2.3	3	35	3.0	3.1	3.0	3	13	4.3	7.0	5.2
			6	25	4.3	2.9	N/A	6	16	4.9	3.9	3.5	4	20	4.0	4.1	4.0	4	7	5.7	9.3	6.9
50PAR36VWFL	2000	55°	2	60	2.1	2.1	N/A	2	39	2.4	3.1	1.2	2	21	2.9	5.7	2.0	2	8	4.2	44.5	3.5
			3	27	3.1	3.1	N/A	3	17	3.6	4.6	1.7	3	9	4.4	8.6	3.0	3	3	6.3	66.8	5.2
			4	15	4.2	4.2	N/A	4	10	4.8	6.1	2.3	4	5	5.9	11.4	4.0	4	2	8.3	89.1	6.9

All data was calculated from each lamp manufacturer's published data and is subject to normal lamp variations. Maximum footcandle is usually at the aiming point, but not always on wider spread lamps. Lamp data supplied by manufacturers is approximate and individual lamp performance may vary.

LITHONIA LIGHTING®
An *Acuity*Brands Company

Sheet #: 125-LOW-GMBR   ©1999 Acuity Lighting Group, Inc. 10/99   125-LOW-GMBR.p65

Lithonia Lighting
Acuity Lighting Group, Inc.
Recessed Downlighting
One Lithonia Way, Conyers, GA 30012
Phone: 800-315-4935 Fax: 770-860-3106
In Canada: 1100 50th Ave., Lachine, Quebec H8T 2V3
www.lithonia.com

LITHONIA LIGHTING®

Catalog Number	
Notes	Type

FEATURES

HOUSING

High quality metal housing.

Available in white (standard) or black finish. A variety of finishes also available.

Removable black matte baffle for relamping.

YOKE

Heavy-gauge steel yoke allows rotation up to 330°.

Pivot mechanism allows adjustment up to 90° from vertical.

ADAPTOR/ELECTRICAL SYSTEM

120V/12V solid-state, electronic transformer standard. Transformer is potted in low-profile, injection-molded adaptor housing which provides easy installation to Lithonia 1 or 2 circuit track. Snap lock secures adaptor to track.

Two-pin porcelain socket on MR16 fixtures. Spaded terminals on lamp leads on PAR36 unit.

LISTING

Fixtures are UL 1574 listed.

Listed and labeled to comply with Canadian Standards.

ACCESSORIES

Accepts a variety of lens and louvers. Shipped separately. See options and accessories tab for more information.

Incandescent Low Voltage

LTC

Bellspot

MR16, PAR36 Lamp

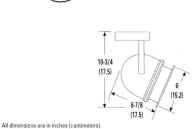

10-3/4 (17.5)

6 (15.2)

6-7/8 (17.5)

All dimensions are in inches (centimeters).

ORDERING INFORMATION

Example: **LTC BLSP MR16 MB WH**

Choose the boldface catalog nomenclature that best suits your needs and write it on the appropriate line. Order accessories as separate catalog numbers (shipped separately).

LTC	BLSP			
Series	**Head Style**	**Lamp Designation**[1]	**Trim Type**	**Finish**[2]
LTC	**BLSP** Bellspot	**MR16** MR16 compatible. 50W maximum. **PAR36** PAR36 compatible. 50W maximum.	**MB** Matte black baffle (standard) **WB** White baffle	**Architectural Colors** (powder finish)[3] **Standard Colors** **WH** White (standard) **DBL** Black **DWHG** Matte white, textured **DBLB** Matte black, textured **Classic Colors** **DMB** Medium bronze **DNA** Natural aluminum **DSS** Sandstone **DGC** Charcoal gray **DTG** Tennis green **DBR** Bright red **DSB** Steel blue **Plated Finishes** **AB** Antique brass **PB** Polished brass **PCHR** Polished chrome

Accessories

Order as separate item

F200 Lens for use with MR16 fixtures.[2]

L200 Honeycomb louver for use with MR16 fixtures.

NOTES

1 For lamp ordering information, refer to options and accessories tab.

2 Yoke mounted fixtures have yokes that match fixtures. White adaptor utilized on white fixtures. Black adaptors on all others. For alternate adaptor color add AWH (white) or ABL (black) after finish color. Example: DMB AWH

3 Additional architectural colors and custom color matches available; please see brochure 794.3.

4 For lens type (color selection information), refer to options and accessories tab.

Downlighting and Track   **Sheet #: 140-LOW-BLSP**   LOW-110

LTC Bellspot

LAMP PERFORMANCE DATA

The lighting performance data charts shown provide lighting levels (footcandles), beam pattern (in feet), rated lamp life.

A Aiming angle	**FC** Footcandles, initial (centerbeam)	**W** Beam width (50% of CB candle power)
D Distance (feet)	**L** Beam length (50% of CB candle power)	**C** Distance to beam center (feet)

Lamp	Rated Life	Beam Spread	0° Aiming Angle					30° Aiming Angle					45° Aiming Angle					60° Aiming Angle				
			D	FC	W	L	C	D	FC	W	L	C	D	FC	W	L	C	D	FC	W	L	C
Q50MR16/C/FL40°-EXN	6000	40°	2	425	1.5	1.5	N/A	2	276	1.7	2.0	1.2	2	150	2.1	3.4	2.0	2	53	2.9	9.7	3.5
			4	106	2.9	2.9	N/A	4	69	3.4	4.1	2.3	3	67	3.1	5.0	3.0	3	24	4.4	14.5	5.2
			6	47	4.4	4.4	N/A	6	31	5.0	6.1	3.5	4	38	4.1	6.7	4.0	4	13	5.8	19.3	6.9
Q50MR16/C/WF55°-FNV	6000	55°	2	225	2.1	2.1	N/A	2	146	2.4	3.1	1.2	2	80	2.9	5.7	2.0	2	28	4.2	44.5	3.5
			4	56	4.2	4.2	N/A	4	37	4.8	6.1	2.3	3	35	4.4	8.6	3.0	3	13	6.3	66.8	5.2
			6	25	6.3	6.3	N/A	6	16	7.2	9.2	3.5	4	20	5.9	11.4	4.0	4	7	8.3	89.1	6.9
50MR16/T/NSP/10	4000	10°	6	319	1.1	1.1	N/A	6	207	1.2	1.4	3.5	4	254	1.0	1.4	4.0	2	160	1.1	2.2	5.2
			10	115	1.8	1.8	N/A	8	117	1.6	1.9	4.6	6	113	1.5	2.1	6.0	4	90	1.4	2.9	6.9
			14	59	2.5	2.5	N/A	10	75	2.0	2.3	5.8	8	64	2.0	2.8	8.0	5	58	1.8	3.6	8.7
50MR16/T/VWFL60	4000	60°	2	250	2.3	2.3	N/A	2	162	2.7	3.5	1.2	2	88	3.3	6.9	2.0	2	31	4.6	N/A	3.5
			4	63	4.6	4.6	N/A	3	72	4.0	5.2	1.7	3	39	4.9	10.4	3.0	3	14	6.9	N/A	5.2
			6	28	6.9	6.9	N/A	4	41	5.3	6.9	2.3	4	22	6.5	13.9	4.0	4	8	9.2	N/A	6.9
50PAR36/CAP/NSP	4000	6°	12	174	1.3	1.3	N/A	8	254	1.0	1.1	4.6	6	246	0.9	1.3	6.0	4	195	0.8	1.7	6.9
			16	98	1.7	1.7	N/A	12	113	1.5	1.7	6.9	10	88	1.5	2.1	10.0	8	49	1.7	3.4	13.9
			20	63	2.1	2.1	N/A	16	63	1.9	2.2	9.2	14	45	2.1	2.9	14.0	12	22	2.5	5.1	20.8
50PAR36NSP	2000	10°	8	172	1.4	1.4	N/A	6	198	1.2	1.4	3.5	4	243	1.0	1.4	4.0	2	344	0.7	1.4	3.5
			12	76	2.1	2.1	N/A	10	71	2.0	2.3	5.8	8	61	2.0	2.8	8.0	4	86	1.4	2.9	6.9
			16	43	2.8	2.8	N/A	14	36	2.8	3.3	8.1	12	27	3.0	4.2	12.0	6	38	2.1	4.3	10.4
50PAR36WFL	2000	39°x27°	2	225	1.4	1.0	N/A	2	146	1.6	1.3	1.2	2	80	2.0	2.0	2.0	2	28	2.8	4.6	3.5
			4	56	2.8	1.9	N/A	4	37	3.3	2.6	2.3	3	35	3.0	3.1	3.0	3	13	4.3	7.0	5.2
			6	25	4.3	2.9	N/A	6	16	4.9	3.9	3.5	4	20	4.0	4.1	4.0	4	7	5.7	9.3	6.9
50PAR36VWFL	2000	55°	2	60	2.1	2.1	N/A	2	39	2.4	3.1	1.2	2	21	2.9	5.7	2.0	2	8	4.2	44.5	3.5
			3	27	3.1	3.1	N/A	3	17	3.6	4.6	1.7	3	9	4.4	8.6	3.0	3	3	6.3	66.8	5.2
			4	15	4.2	4.2	N/A	4	10	4.8	6.1	2.3	4	5	5.9	11.4	4.0	4	2	8.3	89.1	6.9

All data was calculated from each lamp manufacturer's published data and is subject to normal lamp variations. Maximum footcandle is usually at the aiming point, but not always on wider spread lamps. Lamp data supplied by manufacturers is approximate and individual lamp performance may vary.

LITHONIA LIGHTING®
An **Acuity**Brands Company

Sheet #: 140-LOW-BLSP   ©1999 Acuity Lighting Group, Inc. 10/99   140-LOW-BLSP.p65

Lithonia Lighting
Acuity Lighting Group, Inc.
Recessed Downlighting
One Lithonia Way, Conyers, GA 30012
Phone: 800-315-4935 Fax: 770-860-3106
In Canada: 1100 50th Ave., Lachine, Quebec H8T 2V3
www.lithonia.com

Appendix B

Lighting Manufacturers, Distributors, and Suppliers

Control and Equipment Manufacturers

Advance Transformer
http://www.advancetransformer.com

BRK Electronics
http://www.brkelectronics.com

Bryant Electric
http://www.bryant-electric.com

Dexin International
http://www.dexin.com/index_en.asphttp://www.dexin.com

Douglas Lighting Controls
http://www.douglaslightingcontrol.com

Fulham Company
http://www.fulham.com

Honeywell
http://www.honeywell.com

Intelligent Lighting Controls
http://www.ilc-usa.com

Labsphere
http://www.labsphere.com

Leviton Manufacturing
http://www.leviton.com

Litecontrol
http://www.litecontrol.com

LiteTouch
http://www.litetouch.com

Magnetek
http://www.magnetek.com

Novitas
http://www.novitas.com

Pace Technologies
http://www.pacepower.com

Pass & Seymour Legrand
http://www.passandseymour.com

RAB Electric Manufacturing Lighting
http://www.rabweb.com

Sensor Switch
http://www.sensorswitch.com

TORK
http://www.tork.com

The Watt Stopper
http://www.wattstopper.com

Lamp Manufacturers

Broada
http://www.broadalighting.com

Bulbtronics
http://www.bulbtronics.com

DuraLamp USA
http://www.duralamp.com

Eiko
http://www.eiko-ltd.com

GE Lighting
http://www.gelighting.com

Halco Lighting Corporation
http://www.halcolighting.com

LEDtronics
http://www.ledtronics.com

Lights of America
http://www.lightsofamerica.com

Lumenyte International Corporation
http://www.lumenyte.com

Osram Sylvania
http://www.sylvania.com

Panasonic Lighting Corporation
http://www.panasonic.com

Philips Lighting
http://www.lighting.philips.com

Satco Products
http://www.satco.com

Schott-Fostec, LLC (Fiber Optics)
http://www.schott-fostec.com

Westinghouse Lighting Corporation Bulbs
http://www.westinghouselightbulbs.com

Luminaires

AAMSCO Manufacturing Lighting
http://www.aamsco.com

Access Lighting
http://www.accesslighting.com

Alkco Lighting
http://www.alkco.com

The American Glass Light Company
http://www.americanglasslight.com

American Lighting
http://www.americanlighting.net

Arroyo Craftsman Lighting
http://www.arroyo-craftsman.com

Artemide
http://www.artemide.us

ATYS
http://www.atysdesign.com

Banci
http://www.banci.it

Bayworld Industries
http://www.bayworld.com

Bega/US
http://www.bega-us.com

Belfer Lighting Group
http://www.belfergroup.com

Beta-Calco
http://www.betacalco.com

B-K Lighting
http://www.bklighting.com

Boyd Lighting Company
http://www.boydlighting.com

Bruck Lighting Systems
http://www.brucklighting.com

Capri Lighting
http://www.caprilighting.com

Casella
http://www.casellalighting.com/

Chimera
http://www.chimeralighting.com

City Lights Antique Lighting
http://www.citylights.nu

Citybarn Antiques
http://www.citybarnantiques.com

Color Kinetics
http://www.colorkinetics.com

Columbia Lighting
http://www.columbia-ltg.com

Cooper Lighting
http://www.cooperlighting.com

Dabmar Lighting
http://www.dabmar.com

Design Centro Italia
http://www.italydesign.com

Designplan Lighting
http://www.designplan.com

Dyna-Lite Selection
http://www.dynalite.com

ELA Lighting
http://www.ela-lighting.com

ELCO Lighting
http://www.elcolighting.com

Elite Lighting Company
http://www.elitelighting.com

Engineered Lighting Products
http://www.elplighting.com

EYE Lighting International
http://www.eyelighting.com

Fiberstars
http://www.fiberstars.com

Flos
http://www.flos.com

Fontana Arte
http://www.fontanaarte.it

Halo
http://www.haloltg.com

Hampstead Lighting & Accessories
http://www.hampsteadlighting.com

Hans Duus Blacksmith, Inc
http://www.hansduusblacksmith.com

H. E. Williams
http://www.hew.com

Historical Arts & Casting
http://www.historicalarts.com

House of Troy
http://www.houseoftroy.com

Hubbardton Forge & Wood
http://www.vtforge.net

Inlighten Studios
http://inlightenstudios.com

Ivalo Lighting
http://www.ivalolighting.com

Johnson Art Studio
http://www.johnsonartstudio.com

Juno Lighting
http://www.junolighting.com

Justice Design Group
http://www.jdg.com

Kartell
http://www.kartell.com

Kim Lighting
http://www.kimlighting.com

Koch and Lowy
http://www.chapmanco.com

LaMar Lighting
http://www.lamarlighting.com

Lampa
http://www.lampa.com

Latigo Lights
http://www.latigolights.com

LBL Lighting
http://www.lbllighting.com

LED Effects
http://www.ledeffects.com

Lee's Studio
http://www.leesstudio.com

Leucos Lighting
http://www.leucos.com

Lighting by Gregory
http://www.lightingbygregory.com

Lightolier
http://www.lightolier.com

Lightway Industries
http://www.lightwayind.com

Lightworks
http://www.lightworkslighting.com

Limn Company
http://www.limn.com

Lite Energy/Horizon
http://www.liteenergy.com

Lithonia Lighting
http://www.lithonia.com/

Los Angeles Lighting
http://www.lalighting.com

Louis Poulsen Lighting
http://www.louispoulsen.com

LST LSI Lightron
http://www.lsilightron.com

Luceplan
http://www.luceplan.com

Lucifer Lighting Company
http://www.luciferlighting.com

Lumaxam Lubrication
http://www.lumax.com

Lumileds
http://www.lumileds.com

Luminaire
http://www.luminaire.com

Lumux Lighting
http://www.lumux.net

Lutron Electronics
http://www.lutron.com

Luxo Corporation
http://www.luxous.com

Lyn Hovey Studio
http://www.lynhoveystudio.com

Mark Architectural Lighting
http://www.marklighting.com

MaxLite
http://www.maxlite.com

MP Lighting
http://www.mplighting.com

Murano Due
http://www.muranodue.com

Museum of Modern Art Store
http://www.momastore.org

National Specialty Lighting
http://www.nslusa.com

Natural Lighting
http://www.daylighting.com

Nessen Lighting
http://www.nessenlighting.com

Newstamp Lighting
http://www.newstamplighting.com

Nora Lighting
http://www.noralighting.com

Norbert Belfer Lighting
http://www.belfer.com/default.phphttp://
www.belfergroup.com

Norlux Corporation
http://www.norluxcorp.com

Oluce
http://www.oluce.com

Pathway Lighting Products
http://www.pathwaylighting.com

Peerless Lighting
http://www.peerless-lighting.com

Prescolite
http://www.prescolite.com

Prisma Lighting
http://www.prismalighting.com

Progress Lighting
http://www.progresslightingoutlet.com

Promolux Lighting International
http://www.promolux.com

RSA Lighting
http://www.rsalighting.com

SLD Lighting
http://www.sldlighting.com

So-Luminaire Daylighting Systems
http://soluminaire.com

Spectrum Lighting
http://www.spectrum-lighting.com

SPJ Lighting
http://www.spjlighting.com

Steel Partners Inc.
http://www.steelpartnersinc.com

Sternberg Vintage Lighting
http://www.sternberglighting.com

SunLED Corporation
http://www.sunled.com

Sunrise Lighting
http://www.sunriselighting.com

Tech Lighting
http://www.techlighting.com

Times Square Lighting
http://www.tslight.com

Translite Sonoma
http://www.translite.com

Turn of the Century Lighting
http://www.turnofthecenturylighting.com

Vision 3 Lighting
http://www.vision3lighting.com

W.A.C. Lighting
http://www.waclighting.com

Xenon Architectural Lighting
http://www.xenonlight.com

Yankee Craftsman
http://www.yankeecraftsman.com

Zaneen Lighting
http://www.zaneen.com

Zelco
http://www.zelco.com

Recycling Corporations

American Ecology Corporation
(U.S. Ecology)
http://www.americanecology.com

Bethlehem Apparatus Company
http://www.bethlehemapparatus.com

Chemical Waste ManagementProgram
http://www.stanford.edu/dept/EHS/
prod/enviro/waste/

DYNEX Industries
http://www.dynex.com

Earth Protection Services
http://www.earthpro.com

Full Circle Recycling
http://www.fullcirclerecycling.com

Lamp Environmental Industries
http://www.lei-inc.net

Lighting Resources
http://www.lightingresourcesinc.com

Mercury Recovery Services
http://www.dtsc.ca.gov/
HazardousWasteProjects/Mercury_
Recovery.cfm

U.S. Ecology
http://www.americanecology.com

USA Lights & Electric
http://www.usalight.com

Zumtobel Staff
http://www.zumtobelstaff.com

Appendix C

Professional Organizations, Government Agencies, and Trade Associations

ADA Guide
http://www.access-board.gov/adaag/html/adaag.htm

Adaptive Environments
http://www.adaptiveenvironments.org

American Council for an Energy-Efficient Economy
http://www.aceee.org

American Hospital Association
http://www.aha.org

American Hotel & Lodging Association
http://www.ahma.com/

American Institute of Architects
http://www.aia.org

American Institute of Graphic Arts
http://www.aiga.org

American Lighting Association
http://www.americanlightingassoc.com

American National Standards Institute
http://www.ansi.org

American Optometric Association
http://www.aoanet.org

American Society of Civil Engineers
http://www.asce.org

American Society of Furniture Designers
http://www.asfd.com

American Society of Heating, Refrigerating and Air-Conditioning Engineers
http://www.ashrae.org/

American Society of Interior Designers
http://www.asid.org

American Society of Landscape Architects
http://asla.org

American Solar Energy Society
http://www.ases.org

Architectural Lighting
http://www.archlighting.com

Architectural Record
http://www.architecturalrecord.com

ARCOM Master Systems
http://www.arcomnet.com

Arthritis Foundation
http://www.arthritis.org/default.asphttp://www.arthritis.org/resources/home-life/default.asp

Association of Energy Engineers
http://www.aeecenter.org

Association of Energy Services Professionals
http://www.aesp.org

Association of General Contractors of America
http://www.agc.org

Association of Registered Interior Designers of Ontario
http://www.arido.ca

British Contract Furnishing Association
http://www.thebcfa.com

Building Operating Management
http://www.tradespress.com/products/bom

Building Owners & Managers Association
http://www.boma.org

Buildings Magazine
http://www.buildings.com

Business and Institutional Furniture Manufacturer's Association
http://www.bifma.com

Center for Health Design
http://www.healthdesign.org

Chartered Institution of Building Services Engineers
http://www.cibse.org

Color Association of the United States
http://www.colorassociation.com

Color Marketing Group
http://www.colormarketing.org

Construction Specifications Institute
http://www.csinet.org

Construction Symbols and Terminology
http://www.constructionworknews.com

Consulting-Specifying Engineer Magazine
http://www.csemag.com

Contract Lighting Magazine
http://www.contractlighting.net

Contract Magazine
http://www.contractmagazine.com

Cost Estimating Resources
http://cost.jsc.nasa.govt/resources.html

Council for Interior Design Accreditation
http://www.accredit-id.org

EC & M (Electrical Construction & Maintenance) Publications
http://www.ecmweb.com

Electric Power Research Institute (EPRI)
http://www.epri.com

Electrical News
http://www.electricalnews.com

Energy & Environmental Building Association
http://www.eeba.org

Energy & Power Management
http://www.energyandpowermanagement.com

Eyetronics
http://www.eyetronics.com

FabricLink: Educational Resources for Fabrics, Apparel, Home Furnishings and Care
http://www.fabriclink.com

Florida Solar Energy Center
http://www.fsec.ucf.edu

Foundations for Design Integrity
http://www.ffdi.org

Frame Magazine
http://www.framemag.com

Green Building GuidePrimer
http://www.energybuilder.com/greenbld.htm

Green Lights Program
http://www.epa.gov/greenhome-basics.html

Home Furnishings International Association
http://www.hfia.com

Human Systems Integration Information Analysis Center
http://www.hsiiac.org

Illuminating Engineering Society of North America
http://iesna.org

Industrial Designers Society of America
http://www.idsa.org

Institute of Store Planners
http://www.ispo.org/

Interior Design Society
http://www.interiordesignsociety.org

Interior Designers of Canada
http://www.interiordesigncanada.org

International Association of Lighting Designers
http://iald.org

International Code Council
http://www.iccsafe.org

International Colour Authority
http://www.internationalcolourauthority.com

International Commission on Illumination
http://www.cie-usnc.org

International Council of Graphic Designers Associations
http://www.icograda.org/web/home/index.html

International Dark-Sky Association
http://www.darksky.org

International Facility Management Association
http://www.ifma.org

International Furnishings and Design Association
http://www.ifda.com

International Interior Design Association
http://www.iida.org

Intertek Testing Services – ETL SEMKO (Commercial and Electrical)
http://www.etlsemko.com

Lambda Research Corporation
http://www.lambdares.com

LD+A Magazine
http://www.iesna.org/LDA/iesnalda.cfmhttp://www.iesna.org

Lighting Analysts
http://www.lightinganalysts.com

Lighting Dimensions Magazine
http://www.lightingdimensions.com

Lighting Research Center – Rensselaer Polytechnic Institute
http://www.lrc.rpi.edu

Lighting.com (Online Resources for Everything Lighting)
http://www.lighting.com

Lightsearch.com (Lighting Manufacturer and Product Directory)
http://www.lightsearch.com

Live Design Magazine
http://livedesignonline.com

Maintenance Solutions Magazine
http://www.facilitiesnet.com/ms

Metropolis Magazine
http://www.metropolismag.com

Mondo*Arc Magazine
http://www.mondiale.co.uk/

National Association of Homebuilders
Research Center
http://www.nahbrc.org

National Association of Women in
Construction
http://www.nawic.org/

National Council for Interior Design
Qualification
http://www.ncidq.org

National Council on Qualifications for
the Lighting Professions
http://ncqlp.org

National Fire Protection Association
http://www.nfpa.org

National Institute for Occupational
Safety and Health
http://www.cdc.gov/niosh

National Institute of Standards and
Technology – Child Anthropometric
Data
http://www.itl.nist.gov/iaui/ovrt/
projects/anthrokids/ncontent.htm

National Kitchen & Bath Association
http://www.nkba.org

National Lighting Bureau
http://www.nlb.org

National Research Council
http://www.nationalacademies.org/nrc

National Technical Information Service
http://www.ntis.gov

National Trust for Historic
Preservation
http://www.nationaltrust.org

Neocon Trade Shows
http://www.merchandisemart.com

Occupational Safety & Health
Administration
http://www.osha.gov

Pacific Gas and Electric Company
http://www.pge.com

PeopleSize 2000
http://www.openerg.com/psz.htm

Quebec Furniture Manufacturers'
Association
http://www.afmq.com/en

Residential Lighting Magazine
http://www.residentiallighting.com

Retail Construction Magazine
http://www.retailconstructionmag.com

Safework
http://www.safework.com

Underwriter's Laboratories Inc.
http://www.ul.com

U.S. Census Bureau
http://www.census.gov/mcd

Windows and Daylighting Group
http://windows.lbl.gov

References

Chapter 1

Alton, J. (1995). *Painting with Light*. Berkeley, CA: University of California Press.

Benya, J., Heschong, L., McGowan, T., Miller, N., and Rubinstein, F. (2001). *Advanced Lighting Guidelines*. White Salmon, WA: New Buildings Institute.

Bourne, J., and Brett, V. (1991). *Lighting in the Domestic Interior*. London: Sotheby's.

Bowers, B. (1998). *Lengthening the Day: A History of Lighting Technology*. Oxford: Oxford University Press.

Bowmaker, J.K., and Dartnall, H.J. (1980). *Visual pigments of rods and cones in human retina*. Journal of Physiology, 298, 501–511.

Boyce, P.R. (1981). *Human Factors in Lighting*. New York: Macmillan.

Boylan, B.R. (1987). *The Lighting Primer*. Ames, IA: Iowa State University Press.

Coaton, J.R., and Marsden, A.M. (1997). *Lamps and Lighting*, 4th ed. London: Arnold.

Egan, M.D. (1983). *Concepts in Architectural Lighting*. New York: McGraw-Hill.

General Electric (1989). *Lighting Application Bulletin*. Cleveland, OH: General Electric.

Gordon, G. (2003). *Interior Lighting for Designers*, 4th ed. New York: John Wiley & Sons.

Gordon, G., and Nuckolls, J.L. (1995). *Interior Lighting for Designers*. New York: John Wiley & Sons.

Gregory, R.I. (1979). *Eye and Brain: The Psychology of Seeing*, 3rd ed. New York: McGraw-Hill.

Greif, M. (1986). *The Lighting Book*. Pittstown, NJ: The Main Street Press.

Harvey, E.N. (1957). *A History of Luminescence from the Earliest of Times until 1900*. Philadelphia: America Philosophical Society.

Hill, H., and Bruce, V. (1996). *The effects of lighting on the perception of facial surfaces*. Journal of Experimental Psychology: Human Perception and Performance, 22(4), 986–1004.

Hunter, R.S. (1975). *The Measurement of Appearance*. New York: John Wiley & Sons.

Illuminating Engineering Society of North America (IESNA) (2000). *IESNA Lighting Handbook*, 9th ed. New York: Illuminating Engineering Society of North America.

Illuminating Engineering Society of North America (IESNA) (1998). *Lighting for the aged and partially sighted community. Recommended Practice for Lighting and the Visual Environment for Senior Living*, RP-28-98. New York: Illuminating Engineering Society of North America.

Kaufman, J. E. (ed.) (1984). *IES Lighting Handbook Reference Volume 1984*. New York: Illuminating Engineering Society.

Lam, W.C. (1977). *Perception and Lighting as Formgivers for Architecture*. New York: McGraw-Hill.

Lawrence Berkeley National Laboratory (1997). *Lighting Source Book*. Berkeley, CA: Lawrence Berkeley National Laboratory.

Lewis, A.L. (1998). *Equating light sources for visual performance at low luminances*. Journal of the Illuminating Engineering Society, 27(1), 80.

Loe, D.L., Mansfield, J.F., & Rowlands, E. (1994). *Appearance of lit environment and its relevance in lighting design: Environmental study*. Lighting Research & Technology, 26(3), 119–133.

Loe, D.L., and Rowlands, E. (1996). *The art and science of lighting: A strategy for lighting design*. Lighting Research & Technology, 28(4), 153–164.

Lynes, J.A. (1978). *Developments in Lighting—1*. London: Applied Science Publishers Ltd.

Moore, F. (1985). *Concepts and Practice of Architectural Daylighting*. New York: Van Nostrand Reinhold Company.

Phillips, D. (2000). *Lighting Modern Buildings*. Oxford: Architectural Press.

Rosenthal, J., and Wertenbaker, L. (1972). *The Magic of Light*. Boston: Little, Brown and Company.

Veitch, J. (July 9–11, 2000). *Lighting guidelines from lighting quality research*. CIBSE/ILE Lighting 2000 Conference. New York, United Kingdom.

Veitch, J., and Newsham, G. (August, 1996). *Experts' quantitative and qualitative assessment of lighting quality*. Proceedings of the 1996 Annual IESNA Conference. Cleveland, OH. Available at: www.iesna.org.

Watson, L. (1977). *Lighting Design Handbook*. New York: McGraw-Hill.

Weale, R.A. (1961). *Retinal illumination and age*. Illuminating Engineering Society (London), 26(2), 95–100.

Wright, G.A., and Rea, M. S. (1984). *Age, a human factor in lighting*. Proceedings of the 1984 International Conference on Occupational Ergonomics. D.A. Attwood and C. McCann (eds.). Rexdale, Ontario, Canada: Human Factors Association of Canada.

Chapter 2

Allphin, W. (1963). *Sight lines to desk tasks in schools and offices*. Illuminating Engineering, 58(4), 244–249.

Ander, G. (1997). *Daylighting Performance & Design*. New York: John Wiley & Sons.

Benya, J., Heschong, L., McGowan, T., Miller, N., and Rubinstein, F. (2001). *Advanced Lighting Guidelines*. White Salmon, WA: New Buildings Institute.

Bierman, A., and Conway, K. (2000). *Characterizing daylight photosensor systems performance to help overcome market barriers*. Journal of the Illuminating Engineering Society, 29(1), 101–115.

Bleeker, N., and Veenstra, W. (August, 1990). *The performance of four-foot fluorescent lamps as a function of ambient temperature on 60Hz and high frequency ballasts*. Proceedings of the 1990 Annual IESNA Conference. Baltimore, MD.

Borg, N. (March, 1993). *The ABCs of UV*. IAEEL Newsletter.

Bowers, B. (1998). *Lengthening the Day: A History of Lighting Technology*. Oxford: Oxford University Press.

Boyce, P.N., Eklund, N., and Simpson, S. (2000). *Individual lighting control: Task performance, mood and illuminance*. Journal of the Illuminating Engineering Society, 29(1), 131–142.

Boylan, B.R. (1987). *The Lighting Primer*. Ames, IA: Iowa State University Press.

BSI (1992). *Code of Practice for Daylighting*. British Standard BS 8206 Part 2.

Carriere, L., and Rea, M. (1988). *Economics of switching fluorescent lamps*. IEEE Transactions on Industry Applications, 24(3), 370–379.

CIBSE (1987). *Window Design*. CIBSE Applications Manual.

Coaton, J.R., and Marsden, A. M. (1997). *Lamps and Lighting*, 4th ed. London: Arnold.

Davis, R.G. (1987). *Closing the gap: Research, design, and the psychological aspects of lighting*. Lighting Design Applications, 17(5), 14–15; 52.

Ducker Research. (August, 1999). *Lighting quality – key customer values and decision process*. Report to the Light Right Research Consortium.

Egan, M.D. (1983). *Concepts in Architectural Lighting*. New York: McGraw-Hill.

Eklund, N., Boyce, P., and Simpson, S. (2000). *Lighting and sustained performance*. Journal of the Illuminating Engineering Society, 29(1), 116.

Elenbass, W. (1971). *Fluorescent Lamps*, Philips Technical Library, 2nd ed. London: Macmillan.

Flynn, J.E., Segil, A.W., and Steffy, G.R. (1988). *Architectural Interior Systems: Lighting, Acoustics, Air Conditioning*, 2nd ed. New York: Van Nostrand Reinhold.

Flynn, J.E., and Spencer, T.J. (1977). *The effects of light source color on user impression and satisfaction*. Journal of the Illuminating Engineering Society, 6(4), 167–179.

General Electric (1989). *Lighting Application Bulletin*. Cleveland, OH: General Electric.

Gifford, R. (1993). *Scientific evidence for claim about full-spectrum lamps: Past and future*. IRC internal report no. 659.

Gordon, G. (2003). *Interior Lighting for Designers*, 4th ed. New York: John Wiley & Sons.

Gordan, G., and Nuckolls, J. L. (1995). *Interior Lighting for Designers*. New York: John Wiley & Sons.

Greif, M. (1986). *The Lighting Book*. Pittstown, NJ: The Main Street Press.

Henderson, S.T. (1977). *Daylight and Its Spectrum*, 2nd ed. Bristol, England: Adam Hilger.

Heschong Mahone Group (HMG) (1999, August). *Skylighting and Retail Sales, and Daylighting in*

Schools. For Pacific Gas & Electric. URL: http://www.h-m-g.com.

Heschong Mahone Group (HMG) (1997, May). *The Lighting Efficiency Technology Report, vol. I: California Lighting Baseline.* For the California Energy Commission.

Hunter, R.S. (1975). *The Measurement of Appearance.* New York: John Wiley & Sons.

Illuminating Engineering Society of North America (IESNA) (2000). *IESNA Lighting Handbook,* 9th ed. New York: Illuminating Engineering Society of North America.

International Dark-Sky Association (IDA) (1996). *Information sheets 10 and 20.* URL: http://www.dark-sky.org.

Jennings, J.F., Rubinstein, R., and DiBartolomeo, D.R. (2000). *Comparisons of control options in private offices in an advanced lighting controls test bed.* Journal of the Illuminating Engineering Society, 29(2), 39–60.

Ji, Y., Davis, R., and Chen, W. (1999). *An investigation of the effect of operating cycles on the life of compact fluorescent lamps.* Journal of the Illuminating Engineering Society, 28(2), 57–62.

Kaufman, J.E. (ed.) (1984). *IES Lighting Handbook Reference Volume 1984.* New York: Illuminating Engineering Society.

Kay, G.N. (1999). *Fiber Optics in Architectural Lighting.* New York: McGraw-Hill.

Lawrence Berkeley National Laboratory (1997). *Lighting Source Book.* Berkeley, CA: Lawrence Berkeley National Laboratory.

Lewis, A.L. (1998). *Equating light sources for visual performance at low luminances.* Journal of the Illuminating Engineering Society, 27(1), 80.

Lighting Design Lab (1998). *Daylight Models* (video). Seattle, WA: Lighting Design Lab.

Littlefair, P.J. (1996). *Designing with Innovative Daylighting.* London: CRC, Garston.

Littlefair, P.J. (1991). *Site Layout Planning for Daylight and Sunlight: A Guide to Good Practice.* BRE Report BR 209.

Maniccia, D., Rutledge, D., Rea, M., and Morrow, W. (1999). *Occupant use of manual lighting control in private offices.* Journal of the Illuminating Engineering Society, 28(2), 42–56.

Maniccia, D., Von Neida, B., and Tweed, A. (2000). *Analysis of the energy and cost savings potential of occupancy sensors for commercial lighting systems.* Proceedings of the 2000 Annual Conference of the Illuminating Engineering Society of North America.

Mistrick, R., Chen, C., Bierman, B., and Felts, D. (2000). *A comparison of photosensor-controlled electronic dimming systems.* Proceedings of the 2000 Annual Conference of the Illuminating Engineering Society, 29(1), 66–80.

Moore, F. (1985). *Concepts and Practice of Architectural Daylighting. New York:* Van Nostrand Reinhold.

Narendran, A.N., Bullough, J.D., Maliyagoda, N., and Bierman, A. (July/August, 2000). W*hat is useful life for white light LEDs?* Proceedings of the 2000 Annual Conference of the Illuminating Engineering Society of North America. Washington, DC.

National Lighting Product Information Program (NLPIP) (March, 1998). *Specifier reports: Photosensors.*

Navvab, M. (2000). *A comparison of visual performance under high and low color temperature fluorescent lamps.* Proceedings of the 2000 Annual Conference of the Illuminating Engineering Society of North America. Washington, DC.

Phillips Lighting. (1994). *Fluorescent lamps: Correspondence Course, Lesson 9.* Netherlands: Philips Lighting BV.

Phillips, D. (2000). *Lighting Modern Buildings.* Oxford: Architectural Press.

Portland Energy Conservation, I. (1992). *Building Commissioning Guidelines,* 2nd ed. Bonneville Power Administration.

Rea, M.S., and Ouellette, M.J. (1991). *Relative visual performance: A basis for application.* Lighting Research Technology, 23(3), 135–144.

Rea, M.S., Ouellette, M.J., and Kennedy, M.E. (1985). *Lighting and task parameters affecting posture, performance, and subjective ratings.* Journal of Illuminating Engineering Society, 15(1), 231–238.

Rowlands, E., Loe, D.L., McIntosh, R.M., and Mansfield, K. P. (1985). *Lighting adequacy and quality in office interiors by consideration of subjective assessment and physical measurement.* CIE Journal, 4(1), 23–27.

Rundquist, R.A., McDougall, T.G., and Benya, J. (1996). *Lighting Controls: Patterns for Design.* Prepared by R.A. Rundquist Associates for the Electric Power Research Institute and the Empire State Electrical Energy Research Corporation.

Southern California Edison (1999). *Energy Design Resources Case Studies: REMO and Timberland.* Available from: http://www.energydesignresources.com.

Steffy, G.R. (2002). *Architectural Lighting Design,* 2nd ed. New York: Van Nostrand Reinhold.

Stern, R. (1988). *The New Let There Be Neon.* New York: Harry N. Abrams, Inc., Publishers.

U.K. Department of the Environment (1998, March). *Desktop guide to daylighting for architects.* Good Practice Guide 245. Harwell, Oxfordshire, England: ETSU.

Van den Beld, G.J., Begemann, S. H.A., and Tenner, A.D. (1997). *Comparison of preferred lighting levels for two different lighting systems in north-oriented offices.* Light and Engineering, 5(3), 48–52.

Veitch, J., and Newsham, G. (2000). *Exercised control, lighting choices, and energy use: An office simulation experiment.* Journal of Environmental Psychology, 20(3), 219–237.

Veitch, J., and Newsham, G. (1999, June). *Preferred luminous conditions in open-plan offices: implications for lighting quality recommendations.* CIE Proceedings. CIE Pub no. 133, vol. 1, part 2: 4–6.

Veitch, J., and Newsham, G. (1998). *Lighting quality and energy-efficiency effects on task performance, mood, health, satisfaction, and comfort.* Journal of the Illuminating Engineering Society, 27(1), 107.

Waymouth, J.F. (1971). *Electric Discharge Lamps.* Cambridge, MA: MIT Press.

Webb, M. (1984). *The Magic of Neon.* Salt Lake City, UT: Gibbs M. Smith, Inc.

Chapter 3

Albers, J. (1963). *Interaction of Color.* New Haven: Yale University Press.

American Society of Heating, Refrigerating and Air-Conditioning Engineers (1999). *Energy efficient design of new buildings except new low-rise residential buildings,* ASHRAE/IES90.1-1999. Atlanta, GA: ASHRAE.

Benya, J., Heschong, L., McGowan, T., Miller, N., and Rubinstein, F. (2001). *Advanced Lighting Guidelines.* White Salmon, WA: New Buildings Institute.

Birren, F. (1969). *Light, Color and Environment.* New York: Van Nostrand Reinhold.

Boyce, P.R. (1981). *Human Factors in Lighting.* New York: Macmillan.

Boylan, B.R. (1987). *The Lighting Primer.* Ames, IA: Iowa State University Press.

Coaton, J.R., and Marsden, A. M. (1997). *Lamps and Lighting,* 4th ed. London: Arnold.

Egan, M.D. (1983). *Concepts in Architectural Lighting.* New York: McGraw-Hill.

Flynn, J.E. and Spencer, T. J. (1977). *The effects of light source color on user impression and satisfaction.* Journal of the Illuminating Engineering Society, 6(4), 167–179.

General Electric (1989). *Lighting Application Bulletin.* Cleveland, OH: General Electric.

Gordon, G. (2003). *Interior Lighting for Designers,* 4th ed. New York: John Wiley & Sons.

Gordon, G., and Nuckolls, J. L. (1995). *Interior Lighting for Designers.* New York: John Wiley & Sons.

Gregory, R.I. (1979). *Eye and Brain: The Psychology of Seeing,* 3rd ed. New York: McGraw-Hill.

Halse, A.O. (1968). *The Use of Color in Interiors.* New York: McGraw-Hill.

Halstead, M.B. (1997). *Colour.* In J. R. Coaton and A. M. Marsden (eds.), *Lamps and Lighting.* New York: John Wiley & Sons.

Henderson, S.T. (1977). *Daylight and Its Spectrum,* 2nd ed. Bristol, England: Adam Hilger.

Hill, H., and Bruce, V. (1996). *The effects of lighting on the perception of facial surfaces.* Journal of Experimental Psychology: Human Perception and Performance, 22(4), 986–1004.

Hunt, R.W.G. (1991). *Measuring Colour,* 2nd ed. Chichester, England: Ellis Horwood.

Hunter, R.S. (1975). *The Measurement of Appearance.* New York: John Wiley & Sons.

Illuminating Engineering Society of North America (IESNA) (2000). *IESNA Lighting Handbook,* 9th ed. New York: Illuminating Engineering Society of North America.

Illuminating Engineering Society of North America (IESNA) (1998). *Lighting for the aged and partially sighted community. Recommended practice for lighting and the visual environment for Senior Living,* RP-28-98. New York: Illuminating Engineering Society of North America.

Itten, J. (1961). *The Art of Color.* New York: Van Nostrand Reinhold.

Kaufman, J.E. (ed.) (1984). *IES Lighting Handbook Reference Volume 1984.* New York: Illuminating Engineering Society.

Lam, W.C. (1977). *Perception and Lighting as Formgivers for Architecture.* New York: McGraw-Hill.

Littlefair, P. J. (1991). *Site layout planning for daylight and sunlight: a guide to good practice.* BRE Report, BR 209.

Loe, D.L., Mansfield, J.F., and Rowlands, E. (1994). *Appearance of lit environment and its relevance in lighting design: Environmental study.* Lighting Research & Technology, 26(3), 119–133.

Loe, D.L., and Rowlands, E. (1996). *The art and science of lighting: A strategy for lighting design.* Lighting Research & Technology, 28(4), 153–164.

Moore, F. (1985). *Concepts and practice of architectural daylighting.* New York: Van Nostrand Reinhold Company.

Phillips, D. (2000). *Lighting Modern Buildings.* Oxford: Architectural Press.

Rea, M.S. (1986). *Toward a model of visual performance: Foundations and data.* Journal of the Illuminating Engineering Society, 15(2), 41–57.

Rea, M.S., and Ouellette, M.J. (1991). *Relative visual performance: A basis for application.* Lighting Research & Technology, 23(3), 135–144.

Rea, M.S., and Ouellette, M.J. (1988). *Visual performance using reaction times.* Lighting Research & Technology, 20(4), 139–53.

Rosenthal, J., and Wertenbaker, L. (1972). *The Magic of Light.* Boston: Little, Brown and Company.

Rowlands, E.D., Loe, D.L., McIntosh, R.M., and Mansfield, K.P. (1985). *Lighting adequacy and quality in office interiors by consideration of subjective assessment and physical measurement.* CIE Journal, 4(1), 23–37.

Smith F.K., and Bertolone, F. J. (1986). *The Principles and Practices of Lighting Design: Bringing Interiors to Light.* New York: Whitney Library of Design.

Steffy, G.R. (2002). *Architectural Lighting Design,* 2nd ed. New York: Van Nostrand Reinhold.

Tresidder, J. (ed.) (1983). *Mastering Composition and Light.* New York: Time-Life Books.

Varley, H. (1980). *Color.* Los Angeles: Knapp.

Veitch, J. (2000, July). *Lighting guidelines from lighting quality research.* CIBSE/ILE Lighting 2000 Conference. New York, United Kingdom.

Watson, L. (1977). *Lighting Design Handbook.* New York: McGraw-Hill.

Weale, R. A. (1961). *Retinal illumination and age.* Illuminating Engineering Society (London), 26(2), 95–100.

Wilkins, A.J., Nimmo-Smith, I., Slater, A.I., and Bedocs, L. (1989). *Fluorescent lighting, headaches, and eyestrain.* Lighting Research & Technology, 21(1), 11–18.

Wright, G. A., and Rea, M.S. (1984). *Age, a human factor in lighting.* Proceedings of the 1984 International Conference on Occupational Ergonomics. D.A. Attwood, and C. McCann (eds.). Rexdale, Ontario, Canada: Human Factors Association of Canada.

Wright, W.D. (1971). *The Measurement of Colour,* 4th ed. London: Adam Hilger.

Wyszecki, G., and Stiles, W. S. (1967). *Color Science.* New York: John Wiley & Sons.

Chapter 4

Allphin, W. (1961). *BCD appraisals of luminaire brightness in a simulated office.* Illuminating Engineering, 56(1), 31–44.

Ashdown, I. (1998). *Making near-field photometry practical.* Journal of the Illuminating Engineering Society, 27(1), 67–79.

Ballman, T.L., and Levin, R.E. (1987). *Illumination in partitioned spaces.* Journal of the Illuminating Engineering Society, 16(2), 31–49.

Benya, J., Heschong, L., McGowan, T., Miller, N., and Rubinstein, F. (2001). *Advanced Lighting Guidelines.* White Salmon, WA: New Buildings Institute.

Boylan, B.R. (1987). *The Lighting Primer.* Ames, IA: Iowa State University Press.

Bradley, R.D., and Logan, H.L. (1964). *A uniform method for computing the probability of comfort response in a visual field.* Illuminating Engineering, 59(3), 189–206.

Carter, D.J., Sexton, R.C., and Miller, M.S. (1989). *Field measurement of illuminance.* Lighting, Research, & Technology, 21(1), 29–35.

Clark, F. (1968). *Light loss factor in the design process.* Illuminating Engineering, 63(11), 575–581.

Clark, F. (1963). *Accurate maintenance factors.* Illuminating Engineering, 58(3), 124–131.

Coaton, J.R., and Marsden, A.M. (1997). *Lamps and Lighting,* 4th ed. London: Arnold.

Commission Internationale de l'Eclairage (1994). *CIE*

Collections in Photometry and Radiometry. CIE no 114. Vienna, Austria: Bureau Central de la CIE.

DeCusatis, C. (1997). *Handbook of Applied Optometry.* New York: AIP Press.

DiLaura, D.L. (1976). *On the computation of visual comfort probability.* Journal of the Illuminating Engineering Society, 5(4), 207–217.

Egan, M.D. (1983). *Concepts in Architectural Lighting.* New York: McGraw-Hill.

Eklund, N., Boyce, P., and Simpson, S. (2000). *Lighting and sustained performance.* Journal of the Illuminating Engineering Society, 29(1), 116.

Fry, G.A. (1976). *A simplified formula for discomfort glare.* Journal of the Illuminating Engineering Society, 5(1), 10–20.

Gaertner, A.A. (1994). *Photometric and radiometric quantities.* In Course on Photometry, Radiometry, and Colorimetry. NRC 38643. Ottawa, Ontario: National Research Council. Institute for National Measurement Standards.

General Electric (1989). *Lighting Application Bulletin.* Cleveland, OH: General Electric.

Gordon, G. (2003). *Interior Lighting for Designers*, 4th ed. New York: John Wiley & Sons.

Gordon, G., and Nuckolls, J.L. (1995). *Interior Lighting for Designers.* New York: John Wiley & Sons.

Gregory, R.I. (1979). *Eye and Brain: The Psychology of Seeing*, 3rd ed. New York: McGraw-Hill.

Greif, M. (1986). *The Lighting Book.* Pittstown, NJ: The Main Street Press.

Guth, S.K. (1966). *Computing visual comfort ratings for a specific interior lighting installation.* Illuminating Engineering, 61(10), 634–642.

Guth, S.K., and McNelis, J.F. (1961). *Further data on discomfort glare from multiple sources.* Illuminating Engineering, 56(1), 46–57.

Hopkinson, R.G. (1957). *Evaluation of glare.* Illuminating Engineering, 52(6), 305–316.

Hunter, R.S. (1975). *The Measurement of Appearance.* New York: John Wiley & Sons.

Illuminating Engineering Society. Committee on Recommendations of Quality and Quantity of Illumination, Subcommittee on Direct Glare (1966). *Outline of a standard procedure for computing visual comfort ratios for interior lighting.* Report No. 2. Illuminating Engineering, 61(10), 643–666.

Illuminating Engineering Society. Committee on Recommendations of Quality and Quantity of Illumination (1969). *A statement concerning visual comfort probability. (VCP): Naïve vs. experienced observers.* Illuminating Engineering, 64(9), 604.

Illuminating Engineering Society. Committee on Standards of Quality and Quantity for Interior Illumination. (1946). *The interreflection method of predetermining brightness and brightness ratios.* Illuminating Engineering, 41(5), 361–385.

Illuminating Engineering Society. Committee on Testing Procedures. Subcommittee on Guide for Measurement of Photometric Brightness. (1961). *IES guide for measurement of photometric brightness (luminance).* Illuminating Engineering, 56(7), 457–462.

Illuminating Engineering Society. Lighting Design Practice Committee (1968). *Calculation of luminance coefficients based upon zonal-cavity method.* Illuminating Engineering, 63(8), 423–432.

Illuminating Engineering Society. Lighting Design Practice Committee. (1964). *Zonal-cavity method of calculating and using coefficients of utilization.* Illuminating Engineering, 59(5), 309–328.

Illuminating Engineering Society of North America (IESNA) (2000). *IESNA Lighting Handbook*, 9th ed. New York: Illuminating Engineering Society of North America.

Kaufman, J.E. (ed.) (1984). *IES Lighting Handbook Reference Volume 1984.* New York: Illuminating Engineering Society.

Knowles-Middleton, W.E., and Mayo, E.G. (1951). *Variations in the horizontal distribution of light from candlepower standards.* Journal of the Opticians Society of America, 41(8), 513–516.

Lam, W.C. (1977). *Perception and Lighting as Formgivers for Architecture.* New York: McGraw-Hill.

Lawrence Berkeley National Laboratory (1997). *Lighting Source Book.* Berkeley, CA: Lawrence Berkeley National Laboratory.

Levin, R.E. (1982). *The photometric connection: Parts 1–4.* Lighting Design Application, 12(9), 28–35; 12(10), 60-63; 12(11), 42–47; 12(12), 16–18.

Lewis, A.L. (1998). *Equating light sources for visual performance at low luminances.* Journal of the Illuminating Engineering Society, 27(1), 80.

Lighting Design Lab (1998). *Daylight Models* (video). Seattle, WA: Lighting Design Lab.

Littlefair, P.J. (1991). *Site Layout Planning for Daylight and Sunlight: A Guide to Good Practice*. BRE Report BR 209.

Lynes, J.A. (1978). *Developments in Lighting*. London: Applied Science Publishers Ltd.

Moore, F. (1985). *Concepts and Practice of Architectural Daylighting*. New York: Van Nostrand Reinhold.

Murdoch, J.B. (1981). *Inverse square law approximation of illuminance*. Journal of the Illuminating Engineering Society, 10(2), 96–106.

National Bureau of Standards (1991). *The International System of Units (SI)*, 6th ed. NBS Special Publication 330. Gaithersburg, MD: National Bureau of Standards.

O'Brien, P.F., and Balogh, E. (1967). *Configuration factors for computing illumination within interiors*. Illuminating Engineering, 62(4), 169–179.

Phillips, D. (2000). *Lighting Modern Buildings*. Oxford: Architectural Press.

Rosenthal, J., and Wertenbaker, L. (1972). *The Magic of Light*. Boston: Little, Brown and Company.

Smith F.K. and Bertolone, F.J. (1986). *The Principles and Practices of Lighting Design: Bringing Interiors to Light*. New York: Whitney Library of Design.

Steffy, G.R. (2002). *Architectural Lighting Design*, 2nd ed. New York: Van Nostrand Reinhold.

Tresidder, J. (ed.) (1983). *Mastering Composition and Light*. New York: Time-Life Books.

Veitch, J. (2000, July). *Lighting guidelines from lighting quality research*. CIBSE/ILE Lighting 2000 Conference. New York, United Kingdom.

Veitch, J., and Newsham, G. (1999, June). *Preferred luminous conditions in open-plan offices: Implications for lighting quality recommendations*. CIE Proceedings. CIE Pub No. 133, vol. 1, part 2: 4–6.

Veitch, J., and Newsham, G. (1996, August). *Experts' quantitative and qualitative assessment of lighting quality. Proceedings of the 1996 Annual IESNA Conference*. Cleveland, OH. Available at: www.iesna.org.

Ward, L.G., and Shakespeare, R.A. (1998). *Rendering with Radiance: The Art and Science of Lighting Visualization*. San Francisco: Morgan Kaufmann.

Watson, L. (1977). *Lighting Design Handbook*. New York: McGraw-Hill.

Zhang, J.X., and Ngai, P.Y. (1991). *Lighting calculations in a multi-partitioned space*. Journal of the Illuminating Engineering Society, 20(1), 32–43.

Chapter 5

Allphin, W. (1961). *BCD appraisals of luminaire brightness in a simulated office*. Illuminating Engineering, 56(1), 31–44.

Benya, J., Heschong, L., McGowan, T., Miller, N., and Rubinstein, F. (2001). *Advanced Lighting Guidelines*. White Salmon, WA: New Buildings Institute.

Boyce, P.N., Eklund, N., and Simpson, S. (2000). *Individual lighting control: Task performance, mood and illuminance*. Journal of the Illuminating Engineering Society, 29(1), 131–142.

Boyce, P.R. (1981). *Human Factors in Lighting*. New York: Macmillan.

Boylan, B.R. (1987). *The Lighting Primer*. Ames, IA: Iowa State University Press.

Carter, D.J., Sexton, R.C., and Miller, M.S. (1989). *Field measurement of illuminance*. Lighting, Research, & Technology, 21(1), 29–35.

Clark, F. (1968). *Light loss factor in the design process*. Illuminating Engineering, 63(11), 575–581.

Clark, F. (1963). *Accurate maintenance factors*. Illuminating Engineering, 58(3), 124–131.

Coaton, J.R., and Marsden, A.M. (1997). *Lamps and Lighting*, 4th ed. London: Arnold.

Ducker Research (August 1999). *Lighting quality – Key customer values and decision process*. Report to the Light Right Research Consortium.

Egan, M.D. (1983). *Concepts in Architectural Lighting*. New York: McGraw-Hill.

Electric Power Research Institute (EPRI) (1997). *Lighting Retrofit Manual*. Pleasant Hill, CA: Electric Power Research Institute.

Elmer, W.B. (1980). *The Optical Design of Reflectors*. New York: John Wiley & Sons.

Gordan, G., and Nuckolls, J.L. (1995). *Interior Lighting for Designers*. New York: John Wiley & Sons.

Greif, M. (1986). *The Lighting Book*. Pittstown, NJ: The Main Street Press.

Hopkinson, R.G. (1957). *Evaluation of glare*. Illuminating Engineering, 52(6), 305–316.

Illuminating Engineering Society. Committee on Light Control and Equipment Design (1970). *IES guide to design of light control. Part IV: Practical concepts of equipment design*. Illuminating Engineering, 65(8), 479–494.

Illuminating Engineering Society. Lighting Design

Practice Committee. (1968). *Calculation of luminance coefficients based upon zonal-cavity method.* Illuminating Engineering, 63(8), 423–432.

Illuminating Engineering Society of North America (IESNA) (2000). *IESNA Lighting Handbook*, 9th ed. New York: Illuminating Engineering Society of North America.

Kaufman, J.E. (ed.) (1984). *IES Lighting Handbook Reference Volume 1984.* New York: Illuminating Engineering Society.

Lewis, A.L. (1998). *Equating light sources for visual performance at low luminances.* Journal of the Illuminating Engineering Society, 27(1), 80.

Loe, D.L., Mansfield, J.F., and Rowlands, E. (1994). *Appearance of lit environment and its relevance in lighting design: Environmental study.* Lighting Research & Technology, 26(3), 119–133.

Loe, D.L., and Rowlands, E. (1996). *The art and science of lighting: A strategy for lighting design.* Lighting Research & Technology, 28(4), 153–164.

Lynes, J.A. (1978). *Developments in Lighting – 1.* London: Applied Science Publishers.

O'Brien, P.F., and Balogh, E. (1967). *Configuration factors for computing illumination within interiors.* Illuminating Engineering, 62(4), 169–179.

Phillips, D. (2000). *Lighting Modern Buildings.* Oxford: Architectural Press.

Smith F.K., and Bertolone, F.J. (1986). *The Principles and Practices of Lighting Design: Bringing Interiors to Light.* New York: Whitney Library of Design.

Steffy, G.R. (1990). *Architectural Lighting Design.* New York: Van Nostrand Reinhold.

Veitch, J., and Newsham, G. (1998). *Lighting quality and energy-efficiency effects on task performance, mood, health, satisfaction, and comfort.* Journal of the Illuminating Engineering Society, 27(1), 107.

Ward, L.G., and Shakespeare, R.A. (1998). *Rendering with Radiance: The Art and Science of Lighting Visualization.* San Francisco: Morgan Kaufmann.

Watson, L. (1977). *Lighting Design Handbook.* New York: McGraw-Hill.

Chapter 6

American Society of Heating, Refrigerating and Air-Conditioning Engineers (1999). *Energy efficient design of new buildings except new low-rise residential buildings.* ASHRAE/IES90.1–1999. Atlanta, GA: ASHRAE.

Ander, G. (1997). *Daylighting Performance & Design.* New York: John Wiley & Sons.

British Standards Institution (1992). *Code of Practice for Daylighting.* British Standard BS 8206, Part 2.

Benya, J., Heschong, L., McGowan, T., Miller, N., and Rubinstein, F. (2001). *Advanced Lighting Guidelines.* White Salmon, WA: New Buildings Institute.

Bernstien, A., and Conway, K. (2000, March). *The public benefits of California's investments in energy efficiency.* Prepared for the California Energy Commission by the RAND Corporation. MR-1212.0-CEC.

Bierman, A., and Conway, K. (2000). *Characterizing daylight photosensor systems performance to help overcome market barriers.* Journal of the Illuminating Engineering Society, 29(1), 101–115.

Boyce, P.N., Eklund, N., and Simpson, S. (2000). *Individual lighting control: Task performance, mood and illuminance.* Journal of the Illuminating Engineering Society, 29(1), 131–142.

Carriere, L., and Rea, M. (1988). *Economics of switching fluorescent lamps.* IEEE Transactions on Industry Applications, 24(3), 370–379.

Clark, F. (1963). *Accurate maintenance factors.* Illuminating Engineering, 58(3), 124–131.

Coaton, J.R., and Marsden, A.M. (1997). *Lamps and Lighting*, 4th ed. London: Arnold.

Elenbass, W. (1971). *Fluorescent Lamps*, Philips Technical Library, 2nd ed. London: Macmillan.

Energy Information Administration (EIA) (1996). *Annual Energy Outlook, with Projections to 2015.* Washington, DC: U.S. Department of Energy.

Energy Information Administration (EIA) (1995). *Annual Energy Review for 1995.* Washington, DC: U.S. Department of Energy.

Gordon, G., and Nuckolls, J.L. (1995). *Interior Lighting for Designers.* New York: John Wiley & Sons.

Heschong Mahone Group (HMG) (August 1999). *Skylighting and Retail Sales, and Daylighting in Schools.* For Pacific Gas & Electric. http://www.h-m-g.com.

Heschong Mahone Group (HMG). (1997, May). The *Lighting Efficiency Technology Report, Vol. I: California Lighting Baseline.* For the California Energy Commission.

Illuminating Engineering Society, Committee on Light Control and Equipment Design (1970). *IES guide to design of light control. Part IV: Practical concepts of equipment design.* Illuminating Engineering, 65(8), 479–494.

Illuminating Engineering Society of North America (IESNA) (2000). *IESNA Lighting Handbook*, 9th ed. New York: Illuminating Engineering Society of North America.

Interlaboratory Working Group (1997, September). *Scenarios of U.S. Carbon Reductions – Potential Impacts of Energy Technologies by 2010 and Beyond.* Office of Energy Efficiency and Renewable Energy. U.S. Department of Energy.

Jennings, J.F., Rubinstein, R., and DiBartolomeo, D.R. (2000). *Comparisons of control options in private offices in an advanced lighting controls test bed.* Journal of the Illuminating Engineering Society, 29(2), 39–60.

Ji, Y., Davis, R., and Chen, W. (1999). *An investigation of the effect of operating cycles on the life of compact fluorescent lamps.* Journal of the Illuminating Engineering Society, 28(2), 57–62.

Lawrence Berkeley National Laboratory (1992). *Analysis of Federal Policy Options for Improving U.S. Lighting Energy Efficiency.* Berkeley, CA: Lawrence Berkeley National Laboratory.

Littlefair, P.J. (1991). *Site layout planning for daylight and sunlight: A guide to good practice.* BRE Report BR 209.

Maniccia, D., Rutledge, D., Rea, M., and Morrow, W. (1999). *Occupant use of manual lighting control in private offices.* Journal of the Illuminating Engineering Society, 28(2), 42–56.

Maniccia, D., Von Neida, B., and Tweed, A. (2000). *Analysis of the energy and cost savings potential of occupancy sensors for commercial lighting systems.* Proceedings of the 2000 Annual Conference of the Illuminating Engineering Society of North America.

Mistrick, R., Chen, C., Bierman, B., and Felts, D. (2000). *A comparison of photosensor-controlled electronic dimming systems.* Proceedings of the 2000 Annual Conference of the Illuminating Engineering Society, 29(1), 66–80.

Narendrean, N., Yin, T., et al. (2000). *A lamp life predictor for the frequently switched instant-start fluorescent*

systems. Proceedings of the 2000 Annual Conference of the Illuminating Engineering Society of North America.

National Lighting Product Information Program (NLPIP) (1998, March). *Specifier Reports: Photosensors.*

Pacific Gas & Electric Company (1999). *Daylighting Initiative Case Study.* http://www.pge.com.

Phillips, D. (2000). *Lighting Modern Buildings.* Oxford: Architectural Press.

Portland Energy Conservation, I (1992). *Building Commissioning Guidelines*, 2nd ed. Portland, OR: Bonneville Power Administration.

Rundquist, R.A., McDougall, T.G., and Benya, J. (1996). *Lighting Controls: Patterns for Design.* Prepared by R A. Rundquist Associates for the Electric Power Research Institute and the Empire State Electrical Energy Research Corporation.

Rundquist, R.A., Johnson, K., and Aumann, D. (1993). *Calculating lighting and HVAC interactions.* ASHRAE Journal, 35(11), 28.

Southern California Edison (1999). *Energy Design Resources Case Studies: REMO and Timberland.* Available from: http://www.energydesignresources.com

U.K. Department of the Environment (1998, March). *Desktop guide to daylighting for architects.* Good Practice Guide 245. Oxfordshire, United Kingdom: ETSU.

Van Bogaert, G. (1996). *Local control system for ergonomic energy-saving lighting.* Special IAEEEL Edition.

Veitch, J., and Newsham, G. (2000). *Exercised control, lighting choices, and energy use: An office simulation experiment.* Journal of Environmental Psychology, 20(3), 219–237.

Chapter 7

American History Museum of the Smithsonian Institute (2003). *Lighting the Way: A Project at the Smithsonian.* http://americanhistory.si.edu/.

American Society of Heating, Refrigeration and Air-Conditioning Engineers (1999). *Energy efficient design of new buildings except new low-rise residential buildings*, ASHRAE/IES90.1-1999. Atlanta, GA: ASHRAE.

Ander, G. (1997). *Daylighting Performance & Design.* New York: John Wiley & Sons.

BCAP (1999, January). *Energy Conservation and Code Updates: Status of State Energy Codes.* Building Codes Assistance Project, last updated January 1999. http://www.bcap-energy.org/home.php.

Barnes, P.R., Van Dyke, J.W., McConnell, B.W., and Das, S. (1996, July). *Determination Analysis of Energy Conservation Standards for Distribution Transformers.* Oak Ridge, TN: Oak Ridge National Laboratory. ORNL-6847.

Benya, J., Heschong, L., McGowan, T., Miller, N., and Rubinstein, F. (2001). *Advanced Lighting Guidelines.* White Salmon, WA: New Buildings Institute.

Bernstien, A., and Conway, K. (2000, March). *The public benefits of California's investments in energy efficiency.* Prepared for the California Energy Commission by the RAND Corporation. MR-1212.0-CEC.

Bierman, A., and Conway, K. (2000). *Characterizing daylight photosensor systems performance to help overcome market barriers.* Journal of the Illuminating Engineering Society, 29(1), 101–115.

Boyce, P.N., Eklund, N., and Simpson, S. (2000). *Individual lighting control: Task performance, mood and illuminance.* Journal of the Illuminating Engineering Society, 29(1), 131–142.

Boyce, P.N., Eklund, N., and Simpson, S. (1999). *Individual lighting control: Task performance, mood and illuminance.* IESNA Conference Proceedings, 1999. New York: Illuminating Engineering Society of North America.

Boylan, B.R. (1987). *The Lighting Primer.* Ames, IA: Iowa State University Press.

BSI (1992). *Code of Practice for Daylighting.* British Standard BS 8206, Part 2.

California Energy Commission (1999, July). *Building Energy Efficiency Standards.* Title 24 Pt. 6. California Energy Commission.

Carriere, L., and Rea, M. (1988). *Economics of switching fluorescent lamps.* IEEE Transactions on Industry Applications, 24 (3), 370–379.

CIBSE (1987). *Window Design.* CIBSE Applications Manual.

Clark, F. (1963). *Accurate maintenance factors.* Illuminating Engineering, 58(3), 124–131.

Coaton, J.R., and Marsden, A.M. (1997). *Lamps and Lighting* (4th ed.). London: Arnold.

DeCanio, S J. (1998, April). *The efficiency paradox: Bureaucratic and organizational barriers to profitable energy-saving investments.* Energy Policy, 26(5), 441–454.

Delene, J.G., Sheffield, J., Williams, K. A., Reid, R.L., and Hadley, S. (1999, September). *An Assessment of the Economics of Future Electric Power Generation Options and the Implications for Fusion,* ORNL/TM-1999-243, Oak Ridge National Laboratory.

Department of Energy (DOE) (2003). *Resource conservation and recovery act.* http://www.energy.gov.

Energy Information Administration (EIA) (2002). *International Energy Outlook 2002,* Washington, DC: U.S. Department of Energy.

Energy Information Administration (EIA) (December 1998a). *Annual Energy Outlook 1999 with Projections to 2020,* DOE/EIA-0383(99), http://www.eia.doe.gov/oiaf/archive.html, Washington, DC: U.S. Department of Energy.

Energy Information Administration (EIA). (1996). *Annual Energy Outlook, with Projections to 2015.* Washington, DC: U.S. Department of Energy.

Energy Information Administration (EIA) (1995). *Annual Energy Review for 1995.* Washington, DC: U.S. Department of Energy.

Environmental Protection Agency (EPA) (March 1999). *Analysis of Emissions Reduction Options for the Electric Power Industry,* Washington, DC: U.S. Environmental Protection Agency, Office of Air and Radiation. http://www.epa.gov.

Erwine, B., and Heschong, L. (2000, March/April). *Daylight: healthy, wealthy & wise.* Architectural Lighting Magazine. http://www.archlighting.com/architecturallighting/al/index.jsp

Floyd, D.B., Parker, D.S., and Sherwin, J.R. (1996, August). *Measured Field Performance and Energy Savings of Occupancy Sensors: Three Case Studies.* Florida Solar Energy Center, online publication FSEC-PF309.

Goulding, J.R., Lewis, J.O., and Steemers, T.C. (eds.) (1992). *Energy in Architecture: The European Passive Solar Handbook.* London: Batsford.

Henderson, S.T. (1977). *Daylight and Its Spectrum* (2nd ed.). Bristol, England: Adam Hilger.

Heiser, S. (1998). *Controllable ballast retrofit using load shedding and daylight harvesting strategies.* http://powerline.ipcf.org.

Heschong Mahone Group (HMG) (August 1999).

Skylighting and Retail Sales, and Daylighting in Schools. For Pacific Gas & Electric. http://www.h-m-g.com.

Heschong Mahone Group (HMG) (1997, May). *The Lighting Efficiency Technology Report, Vol. I: California Lighting Baseline.* For the California Energy Commission.

Illuminating Engineering Society, Lighting Design Practice Committee (1968). *Calculation of luminance coefficients based upon zonal-cavity method.* Illuminating Engineering, 63(8), 423–432.

Illuminating Engineering Society of North America (IESNA) (2000). *IESNA Lighting Handbook* (9th ed.). New York: Illuminating Engineering Society of North America.

Interlaboratory Working Group. (2000, November). *Scenarios for a Clean Energy Future* (Oak Ridge, TN: Oak Ridge National Laboratory and Berkeley, CA: Lawrence Berkeley National Laboratory), ORNL/CON-476 and LBNL-44029.

Interlaboratory Working Group (1997, September). *Scenarios of U.S. Carbon Reductions—Potential Impacts of Energy Technologies by 2010 and Beyond.* Office of Energy Efficiency and Renewable Energy, U.S. Department of Energy.

International Association of Energy-Efficient Lighting (IAEEL) (2000). *Global lighting: 1000 power plants.* IAEEL Newsletter, 1-2/00, 1–4.

International Dark-Sky Association (IDA) (1996). *Information Sheets 10 and 20.* http://www.darksky.org.

Jennings, J.F., Rubinstein, R., and DiBartolomeo, D.R. (2000). *Comparisons of control options in private offices in an advanced lighting controls test bed.* Journal of the Illuminating Engineering Society, 29(29), 39–60.

Koomey, J., Sanstad, A. H., and Shown, L.J. (1996, July). *Energy-efficient lighting: market data, market imperfections, and policy success.* Contemporary Economic Policy. Vol. XIV, no. 3 (Also LBL-37702.REV). 98-111.

Lawrence Berkeley National Laboratory (1997). *Lighting Source Book.* Berkeley, CA: Lawrence Berkeley National Laboratory.

Lawrence Berkeley National Laboratory. (1992). *Analysis of Federal Policy Options for Improving U.S. Lighting Energy Efficiency.* Berkeley, CA: Lawrence Berkeley National Laboratory.

Lee, E.S., DiBartolomeo, D.L., and Selkowitz, S.S. (2000, August). *Electrochromic glazings for commercial buildings: Preliminary results from a full-scale testbed.* ACEEE 2000 Summer Study on Energy Efficiency in Buildings, Efficiency and Sustainability. CA: Pacific Grove.

Lee, E.S., Selkowitz, M.S., Levi, S.L., Blanc, E., McConahey, M., McLintock, P., Hakkarainen, N.L., Myer, M.P., and May, (2002, August). *Active load management with advanced window wall systems: Research and industry perspectives.* ACEEE 2002 Summer Study on Efficiency in Buildings. CA: Pacific Grove.

Lewin, I. (1999, August). *Light trespass: Research, results, and recommendations.* IESNA Annual Conference Proceedings, 107.

Lewis, I. (2000, April). *Light Trespass Research, Final Report: TR-114914.* Electric Power Research Institute.

Lighting Design Lab (1998). *Daylight Models* (video). Seattle, WA: Lighting Design Lab.

Littlefair, P.J. (1991). *Site layout planning for daylight and sunlight: A guide to good practice.* BRE Report BR 209.

Maniccia, D., Rutledge, D., Rea, M., and Morrow, W. (1999). *Occupant use of manual lighting control in private offices.* Journal of the Illuminating Engineering Society, 28(2), 42–56.

Maniccia, D., Von Neida, B., and Tweed, A. (2000). *Analysis of the energy and cost savings potential of occupancy sensors for commercial lighting systems.* Proceedings of the 2000 Annual Conference of the Illuminating Engineering Society of North America.

Mistrick, R., Chen, C., Bierman, B., and Felts, D. (2000). *A comparison of photosensor-controlled electronic dimming systems.* Proceedings of the 2000 Annual Conference of the Illuminating Engineering Society, 29(1): 66–80.

Moore, F. (1985). *Concepts and Practice of Architectural Daylighting.* New York: Van Nostrand Reinhold.

National Lighting Product Information Program (NLPIP) (1998, March). *Specifier Reports: Photosensors.*

NREL (1998, September). *Photovoltaics and Commercial Buildings—A Natural Match.* Golden, CO: Produced for the U.S. Department of Energy by the National Renewable Energy Laboratory.

Office of Fossil Energy (1999, May). *Coal and Power Systems: Strategic Plan & Multi-Year Program Plans.* U.S. Department of Energy, Washington, DC.

Pacific Gas & Electric Company (2000). *Lighting Controls:*

Codes and Standards Enhancement (CASE) Study. San Francisco, CA: Pacific Gas & Electric Company.

Pacific Gas & Electric Company (1999). *Daylighting Initiative Case Study.* http://www.pge.com/pec/daylight.

Pacific Gas & Electric Company (1998). *Case study—occupancy sensor commissioning.* 1998 Building Commissioning and Building Performance Tools Program.

Phillips, D. (2000). *Lighting Modern Buildings.* Oxford: Architectural Press.

Portland Energy Conservation, I. (1992). *Building Commissioning Guidelines* (2nd ed.). Portland, OR: Bonneville Power Administration.

Rea, M.S. (1998). *The quest for the ideal office controls system.* LRC Lighting Futures, 1998 3 (3).

Richman, E.E., Dittmer, A.L., and Keller, J.M. (1994, Winter). *Field analysis of occupancy sensor operation: Parameters affecting lighting energy savings.* Journal of Illuminating Engineering Society.

Rubinstein, F., and Pettler, P. (2001). *Final report on Internet addressable light switch. High Performance Commercial Building Systems.* CA: California Energy Commission.

Rundquist, R.A., Johnson, K., and Aumann, D. (1993). *Calculating lighting and HVAC interactions.* ASHRAE Journal, 35(11), 28.

Rundquist, R.A., McDougall, T.G., and Benya, J. (1996). *Lighting Controls: Patterns for Design.* Prepared by R.A. Rundquist Associates for the Electric Power Research Institute and the Empire State Electrical Energy Research Corporation.

Selkowitz, S., and Lee, E.S. (1998, May). *Advanced fenestration systems for improved daylight performance.* Daylighting E98 Conference Proceedings, Canada: Ottawa, Ontario.

Slater, A., Bordass, B., and Heasman, T. (1996, March). *Give people control of lighting controls.* IAELL Newsletter.

Smiley, F. (1996, February). *Durant middle school.* Architectural Lighting Magazine. http://www.arch-lighting.com/architecturallighting/al/index.jsp

Steffy, G.R. (1990). *Architectural Lighting Design.* New York: Van Nostrand Reinhold.

Southern California Edison (1999). *Energy Design Resources Case Studies: REMO and Timberland.* http://www.energydesignresources.com.

U.K. Department of the Environment (1998, March). *Desktop guide to daylighting for architects.* Good Practice Guide 245. Oxfordshire, England: ETSU.

U.S. Environmental Protection Agency (EPA) (2001). *Design for the Environment.* http://www.epa.gov/.

U.S. Office of Technology Assessment (1992). *Green Products by Design: Choices for a Cleaner Environment.* Washington, DC: Office of Technology Assessment.

Van Bogaert, G. (1996). *Local control system for ergonomic energy-saving lighting.* Special IAEEEL Edition.

Van den Beld, G.J., Begemann, S.H.A., and Tenner, A.D. (1997). *Comparison of preferred lighting levels for two different lighting systems in north-oriented offices.* Light and Engineering, 5(3), 48–52.

Veitch, J. (2000, July). *Lighting guidelines from lighting quality research.* CIBSE/ILE Lighting 2000 Conference. New York, U.K.

Veitch, J., and Newsham, G. (2000). *Exercised control, lighting choices, and energy use: An office simulation experiment.* Journal of Environmental Psychology, 20(3), 219–237.

Veitch, J., and Newsham, G. (1999, January). *Individual control can be energy efficient.* IAEEL Newsletter.

Veitch, J., and Newsham, G. (1998). *Lighting quality and energy-efficiency effects on task performance, mood, health, satisfaction, and comfort.* Journal of the Illuminating Engineering Society, 27(1), 107.

Webber, C.A., and Brown, R.E. (1998). *Savings potential of ENERGY STAR voluntary labeling programs.* Proceedings of the 1998 ACEEE Summer Study on Energy Efficiency in Buildings. Asilomar, CA: American Council for an Energy Efficient Economy, Washington, DC (also LBNL-41972).

Chapter 8

Ander, G. (1997). *Daylighting Performance & Design.* New York: John Wiley & Sons.

Archea, J. (1985). *Environmental factors associated with stair accidents by the elderly.* Clinics in Geriatric Medicine, 1, 555–569.

Arendt, J., and Broadway, J. (1987). *Light and melatonin as zeitgebers in man.* Chronobiology International, 4, 273–282.

Averill, J.R. (1973). *Personal control over aversive stimuli and its relationship to stress.* Psychological Bulletin, 80, 286–303.

Banbury, S., Macken, W., Tremblay, S., and Jones, D. (2001). *Noise distraction affects memory.* Human Factors, 43(1), 12–29.

Barnes, R.D. (1981). *Perceived freedom and control in the built environment.* In J.H. Harvey, (ed.), Cognition, Social Behavior, and the Environment. Hillsdale, NJ: Erlbaum, pp. 409–422.

Baron, R.A., and Rea, M.S. (1991). *Lighting to soothe the mood.* Lighting Design and Application, 12, 30–32.

Baron, R.A., Rea, M.S., and Daniels, S.G. (1992). *Effects of indoor lighting (illuminance and spectral distribution) on the performance of cognitive tasks and interpersonal behaviors: The potential mediating role of positive affect.* Motivation and Emotion, 16, 1–33.

Beach, L.R., Wise, B.K., and Wise, J.A. (1988). *The human factors of color in environmental design: A critical review.* Technical Report, NASA Ames Research Center, Moffett Field, CA.

Beauchemin, K.M., and Hays, P. (1996). *Sunny hospital rooms expedite recovery from severe and refractory depressions.* Journal of Affective Disorders, 40, 49–51.

Begemann, S.H.A., Aarts, M.P.J., and Tenner, A.D. (1994, November). *Daylight, artificial light, and people.* Paper presented at the 1994 Annual Conference of the Illuminating Engineering Society of Australia and New Zealand, Melbourne, Australia.

Belcher, M.C., and Kluczny, R. (1987, June). *The effects of light on decision making: Some experimental results.* Proceedings of CIE 21st Session, Venice, Italy: Central Bureau of CIE.

Benya, J., Heschong, L., McGowan, T., Miller, N., and Rubinstein, F. (2001). *Advanced Lighting Guidelines.* White Salmon, WA: New Buildings Institute.

Berry, J.L. (1983). *Work efficiency and mood states of electronic assembly workers exposed to full-spectrum and conventional fluorescent illumination.* Dissertation Abstracts International, 44, 635B.

Bierman, A., and Conway, K. (2000). *Characterizing daylight photosensor systems performance to help overcome market barriers.* Journal of the Illuminating Engineering Society, 29(1), 101–115.

Birren, F. (1969). *Light, Color and Environment.* New York: Van Nostrand Reinhold.

Blackwell, H.M. (1946). *Contrast thresholds of the human eye.* Journal of the Optical Society of America, 36, 624–643.

Blehar, M.C., and Rosenthal, N.E. (eds.) (1989). *Seasonal Affective Disorders and Phototherapy.* New York: Guilford Press.

Boray, P., Gifford, R., and Rosenblood, L. (1989). *Effects of warm white, cool white and full-spectrum fluorescent lighting on simple cognitive performance, mood and ratings of others.* Journal of Environmental Psychology, 9, 297–308.

Boubekri, M., Hull IV, R.B., and Boyer, L.L. (1991). *Impact of window size and sunlight penetration on office workers' mood and satisfaction: A novel way of assessing sunlight.* Environment and Behavior, 23, 474–493.

Bowmaker, J.K., and Dartnall, H.J. (1980). *Visual pigments of rods and cones in human retina.* Journal of Physiology, 298, 501–511.

Boyce, P.N., Eklund, N., and Simpson, S. (2000). *Individual lighting control: Task performance, mood and illuminance.* Journal of the Illuminating Engineering Society, 29(1), 131–142.

Boyce, P.N., Eklund, N., and Simpson, S. (1999). *Individual lighting control: Task performance, mood and illuminance.* IESNA Conference Proceedings, 1999. New York: Illuminating Engineering Society of North America.

Boyce, P.R. (1987). *Lighting research and lighting design: Bridging the gap.* Lighting Design and Application, 17(5), 10–12 and 50–51; 17(6), 38–44.

Boyce, P.R. (1981). *Human Factors in Lighting,* New York: Macmillan.

Boyce, P.R. (1973). *Age, illuminance, visual performance, and preference.* Lighting Research and Technology, 5, 125–139.

Boyce, P.R., Akashi, Y., Hunter, C.M., and Bullough, J.D. (2003). *The impact of spectral power distribution on the performance of an achromatic visual task.* Lighting Research and Technology, 35(2), 141–161.

Boynton, R.M., and Boss, D.E. (1971). *The effect of background luminance and contrast upon visual search performance.* Illuminating Engineering, 66, 173–186.

Bradley, R.D., and Logan, H.L. (1964). *A uniform method for computing the probability of comfort response in a visual field.* Illuminating Engineering, 59(3), 189–206.

Brainard, G.C., and Bernecker, C.A. (1995, November). *The effects of light on physiology and behavior.* Proceedings of CIE 23rd Session, Vol. 2. New Delhi, India: Central Bureau of CIE.

Brody, L.R., and Hall, J.A. (1993). *Gender and emotion.* In M. Lewis and J.M. Havilands (eds.), Handbook of Emotions. New York: Guilford, pp. 447–460.

Bureau of the Census (1997). *Statistical Abstract of the United States: 1997,* Vol. 117. Washington, DC: Bureau of the Census, p. 143.

Butler, D.L., and Biner, P. M. (1990). *A preliminary study of skylight preferences.* Environment and Behavior, 22, 119–140.

Butler, D.L., and Biner, P.M. (1989). *Effects of setting on window preferences and factors associated with those preferences.* Environment and Behavior, 21, 17–31.

Campbell, S.S., and Murphy, P.J. (1998). *Extraocular circadian phototransduction in humans.* Science, 279, 396–399.

Carter, D.J., Slater, A.I., and Moore, T. (1999, June). *A study of occupier-control lighting systems.* Proceedings of the 24th Session of the Commission Internationale de l'Eclairage, Warsaw, Poland. Vol. 1, Part 2. Vienna, Austria: CIE Central Bureau, pp. 108–110.

Cohen, S., Evans, G.W., Stokols, D., and Krantz, D.S. (1986). *Behavior, Health, and Environmental Stress.* New York: Plenum.

Cohen-Mansfield, J., Werner, P., and Freedman, L. (1995). *Sleep and agitation in agitated nursing home residents: An observational study.* American Sleep Disorders Association and Sleep Research Society, 18(8), 674–680.

Collins, K.W. (1980). *Effects of conversational noise, coping techniques, and individual differences on the performance of academic tasks.* Dissertation Abstracts International, 41, (1-B), 386–387.

Dalgleish, T., Rosen, K., and Marks, M. (1996). *Rhythm and blues: The theory and treatment of seasonal affective disorders.* British Journal of Clinical Psychology, 35, 163–182.

DeCusatis, C. (1997). *Handbook of Applied Optometry.* New York: AIP Press.

Delay, E.R., and Richardson, M.A. (1981). *Time estimation in humans: Effects of ambient illumination and sex.* Perceptual and Motor Skills, 53, 747–750.

Department of Health and Human Services (1997). *A Profile of Older Americans: 1997.* Washington, DC: Department of Health and Human Services, p. 5.

Ducker Research. (1999, August). *Lighting quality – Key customer values and decision process.* Report to the Light Right Research Consortium.

Eklund, N., Boyce, P., and Simpson, S. (2000). *Lighting and sustained performance.* Journal of the Illuminating Engineering Society, 29(1), 116.

Ellis, H.C., and Ashbrook, P.W. (1991). *The "state" of mood and memory research: A selective review.* In D. Kuiken (ed.), Mood and Memory, Theory, Research and Applications. London: Sage Publications, pp. 1–21.

Erwine, B., and Heschong, L. (2000, March/April). *Daylight: healthy, wealthy & wise.* Architectural Lighting Magazine.

Evans, G.W. (1997). *Environmental stress and health.* In A. Baum, T. Revenson, and J.E. Singer (eds.), Handbook of Health Psychology. Hillsdale, NJ: Earlbaum.

Evans, G.W. (ed.) (1982). *Environmental Stress.* Cambridge: Cambridge University Press.

Evans, G.W., and Cohen, S. (1987). *Environmental Stress.* In D. Stokols and I. Altman (eds.), Handbook of Environmental Psychology. New York: John Wiley & Sons, pp. 571–610.

Figueiro, M.G., Eggleston, G., and Rea, M.S. (2002). *Effects of light exposure on behavior of Alzheimer's patients: A pilot study.* Paper presented at the Fifth International LRO Lighting Research Symposium, Orlando, FL.

Figueiro, M.G., and Stevens, R. (2002). *Daylight and productivity: A possible link to circadian regulation.* Poster Session at the Fifth International LRO Lighting Research Symposium, Orlando, FL.

Flynn, J.E. (1977). *A study of subjective responses to low energy and nonuniform lighting systems.* Lighting Design and Application, 7, 6–15.

Flynn, J.E., and Spencer, T.J. (1977). *The effects of light source color on user impression and satisfaction.* Journal of the Illuminating Engineering Society, 6(4), 167–179.

Food and Drug Administration. (1986, September). *Lamp's labeling found to be fraudulent.* FDA Talk Paper (No. T86-69). Rockville, MA: U.S. Department of Health and Human Services.

Garling, T., Book, A., and Lindberg, E. (1986). *Spatial orientation and wayfinding in the designed environment:*

A conceptual analysis and some suggestions for postoccupancy evaluation. Journal of Architectural and Planning Research, 3, 55–64.

Gawron, V.J. (1982). *Performance effects of noise intensity, psychological set, and task type and complexity.* Human Factors, 24, 225–243.

Gifford, R. (1988). *Light, décor, arousal, comfort and communication.* Journal of Environmental Psychology, 8, 177–189.

Giradin, B.W. (1992). *Lightwave frequency and sleep-wake frequency in well, full-term neonates,* Holistic Nursing Practice, 6(4), 57–66.

Glass, D.C., and Singer, J.E. (1972). *Urban Stress.* New York: Academic Press.

Graham, R., and Michel, A. (2003). *Impact of dementia on circadian patterns. Lighting and circadian rhythms and sleep in older adults* (Technical Memorandum 1007708) Palo Alto, CA: Electric Power Research Institute (EPRI).

Graham, R., and Michel, A. (2003). *Sundowning: Lighting and circadian rhythms and sleep in older adults* (Technical Memorandum 1007708) Palo Alto, CA: Electric Power Research Institute (EPRI).

Gregory, R.I. (1979). *Eye and brain: The Psychology of Seeing,* 3rd ed. New York: McGraw-Hill.

Hall, E.T. (1966). *The Hidden Dimension.* New York: Doubleday.

Hedge, A., Erickson, W., and Rubin, G. (1992). *Effects of personal and occupational factors on sick building syndrome reports in air conditioning offices.* In J.C. Quirk, L.R. Murphy, and J.J. Hurrell (eds.), Stress and well-being at work. Washington, DC: American Psychological Association, pp. 286-298.

Henderson, J. (1986). *Light as nutrient: a design update.* Interiors, 146, 50.

Heschong Mahone Group (HMG) (1999, August). *Skylighting and retail sales, and daylighting in schools.* For Pacific Gas & Electric. URL: http://www.h-m-g.com.

Heschong Mahone Group (HMG) (1997, May). *The lighting efficiency technology report, vol. I: California Lighting Baseline.* For the California Energy Commission.

Hiatt, L. (1991). *Nursing home renovation designed for reform.* Boston: Butterworth.

Hill, H., and Bruce, V. (1996). *The effects of lighting on the perception of facial surfaces.* Journal of Experimental Psychology: Human Perception and Performance, 22(4), 986–1004.

Hughes, P.C. (1980). *The use of light and color in health.* In A.C. Hastings, J. Fadiman, and J.S. Gordon (eds.), The Complete Guide to Holistic Medicine: Health for the Whole Person. Boulder, CO: Westview Press, pp. 294–308.

Hughes, P.C., and McNelis, J.F. (1978). *Lighting, productivity, and the work environment.* Lighting Design and Application, 8(12), 32–38.

Hygge, S. (1991). *The interaction of noise and mild heat on cognitive performance and serial reaction time.* Environment International, 17, 229–234.

Illuminating Engineering Society of North America (IESNA) (2000). *IESNA Lighting Handbook,* 9th ed. New York: Illuminating Engineering Society of North America.

Illuminating Engineering Society of North America. (1998). *Lighting for the aged and partially sighted community. Recommended Practice for Lighting and the Visual Environment for Senior Living,* RP-28-98. New York: Illuminating Engineering Society of North America.

Isen, A.M., Daubman, K.A., and Nowicki, G.P. (1987). *Positive affect facilitates creative problem solving.* Journal of Personality and Social Psychology, 52(6), 1122–1131.

Kleeman, W.B. (1981). *The Challenge of Interior Design.* Boston: CBI Publishing.

Knez, I. (2001). *Effects of colour of light on nonvisual psychological processes.* Journal of Environmental Psychology, 21(2), 201–208.

Knez, I. (1997, November). *Changes in females' and males' positive and negative moods as a result of variations in CCT, CRI and illuminance levels.* Proceedings of Right Light: 4th European Conference on Energy Efficient Lighting, Copenhagen, Denmark, 1, 149–154.

Knez, I. (1995). *Effects of indoor lighting on mood and cognition.* Journal of Environmental Psychology, 15, 39–51.

Knez, I., and Enmarker, I. (1998). *Effects of office lighting on mood and cognitive performance and a gender effect in work-related judgment.* Environment and Behavior, 4, 553–567.

Knez, I., and Hygge, S. (in press). *The circumplex structure* of affect: A Swedish version. Scandinavian Journal of Psychology.

Knez, I., and Kers, C. (2000). *Effects of indoor lighting, gender and age on mood and cognitive performance.* Environment and Behavior, 32, 817–831.

Kwallek, N., and Lewis, C.M. (1990). *Effects of environmental colour on males and females: A red or white or green office.* Applied Economics, 21, 275–278.

Lam, R.W., Kripke, D.F., and Gillin, J.C. (1989). *Phototherapy for depressive disorders: A review.* Canadian Journal of Psychiatry, 34, 140–147.

Lam, W.C. (1977). *Perception and Lighting as Formgivers for Architecture.* New York: McGraw-Hill.

Lewy, A.J., Wehr, T.A., Goodwin, F.K., Newsome, D.A., and Markey, S.P. (1980). *Light suppresses melatonin secretion in humans.* Science, 210, 1267–1269.

Lockely, S. (2002). *Light and human circadian regulation: Night work, day work, and jet lag.* Paper presented at the Fifth International LRO Lighting Research Symposium, Orlando, FL.

Maas, J.B., Jayson, J.K., and Kleiber, D.A. (1974). *Effects of spectral differences in illumination on fatigue.* Journal of Applied Psychology, 59, 524–526.

Marans, R.W., and Yan, X. (1989). *Lighting quality and environmental satisfaction in open and enclosed offices.* Journal of Architectural and Planning Research, 6, 118–131.

Martin, L.E., Marler, M., Shochat, T., and Ancoli-Israel, S. (2000). *Circadian rhythms of agitation in institutionalized patients with Alzheimer's disease.* Chronobiology International, 17(3), 405–418.

McClaughan, C.L.B., Aspinall, P.A., and Webb, R.S. (1996, March/April). *The effects of lighting upon mood and decision making,* Proceedings of CIBSE National Lighting Conference, University of Bath, Bath, UK, pp. 237–245.

Megaw, E. (1992). *The visual environment.* In A.P. Smith and D.M. Jones (eds.), Handbook of Human Performance, Volume 1: The Physical Environment. London: Academic Press, pp. 261–296.

Miller, C.L., White, R., Whitman, T.L., O'Callaghn, M.F., and Maxwell, S.E. (1995). *The effects of cycled versus noncycled lighting on the growth and development in preterm infants.* Infant Behavior and Development, 18(1), 87–95.

Miller, N. (2002). *Lighting for seniors: Obstacles in applying the research.* Paper presented at the Fifth International LRO Lighting Research Symposium, Orlando, FL.

Mishimia, K., Okawa, M., Hiskikawa, Y., Hozumi, S., Hori, H., and Takashi, (1994). *Morning bright therapy for sleep and behavior disorders in elderly patients with dementia.* Acta Psychiatry Scandinavia, 89, 1–7.

National Lighting Bureau (1988). *Office Lighting and Productivity.* Washington, DC: National Lighting Bureau.

National Mental Health Association (2003). *Seasonal Affective Disorders.* http://www.nmha.org. Retrieved May 8, 2003.

Navvab, M. (2000). *A comparison of visual performance under high and low color temperature fluorescent lamps.* Proceedings of the 2000 Annual Conference of the Illuminating Engineering Society of North America. Washington, D.C.

Nelson, T.M., Nilsson, T.H., and Johnson, M. (1984). *Interaction of temperature, illuminance and apparent time of sedentary work fatigue.* Ergonomics, 27, 89–101.

Noelle-Waggoner, E. (2002). *Let there be light, or face the consequences: A national concern for our aging population.* Paper presented at the Fifth International LRO Lighting Research Symposium, Orlando, FL.

Passini, R. (1984). *Wayfinding in Architecture.* New York: Van Nostrand Reinhold.

Passini, R., Pigot, H., Rainville, C., and Tetreault, M.H. (2000). *Wayfinding in a nursing home for advanced dementia of the Alzheimer's type.* Environment and Behavior, 32(5), 684–710.

Passini, R., Rainville, C., Marchand, N., and Joanette, Y. (1998). *Wayfinding and dementia: Some research findings and a new look at design.* Journal of Architectural and Planning Research, 15(2), 133–151.

Phelps, D.L., and Watts, J.L. (1997). *Early light reduction for preventing retinopathy of prematurity in very low birth weight infants.* Cochrane Library Issue 2.

Quinn, G.C., Shin, M., Maguire, M., and Stone, R. (1999, May). *Myopia and ambient lighting at night.* Nature, 113.

Rea, M.S. (2002). *Light – much more than vision.* (Keynote). Light and Human Health: EPRI/LRO5 International Lighting Research Symposium. Palo Alto, CA: Lighting Research Office of the Electric Power Research Institute, 1–15.

Rea, M.S. (1988). *Population data on near field visual acuity for use with the vision and lighting diagnostic (VALiD) Kit* (report no. CR5544.3). Ottawa, ON: National Research Council of Canada.

Rea, M.S. (1986). *Toward a model of visual performance: Foundations and data.* Journal of the Illuminating Engineering Society, 15(2), 41–57.

Rea, M.S., Bullough, J.D., and Figueiro, M.G. (2002). *Phototransduction for human melatonin suppression.* Journal of Pineal Research, 32, 209–213.

Rea, M.S., Figueiro, M.G., and Bullough, J.D. (2002). *Circadian photobiology: An emerging framework for lighting practice and research.* Lighting Research and Technology, 34(3), 177–190.

Rea, M.S., and Ouellette, M.J. (1991). *Relative visual performance: A basis for application.* Lighting Research & Technology, 23(3), 135–144.

Rea, M.S., and Ouellette, M.J. (1988). *Visual performance using reaction times.* Lighting Research & Technology, 20(4), 39–53.

Research Group for Inclusive Environments (RGIE). *Task lighting for visually impaired people in an office environment.* Research Group for Inclusive Environments (RGIE). http://www.rdg.ac.uk. Retrieved: December 18, 2002.

Reynolds, J.D., Hardy, R.J., Kennedy, K.A., Spencer, R., van Heuven, W.A.J., and Fielder, A.R. (1998). *Lack of efficacy of light reduction in preventing retinopathy of prematurity.* The New England Journal of Medicine, 338(22), 1572–1576.

Rothman, M. (1987). *Designing work environments to influence productivity,* Journal of Business and Psychology. 1, 390–550, 395.

Rowlands, E.D., Loe, D.L., McIntosh, R.M., and Mansfield, K.P. (1985). *Lighting adequacy and quality in office interiors by consideration of subjective assessment and physical measurement.* CIE Journal, 4(1), 23–37.

Saegert, S. (1976). *Stress-inducing and stress-reducing qualities of environment.* In H.M. Proshansky, W.H. Ittelson, and L. Rivlin (eds.), Environmental Psychology, 2nd ed. New York: Holt, pp. 218–223.

Sanders, P.A., and Bernecker, C.A. (1990). *Uniform veiling luminance and display polarity affect VDU user performance.* Journal of the Illuminating Engineering Society, 19(2), 113–123.

Satlin, A., Volicer, L., Ross, V., Herz, L., and Campbell, S. (1992). *Bright light treatment of behavioral and sleep disturbances in patients with Alzheimer's disease.* American Journal of Psychiatry, 149(8), 1028–1032.

Sherrod, D., and Cohen, S. (1979). *Density, personal control, and design.* In J. Aliello and A. Baum (eds.), Residential Crowding and Design. New York: Plenum, pp. 217–228.

Simonson, E., and Brozek, J. (1948). *Effects of illumination level on visual performance and fatigue.* Journal of the Optical Society of America, 38, 384–397.

Skwerer, R.G., Jacobsen, F.M., Duncan, C.C., Kelly, K.A., Sack, D.A., Tamarkin, L., Gaist, P. A., Kasper, S., and Rosenthal, N.E. (1989). *Neurobiology of seasonal affective disorders and phototherapy.* In M.C. Blehar and N.E. Rosenthal (eds.), Seasonal Affective Disorders and Phototherapy. New York: Guilford Press, pp. 311–332.

Smith, A.P., and Broadbent, D.E. (1980). *Effect of noise on performance of embedded figures tasks.* Journal of Applied Psychology, 2, 246–248.

Sommer, R. (1969). *Personal Space.* Englewood Cliffs, NJ: Prentice-Hall.

Stevens, R. (2002). *Epidemiological evidence indicating light exposure is linked to human cancer development.* Paper presented at the Fifth International LRO Lighting Research Symposium, Orlando, FL.

Stokols, D., and Altman, I. (1987). *Introduction.* In D. Stokols and I. Altman (eds.), Handbook of Environmental Psychology, Vol. 1. New York: John Wiley & Sons, pp 1–4.

Taylor, R.B. (1988). *Human Territorial Functioning.* New York: Cambridge University Press.

Veitch, J. (2000, July). *Lighting guidelines from lighting quality research.* CIBSE/ILE Lighting 2000 Conference. New York, United Kingdom.

Veitch, J.A. (1997). *Revisiting the performance and mood effects of information about light and fluorescent lamp type.* Journal of Environmental Psychology, 17(1), 253-262.

Veitch, J.A., and Gifford, R. (1996a). *Assessing beliefs about lighting effects on health, performance, mood and social behavior.* Environment and Behavior, 28, 446–470.

Veitch, J.A., and Gifford, R. (1996b). *Choice, perceived control, and performance decrements in the physical environment.* Journal of Environmental Psychology, 16, 269–276.

Veitch, J.A., Gifford, R., and Hine, D.W. (1991). *Demand characteristics and full spectrum lighting effects on performance and mood.* Journal of Environmental Psychology, 11, 87–95.

Veitch, J.A., and McColl, S. (2001). *Evaluation of full-spectrum fluorescent lighting.* Ergonomics, 44(3), 255–279.

Veitch, J.A., and McColl, S. (1995). *On the modulation of fluorescent light: Flicker rate and spectral distribution effects on visual performance and visual comfort.* Light Research and Technology, 27, 243–256.

Veitch, J.A., and Miller, N., McKay, H., and Jones, C.C. (1996, August). *Lighting System Effects on Judged Lighting Quality and Facial Appearance.* Paper presented at the 1996 Annual Conference of the Illuminating Engineering Society of North America, Cleveland, OH.

Veitch, J., and Newsham, G. (2000). *Exercised control, lighting choices, and energy use: An office simulation experiment.* Journal of Environmental Psychology 20(3), 219–237.

Veitch, J.A., and Newsham, G.R. (1999, June). *Preferred luminous conditions in open-plan offices: Implication for lighting quality recommendations.* Proceedings of the Commission Internationale de l'Eclairage (CIE) 24th Session, Warsaw, Poland, Vol. 1, Part 2, Vienna, Austria: CIE Central Bureau, pp. 4–6.

Veitch, J., and Newsham, G. (January, 1999). *Individual control can be energy efficient.* IAEEL Newsletter.

Veitch, J.A., and Newsham, G.R. (1998a). *Experimental Investigations of Lighting Quality, Preferences and Control Effects on Task Performance and Energy Efficiency: Experiment 2, Primary Analyses – Final Report* (IRC Internal Report No. 767/Client Report No. A3546.5). Ottawa, ON: National Research Council Canada, Institute for Research in Construction.

Veitch, J.A., and Newsham, G. (1998). *Consequences of the perception and exercise of control over lighting.* 106th Annual Convention of the American Psychological Association, August 1998. San Francisco, CA.

Veitch, J., and Newsham, G. (1996, August). *Experts' quantitative and qualitative assessment of lighting quality.* Proceedings of the 1996 Annual IESNA Conference. Cleveland, OH. Available at: www.iesna.org.

Veitch, J.A., and Newsham, G.R. (1996). *Determinants of Lighting Quality II: Research and Recommendations.* Paper presented at the 104th Annual Convention of the American Psychological Association. Toronto, Ontario, Canada (ERIC Document Reproduction Service No. ED408543).

Veitch, J.A., and Newsham, G.R. (1988b). *Lighting quality and energy-efficiency effects on task performance, mood, health, satisfaction and comfort.* Journal of the Illuminating Engineering Society, 27(1), 107–129.

Wapner, S., and Demick, J. (2002). *The increasing contexts of context in the study of environment behavior relations.* In R. Bechtel and A. Churchman (eds.), Handbook of Environmental Psychology. New York: Wiley.

Weisman, G. (1981). *Evaluating architectural legibility.* Environment and Behavior, 13, 189–204.

Weston, H.C. (1962). *Sight, Light, and Work,* 2nd ed. London: Lewis.

Wilson, S., and Hedge, A. (1987). *The Office Environment Survey.* London: Building Use Studies Ltd.

Winchip, S.M. (1990). *Dementia health care facility design.* Journal of Interior Design Education and Research, 16(2), 39–46.

Wineman, J.D. (1982). *The office environment as a source of stress.* In G.W. Evans (ed.), Environmental Stress. New York: Cambridge University Press, pp. 256–285.

Wright, G.A., and Rea, M.S. (1984). *Age, a human factor in lighting.* Proceedings of the 1984 International Conference on Occupational Ergonomics. D.A. Attwood and C. McCann (eds.). Rexdale, Ontario, Canada: Human Factors Association of Canada.

Wu, W., and Ng, E. (2003). *A review of the development of daylighting in schools.* Lighting Research and Technology, 35(2), 111–125.

Zeisel, J. (2000). *Environmental design effects on Alzheimer symptoms in long term care residences.* World Hospitals and Health Service, 36(3), 27–31.

Chapter 9

Albers, J. (1963). *Interaction of Color.* New Haven, CT: Yale University Press.

American Institute of Architects (2000). *Architectural Graphics Standards,* 10th ed. New York: John Wiley & Sons.

Ander, G. (1997). *Daylighting Performance & Design.* New York: John Wiley & Sons.

Archea, J. (1985). *Environmental factors associated with*

stair accidents by the elderly. Clinics in Geriatric Medicine, 1, 555–569.

Baron, R.A., and Rea, M.S. (1991). *Lighting to soothe the mood.* Lighting Design and Application, 12, 30–32.

Benya, J., Heschong, L., McGowan, T., Miller, N., and Rubinstein, F. (2001). *Advanced Lighting Guidelines.* White Salmon, WA: New Buildings Institute.

Blakemore, R.G. (1997). *History of Interior Design and Furniture: From Ancient Egypt to Nineteenth-Century Europe.* New York: John Wiley & Sons.

Bradtmiller, B., and Annis, J. (1997). *Anthropometry for Persons with Disabilities: Needs for the Twenty-First Century.* Washington, DC: U.S. Architectural and Transportation Barriers Compliance Board (http://www.access-board.gov/research&training/Anthropometry/anthro.htm).

Clark, C. (2001). *Computers are causing health problems.* Journal of End User Computing, 13(1), 34–45.

Clodagh (2001). *Total Design: Contemplate, Cleanse, Clarify, and Create your Personal Space.* New York: Clarkson/Potter Publishers.

Deason, V. (1997). *Anthropometry: The human dimension.* Optics and Lasers in Engineering, 28, 83–88.

Diffrient, N., Tilley, A.R., and Bardagjy, J.C. (1974). *Humanscale 1/2/3.* Cambridge: The MIT Press.

Diffrient, N., Tilley, A.R., and Harman, D. (1981). *Humanscale 4/5/6.* Cambridge: The MIT Press.

Dreyfuss, H. (1960). *The Measure of Man – Human Factors in Design.* New York: Whitney Publications.

Fry, G.A. (1976). *A simplified formula for discomfort glare.* Journal of the Illuminating Engineering Society, 8(1), 10–20.

General Electric (1989). *Lighting Application Bulletin.* Cleveland, OH: General Electric.

Gordon, J.E.H. (1891). *Decorative Electricity.* London: Sampson Low, Marston, Searle, & Rivington.

Grandjean, E. (1987). *Ergonomics in Computerized Offices.* Philadelphia: Taylor & Francis.

Hall, E.T. (1966). *The Hidden Dimension.* New York: Doubleday.

Halse, A.O. (1968). *The Use of Color in Interiors.* New York: McGraw-Hill.

Halstead, M.B. (1997). *Colour.* In J.R. Coaton and A.M. Marsden (eds.), Lamps and Lighting. New York: John Wiley & Sons.

Hammond, R. (1884). *The Electric Light in Our Homes.* New York: R. Worthington.

Hill, H., and Bruce, V. (1996). *The effects of lighting on the perception of facial surfaces.* Journal of Experimental Psychology: Human Perception and Performance, 22(4), 986–1004.

Hopkinson, R.G. (1957). *Evaluation of glare.* Illuminating Engineering, 52(6), 305–316.

Human Factors Society (1988). *American National Standard for Human Factors Engineering of Visual Display Terminal Workstations* (ANSI/HFS 100-1988). Santa Monica, CA.

Illuminating Engineering Society of North America (IESNA) (2000). *IESNA Lighting Handbook*, 9th ed. New York: Illuminating Engineering Society of North America.

Illuminating Engineering Society of North America (IESNA) (1998). *Lighting for the aged and partially sighted community. Recommended Practice for Lighting and the Visual Environment for Senior Living,* RP-28-98. New York: Illuminating Engineering Society of North America.

Lam, W.M. (1986). *Sunlighting as Formgivers for Architecture.* New York: Van Nostrand Reinhold.

Lighting Controls Association (1999). *The National Dimming Initiative.* Advance Transfer Co.

Littlefair, P.J. (1996). *Designing with Innovative Daylighting.* London: CRC, Garston.

McClaughan, C.L.B., Aspinall, P.A., and Webb, R.S. (March 31–April 13, 1996). *The effects of lighting upon mood and decision-making.* Proceedings of CIBSE National Lighting Conference, University of Bath, pp. 237–245.

Miller, C.L., White, R., Whitman, T.L., O'Callaghn, M.F., and Maxwell, S.E. (1995). *The effects of cycled versus noncycled lighting on the growth and development in preterm infants.* Infant Behavior and Development, 18(1), 87–95.

Mistrick, R., Chen, C., Bierman, B., and Felts, D. (2000). *A comparison of photosensor-controlled electronic dimming systems.* Proceedings of the 2000 Annual Conference of the Illuminating Engineering Society, 29(1), 66–80.

Mount, C.M. (1992). *Residential Interiors.* Glen Cove, NY: P.B.C. International.

NASA (1978). *Anthropometric Source Book.* NASA Reference Publication 1024. Washington, DC: U.S. National Aeronautics and Space Administration.

Nielsen, J. (1993). *Usability Engineering*. Boston: Academic Press.

O'Dea, W.T. (1958). *The Social History of Lighting*. London: Routledge and Kegan Paul.

Panero, J., and Zelnik, M. (1979). *Human Dimension, Interior Space*. New York: Whitney Library of Design.

Pheasant, S. (1996). *Bodyspace: Anthropometry, Ergonomics and the Design of Work*, 2nd ed. Bristol, England: Taylor & Francis.

Phillips, D. (1997). *Lighting Historic Buildings*. New York: McGraw-Hill.

Raschko, B. (1982). *Housing Interiors for the Disabled and Elderly*. New York: Van Nostrand Reinhold.

Rowlands, E.D., Loe, D.L., McIntosh, R.M., and Mansfield, K.P. (1985). *Lighting adequacy and quality in office interiors by consideration of subjective assessment and physical measurement*. CIE Journal, 4(1), 23–37.

Rundquist, R.A., McDougall, T.G., and Benya, J. (1996). *Lighting Controls: Patterns for Design*. Prepared by R.A. Rundquist Associates for the Electric Power Research Institute and the Empire State Electrical Energy Research Corporation. Northampton, MA.

Smith F.K., and Bertolone, F.J. (1986). *The Principles and Practices of Lighting Design: Bringing Interiors to Light*. New York: Whitney Library of Design.

Society of Automotive Engineers (1977). *Anthropometry of Infants, Children and Youths to Age 18 for Product Safety Design*. SP-450. Warrendale, PA.

Sommer, R. (1969). *Personal Space*. Englewood Cliffs, NJ: Prentice-Hall.

Steffy, G.R. (1990). *Architectural Lighting Design*. New York: Van Nostrand Reinhold.

Stoudt, H.W. (1981). *Anthropometry of the elderly*. Human Factors Society Bulletin, 23, (1).

U.K. Department of the Environment (March 1998). *Desktop guide to daylighting for architects*. Good Practice Guide 245. Harwell, Oxfordshire, England: ETSU.

U.S. Department of Health, Education, and Welfare (1979). *Weight and height of adults 18–74 years of age: United States, 1971–1974*. Vital and Health Statistics, Series 11, no. 211. Washington DC: U.S. Government Printing Office.

U.S. Department of Health, Education, and Welfare (1966). *Weight, height, and selected body dimensions of adults: United States, 1960–1962*. Vital and Health Statistics, Series 11, no. 8. Washington, DC.: U.S. Government Printing Office.

U.S. Department of Housing and Urban Development (1972). *A Design Guide for Home Safety*. Washington D.C.; U.S. Government Printing Office.

U.S. Department of Justice (1991). *Americans with disabilities act – Title III*. Federal Register [28 CFR Part 36], vol. 56, no. 144. Washington, DC: U.S. Government Printing Office.

Veitch, J., and Newsham, G. (January 1999). *Individual control can be energy efficient*. IAEEL Newsletter.

Whiton, S., and Abercrombie, S. (2002). *Interior Design & Decoration*, 5th ed. Upper Saddle River, NJ: Prentice-Hall.

Wright, G.A., and Rea, M.S. (1984). *Age, a human factor in lighting*. Proceedings of the 1984 International Conference on Occupational Ergonomics. D.A. Attwood and C.McCann (eds.). Rexdale, Ontario, Canada: Human Factors Association of Canada.

Chapter 10

Abercrombie, S. (1998). *Corporate Interiors*, No. 2. New York: Retail Reporting Corporation.

Allphin, W. (1961). *BCD appraisals of luminaire brightness in a simulated office*. Illuminating Engineering, 56(1), 31–44.

American Hotel & Lodging Association (2003). *2003 Lodging Industry Profile*. Washington, DC: American Hotel & Lodging Association.

Ander, G. (1997). *Daylighting Performance & Design*. New York: John Wiley & Sons.

Archea, J. (1985). *Environmental factors associated with stair accidents by the elderly*. Clinics in Geriatric Medicine, 1, 555–569.

Ballman, T.L., and Levin, R.E. (1987). *Illumination in partitioned spaces*. Journal of the Illuminating Engineering Society, 16(2), 31–49.

Baraban, R.S., and Durocher, J.F. (2001). *Successful Restaurant Design*. 2d ed., New York: John Wiley & Sons.

Barr, W., and Broudy, C. (1985). *Designing to Sell: A Complete Guide to Retail Store Planning and Design*. New York: McGraw-Hill.

Beauchemin, K.M., and Hays, P. (1996). *Sunny hospital*

rooms expedite recovery from severe and refractory depressions. Journal of Affective Disorders, 40, 49–51.

Benya, J.R. (December 1–6, 2001). *Lighting for Schools.* Washington, DC: National Clearinghouse for Educational Facilities.

Benya, J., Heschong, L., McGowan, T., Miller, N., and Rubinstein, F. (2001). *Advanced Lighting Guidelines.* White Salmon, WA: New Buildings Institute.

Bernstien, A., and Conway, K. (March 2000). *The Public Benefits of California's Investments in Energy Efficiency.* Prepared for the California Energy Commission by the RAND Corporation. MR-1212.0-CEC.

Bornholdt, D. (2001). *Green Suites International & GE Lighting Team to Bring Solid Energy Savings to Light.* http://www.hospitalitynet.org.

Boubekri, M., Hull IV, R.B., and Boyer, L.L. (1991). *Impact of window size and sunlight penetration on office workers' mood and satisfaction: A novel way of assessing sunlight.* Environment and Behavior, 23, 474–493.

Boyce, P.N., Eklund, N., and Simpson, S. (2000). *Individual lighting control: Task performance, mood and illuminance.* Journal of the Illuminating Engineering Society, 29(1), 131–142.

Boyce, P.N., Eklund, N., and Simpson, S. (1999). *Individual lighting control: Task performance, mood and illuminance.* IESNA Conference Proceedings, 1999. New York: Illuminating Engineering Society of North America.

Boykin, P.J. (1991). *Hotel Guestroom Design.* Dubuque, IA: Kendall/Hunt Publishing.

British Standards Institution (1992). *Code of Practice for Daylighting.* British Standard BS 8206 Part 2.

Building Codes Assistance Project (January 1999). *Energy Conservation and Code Updates: Status of State Energy Codes.* Last updated January 1999. http://www.bcap-energy.org/home.php.

Bush-Brown, A. (1992). *Hospitable Design for Healthcare and Senior Communities.* New York: Van Nostrand Reinhold.

California Energy Commission (July 1999). *Building Energy Efficiency Standards.* Title 24 Pt. 6.

Chartered Institution of Building Services Engineers (1987). *Window Design.* CIBSE Applications Manual. London: CIBSE.

Clark, C. (2001). *Computers are causing health problems.* Journal of End User Computing, 13(1), 34–45.

Coaton, J.R., and Marsden, A.M. (1997). *Lamps and Lighting,* 4th ed. London: Arnold.

Cohen, E.L., and Emery, S.R. (1984). *Dining by Design.* New York: Van Nostrand Reinhold.

Dorf, M.E. (August 1992). *Restaurants that Work.* New York: Whitney Library of Design.

Ducker Research (1999). *Lighting Quality – Key Customer Values and Decision Process.* Report to the Light Right Research Consortium.

Duro-Test Lighting (2003). *Importance of Lighting in Schools.* http://www.full-spectrum-lighting.com. 1–3.

Fannin, J. (2003). *Hotel safety: Consumer demand presents a marketing opportunity.* HSMAI Marketing Review, Spring, 27–33.

Fitch, R., and Knobel, L. (1990). *Retail Design.* New York: Whitney Library of Design.

Flynn, J.E. (1977). *A study of subjective responses to low energy and nonuniform lighting systems.* Lighting Design and Application, 7, 6–15.

Flynn, J.E., and Spencer, T.J. (1977). *The effects of light source color on user impression and satisfaction.* Journal of the Illuminating Engineering Society. 6(4), 167–179.

Garling, T., Book, A., and Lindberg, E. (1986). *Spatial orientation and wayfinding in the designed environment: A conceptual analysis and some suggestions for postoccupancy evaluation.* Journal of Architectural and Planning Research, 3, 55–64.

Gosling, D., and Maitl, B. (1976). *Design and Planning of Retail Systems.* New York: Whitney Library of Design.

Grabois, E., Nosek, M., and Rossi, C. (1999). *Accessibility in physicians' offices.* Archives of Family Medicine, 8(1), 44–51.

Green Suites International (2001). *Green Suites International & GE Lighting Team to Bring Solid Energy Savings to Light.* http://www.hospitalitynet.org.

Herzog, T., Black, A., Fountaine, K., and Knotts, D. (1997). *Benefits of restorative environment.* Journal of Environmental Psychology, 17(2), 165–170.

Heschong Mahone Group (HMG) (August 1999). *Skylighting and Retail Sales, and Daylighting in Schools.* For Pacific Gas & Electric. http://www.h-m-g.com.

Heschong Mahone Group (HMG) (May 1997). *The Lighting Efficiency Technology Report, vol. I: California Lighting Baseline.* For the California Energy Commission.

Hiatt, L. (1991). *Nursing Home Renovation Designed for Reform.* Boston: Butterworth.

Hill, H., and Bruce, V. (1996). *The effects of lighting on the perception of facial surfaces.* Journal of Experimental Psychology: Human Perception and Performance, 22(4), 986–1004.

Howell, S., and Ira C. (1987). *Designing for Aging: Patterns of Use.* Cambridge, MA: MIT Press.

Hughes, P.C. (1980). *The use of light and color in health.* In A.C. Hastings, J. Fadiman, and J.S. Gordon (eds.), The Complete Guide to Holistic Medicine: Health for the Whole Person. Boulder, CO: Westview Press, pp. 294–308.

Hughes, P.C., and McNelis, J.F. (1978). *Lighting, productivity, and the work environment.* Lighting Design and Application, 8(12), 32–38.

Illuminating Engineering Society of North America (IESNA) (2000). *IESNA Lighting Handbook,* 9th ed. New York: Illuminating Engineering Society of North America.

Institute of Store Planners (2002). *Stores and Retail Spaces.* Cincinnati, OH: ST Publications.

Institute of Store Planners (2001). *Stores and Retail Spaces.* Cincinnati, OH: ST Publications.

Kreith, F., and West, R.E. (1996). *CRC Handbook of Energy Efficiency.* London: CRC Press.

Kuller, R., and Laike, T. (1998). *The impact of flicker fluorescent lighting on well-being, performance and physiological arousal.* Ergonomics, 4, 433–447.

Kwallek, N., and Lewis, C.M. (1990). *Effects of environmental colour on males and females: A red or white or green office.* Applied Economics, 21, 275–278.

Lamarre, L. (1995). *Lighting the office environment.* EPRI Journal, 20(3), 22–27.

Lane, M. (1996). *School Classrooms. Lighting Design Lab.* http://www.lightingdesignlab.com/articles/old_articles.htm. 1–2.

Lang, S. (2003). *Good lighting for healthcare buildings. Business Briefing: Hospital Engineering & Facilities Management.* Berkeley, CA: Lawrence Berkeley National Laboratory.

Lawrence Berkeley National Laboratory (2003). *Lighting Energy Savings Opportunities in Hotel Guest Rooms: Results from a scoping study at the Redondo Beach Crown Plaza.* http://www.lbl.gov.

Lawrence Berkeley National Laboratory. (1992). *Analysis of Federal Policy Options for Improving U.S. Lighting Energy Efficiency.* Berkeley, CA: Lawrence Berkeley National Laboratory.

Leibrock, C.A. (2000). *Design Details for Health: Making the Most of Interior Design's Healing Potential.* New York: John Wiley & Sons.

Lerum, V., and Buvik, K. (2000). *Sun, light, and air: Monitoring the energy performance of the new Grong school building.* ASES Solar 2000 Conference, Madison, WI. 493–497.

Littlefair, P.J. (1996). *Designing with Innovative Daylighting.* London: CRC, Garston.

Littlefair, P.J. (1991). *Site Layout Planning for Daylight and Sunlight: A Guide To Good Practice.* BRE Report BR 209.

Lodging Magazine. (March, 1–4, 2003). *Lodging trends.* Lodging Magazine, http://www.lodgingmagazine.com, 1-4.

Malkin, J. (2002). *Medical & Dental Space Planning: A Comprehensive Guide to Design, Equipment, & Clinical Procedures.* New York: John Wiley & Sons.

Malkin, J. (1992). *Hospital Interior Architecture: Creating Healing Environments.* New York: Van Nostrand Reinhold.

Maniccia, D., Rutledge, D., Rea, M., and Morrow, W. (1999). *Occupant use of manual lighting control in private offices.* Journal of the Illuminating Engineering Society 28(2), 42–56.

Maniccia, D., Von Neida, B., and Tweed, A. (2000). *Analysis of the energy and cost savings potential of occupancy sensors for commercial lighting systems.* Proceedings of the 2000 Annual Conference of the Illuminating Engineering Society of North America.

Marans, R.W., and Yan, X. (1989). *Lighting quality and environmental satisfaction in open and enclosed offices.* Journal of Architectural and Planning Research, 6, 118–131.

Mattila, A.S. (2001). *Creating customer loyalty in restaurants.* Cornell Hotel and Restaurant Administration Quarterly, 42(6), 73–79.

Mazzurco, P. (1986). *Bath Design.* New York: Whitney Library of Design.

McGowan, J. (June, 2002). *Buildings online.* Energy User News. http://www.energyusernews.com.

Mishimia, K., Okawa, M., Hiskikawa, Y., Hozumi, S., Hori, H., and Takashi, M. (1994). *Morning bright therapy for sleep and behavior disorders in elderly patients with dementia.* Acta Psychiatry Scandinavia, 89, 1–7.

National Lighting Bureau (1988). *Office Lighting and Productivity*. Washington, DC: National Lighting Bureau.

Northeast Energy Efficiency Partnership (2002). *Combining Quality Design and Energy Efficiency for Private Offices, Open-Plan Offices, Office Corridors*. www.neep.org.

Northeast Energy Efficiency Partnership (2002). *"Energy Effective" Lighting for Classrooms: Combining Quality Design and Energy Efficiency*. www.neep.org.

Northeast Energy Efficiency Partnership (2000). *Combining Quality Design and Energy Efficiency for Retail and Grocery Daylighting*. www.neep.org.

Northeast Energy Efficiency Partnership (2000). *Combining Quality Design and Energy Efficiency for Small Retail Lighting*. www.neep.org.

Novak, A. (1977). *Store Planning and Design*. New York: Lebhar Friedman.

Passini, R. (1984). *Wayfinding in Architecture*, New York: Van Nostrand Reinhold.

Passini, R., Pigot, H., Rainville, C., and Tetreault, M.H. (2000). *Wayfinding in a nursing home for advanced dementia of the Alzheimer's type*. Environment and Behavior, 32(5), 684–710.

Pegler, M.M. (2001). *Stores of the Year, No.13*. New York: Visual Reference Publications.

Pile, J. (1978). *Open Office Planning: A Handbook for Interior Designers and Architects*. New York: Whitney Library of Design.

Piotrowski, C., and Rogers, E. (1999) *Designing Commercial Interiors*. New York: John Wiley & Sons.

Plympton, P., Conway, S., and Epstein, K. (2000). *Daylighting in schools: Improving student performance and health at a price schools can afford*. ASES Solar 2000 Passive Conference, Madison, WI., 487–492.

Ravetto, A. (1994). *Daylighting schools in North Carolina*. Solar Today, 8(2), 22–24.

Rea, M.S. (1998). *The quest for the ideal office controls system*. LRC Lighting Futures 1998, (3).

Research Group for Inclusive Environments (RGIE). *Task lighting for visually impaired people in an office environment*. Research Group for Inclusive Environments (RGIE). http://www.rdg.ac.uk

Rothman, M. (1987). *Designing work environments to influence productivity*. Journal of Business and Psychology, 1, 390–550.

Russell, B. (1981). *The Interiors Book of Shops and Restaurants*. New York: Watson-Guptill.

Siguaw, J.A., and Enz, C.A. (1999). *Designing hotel restaurants for profitability*. Cornell Hotel and Restaurant Administration Quarterly, 40(5), 50–57.

Simeonova, M. (2003). *Healthy lighting*. The Center for Health Design. http://www.healthdesign.org. 1-3.

Slater, A., Bordass, B., and Heasman, T. (March 1996). *Give people control of lighting controls*. IAELL Newsletter.

Sleep Foundation (2003). *The Impact of Sleep Problems*. http://www.sleepfoundation.org, 1-12.

Sorcar, P.C. (1987). *Architectural Lighting for Commercial Interiors*. New York: John Wiley & Sons.

Thayer, B. (1995). *A daylight school in North Carolina*. Solar Today, 9(6), 36–39.

Thompson, G.M. (2002). *Planning restaurant seating*. Cornell Hotel and Restaurant Administration Quarterly, 43(4), 48–57.

United States Environmental Protection Agency (EPA) (2001). *Design for the Environment*. http://www.epa.gov/.

Veitch, J., and Newsham, G. (2000). *Exercised control, lighting choices, and energy use: An office simulation experiment*. Journal of Environmental Psychology 20(3), 219–237.

Veitch, J.A., and Newsham, G.R. (June 24–30, 1999). *Preferred luminous conditions in open-plan offices: Implications for lighting quality recommendations*. Proceedings of the Commission Internationale de l'Eclairage (CIE) 24th Session, Warsaw, Poland, Vol. 1, Part 2, Vienna, Austria: CIE Central Bureau, pp. 4–6.

Veitch, J., and Newsham, G. (January 1999). *Individual control can be energy efficient*. IAEEL Newsletter.

Weinhold, V. (1988). *Interior Finish Materials for Health Care Facilities*. Springfield, IL: Charles C. Thomas.

Weishar, J. (1992). *Design for Effective Selling Space*. New York: McGraw-Hill.

Whitehead, R. (2002). *Lighting Design Sourcebook*. Gloucester, MA: Rockport Publishers.

Chapter 11

Alderman, R.L. (1997). *How to Prosper as an Interior Designer: A Business and Legal Guide*. New York: John Wiley & Sons.

Allen, P.S., Jones, L.M., and Stimpson, M.F. (2004).

Beginnings of Interior Environments, 9th ed. Upper Saddle River, NJ: Pearson/Prentice Hall.

American Institute of Architects (2000). *Architectural Graphics Standards*, 10th ed. New York: John Wiley & Sons.

Benya, J., Heschong, L., McGowan, T., Miller, N., and Rubinstein, F. (2001). *Advanced Lighting Guidelines.* White Salmon, WA: New Buildings Institute.

Birnberg, H.G. (1999). *Project Management for Building Designers and Owners.* Boca Raton, FL: CRC Press.

Burde, E. (1992). *Design Presentation Techniques.* New York: McGraw-Hill.

Burstein, D., and Stasiowski, F. (1982). *Project Management for the Design Professional.* New York: Watson-Guptill.

Ching, F.D.K. (2003). *Architectural Graphics*, 4th ed. New York: John Wiley & Sons.

Coleman, C. (ed.) (2001). *Interior Design Handbook of Professional Practice.* New York: McGraw-Hill.

Doyle, M.E. (1999). *Color Drawing: Design Skills and Techniques for Architects, Landscape Architects, and Interior Designers*, 2nd ed. New York: John Wiley & Sons.

Farren, C.E. (1999). *Planning and Managing Interior Projects*, 2nd ed. Kingston, MA: R.S. Means.

Getz, L. (1986). *Business Management in the Smaller Design Firm.* Newton, MA: Practice Management Associates.

Gibbs, J. (1997). *A Handbook for Interior Designers.* London: Sterling Publications.

Illuminating Engineering Society of North America (IESNA) (2000). *Document DG-3-00: Application of Luminaire Symbols on Lighting Design Drawings.* New York: Illuminating Engineering Society of North America.

International Association of Lighting Designers (IALD) (2002). *Guidelines for Specification Integrity.* Chicago: International Association of Lighting Designers.

Kilmer, R., and Kilmer, W.O. (1992). *Designing Interiors.* New York: Harcourt Brace.

Kliment, S.A. (1998). *Writing for Design Professionals.* New York: W. W. Norton.

Knackstedt, M.V. (2002). *The Interior Design Business Handbook.* New York: John Wiley & Sons.

Koenig, P.A. (2000). *Design Graphics: Drawing Techniques for Design Professionals.* Upper Saddle River, NJ: Pearson Education/Prentice Hall.

Koomen-Harmon, S., and Kennon, K. (2001). *The Codes Guidebook for Interiors*, 2nd ed. New York: John Wiley & Sons.

Kriebel, T.M., Birdsong, C., and Sherman, D.J. (1991). *Defining interior design programming.* Journal of Interior Design Education and Research, 17(1), 29–36.

Liebing, R.W. (1999). *Architectural Working Drawings*, 4th ed. New York: John Wiley & Sons.

Mitton, M. (1999). *Interior Design Visual Presentations: A Guide to Graphics, Models, and Presentation Techniques.* New York: John Wiley & Sons.

Nissen, L., Faulkner, R., and Faulkner, S. (1994). *Inside Today's Home*, 6th ed. New York: Harcourt Brace.

O'Leary, A.F. (1992). *Construction Administration in Architectural Practice.* New York: McGraw-Hill.

Pile, J.F. (2003). *Interior Design*, 3rd ed. New York: Harry N. Abrams.

Pile, J.F. (1995). *Interior Design*, 2nd ed. New York: Harry N. Abrams.

Pile, J.F. (1988). *Interior Design.* New York: Harry N. Abrams.

Piotrowski, C.M. (2002). *Professional Practice for Interior Designers*, 3rd ed. New York: John Wiley & Sons.

Piotrowski, C.M. (1992). *Interior Design Management: A Handbook for Owners and Managers.* New York: John Wiley & Sons.

Ramsey, C.G., and Sleeper, H. R. (2000). *Architectural Graphic Standards*, 10th ed. New York: John Wiley & Sons.

Reznikoff, S.C. (1989). *Specifications for Commercial Interiors: Professional Liabilities, Regulations, and Performance Criteria.* New York: Whitney Library of Design.

Reznikoff, S.C. (1986). *Interior Graphic and Design Standards.* New York: Whitney Library of Design.

Siegel, H., and Siegel, A. (1982). *A Guide to Business Principles and Practices for Interior Designers.* New York: Whitney Library of Design.

Smith, W.D., and Smith, L.H. (2001). *McGraw-Hill On-Site Guide to Building Codes 2000: Commercial and Residential Interiors.* New York: McGraw-Hill.

Stasiowski, F., and Burnstein, D. (1982). *Project Management for the Design Professional.* New York: Whitney Library of Design/Watson-Guptill Publications.

Steffy, G.R. (2002). *Architectural Lighting Design*, 2nd ed. New York: Van Nostrand Reinhold.

Thompson, J.A. (ed.) (1992). *ASID Professional Practice Manual.* New York: Whitney Library of Design.

Veitch, R.M., Jackman, D.R., and Dixon, M.K. (1990). *Professional Practice: A Handbook for Interior Designers.* Winnipeg, Canada: Peguis Publishers.

Wakita, O.A., and Linde, R.M. (2003). *The Professional Practice of Architectural Working Drawings,* 3rd ed. New York: John Wiley & Sons.

Williams, D.J. (1996). *Preparing for Project Management.* New York: American Society of Civil Engineers.

Chapter 12

Alderman, R.L. (1997). *How to Prosper as an Interior Designer: A Business and Legal Guide.* New York: John Wiley & Sons.

Allen, P.S., Jones, L.M., and Stimpson, M.F. (2004). *Beginnings of Interior Environments,* 9th ed. Upper Saddle River, NJ: Pearson/Prentice Hall.

American Institute of Architects. (2000). *Architectural Graphics Standards,* 10th ed. New York: John Wiley & Sons.

Benya, J., Heschong, L., McGowan, T., Miller, N., and Rubinstein, F. (2001). *Advanced Lighting Guidelines.* White Salmon, WA: New Buildings Institute.

Binggeli, C. (2002). *Building Systems for Interior Designers.* New York: John Wiley & Sons.

Birnberg, H.G. (1999). *Project Management for Building Designers and Owners.* Boca Raton, FL: CRC Press.

Browning, H.C. (1996). *The Principles of Architectural Drafting.* New York: Whitney Library of Design.

Burstein, D., and Stasiowski, F. (1982). *Project Management for the Design Professional.* New York: Watson-Guptill.

Burde, E. (1992). *Design Presentation Techniques.* New York: McGraw-Hill.

Ching, F.D.K. (2003). *Architectural Graphics,* 4th ed. New York: John Wiley & Sons.

Ching, F.D.K. (2002). *Building Construction illustrated,* 3rd ed. New York: John Wiley & Sons.

Clough, R.H. (1986). *Construction Contracting,* 5th edition. New York: John Wiley & Sons.

Coleman, C. (ed.) (2001). *Interior Design Handbook of Professional Practice.* New York: McGraw-Hill.

Crawford, T., and Bruck, E.D. (2001). *Business and Legal Forms for Interior Designers.* New York: Allworth Press.

Doyle, M.E. (1999). *Color Drawing: Design Skills and Techniques for Architects, Landscape Architects, and Interior Designers,* 2nd ed. New York: John Wiley & Sons.

Farren, C.E. (1999). *Planning and Managing Interior Projects,* 2nd ed. Kingston, MA: R.S. Means.

Fielder, W.J., and Frederick, H.J. (2001). *The Lit Interior.* Boston: Architectural Press.

Getz, L. (1986). *Business Management in the Smaller Design Firm.* Newton, MA: Practice Management Associates.

Gibbs, J. (1997). *A Handbook for Interior Designers.* London: Sterling Publications.

Gorman, J. (1995). *Detailing Light: Integrated Lighting Solutions for Residential and Contract Design.* New York: Whitney Library of Design.

Illuminating Engineering Society of North America (IESNA) (2000). *Document DG-3-00: Application of Luminaire Symbols on Lighting Design Drawings.* New York: Illuminating Engineering Society of North America.

International Association of Lighting Designers (IALD) (2002). *Guidelines for specification integrity.* Chicago: International Association of Lighting Designers.

International Interior Design Association (1999). *Forms and Documents Manual.* Chicago: International Interior Design Association.

Kilmer, R., and Kilmer, W.O. (1992). *Designing Interiors.* New York: Harcourt Brace.

Kliment, S.A. (1998). *Writing for Design Professionals.* New York: W.W. Norton.

Knackstedt, M.V. (2002). *The Interior Design Business Handbook.* New York: John Wiley & Sons.

Koenig, P.A. (2000). *Design Graphics: Drawing Techniques for Design Professionals.* Upper Saddle River, NJ: Pearson Education/ Prentice Hall.

Koomen-Harmon, S., and Kennon, K. (2001). *The Codes Guidebook for Interiors,* 2nd ed. New York: John Wiley & Sons.

Kriebel, T.M., Birdsong, C., and Sherman, D.J. (1991). *Defining interior design programming.* Journal of Interior Design Education and Research, 17(1), 29-36.

Lamit, L.G. (1994). *Technical Drawing and Design.* Minneapolis/St. Paul: West Publishing Company.

Laseau, P. (2001). *Graphic Thinking for Architects & Designers,* 3rd ed. New York: John Wiley & Sons.

Liebing, R.W. (1999). *Architectural Working Drawings,* 4th ed. New York: John Wiley & Sons, Inc.

Lohmann, W.T. (1992). *Construction Specifications: Managing the Review Process.* Boston: Butterworth Architecture.

McGowan, M., and Kruse, K. (2003). *Interior Graphic Standards.* New York: John Wiley & Sons.

Mitton, M. (1999). *Interior Design Visual Presentations: A Guide to Graphics, Models, and Presentation Techniques.* New York: John Wiley & Sons.

Nissen, L., Faulkner, R., & Faulkner, S. (1994). *Inside Today's Home,* 6th ed. New York: Harcourt Brace.

O'Leary, A.F. (1992). *Construction Administration in Architectural Practice.* New York: McGraw-Hill.

Pile, J.F. (2003). *Interior Design,* 3rd ed. New York: Harry N. Abrams Inc.

Pile, J.F. (1995). *Interior Design,* 2nd ed. New York: Harry N. Abrams Inc.

Pile, J.F. (1988). *Interior Design.* New York: Harry N. Abrams Inc.

Piotrowski, C.M. (2002). *Professional Practice for Interior Designers,* 3rd ed. New York: John Wiley & Sons.

Piotrowski, C.M. (1992). *Interior Design Management: A Handbook for Owners and Managers.* New York: John Wiley & Sons.

Preiser, W., Rabinowitz, H., and White, E. (1988). *Post-Occupancy Evaluation.* New York: Van Nostrand Reinhold.

Ramsey, C.G., and Sleeper, H.R. (2000). *Architectural Graphic Standards,* 10th ed. New York: John Wiley & Sons.

Reznikoff, S.C. (1989). *Specifications for Commercial Interiors: Professional Liabilities, Regulations, and Performance Criteria.* New York: Whitney Library of Design.

Reznikoff, S.C. (1986). *Interior Graphic and Design Standards.* New York: Whitney Library of Design.

Siegel, H., and Siegel, A. (1982). *A Guide to Business Principles and Practices for Interior Designers.* New York: Whitney Library of Design.

Smith, F.K., and Bertolone, F.J. (1986). *The Principles and Practices of Lighting Design: Bringing Interiors to Light.* New York: Whitney Library of Design.

Smith, W.D., and Smith, L.H. (2001). *McGraw-Hill On-Site Guide to Building Codes 2000: Commercial and Residential Interiors.* New York: McGraw-Hill.

Stasiowski, F., and Burnstein, D. (1982). *Project Management for the Design Professional.* New York: Whitney Library of Design/Watson-Guptill Publications.

Steffy, G.R. (2002). *Architectural Lighting Design,* 2nd ed. New York: Van Nostrand Reinhold.

Thompson, J.A. (ed.) (1992). *ASID Professional Practice Manual.* New York: Whitney Library of Design.

Travisono, J. (ed.) (1997). *E Source Technology Atlas Series: Lighting.* Boulder, CO: E Source.

Veitch, R.M., Jackman, D.R., and Dixon, M.K. (1990). *Professional Practice: A Handbook for Interior Designers.* Winnipeg, Canada: Peguis Publishers.

Wakita, O.A., and Linde, R.M. (2003). *The Professional Practice of Architectural Working Drawings,* 3rd ed. New York: John Wiley & Sons.

Wang, C. (1979). *Plan & Section Drawing.* New York: Van Nostrand Reinhold.

Williams, D.J. (1996). *Preparing for Project Management.* New York: American Society of Civil Engineers.

Index

Credits

Chapter 1

Figure 1.1 – © Jane Hurd/Phototakeusa.com

Figure 1.3 – Photograph © Danny Lehman/ Corbis

Figure 1.4 – Photograph © Paul Colangelo/ Corbis

Figure 1.7 – Photograph © Peter Aaron/Esto

Figure 1.8 – Photograph © Tom Leighton/Elizabeth Whiting & Assoc./Corbis

Figure 1.9 – Photograph © John Credland / Alamy

Figure 1.10 – Photograph © Elizabeth Whiting & Assoc./ Corbis

Figure 1.11 – Photograph © rhythmic image / Alamy

Figure 1.12 – Photograph © Arcaid /Alamy

Chapter 2

Figure 2.1 – Photograph Brand X Pictures / Alamy

Figure 2.3 – Photograph © Kevin Matthews/Greatbuildings.com

Table 2.1 – Adapted from GE Lighting Lamp Products Catalog, 2004

Figure 2.5 – Courtesy of Philips Lighting Company

Figure 2.11 – Photograph Lumitex, Inc., manufacturers of fiber optic lighting

Figure 2.12a – Photograph © George B. Diebold/Corbis

Figure 2.12b – Photograph © Brownie Harris/Corbis

Figure 2.14 – Photograph Schott

Figure 2.15 – Photograph © Getty Images

Figure 2.16 – Photograph © Red Cover/Mark York

Chapter 3

Figure 3.1a – Photograph © Alexander Burkatowski/Corbis

Figure 3.1b – Photograph © Burstein Collection/Corbis

Figure 3.3 – Adapted from a chart developed by General Electric

Figure 3.6 – Photograph © Image Source/Corbis

Table 3.2 – Reprinted from IESNA Lighting Handbook (9th ed.) pp. 1–22, with permission from the Illuminating Engineering Society of North America

Table 3.3 – Reprinted from IESNA Lighting Handbook (9th ed.) pp. 18–22, with permission from the Illuminating Engineering Society of North America

Chapter 4

Figure 4.2 – Prudential Lighting

Table 4.2 – Reprinted from IESNA Lighting Handbook (9th ed.) pp. 9–20, with permission from the Illuminating Engineering Society of North America

Figure 4.5 – Courtesy of Philips Lighting Company

Figure 4.10 – Photograph © Reto Guntli/zapaimages.com

Chapter 5

Figure 5.1 – Photograph © David Reed/Corbis

Figure 5.13 – www.lighting.com

Chapter 6

Figure 6.3 – Photograph © John Madere/ Corbis

Chapter 7

Figure 7.1 – Source: Energy Information Administration.

Figure 7.2 – Source: Energy Information Administration.

Figure 7.3 – Source: Energy Information Administration.

Table 7.1 – Source: Energy Information Administration.

Figure 7.4 – Reprinted from IESNA Lighting Handbook (9th ed.) with permission from the Illuminating Engineering Society of North America

Figure 7.5 – Source: Energy Information Administration

Figure 7.6 – Design for the Environment, US Environmental Protection Agency

Chapter 8

Figure 8.1 – Photograph Reprinted with permission of the United States Holocaust Memorial Museum "The views or opinions expressed in this book and the context in which the images are used, do not necessarily reflect the views or policy of, nor imply approval or endorsement by, the United States Holocaust Memorial Museum."

Figure 8.2 – Photograph The Anglepoise © model 1227 designed by George Carwardine/ Anglepoise LTD.

Chapter 10

Figure 10.1 – Photograph © Corbis

Figure 10.2 – Photograph © Jack Hollingsworth/Corbis

Figure 10.3 – Photograph © plainpicture GmbH & Co. KG / Alamy

Figure 10.4 – Photograph © Richard Lee Johnson/Beateworks/Corbis

Figure 10.6 – Photograph © Paul Chesley/Stone/Getty Images

Figure 10.7 – Photograph © Chuck Pefley/Alamy

Chapter 11

Figure 11.9 – Courtesy Domingo Gonzalez Associates

Appendix A

Page 263   Courtesy of Philips Lighting Company

Page 264   Courtesy of Philips Lighting Company

Page 265   Courtesy of Philips Lighting Company

Page 266   Courtesy of Philips Lighting Company

Page 267   Reprinted by permission Lithonia Lighting

Page 268   Reprinted by permission Lithonia Lighting

Page 269   Reprinted by permission Lithonia Lighting

Page 270   Reprinted by permission Lithonia Lighting

Page 271   Reprinted by permission Lithonia Lighting

Page 272   Reprinted by permission Lithonia Lighting